MW01069110

FOOD AND LITERATURE

This volume examines food as subject, form, landscape, polemic, and aesthetic statement in literature. With chapters analyzing food and race, queer food, intoxicated poets, avant-garde food writing, vegetarianism, the recipe, the supermarket, food comics, and vampiric eating, this collection brings together fascinating work from leading scholars in the field. It is the first volume to offer an overview of literary food studies and reflect on its origins, developments, and applications. Taking up maxims such as "we are what we eat," it traces the origins of literary food studies and examines key questions in cultural texts from different global literary traditions. It charts the trajectories of the field in relation to work in critical race studies, postcolonial studies, and children's literature, positing an omnivorous method for the field at large.

GITANJALI G. SHAHANI is Associate Professor of English at San Francisco State University. She has coedited *Emissaries in Early Modern Literature and Culture* (2009). Her articles have appeared in *JEMCS*, *Shakespeare*, *Shakespeare Studies*, and several edited collections. Her book, *Tasting Difference*, on food, race, and colonialism in the early modern period, is forthcoming in 2019.

CAMBRIDGE CRITICAL CONCEPTS

Cambridge Critical Concepts focuses on the important ideas animating twentieth- and twenty-first-century literary studies. Each concept addressed in the series has had a profound impact on literary studies, as well as on other disciplines, and already has a substantial critical bibliography surrounding it. This series captures the dynamic critical energies transmitted across twentieth- and twenty-first-century literary landscapes: the concepts critics bring to reading, interpretation and criticism. By addressing the origins, development and application of these ideas, the books collate and clarify how these particular concepts have developed, while also featuring fresh insights and establishing new lines of enquiry.

Cambridge Critical Concepts shifts the focus from period- or genre-based literary studies of key terms to the history and development of the terms themselves. Broad and detailed contributions cumulatively identify and investigate the various historical and cultural catalysts that made these critical concepts emerge as established twenty-first-century landmarks in the discipline. The level will be suitable for advanced undergraduates, graduates and specialists, as well as to those teaching outside their own research areas, and will have cross-disciplinary relevance for subjects such as history and philosophy.

Published Titles

Animals, Animality, and Literature
Edited by Bruce Boehrer, Molly Hand and Brian Massumi
Florida State University, University of Montreal

Food and Literature
Edited by Gitanjali Shahani
San Francisco State University

Time and Literature
Edited by Thomas M. Allen
University of Ottawa

The Global South and Literature
Edited by Russell West-Pavlov
University of Tübingen

Trauma and Literature
Edited by Roger Kurtz
The College at Brockport, State University of New York

Law and Literature
Edited by Kieran Dolin
University of Western Australia

Terrorism and Literature
Edited by Peter Herman
San Diego State University

(continued after the Index)

FOOD AND LITERATURE

EDITED BY

GITANJALI G. SHAHANI

San Francisco State University

CAMBRIDGE
UNIVERSITY PRESS

CAMBRIDGE
UNIVERSITY PRESS

University Printing House, Cambridge CB2 8BS, United Kingdom

One Liberty Plaza, 20th Floor, New York, NY 10006, USA

477 Williamstown Road, Port Melbourne, VIC 3207, Australia

314–321, 3rd Floor, Plot 3, Splendor Forum, Jasola District Centre, New Delhi – 110025, India

79 Anson Road, #06-04/06, Singapore 079906

Cambridge University Press is part of the University of Cambridge.

It furthers the University's mission by disseminating knowledge in the pursuit
of education, learning, and research at the highest international levels of excellence.

www.cambridge.org
Information on this title: www.cambridge.org/9781108426329
DOI: 10.1017/9781108661492

© Cambridge University Press 2018

First published 2018

Printed in the United States of America by Sheridan Books, Inc

A catalogue record for this publication is available from the British Library.

Library of Congress Cataloging-in-Publication Data
Names: Shahani, Gitanjali, editor.
Title: Food and literature / edited by Gitanjali Shahani.
Description: Cambridge: Cambridge University Press, 2018. |
Series: Cambridge critical concepts
Identifiers: LCCN 2018002371 | ISBN 9781108426329 (hardback)
Subjects: LCSH: Food in literature. | Food – Social aspects. |
Gastronomy in literature. | Food habits in literature.
Classification: LCC PN56.F59 F65 2018 | DDC 809/.933559–dc23
LC record available at https://lccn.loc.gov/2018002371

ISBN 978-1-108-42632-9 Hardback

Contents

Notes on Contributors

TOMOKO AOYAMA is Associate Professor of Japanese at the University of Queensland, Australia. Her research interests include parody, humor, and intertextuality in modern and contemporary Japanese literature and culture, including girls' manga. Her publications include: "Literary Daughters' Recipes" (2000), "Appropriating Bush Tucker: Food in Inoue Hisashi's *Yellow Rats*" (2006), *Reading Food in Modern Japanese Literature* (2008), "Queering the Cooking Man: Food and Gender in Yoshinaga Fumi's (BL) Manga" (2015) and many others. She has also coedited *Girl Reading Girl in Japan* (2010) and *Configurations of Family in Contemporary Japan* (2015), and co-translated Kanai Mieko's novels: *Indian Summer* (2012) and *Oh, Tama!* (2014).

ROBERT APPELBAUM received his PhD from the University of California, Berkeley, and is currently Professor of English Literature at Uppsala University, Sweden. He has been a fellow of Arts and Humanities Research Council, the Leverhulme Foundation, and the Stellenbosch Institute for Advanced Study, South Africa. His books include *Aguecheek's Beef, Belch's Hiccup and Other Gastronomic Interjections: Literature, Culture and Food among the Early Moderns* (2006), winner of the 2007 Roland H. Bainton Prize, *Working the Aisles: A Life in Consumption* (2014), and *Terrorism before the Letter: Mythography and Political Violence in England, Scotland and France 1559–1642* (2015).

DEEPIKA BAHRI is Professor in the English department at Emory University. She is the author of *Native Intelligence: Aesthetics, Politics, and Postcolonial Literature* and *Postcolonial Biology: Psyche and Flesh after Empire*. She has also edited two collections, *Between the Lines: South Asians and Postcoloniality* and *Realms of Rhetoric: Inquiries into the Prospects of Rhetoric Education*. Her research and teaching center on aesthetics and the socio-political context of art.

ALLISON CARRUTH is Associate Professor in the English Department, Institute for Society and Genetics, and Institute of the Environment and Sustainability at UCLA, where she directs the Laboratory for Environmental Narrative Strategies. She is the author of *Global Appetites: American Power and the Literature of Food* (Cambridge University Press, 2013) and co-author with Amy L. Tigner of *Literature and Food Studies* (2018). Her articles have appeared in places such as *American Literary History, Modernism/modernity, Modern Fiction Studies, Public Books, Public Culture,* and *PMLA*.

ROHIT CHOPRA is Associate Professor in the Department of Communication at Santa Clara University. He is the author of *Technology and Nationalism in India* (2008) and coeditor of *Global Media, Culture, and Identity* (2011). He has also published articles in numerous journals, including *Cultural Studies, New Media and Society,* and the *Journal of International Communication,* as well as book chapters in edited volumes. His chapter "Global Food, Global Media, Global Culture: Representations of the New Indian Cuisine in Indian Media" has been published in *The Bloomsbury Handbook of Food and Popular Culture*. His current research projects address the relationship between memory, media, and violence and the impact of the internet on the sense of our past. He is also working on a trade publication on Hindu nationalism and new media.

J. MICHELLE COGHLAN is Lecturer in American Literature at the University of Manchester. She is the author of *Sensational Internationalism: The Paris Commune and the Remaking of American Memory in the Long Nineteenth Century,* which won the 2017 Arthur Miller Centre First Book Prize in American Studies. Recent work has appeared in *Arizona Quarterly,* the *Henry James Review,* and *Resilience;* she guest-edited "Tasting Modernism," the Winter 2014 special issue of *Resilience: Journal of the Environmental Humanities*. Her new project, *Culinary Designs,* chronicles the rise of American food writing and the making of American taste in the long nineteenth century.

FRANCES E. DOLAN is Distinguished Professor of English at the University of California, Davis. Her research and teaching focus on sixteenth- and seventeenth-century literature and children's literature. She is the author of numerous articles and four books, most recently *True Relations: Reading, Literature, and Evidence in Seventeenth-Century England* (2013), which won the John Ben Snow prize from the North American Conference on British Studies. A former president of the

Shakespeare Association of America and an award-winning teacher, she has also prepared many texts for classroom, including *Twelfth Night: Language and Writing* (2014) and *The Taming of the Shrew: Texts and Contexts* (1996).

DENISE GIGANTE teaches British literature, mainly from the eighteenth and nineteenth centuries, at Stanford University. She is the author of *Taste: A Literary History* (2005). She has, more recently, published a chapter on Milton and the making of aesthetic taste in *Milton in the Long Restoration*, edited by Blair Hoxby and Ann Baynes Coiro (2016) and "Coffee in the Age of Gastronomy: A Chapter in the History of Taste," in *The Taste Culture Reader: Experiencing Food and Drink*, edited by Carolyn Korsmeyer (2017). She is the editor of *Gusto: Essential Writings in Nineteenth-Century Gastronomy* (2005) and "Romantic Gastronomies," a special issue of *Romantic Circles Praxis* (2007).

SANDRA M. GILBERT is Distinguished Professor of English Emerita at the University of California, Davis. She is the author of eight collections of poetry: *In the Fourth World, The Summer Kitchen, Emily's Bread, Blood Pressure, Ghost Volcano*, and *Kissing the Bread: New and Selected Poems 1969–1999, The Italian Collection*, and *Belongings*. Her most recent volume of poems, *Aftermath*, was published in 2011. She is the author of *The Culinary Imagination: From Myth to Modernity* (2014).

DARRA GOLDSTEIN is the Willcox B. and Harriet M. Adsit Professor of Russian, Emerita at Williams College and the founding editor of *Gastronomica: The Journal of Food and Culture*, named the 2012 Publication of the Year by the James Beard Foundation. She has published widely on literature, culture, art, and cuisine. In addition to serving as series editor of California Studies in Food and Culture, she is the author of five award-winning cookbooks. She has consulted for the Council of Europe as part of an international group exploring ways in which food can be used to promote tolerance and diversity, and under her editorship the Council published *Culinary Cultures of Europe: Identity, Diversity and Dialogue*. In 2013 she served as Distinguished Fellow in Food Studies at the Jackman Humanities Institute, University of Toronto, and in 2016 was named a Macgeorge Fellow in Food Studies at the University of Melbourne.

DAVID B. GOLDSTEIN is a poet, critic, and food writer. His first monograph, *Eating and Ethics in Shakespeare's England*, shared the 2014 biennial Shakespeare's Globe Book Award. He has also published two books of poetry and has coedited two essay collections: *Culinary Shakespeare* (with Amy Tigner) and *Shakespeare and Hospitality* (with Julia Reinhard Lupton). His essays on early modern literature, Emmanuel Levinas, food studies, ecology, and contemporary poetry have appeared in *Studies in English Literature, Shakespeare Studies, Gastronomica*, and numerous other journals and collections. David teaches at York University in Toronto, where he is Associate Professor of English.

KARA K. KEELING is a past president of the Children's Literature Association and serves as Professor of English at Christopher Newport University, in Newport News, Virginia, where she teaches courses on children's and young adult literature. She co-authored, with Marsha Sprague, *Discovering a Voice: Engaging Adolescent Girls with Young Adult Literature* (2007), and coedited, with Scott T. Pollard, *Critical Approaches to Food in Children's Literature* (2009). She and Pollard have written on food in children's literature in texts by a number of children's authors (including Pamela Muñoz Ryan, Polly Horvath, Neil Gaiman, Beatrix Potter, and Maurice Sendak) and are engaged in a book-length study of food and children's literature.

CATHERINE KEYSER is Associate Professor in the English Department at the University of South Carolina. The author of *Playing Smart: New York Women Writers and Modern Magazine Culture* (2010), Keyser has published on food and US culture in the *Journal of Modern Periodical Studies, Transition, Modernism/modernity*, and *Modern Fiction Studies*. Her current project, *Artificial Color: Modern Food and Racial Fictions*, argues that twentieth-century US literature creates racial imaginaries and critiques whiteness through food technologies, geographies, and regimens.

VALÉRIE LOICHOT is Professor of French and English and a core member of Comparative Literature at Emory University. She is the author of *Orphan Narratives: The Postplantation Literatures of Faulkner, Glissant, Morrison, and Saint-John Perse* (2007) and *The Tropics Bite Back: Culinary Coups in Caribbean Literature* (2013). She is the winner of the Aldo and Jeanne Scaglione Prize for French and Francophone Studies, 2015. She has directed a special issue of *La Revue des Sciences humaines* in honor of her former mentor Édouard Glissant (*Entours d'Édouard Glissant*, 2013). In addition, Loichot has authored numerous articles on Caribbean literature and culture, Southern literature, creolization theory, transatlantic studies, feminism and exile, and food studies published in journals including *Callaloo, Études francophones, French Cultural Studies*,

French Review, International Journal of Francophone Studies, Mississippi Quarterly, and *Small Axe: A Caribbean Platform for Criticism.*

MIRIAM O'KANE MARA is Associate Professor of English at Arizona State University. Her research interests include Irish literature and film, postcolonial literatures, gender studies, and food studies. In particular, her work often examines the fiction of Edna O'Brien, Nuala O'Faolain, Anne Enright, and Colum McCann. A second research stream investigates intersections of medical texts, cultural representations of health and illness including novels and film, and gendered bodies. Recent publications have appeared in *New Hibernia Review* and *Nordic Irish Studies,* and she is currently at work on a book investigating ill female bodies.

JENNIFER PARK is Assistant Professor of English at the University of North Carolina at Greensboro. Her research interests include early modern literature, science and medicine, recipe culture, and performance in early modern England. She is working on a book manuscript on vital preservation which examines early modern preservative cultures in metaphor and on stage. Her previous research has been published in *Studies in Philology, Renaissance and Reformation,* and *Performance Matters.*

SCOTT T. POLLARD is Professor of English at Christopher Newport University. With Kara K. Keeling, he coedited *Critical Approaches to Food in Children's Literature* (2009). Together they have written and published articles on food in children's literature in texts by a number of children's authors (including Pamela Muñoz Ryan, Polly Horvath, Neil Gaiman, Beatrix Potter, and Maurice Sendak), and they are currently engaged in a book-length study of food and children's literature. Pollard also coedited with Margarita Marinova her translation from the Russian of Mikhail Bulgakov's dramatic adaptation of *Don Quixote* (2014), and he edited a special volume of *Children's Literature Association Quarterly* on disability in 2013.

ELSPETH PROBYN is Professor of Gender and Cultural Studies at the University of Sydney. She has taught media, cultural studies, and sociology and has held several prestigious visiting appointments around the world. Probyn is the author of several groundbreaking monographs: on subjectivity and gender in cultural studies (*Sexing the Self: Gendered Positions in Cultural Studies*), on queer desire and belonging (*Outside Belonging*), on eating and identity (*FoodSexIdentity*), on affect and emotion (*Blush: Faces on Shame*). She has also published well over 150 articles and chapters across the fields of gender, media, and cultural studies, sociology, philosophy, cultural geography, anthropology, and critical psychology. She has recently been researching Sustainable Fish: a material analysis of cultures of consumption and production that analyzes the sustainability of the production and consumption of fish, or "more-than-human" sustainable fish communities, the results of which have been published in a book, *Eating the Ocean* (2016).

PARAMA ROY is Professor of English at the University of California, Davis. She is the author of *Alimentary Tracts: Appetites, Aversions, The Postcolonial*, and *Indian Traffic: Identities in Question in Colonial and Postcolonial India*, and coeditor of *States of Trauma: Gender and Violence in South Asia*.

GITANJALI G. SHAHANI is Associate Professor of English at San Francisco State University, where she teaches courses on Shakespeare studies, postcolonial studies, and food studies. Her work has been published in numerous collections and journals, including *Shakespeare, Shakespeare Studies*, and *The Journal of Early Modern Cultural Studies*. She has coedited *Emissaries in Early Modern Literature and Culture* (2009) and guest edited a special issue of *Shakespeare Studies* on "Diet and Identity in Shakespeare's England" (2014). Her book, *Tasting Difference*, on food, race, and colonial encounters in the early modern period is forthcoming in 2019.

ANDREW WARNES is Reader in American Studies at the University of Leeds. His first monograph *Hunger Overcome?* (2004) draws attention to images of abundance and avoidable want in African-American writings after 1900. A second book, *Savage Barbecue: Race, Culture, and the Invention of America's First Food* (2008), explores imperial mythologies of barbecue, and shows how these invented etymologies merge distinctive Indian cultures into a single myth of antithetical savagery. His more recent research focuses on the cultural grammar of consumer desire and commodity flow in American life. This has led to *American Tantalus: Horizons, Happiness and the Impossible Pursuits of US Literature and Culture* (2014) and, most recently, a cultural history of the supermarket cart, which will be published in 2019.

Introduction
Writing on Food and Literature
Gitanjali G. Shahani

Books to Taste and Books to Chew

Some books are to be tasted, others to be swallowed, and some few to be chewed and digested.

Francis Bacon, "Of Studies"

I begin here with a quotation from Francis Bacon, which gives this section its title, but the possibilities for food epigraphs are endless. Indeed, it has become something of a critical convention to start a volume on food with one of many food aphorisms available to scholars in the field. We might start, as Terry Eagleton does, with the Bacon quotation above, on the process of devouring a book. Or we might start with Eagleton himself, whose pithy maxims about food and literary interpretation inaugurate several works: "If there is one sure thing about food, it is that it is never just food ... Like the post-structuralist text, food is endlessly interpretable, as gift, threat, poison, recompense, barter, seduction, solidarity, suffocation."[1] We might turn to the structuralists with Levi-Strauss' formulation that food is good to think with.[2] Or to Roland Barthes on the semiotics of food: "For what is food? It is not only a collection of products ... It is also, and at the same time, a system of communication, a body of images, a protocol of usages, situations, and behavior."[3] We might begin with authors like Ben Jonson, whose character of the Cook in turn asks us to begin all thought and understanding in the kitchen, for "The art of poetry was learned and

---

[1] Terry Eagleton, "Edible Ecriture," *Times Higher Education*, October 24, 1997, www.timeshighereducation.co.uk/features/edible-ecriture/104281.article.

[2] Claude Lévi-Strauss, "The Culinary Triangle," *Partisan Review* 33.4 (1966): 586–95. Elspeth Probyn and Sandra Gilbert have pointed out that the origin of the quote is vexed and was probably made in connection with taboos on eating totem animals, rather than eating and thinking generally. Elspeth Probyn, *Carnal Appetites: FoodSexIdentities* (New York: Routledge, 2000); Sandra M. Gilbert, *The Culinary Imagination: From Myth to Modernity* (New York: Norton, 2014).

[3] Roland Barthes, "Toward a Psychosociology of Contemporary Food Consumption," in *Food and Culture: A Reader*, edited by Carole Counihan and Penny Van Esterik (New York: Routledge, 2008), 29.

I

found out ... the same day with the art of cookery."⁴ We could pay homage to the eighteenth-century gastronome, Brillat-Savarin, whose oft-quoted truism on food and identity – "tell me what you eat: I will tell you what you are" – is now what one scholar calls "a chestnut of food studies scholarship."⁵ Or we might turn to more recent writers like Hemingway, as Sandra Gilbert does, in order to understand "why and how we read, write, work and play with food in the gastronomically obsessed twenty-first century."⁶ Hemingway, who reminisces about eating Chinese sea slugs and hundred-year-old eggs, might offer us a reason for our food studies endeavors: "there is romance in food when romance has disappeared from everywhere else."⁷

I offer these quotations not simply to continue the tradition of the food epigraph, but to suggest that the tradition itself speaks to an important relationship between food and word that literary scholars have identified in a range of recent works. These epigraphs point to an intricate relationship between eating and writing and the writing on eating. Their persistent appearance in volumes, whether in work on food and children's literature, food and Asian American literature, or food and early modern literature, might be treated as a call for an overarching method for thinking about food in relation to the literary text. Implicit in each maxim at the outset of each work is a method. Thus, for instance, Bacon's quotation in Eagleton's work compels us to think about the process of consuming the book and the process of consuming in the book. It articulates ways in which we take in a book. And Eagleton, extrapolating on Bacon's aphorism, in turn asks us to think of the process of creating the book as a process of cooking it up: "writing is a processing of raw speech just as cooking is a transformation of raw materials."⁸ This volume examines such moments of culinary transformation in literature. It turns to food as subject, as form, as landscape, as polemic, as political movement, as aesthetic statement, and as key ingredient in literature. It looks at food in the literary text, food text as literature, and literature as food for thought. It asks: what if we think of the tasting, chewing, and digesting of Bacon's maxim as a kind of theme and method? Or even as a mandate – some books *are to be* tasted, others *are to*

---

⁴ Ben Jonson, "Neptune's Triumph," in *The Works of Ben Jonson with a Biographical Memoir*, edited by William Gifford (New York: D. Appleton: 1879), 758.
⁵ Anthelme Brillat-Savarin, *The Physiology of Taste; or, Meditations on Transcendental Gastronomy*, translated by M. F. K. Fisher (New York: Heritage Press, 1949), 1; Kyla Wazana Tompkins, *Racial Indigestion: Eating Bodies in the Nineteenth Century* (New York: New York University Press, 2012), 3.
⁶ Gilbert, *Culinary Imagination*, xv.
⁷ Quoted in ibid.
⁸ Eagleton, "Edible Ecriture."

be chewed? How does eating work in the text and how do we, as readers and critics, consume the process of eating in the text?

After all, as Mervyn Nicholson noted in an early article on food and writing, literary characters do not need to eat to stay "alive."[9] Food in the literary text is not what Barthes has called a "first need."[10] And yet, characters do eat. Some of their most memorable words and scenes are gastronomic. Proust begins *Remembrance of Things Past* with a recollection of tea and cakes, a meditation on the "petites madeleines" of memory. Swift's satire is most biting in his recommendation that his countrymen eat their babies. Titus Andronicus' revenge is most gruesome when he serves Tamora her sons in a pie. Prufrock's visions and revisions are most painful when he dares to eat a peach. Salman Rushdie's historiographic metafiction rests on Saleem's cooked up chutneys and his "chutnification of history," with each chapter lined up as a label on a pickle jar at the end of *Midnight's Children*. Food is memory, food is irony, food is drama, food is symbol, food is form. It is "endlessly interpretable." It is good to think with. We return again to the food maxims.

But to ponder these maxims more carefully, we might ask if food is good to think with (and not simply good to eat), as Levi-Strauss suggests, how should we think of food in the literary text? What do food words and food scenes do for the literary text? How does food function as a formal device? Can we think in terms of a food ekphrasis in which we pause to read descriptions of feasts, banquets, kitchen scenes, and fictional dishes? What are characters really saying when they say things about food – food that they don't need to eat and food that the reader cannot really share? In *Midnight's Children*, for instance, Rushdie's ever-digressing Tristram Shandy-like narrator interrupts his tale at a critical juncture in the final chapter to contemplate the process of pickling. "What is required for chutnification? Raw materials, obviously – fruit, vegetables, fish, vinegar, spices. Daily visits from Koli women with their saris hitched up between their legs. Cucumbers aubergines mint," Saleem tells us.[11] While expounding at length on chutneys, Saleem is also, of course, contemplating the form of the novel itself. His narrative, and by extension, Rushdie's, is a pickling and preserving of history, with adequate masala thrown in for good measure. (And as subcontinental readers are well aware, "masala" is also exaggeration – spice that is arguably superfluous in any dish or tale,

[9] Mervyn Nicholson, "Food and Power: Homer, Carroll, Atwood and Others," *Mosaic* 20.3 (1987): 107.
[10] Barthes, "Psychosociology of Contemporary Food Consumption," 30.
[11] Salman Rushdie, *Midnight's Children* (New York: Random House, 2006), 530.

yet neither would be quite palatable without it.) As we approach the end, he is careful to leave one jar empty, "for the process of revision should be constant and endless," as history will continue to seep into it long after his story ends. What we have here is food as form. As one of the earliest post-colonial novels to emerge from the Indian subcontinent, it is fitting that Rushdie turns to the trope of "chutnification" to elucidate his technique – a technique which Linda Hutcheon would later call historiographic metafic-tion.[12] Rushdie's work was among the earliest in this form and his pickling metaphors were, in fact, integral to it. Pickling *was* the form.

Scholarship in literary food studies is attuned to these culinary moments in a text. They are often to be found in digressions and asides, seemingly incidental to the text. Yet they are critical to the writer's form and imagina-tive landscape. In the wonderfully titled *Aguecheek's Beef, Belch's Hiccup and Other Gastronomic Interjections*, Robert Appelbaum argues that "The writer interjects something about food in order to score a point regarding something else, yet the interjection is, finally, about food too – about what we do with it, what we want from it, what it means."[13] For Appelbaum, the interjection tells us something about the writer, the character, the writing, the culture, and ultimately about food in a given culture. To study the gastronomic interjection is then to study the literary, material, and cultural contexts in which it was uttered.

Hamlet's wry remark to Horatio about his mother's nuptials following so close at the heels of his father's funeral, that "The funeral baked meats / Did coldly furnish forth the marriage tables" is one such gastronomic interjection that has elicited interest from literary scholars and food historians alike (*Hamlet*, 1.2.179–80).[14] While Stephen Greenblatt notes the "economy of calculation and equivalence" in Hamlet's jest, Ken Albala notes that the jest itself draws from the fact that the pastry shells used to preserve such baked meats were often referred to as "coffins."[15] Encasing everything from dead bodies, to meat, to jewelry, coffins or coffers were variously meant to protect the contents from decay, theft, and corruption. In the absence of our modern-day distinction between "coffin" and "coffer,"

[12] Linda Hutcheon, "Historiographic Metafiction Parody and the Intertextuality of History," in *Intertextuality and Contemporary American Fiction*, edited by Patrick O'Donnell and Robert Con Davis (Baltimore: Johns Hopkins University Press, 1989), 3–32.
[13] Robert Appelbaum, *Aguecheek's Beef, Belch's Hiccup, and Other Gastronomic Interjections* (Chicago: University of Chicago Press, 2006), xii.
[14] *The Norton Shakespeare*, edited by Stephen Greenblatt et al. (New York: Norton, 2008).
[15] Greenblatt quoted in Appelbaum, *Aguecheek's Beef*, 17; Ken Albala, "Shakespeare's Culinary Metaphors," *Shakespeare Studies* 42 (2014): 64.

Hamlet's bitter interjection about the marriage banquet takes on a more gruesome meaning.

Early modernists would, in fact, be quick to note that the word "bitter" itself as describing character comes from a physiognomic understanding of character as constituted in large part through diet. Lady Macbeth's liquid imagery in conceiving of her husband as "too full o'th' milk of human kindness" and soon after, calling on the spirits to come to her "woman's breast" and take her "milk for gall" is yet another macabre Shakespearean interjection that relies on an understanding of early modern humoral and dietary frameworks for its full effect (*Macbeth* 1.5.15, 45–46).[16] To parse these lines is to reckon with the systems of meaning that food holds, as much in the dramatist's imagination as in his audience's. Such readings, while hitherto confined to the footnotes of authoritative Shakespearean editions, take center stage in recent work that draws on the methods of food studies, bringing new perspectives to the writings of the early moderns as revealed in their "gastronomic interjections."

As a term, the "gastronomic interjection" also adds to what is part of a growing critical vocabulary that allows us to think with food. In her recent work, *The Culinary Imagination*, Sandra Gilbert offers us yet another term, what she calls the "*eating* words of novelists and memoirists, poets and polemicists."[17] Eating words emerge from a range of food texts and contexts. If we learn to think with food, we see that eating words pepper all kinds of works, even works that are not, strictly speaking, about food. As descriptors, eating words give us a way to trace the processes by which ingredients work together to create the literary text. Gilbert is especially interested in the imperative – "Add food and *stir*" – that informs so many works in which "We stir readers when we add food because we remind them of their place at the complicated buffet of self, family, culture."[18] (Perhaps another maxim to add to our list?)

Thus, for instance, in the opening pages of *The Namesake*, Jhumpa Lahiri's homesick protagonist cobbles together a favorite Indian street snack in the kitchen of her Boston apartment, longing for the foods and flavors of the home she left behind in Calcutta.

> On a sticky August evening two weeks before her due date, Ashima Ganguly stands in the kitchen of her Central Square apartment, combining Rice Krispies and Planter peanuts and chopped red onion in a bowl. She adds

---

[16] *Norton Shakespeare.*
[17] Gilbert, *Culinary Imagination*, xv.
[18] Ibid., 8.

salt, lemon juice, thin slices of green chili pepper, wishing there were mus-
tard oil to pour into the mix. Ashima has been consuming this concoction throughout her pregnancy, a humble approximation of the snack sold
for pennies on Calcutta sidewalks and railway platforms throughout India,
spilling from newspaper cones ... Tasting from cupped palms, she frowns;
as usual, there's something missing.[19]

The food scene of Lahiri's novel invites readers to participate in the preparation of the snack, the partaking of it, and in the sense of cultural longing
and loneliness associated with it. The synesthetic effect of the passage is
evident. As Carolyn Daniel argues in her work *Voracious Children*, "Food
descriptions in fiction, like menus in restaurants and television cookery
programs, produce visceral pleasure, a pleasure which notably involves
both intellect and material body working in synaesthetic communion."[20]
In crucial ways, this synesthetic function of food description accounts
not only for the continuing preoccupation with food in the literary text
but also with the food text – by which we might mean recipes, menus,
foodoirs, food blogs – as literature. The food text, the food scene in the
literary text, the "eating words" – all function in similar ways. They ask us,
as Lynne Vallone puts it, to "taste the words with our eyes."[21] In Lahiri's
introductory passage too, we taste with our eyes, but interestingly we do
so at two levels. We see Ashima cooking the first of many snacks in the
novel, but we also scan her recipe for the snack. We note the food context
in the literary text, but we also note the food text in the literary context. In
reading about the preparation of *bhelpuri*, we follow a recipe of sorts – an
itemized list of heuristic instructions that straddle the realm of the culinary
and the literary. The narrative offers a recipe, but the recipe is also in and
of itself a narrative.

Perhaps this point is most poignantly brought home in the collection
of recipes that a group of women compiled from the constraints of the
Czechoslovakian concentration camp of Terezin in the mid-twentieth century. As they neared their death, they fantasized about food, shared recipes
from their bunks late at night, on occasion, even broke into arguments
about the appropriate way to prepare dishes they would never eat again.
"We called it 'cooking with the mouth,'" writes one woman who survived
Terezin and Auschwitz, "Everybody did it. And people got very upset if
they thought you made a dish the wrong way or had the wrong recipe for

[19] Jhumpa Lahiri, *The Namesake* (New York: First Mariner Books, 2003), 1.
[20] Carolyn Daniel, *Voracious Children: Who Eats Whom in Children's Literature* (New York: Routledge, 2006), 2.
[21] Quoted in Daniel, *Voracious Children*, 2.

it."[22] With paper hard to come by, they put down their recipes on whatever scraps were available, including propaganda leaflets and photographs of Hitler. The recipes give instructions for making beloved dishes in the Czech tradition. But to whom were these instructions directed? What could these recipes mean to women who were dying of starvation and had little hope of entering a kitchen or partaking of the offerings they had dreamed up? Perhaps the cookbook, even in the absence of an audience that would benefit from its heuristic instructions, was a way of preserving traditions that they knew were soon to disappear. Perhaps the recipes therein constitute a collective narrative from what has been called "the darkest kitchen of the twentieth century."[23] As Cara De Silva observes in her edition of the Terezin recipes, *In Memory's Kitchen*, "whatever its explicit or implicit functions, Mina's cookbook – and the others – make it clear that half a century after the Holocaust, when we thought we were familiar with all the creative ways in which human beings expressed themselves during the long years of the horror, at least one small genre, the making of cookbooks, has gone largely unnoticed."[24] Whether as cookbook, memoir, or testimony, the manuscripts from Terezin defy the boundaries of conventional food genres. They create new vocabularies of hunger and new forms of expression to endure, even defy, it. If, as Primo Levi has argued, the Holocaust required a new language to signal "hunger," "fear," "pain" – these being mere words "created and used by free men who lived in comfort" – it might be in these memories of meals and recipes for them that we find such a language evolving.[25]

Early work on the food text, work that did not necessarily identify itself as part of a well-defined field called food studies, pointed to the narrative function within food genres such as the recipe book. Of course, the recipe has for some years been the subject of several scholarly volumes, especially in early modern literary studies, which has turned to seventeenth-century receipt collections, such as those by Hannah Woolley, to find important evidence of women's textual production in the period. But over twenty years ago, when Susan Leonardi began her essay in *PMLA* by sharing a recipe, such work was in a fledgling stage.[26] In "Recipes for Reading: Summer

[22] Cara De Silva, ed. *In Memory's Kitchen* (Northvale, NJ: Jason Aronson, 1996), xix.
[23] Gilbert, *Culinary Imagination*, 23.
[24] De Silva, *In Memory's Kitchen*, xxxiii.
[25] See Michael Berenbaum's Foreword in ibid., xv.
[26] For work on the early modern receipt collections see Michelle DiMeo and Sara Pennell, eds., *Reading and Writing Recipe Books 1550–1800* (Manchester: Manchester University Press, 2013); Robert Appelbaum, "Rhetoric and Epistemology in Early Printed Recipe Collections," *Journal for Early Modern Cultural Studies* 3.2 (Fall/Winter 2003): 1–35; David Goldstein, "Woolley's Mouse: Early

Pasta, Lobster à la Riseholme, and Key Lime Pie," Leonardi started by offering her readers a recipe for summer pasta and in the remainder of the article invited them to explore this act as one that brings the reading and writing mind together in an active relationship. Leonardi went on to examine the narratives embedded in a range of recipe books, looking at the literary and culinary techniques by which they were shared with audiences. She ended with an interesting reflection on the dissemination and reception of the recipe as text:

> I want to return for a moment to the summer pasta. It was this process of thinking about the meaning of recipes and recipe giving that made me want to begin this text with a recipe, to embed a recipe in a text that mediates on the recipe as embedded discourse. I wanted to begin with a recipe in hopes ... of creating a persona readers could identify and trust, in hopes of creating readers who would, therefore, willingly suspend for a few pages not so much disbelief as academic skepticism.[27]

What we see here are several foundational ideas for the field that we now call literary food studies. Leonardi gives us one of the earliest methods for thinking about food and text by sharing a method from a food text. She evokes a food scene, makes a case for the study of a food genre, and close reads the literary techniques at work in its dissemination. Importantly, Leonardi tests the limits and licenses of her method, even anticipating academic skepticism. Such skepticism would persist in the field for years to come.

In 1999 an op-ed piece in the *Chronicle of Higher Education* compared the trend for food studies to the new yuppie trend for humble kitchen fare: "Food studies is much like rice: once shunned as too ordinary, it's now a hot commodity, available in countless varieties." While the piece goes on to offer a balanced assessment of serious work in the field, along with some of the "half-baked" projects out there (the pun, we gather, is intentional), its lede sentence about food studies as "scholarship lite" has become something of a maxim in itself, plaguing the field much more than is warranted.[28] Anita Mannur, in her work *Culinary Fictions*, tackles such criticism head on, arguing that the ambivalence about food studies as a discipline "speaks more to the anxiety about placing something as seemingly superficial as food into the center of critical analysis ... than it does

---

Modern Recipe Books and the Uses of Nature," in *Ecofeminist Approaches to Early Modernity* edited by Jennifer Munroe and Rebecca Laroche (New York: Palgrave Macmillan, 2011), 105–28.

[27] Susan Leonardi, "Recipes for Reading: Summer Pasta, Lobster à la Riseholme, and Key Lime Pie," *PMLA* 104.3 (1989): 347.

[28] Jennifer K. Ruark, "A Place at the Table," *Chronicle of Higher Education* 45.44 (1999): A17–A19.

to the seriousness of food per se."[29] But rather than mounting an elaborate defense against accusations of "scholarship lite," Mannur suggests that "we would do well to attend instead to the contradictory perplexities which animate the doubts leveled against 'food studies.'"[30] To probe these anxieties is to reckon with long and mired disciplinary histories.

What accounts for these early reservations about food as a legitimate object of academic inquiry? Why have disciplines like anthropology and sociology been regarded as a more natural home for food studies than literature? What sort of assumptions have worked to implicitly apportion particular fields to particular genders, so that food studies is considered a natural fit with women's studies? Perhaps, as one commentator in the *Chronicle* article suggests, it is the quotidian nature of food and its long association with women in the kitchen that results in the labeling of it as "scholarship lite." "Real men don't eat quiche, and real men certainly don't write about quiche."[31] The objection is, no doubt, intentionally facetious. But as Carole Counihan and Penny Van Esterik point out in their landmark collection *Food and Culture*, scholars in women's studies have had to do much work in changing such attitudes, by "legitimizing a domain of human behavior so heavily associated with women over time." Equally, the increased politicization of food and the expansion of social movements associated with food have created an increased awareness of food consumption and food production, contributing to the respectability of scholarly endeavors on food. According to Counihan and Van Esterik, having gained such legitimacy as a topic of scholarly research, "its novelty, richness, and scope provided limitless grist for the scholarly mill – as food links body and soul, self and other, the personal and the political, the material and the symbolic."[32]

We might, of course, ask a different set of questions about this newfound legitimacy and popularity of the field. In recent years, why has the field gained such wide appeal? What are we to make of the ubiquity of food texts and food approaches and food discourses in general? Typical explanations tend to reiterate some version of the following: food is fundamental; we all have to eat it; we eat it together. More speculative explanations suggest that this popularity has something to do with what

---

[29] Anita Mannur, *Culinary Fictions: Food in South Asian Diasporic Culture* (Philadelphia: Temple University Press, 2010), 10.
[30] Ibid., 12.
[31] Ruark, "Place at the Table."
[32] Carole Counihan and Penny Van Esterik, eds., *Food and Culture: A Reader* (New York: Routledge, 2008), 1–2.

Michael Pollan has called "the decline and fall of home cooking," while more existential explanations suggest that we have not much else left to speculate on.[33] Perhaps, as Elspeth Probyn argues, food is "the last bastion of authenticity in our lives."[34] In the wake of postmodern tenets that our identities are fragmented and tenuous, food becomes the only remaining marker of selfhood. If we write about food on an unprecedented scale, it is to grapple with these changing identities and nostalgically hark back to lost ones. Thus it is that we have foodoirs, food wars, food flicks, food nets, food porn, food art, food for thought. Essentially, as Gilbert puts it, we have "food on the mind, everywhere."[35]

British celebrity food chef Nigella Lawson has claimed that gastroporn is our last allowable excess, that we are all, in effect, "gastropornographers."[36] The mingling of food and sex in literary and cultural forms such as the food show, the foodoir, and the coming of age food novel are all, in a sense, testament to Lawson's claim. How might such an obsession look in terms of a larger historical perspective? How might it compare with the foodways and food words of other historical epochs? Certainly, our "*fin de siècle* craze for food," as Probyn notes, seems to echo Foucault's description of the Greeks for whom "the question of foods ... was a great deal more important than sexual activity."[37] Perhaps we can take recourse to yet another pithy maxim, from a *New York Times* piece, which sums up this new trend by declaring, "Food Is the New Sex." This nugget in the *Times* is part of a larger piece that looks at the "transvaluation" of rules and taboos typically associated with sex onto food that is unique to our own historical moment, so that the morality accruing around the former now derives from the latter.[38] But sensational headlines aside, it is worth asking how dietary regimes and sexual regimes intersect in literature and culture at large and how scholarly work in the field has mapped these intersections. "If much of cultural theory over the last decade has revolved around sex as that which secures identity," writes Probyn in a work that is appropriately sub-titled *FoodSexIdentities*, "it seems to me that the sensual nature of eating now constitutes a privileged optic through which to consider how identities and the relations between sex, gender and power are being

---

[33] See Gilbert, *Culinary Imagination*, 5–6. The existential explanation is posed by Joe-Anne McLaughlin in her poem "Existentially Speaking," which Gilbert discusses on page 5.
[34] Probyn, *Carnal Appetites*, 12.
[35] Gilbert, *Culinary Imagination*, 4.
[36] Probyn, *Carnal Appetites*, 59.
[37] Ibid., 6.
[38] "Food Is the New Sex," *New York Times*, February 10, 2009, http://ideas.blogs.nytimes.com/2009/02/10/food-is-the-new-sex/?_r=0.

renegotiated."[39] The eating body, the pleasures and taboos it endures, is thus an important focal point in recent work on literary food studies.

In Fannie Flagg's American cult classic from the late eighties, *Fried Green Tomatoes at the Whistle Stop Cafe*, we partake of the pleasures that lie at the intersection of food and sex. Through the polyphony of narrative voices, we hear the stories of two generations of Southern women, their relationships with food and each other. The novel's queering of food is most apparent in its narrative of Ruth and Idgie, whose intimacy emerges in the many food scenes of the novel. It is honey that allows the women to articulate their sexual longing for each other and it is in their shared rituals around food preparation at the Whistle Stop Café that their relationship unfolds. As Laura Lindenfeld points out, "By subverting the traditional model of the woman server and caretaker and turning the role of feeder into a means of overthrowing male dominance *Fried Green Tomatoes* challenges traditional concepts of power." Rather than a form of female oppression, "Food and servitude thus become sources of strength throughout the Idgie/Ruth narrative."[40] By contrast, Evelyn's eating disorder in the frame tale depicts a more troubled relationship with food and sex. We see her approaching menopause, staring at cartons of ice cream or unwrapping candy bars in solitude. Food evidently takes the place of any kind of intimacy or community, which she cannot find with her husband, her Tupperware groups, or the Women's Community Center, the last of which she abandons in a humorous episode when called upon to study her own vagina. Both the narrative strands of the novel are brought together around the rituals of "eating sex" – a term we might borrow from Probyn to describe the mingling of alimentary and sexual regimes in the novel.

Such readings of "eating sex" allow us to queer food studies, a move called for by Julia C. Ehrhardt and others, who examine the foodways that negotiate (variously reinforcing and resisting) heterosexual gender ideologies.[41] The mouth, in particular, becomes an important locus in such an analysis of appetite and desire. For Kyla Wazana Tompkins, it is a site of "*queer alimentarity*" – "a space with a cultural and erotic history of its own, one that ... offers glimpses of a presexological mapping of desire, appetite, and vice."[42] To take up forms of queer alimentarity is to focus on the ways

[39] Probyn, *Carnal Appetites*, 6–7.
[40] Laura Lindenfeld, "Women Who Eat Too Much: Femininity and Food in *Fried Green Tomatoes*," in *From Betty Crocker to Feminist Food Studies: Critical Perspectives on Women and Food*, edited by Arlene V. Avakian and Barbara Haber (Amherst: University of Massachusetts Press, 2005), 230.
[41] Julia C. Ehrhardt, "Towards Queering Food Studies: Foodways, Heteronormativity, and Hungry Women in Chicana Lesbian Writing," *Food and Foodways* 14.2 (2006): 91–109.
[42] Tompkins, *Racial Indigestion*, 5.

in which the mouth and its acts of tasting, touching, and ingesting are constituted in particular literary and cultural texts. Through its incorporation of the external, the mouth also becomes one of the body's most vulnerable orifices. Bakhtin, whom we will return to later in this introduction, notes that it is in the act of eating that the body most reveals its own openness, "Here man tastes the world, introduces it into his own body, makes it part of himself."[43] The mouth then marks the threshold through which the other becomes part of the self, transforming the self in the process. As Maggie Kilgour notes in *From Cannibalism to Communion*, "The basic model for all forms of incorporation is the physical act of eating, and food is the most important symbol for other external substances that are absorbed."[44] The mouth registers (both in the act of eating and speaking) the body's exchange and communion with others.

Ingestion thus opens up the body to forms of contact and commerce with the other. It threatens bodily boundaries in ways that cultures have deliberated through the ages. Elsewhere, I have examined the disciplinary imperatives of seventeenth-century English conduct literature, domestic manuals, and dietaries that in the wake of the East India trade came to be preoccupied with the entry of foreign spices into the mouth and its perceived threat of racial contamination from "Blackamores" and "Bantamen."[45] Equally, this threat is projected on to the other, who in early colonial narratives is routinely conjured up as the cannibalistic figure that threatens to devour and annihilate the self. According to Kilgour, "To accuse a minority that resists assimilation into the body politic of that body's own desire for total incorporation is a recurring tactic: during the Middle Ages the Jews were accused of cannibalism, after the Reformation the Catholics were."[46] In this tension between the eating body and the eaten body, the mouth marks the threshold between self and other.

It is also in the mouth's craving of the other that we can register the intersections between food studies and critical race studies. In "Eating the Other" bell hooks contends that contemporary mass culture increasingly thrives on the idea that there is pleasure to be found in the fetishization of racial difference: "The commodification of Otherness has been

---

[43] Mikhail Bakhtin, *Rabelais and His World*, translated by Helene Iswolsky (Cambridge, MA: MIT Press, 1968), 281.

[44] Maggie Kilgour, *From Communion to Cannibalism: An Anatomy of Metaphors of Incorporation* (Princeton: Princeton University Press, 1990), 6.

[45] Gitanjali Shahani, "The Spicèd Indian Air in Early Modern England," in *Shakespeare Studies* 42 (2014): 122–37.

[46] Kilgour, *From Communion to Cannibalism*, 5.

so successful because it is offered as a new delight, more intense, more satisfying than normal ways of doing and feeling."[47] Tompkins turns to an earlier period in *Racial Indigestion*, examining the trope of the edible black body in nineteenth-century US literature. Opening with a description of a silent gag film from the 1900s in which a black child is eaten by an alligator, Tompkins proceeds to explore a rich archive of trading cards, children's literature, advertisements, and other primary documents in which black and Asian bodies are inscribed "with the marks of race and food."[48] *Racial Indigestion* thus provides us with new critical paradigms for examining the consumption of otherness in discursive productions of the culinary and gastronomic.

The turn to food has also empowered scholars to write colonial histories anew through food. Work in postcolonial studies, for instance, has recognized ways in which particular foods and drugs like spices, sugar, tea, and opium – what Parama Roy has called the "psychopharmacopoeia of empire" – have shaped colonial encounters in different parts of the world.[49] Marx's image of vampire capitalism might be harnessed to an image of cannibal colonialism in order to understand the appetites that drove colonial regimes. For Roy, "Colonial politics often spoke in an indisputably visceral tongue: its experiments, engagements, and traumas were experienced in the mouth, belly, olfactory organs, and nerve endings, so that the stomach served as a kind of somatic political unconscious in which the phantasmagoria of colonialism came to be embodied."[50] Thus it is that the colonial mouth as much as the colonial gaze has become the focus of recent work in food studies and postcolonial studies, most recently exemplified in Valérie Loichot's *The Tropics Bite Back*.[51] Equally, postcolonial studies has turned its attention to anti-colonial movements that have drawn on the symbolic power of food and abstinence. We might think of chapattis in the Mutiny, salt in the Satyagraha march, and fasts in Gandhi's protest movements as important examples from the Indian context. To reckon with food and eating in these contexts is to reckon with long and complex histories of encounter and resistance in a kind of alimentary contact zone.

[47] bell hooks, "Eating the Other: Desire and Resistance," in *Black Looks: Race and Representation* (Cambridge, MA: South End, 1999), 21.
[48] Tompkins, *Racial Indigestion*, 1.
[49] Parama Roy, *Alimentary Tracts: Appetites, Aversions, and the Postcolonial* (Durham: Duke University Press, 2010), 7.
[50] Ibid.
[51] Valérie Loichot, *The Tropics Bite Back: Culinary Coups in Caribbean Literature* (Minneapolis: University of Minnesota Press, 2013).

Popular commodity histories have often chronicled the "rise" of commodities like chocolate and sugar, typically evacuating such narratives of their colonial underpinnings. Scholars like Bruce Robbins have extensively documented the commodity fetish at work in these popular histories, observing the rhetorical flourish in titles such as *Corn and Capitalism: How a Botanical Bastard Grew to Global Dominance* or *The World of Caffeine: The Science and Culture of the World's Most Popular Drug.* The "hero" of every such story tends to be global capitalism itself. Its narrative arc is predictable. We typically begin with a commodity like coffee or chocolate, which is restricted to courtly circles for reasons that have to do with its price and rarity; along comes an underdog who valiantly fights to bring it to the masses; we then have villains fighting its spread for reasons that have to do with avarice or moral outrage, but they are ultimately vanquished. Capitalism triumphs and the consumer is rewarded. "What a wondrous system this is, you are told, that has brought to your doorstep or breakfast table all these things you would have never known existed, yet things without which you would not, you suddenly realize, be yourself," Robbins sums up the moral of the story.[52] By contrast, academic projects on food commodities have taken a more nuanced approach. Timothy Morton's work on the poetics of spices and Kim F. Hall's on the politics of sugar have refused the commodity fetishism of popular narratives.[53] Hall's work, for instance, has made important interventions in early modern food studies through her examination of race, gender, and material culture in the Anglo-Caribbean sugar trade.

The attention to changing ecologies that result from colonial and plantation economies has also resulted in a rich dialogue between postcolonial and ecocritical studies, which, in turn, has drawn new attention to local food practices, cultivation, and consumption. In the words of eco-theorist Pablo Mukherjee:

> Surely any field purporting to theorize the global conditions of imperialism and colonialism (let us call it postcolonial studies) cannot but consider the complex interplay of environmental categories such as water, land, energy, habitat, migration with political or cultural categories such as state, society, conflict, literature, theater, visual arts. Equally, any field purporting to attach interpretive importance to environment (let us call it eco/environmental

---

[52] Bruce Robbins, "Commodity Histories," *PMLA* 120.2 (2005): 456.
[53] Timothy Morton, *The Poetics of Spice: Romantic Consumerism and the Exotic* (Cambridge: Cambridge University Press, 2000); Kim F. Hall, "'Extravagant Viciousness': Slavery and Gluttony in the Works of Thomas Tryon," in *Writing Race across the Atlantic World: Medieval to Modern*, edited by Philip D. Beidler and Gary Taylor (New York: Palgrave Macmillan, 2005), 93–111.

studies) must be able to trace the social, historical and material coordinates of categories such as forests, rivers, bio-regions and species.[54]

To this we might add, any field purporting to mine these intersections might consider the colonial and environmental impact of imperial expansion on global and indigenous foodways and agricultural practices. It was, after all, Karl Marx who reminded us that two centuries ago "nature, which does not trouble herself about commerce, had planted neither sugar-cane nor coffee trees" in the West Indies.[55]

Chronicling the colonial and ecological histories of such commodities, we might turn to novellas like Julia Alvarez's *A Cafecito Story* and other work that addresses the environmental and political implications of food and tourism or food and agribusiness. In Alvarez's eco fable, we travel with a Nebraskan farmer on his journey to discover fair trade coffee, after his own family farm has caved under the forces of agribusiness. When Joe's land is eventually razed to make way for parking lots and strip malls, he ventures to the Dominican Republic, where he learns about the return to traditional methods of shade-grown coffee and stays to start his own cooperative. Critics have often pointed out that the novella, while ostensibly clearing space for a new future for Dominican coffee growers, "reinscribes the US expansion project of Manifest Destiny."[56] Yet in the tensions that such a work provokes, we might find fertile territory for conversations about the global movements of people and foods in relation to one another. Particularly valuable here are the theoretical paradigms formulated by scholars such as Allison Carruth, whose *Global Appetites: American Power and the Literature of Food* brings together work in food studies, food policy, agriculture history, social justice, and the environmental humanities.[57]

Eating is "an agricultural act" insists Wendell Berry, the American novelist, farmer, and environmental activist. Yet, as Berry points out, most eaters are at a remove from the cycle of food cultivation, thinking of themselves as consumers of an industrial product. Consequently, they ignore key questions: "How pure or clean is it, how free of dangerous chemicals? How far was it transported, and what did transportation add to the cost?

---

[54] Quoted in Graham Huggan and Helen Tiffin, *Postcolonial Ecocriticism: Literature, Animals, Environment* (London: Routledge, 2010), 2.

[55] David McLellan, ed., *Karl Marx: Selected Writings* (Oxford: Oxford University Press, 2000), 295.

[56] See Trenton Hickman, "Coffee and Colonialism in Julia Alvarez's *A Cafecito Story*," in *Caribbean Literature and the Environment: Between Nature and Culture*, edited by Elizabeth M. DeLoughrey, Renée K. Gosson, and George B. Handley (Charlottesville: University of Virginia Press, 2005), 70.

[57] Allison Carruth, *Global Appetites: American Power and the Literature of Food* (New York: Cambridge University Press, 2013).

How much did manufacturing or packaging or advertising add to the cost? When the food product has been manufactured or 'processed' or 'precooked,' how has that affected its quality or price or nutritional value?"[58] Berry's concerns are taken up in the work of several other food activists. Work on the ethics of eating right might constitute a field of inquiry in itself and lead us to a study of new food genres such as the polemics and manifestos of Carlo Petrini and Michael Pollan. Their incisive critiques of our foodways have spawned new food movements and food activism, particularly directed at the impact of the fast food industry. In *Fast Food Nation: The Dark Side of the All-American Meal*, Eric Schlosser paints a grim picture, imagining briefly how America's foodways will appear to future civilizations:

> And should Armageddon come, should a foreign enemy someday shower the United States with nuclear warheads, laying waste to the whole continent, entombed within Cheyenne Mountain, along with the high-tech marvels, the pale blue jumpsuits, comic books, and Bibles, future archeologists may find other clues to the nature of our civilization – Big King wrappers, hardened crusts of Cheesy Bread, Barbeque Wing bones, and the red, white, and blue of a Domino's pizza box.[59]

In this foodscape of wrappers, cafeteria trays, and cardboard containers, food production is imagined as an industrial process and eating as an empty, transient activity. Petrini's *Slow Food Manifesto* with its injunctions to resist the "fast life" and revive food traditions, as much as Berry's pleas to participate in the cycles of food production and preparation suggest alternative relationships between food and the self in the industrialized West.[60]

Such work will render hollow accusations that the scholarly turn to food is the result of a cynical, we-have-nothing-left-to-turn-to boredom. As a field, food studies reveals itself to be less concerned with food fetishes and food fads than it is with recovering important stories and histories that cannot be told without food. Recent work has also been more skeptical about the food fetishes of the field, resisting the more populist and problematic strains in work on food. Mannur, for instance, compels us to question why food is so often assumed to be an appropriate lens for the description of ethnicity, with food illustrations gracing the covers of Asian

---

[58] Wendell Berry, "What Are People For?," in *Eating Words: A Norton Anthology of Food Writing*, edited by Sandra M. Gilbert and Roger J. Porter (New York: Norton, 2015), 382.

[59] Eric Schlosser, "Fast Food Nation: The Dark Side of the All-American Meal," *New York Times*, www.nytimes.com/books/first/s/schlosser-fast.html.

[60] Carlo Petrini, "Slow Food Manifesto," in *Eating Words: A Norton Anthology of Food Writing*, edited by Sandra M. Gilbert and Roger J. Porter (New York: Norton, 2015), 408.

American fiction that is only loosely about food, and food metaphors appearing in reviews of South Asian fiction that isn't even remotely about curry.[61] She contends that the popularity of the culinary here is a way of rendering racial and ethnic difference "more palatable."[62] Others such as Tompkins have called for a shift from food studies to *critical eating studies*," in a move that seeks to resist the fetishization of the food commodity. Without lending credence to the "scholarship lite" accusation, we might do well to heed her call to "nudge food studies' interests and methods away from an unreflective collaboration in the object-based fetishism of single-commodity histories and ideologically worrisome localist politics," turning instead to critical eating studies and its intersections with feminist, queer, and gender studies as well as to critical race studies.[63]

Such an approach allows literary food studies to formulate a theoretical framework in relation to other fields and critical approaches that have placed the body and its political, racial, and gendered economies at the crux of analysis. It allows us to recognize, as Mannur does, that literary food scholars will necessarily engage in what Brad Epps has called a kind of "promiscuity," drawing from and deploying interdisciplinary methods.[64] Of course, literary critics have and will continue to simultaneously create their own methodologically consistent ways to approach the culinary text. In the end, to use yet another eating word, we will have to be omnivorous in our methods, as we look at books to taste and books to chew, both in terms of approaches culled from our own field and others.

Toward an Omnivorous Method

The essays in *Food and Literature* aim to posit such an omnivorous method for the field at large. If we began the previous section with a more abstract consideration of food (as language, as metaphor, as form, as sex), with Eagleton's stipulation that "it is that it is never just food," we nevertheless found our way to a consideration of food as material substance (the stuff of colonial loot, of agricultural cycles, of industrial plants). We traced its intersections with work in critical race studies, queer theory, postcolonial studies, and other fields that have shaped its central concerns. Along the way, we examined the possibilities for the applications of its methods in different literary and cultural texts. What I have offered in the previous

---

[61] Mannur, *Culinary Fictions*, 14.
[62] Ibid.
[63] Tompkins, *Racial Indigestion*, 2–3.
[64] Mannur, *Culinary Fictions*, 18.

section, then, is a method and structuring principle for the volume as a whole that imagines the possibilities for different approaches and objects of inquiry in literary food studies.

As a collection, *Food and Literature* is well timed to reflect on the origins of the field, trace important developments, and suggest practical applications for future work. It is one of the first collections to take up food and literature as theme and method. Most early volumes in food studies have been either interdisciplinary in rationale and scope or quite specifically focused on work in the social sciences. Counihan and Van Esterik's seminal work on *Food and Culture*, first printed in 1997 and then again in 2008, is quite explicit in its intent to offer "classic papers" in the social sciences.[65] The editors agree upon the centrality of cultural anthropology to the field of food studies, thus anthologizing valuable foundational essays by Margaret Mead on changing food habits; Lévi Strauss on the culinary triangle; Sidney Mintz on sugar, slavery, and global trade; among others. With the exception of Jack Goody's "The Recipe, the Prescription and the Experiment" and Arjun Appadurai's "Cookbooks in Contemporary India," observations about food texts and literary texts emerge only incidentally. Even though the introduction does note the "countless" new works on food in literature "from the study of eating and being eaten in children's literature ... to food symbols in early modern American fiction ... to post-Freudian analysis of literary orality," we sample very little fare along these lines in the anthologized essays. Likewise, *The Cultural Politics of Food and Eating*, published in 2005, clearly sets out to reach a "transdisciplinary" readership. The editors note that contributors to the volume are not anthropologists of "the card-carrying, degree-holding type," but the literary text remains beyond the scope of the volume.[66] As such, the foundational volumes in food studies have been valuable to literary scholars, but have not specifically taken up literary texts for analysis. Where the literary text is the focus of analysis, as in *The Table is Laid: The Oxford Anthology of South Asian Food Writing*, we have a collection of primary texts on food, with anthologized fiction and non-fiction from writers such as Sara Suleri and Kiran Desai, but the focus here remains on making primary texts in South Asian studies available to an audience, rather than theorizing the field at large.[67]

[65] Counihan and Van Esterik, *Food and Culture*, 3.
[66] James I. Watson and Melissa I. Caldwell, eds., *The Cultural Politics of Food and Eating: A Reader* (Malden, MA: Blackwell, 2005), 2.
[67] John Thieme and Ira Raja, eds. *The Table Is Laid: The Oxford Anthology of South Asian Food Writing* (New Delhi: Oxford University Press, 2009).

Of course, this is not to suggest a dearth of monographs, edited volumes, and special issues on food in particular literary periods or in relation to particular authors. In Shakespeare studies alone, which I cite mainly since it has allowed for my own points of entry into food studies, one can produce a long list that includes Ken Albala's *Eating Right in the Renaissance* (2002), Robert Appelbaum's *Aguecheek's Beef, Belch's Hiccup, and Other Gastronomic Interjections* (2006), Joan Fitzpatrick's *Food in Shakespeare: Early Modern Dietaries and the Plays* (2007), and David Goldstein's *Eating and Ethics in Shakespeare's England* (2013).[68] Edited collections and special issues such as *Renaissance Food from Rabelais to Shakespeare* (2010), *Diet and Identity in Shakespeare's England* (2014), and *Culinary Shakespeare* (2016) have been devoted to different aspects of food and eating in the plays and the period at large.[69] Work on food genres (such as recipe books, household manuals, and dietaries) and foodstuffs (such as sugar, spice, and sack) has emerged in stand-alone essays and as parts of larger work on subjects as wide-ranging as Shakespeare and early modern domesticity, Shakespeare and early modern medicinal practice, as well as Shakespeare and early modern colonial ventures.[70] Any foray into other areas of literary study would produce comparable bibliographies. Kara K. Keeling and Scott T. Pollard's introduction in *Critical Approaches to Food in Children's Literature*, for instance, offers an extensive list of citations that includes articles, single-work studies, and scholarly monographs that take up everything from eating disorders in *Mrs. Piggle Wiggle*, to psychoanalytic readings of Maurice Sendak, to the power relations in children's texts on eating and being eaten.[71]

This is all to say that there is a rich archive of work on food in particular subfields of literature, but a work that looks at the entire field systematically,

[68] See Ken Albala, *Eating Right in the Renaissance* (Berkeley: University of California Press, 2002); Appelbaum, *Aguecheek's Beef*; Joan Fitzpatrick, ed., *Food in Shakespeare: Early Modern Dietaries and the Plays* (London: Ashgate, 2007); David B. Goldstein, *Eating and Ethics in Shakespeare's England* (Cambridge: Cambridge University Press, 2013).

[69] See Joan Fitzpatrick, ed., *Renaissance Food from Rabelais to Shakespeare: Culinary Readings and Culinary Histories* (Aldershot, UK: Ashgate, 2010); Kimberly Ann Coles and Gitanjali Shahani, "Diet and Identity in Shakespeare's England," Shakespeare Studies 42 (2014): 21–31; David B. Goldstein and Amy L. Tigner, *Culinary Shakespeare* (Pittsburgh, PA: Duquesne University Press, 2016).

[70] See Kim F. Hall's chapter on sugar, "Culinary Spaces, Colonial Spaces: The Gendering of Sugar in the Seventeenth Century," in *Feminist Readings of Early Modern Culture: Emerging Subjects*, edited by Valerie Traub, M. Lindsay Kaplan, and Dympna Callaghan (Cambridge: Cambridge University Press, 1996), 168–90; on spices, Shahani, "Spicèd Indian Air"; and on sack, Barbara Sebek, "'More Natural to the Nation': Situating Shakespeare in the 'Querelle de Canary,'" *Shakespeare Studies* 42 (2014): 106–21.

[71] Kara K. Keeling and Scott T. Pollard, "Introduction: Food in Children's Literature," in *Critical Approaches to Food in Children's Literature*, edited by Kara K. Keeling and Scott T. Pollard (New York: Routledge, 2009), 3–18.

comprehensively, and methodologically has yet to be published. *Food and Literature* seeks to fill this void. It does not limit itself to particular authors, genres, time periods, or regions in the way that earlier collections and monographs have had to. Coming as it does at this particular juncture in food studies scholarship, it is unhampered by justifications and defenses about food as a legitimate object of academic inquiry. It is able to look at the disciplinary and interdisciplinary moorings of literary food studies and offer new ways in which food can animate our field. It brings together scholars from a range of subfields in literary food studies to present an ongoing conversation about food as subject and food as method. It hopes to achieve for literary studies what earlier volumes such as *Food and Culture* achieved for anthropology and other disciplines in the social sciences, offering a collection that charts the origins, developments, and applications of methods in the field.

Structure and Organization

The structure for this volume follows the organizational framework of the Cambridge Critical Concepts series as a whole. It includes sections on the origins, developments, and applications of food studies in literary studies. Below is a brief description of each section and the ways in which it executes the objectives of the volume and the series as a whole.

Origins

It is hard to pinpoint originary moments even in a field as recent as literary food studies. The search for Ur-texts has variously led scholars to the earliest book-length studies on food in literature, such as James Brown's *Fictional Meals and Their Function in the French Novel*, or to canonical work on the eating body, such as Mikhail Bakhtin's *Rabelais and His World*.[72] Several scholars cite Roland Barthes' ideas on the semiotics of food as a starting point for thinking about food and language. Others turn to publication history, by looking at the founding of *Gastronomica: The Journal of Food and Culture* as a key moment for the study of food in the humanities. Still others look to founding figures like Warren Belasco in tracing the trajectories of the field. This volume takes a well-known food maxim as its originary moment, turning to Brillat-Savarin's "tell me what you

---

[72] James W. Brown, *Fictional Meals and their Function in the French Novel 1789–1848* (Toronto: University of Toronto Press, 1984); Bakhtin, *Rabelais and His World*.

eat: I will tell you what you are" as its starting point.[73] The eighteenth-century gastronome's quotation is by now, of course, something of a cliché. Watered down versions of it figure in advertisements, popular diets, and elementary school notice boards, all of which warn, "you are what you eat." But it is the testing of this cliché that I find valuable as a starting point. Literary food studies has articulated some its most important questions in the process of reevaluating it.

"Do we eat what we are, or are we what we eat? Do we eat or are we eaten? … in eating do we confirm our identities, or are our identities reforged, and refracted by what and how we eat?" asks Probyn in a reworking of Brillat-Savarin's aphorism that is grounded in questions of food and identity politics.[74] Gilbert rewrites the aphorism to ask a set of questions about the gastronomic fantasies that are at the heart of our culinary imagination: "*Tell me what you read and write about what you eat, and I shall tell you more about what you are. Tell me how you envision food in stories and poems, memoirs and biographies, films and pictures and fantasies, and we shall begin to understand how you think about your life.*"[75] Here is a method, indeed the *raison d'être* of literary food studies that emerges in the process of engaging with the quotation. Tompkins asks a new set of questions via the aphorism. It is not simply the "what" of what one eats that matters:

> It is the "where" of where we eat and where food comes from; the "when" of historically specific economic conditions and political pressures; the "how" of how food is made; and the "who" of who makes and who gets to eat. Finally, and most important, it is the many "whys" of eating – the differing imperatives of hunger necessity, pleasure, nostalgia and protest – that most determine its meaning.[76]

It is in these theoretical reformulations of Brillat-Savarin's aphorism that we might find a manifesto of sorts for the field. And it is these questions and reformulations that guide Part 1, on "Origins." The chapters in Part 1 take up the how, the why, the when, and the where of literary food studies. Collectively, they address central questions that have constituted the field, as we know it today. Rather than following a chronological format that moves from an examination of food in one literary time period to the next, this part of the book follows the key theoretical questions that animate the field of literary food studies. It eschews such linearity since the field of food

---

[73] Brillat-Savarin, *Physiology of Taste*, 3.
[74] Probyn, *Carnal Appetites*, 11.
[75] Gilbert, *Culinary Imagination*, 6.
[76] Tompkins, *Racial Indigestion*, 4.

studies itself has grown in ways that aren't necessarily linear or chronological. While it does take a historical overview of the field, it does so by
probing the how, the what, and the when of food and eating in a range of
literary traditions and time periods.

David B. Goldstein's chapter opens Part I with an exploration of commensality – the "how" of eating. In **"Commensality,"** Goldstein contends
that literary and historical studies have tended to focus primarily on what
social scientists call the culinary, or the "what of eating" – the food on our
plates, how it got there, and what it does to us. But of equal importance
is the commensal, or the "how of eating" – how acts of sharing food help
construct self–other relationships, group interactions, and indeed whole
societies. His chapter considers the role of commensality in literature
through several lenses, using illustrations from the works of the Greeks
to the contemporary period. He argues that "Literature has always been
exquisitely attuned to commensality, even if Western philosophy notably
has not. This is because literature has always been concerned with social
relationships and with larger webs of connection." While literary criticism,
"blinded by the biases of philosophy," has only recently begun to explore
the importance of the commensal, it is, Goldstein insists, "among the best
equipped hermeneutics to uncover and articulate these conceptions." He
thereby articulates an important method for literary food studies.

From a consideration of the "how" in Goldstein's work, we move to
an examination of the "where" in Andrew Warnes' analysis of literary
foodscapes. In **"The Drive-Thru Supermarket: Shopping Carts and
the Foodscapes of American Literature,"** Warnes analyzes the work of
writers like Ginsberg, Jarrell, and others, who call attention not only to
the gleaming and vibrant commodities to be chosen from the supermarket
shelf, but also to the clattering functionality of the borrowed cart, which
then holds these choices before presenting them to the checkout. They
attribute to such carts a different mode of walking, quite unlike the leisurely strolling of earlier or *fin de siècle* modes of shopping. A new and
anxious need to return home instead underpins their movement in the
supermarket. This new compulsion becomes associated in their work with
their failure to occupy the foodscape, and the world, they move through.
While scholarship in the social sciences has for a while focused on the
supermarket, Daniel Miller's "Making Love in Supermarkets" and Frank
Cochoy and Catherine Grandclément-Chaffy's "Publicizing Goldilock's
Choice at the Supermarket" being important cases in point, Warnes'
chapter offers an important literary method for the study of foodspaces
that might include restaurants, kitchens, or cafeterias in other literary

texts.[77] Immigrant writing, in particular, has dwelt on the tensions that arise as diasporic communities are compelled to negotiate spaces such as supermarkets and school cafeterias in their adopted land. Writing by Lahiri and Eddie Huang, both of whom address the loneliness of the immigrant in hostile foodscapes, is ripe for analysis in these terms.[78]

The next chapter approaches the "when," "where," and "what" of food in its consideration of early dietary injunctions that we now call "vegetarianism." "In any global history of vegetarianism, most roads lead to the Indian subcontinent at some point or another," Parama Roy begins her chapter, taking us first as far back as 326 BCE when Alexander first visited the Indian subcontinent. In **"Gothic Vegetarianism,"** Roy examines the travel accounts from the late sixteenth and seventeenth centuries of European travelers to the coastal cities of western India. To many of these European observers the "Gentiles" they saw were distinguished by a religiously mandated compassion toward nonhuman life that functioned as a rebuke to the ways of their putatively more bloodthirsty European compatriots. Such seemingly extreme or perverse forms of vegetarianism or nonviolence coexisted, as many noted, with unusual and perverse forms of cruelty, especially against widows and carnivores, and gave subcontinental vegetarianism a strikingly gothic character. Roy's chapter enables us to think of originary moments when the foodways of the subcontinent permeated Western consciousness and shaped debates about food choices for centuries to come. She thus contributes to a growing body of work in literary food writing on vegetarianism that authors and activists like Tristram Stuart have taken as the subject of their work.[79] Her chapter opens up interesting possibilities for future work at the intersection of food studies, animal studies, and work on the nonhuman.

Denise Gigante's chapter, in formulating a theory of taste, takes us to the creation of the gastronome as a figure in literary discourse. In **"Good Taste, Good Food, and the Gastronome,"** Gigante reflects on the history of taste as a culinary preference and an aesthetic category. She chronicles how taste philosophers struggled with

---

[77] See Daniel Miller, *A Theory of Shopping* (Cambridge: Polity, 1998); Frank Cochoy and Catherine Grandclément-Chaffy, "Publicizing Goldilock's Choice at the Supermarket: The Political Work of Product Packs, Carts and Talk," in *Making Things Public: Atmospheres of Democracy*, edited by Bruno Latour and Peter Weibel (Cambridge, MA: MIT Press, 2005): 646–59.

[78] See in particular, stories like "Mrs. Sen's" from Jhumpa Lahiri, *Interpreter of Maladies* (Boston: Houghton Mifflin Harcourt, 1999) and Eddie Huang, *Fresh Off the Boat: A Memoir* (New York: Spiegel & Grau, 2013).

[79] Tristram Stuart, *The Bloodless Revolution: A Cultural History of Vegetarianism from 1600 to Modern Times* (New York: Norton, 2007).

the metaphor (*goût, gusto,* taste) given by the modern languages to aesthetic experience. What could the intellectual activity of objective, disinterested judgment have to do with the salivary organs of the mouth – seat of
instinctive, unthinking sensation? The purpose of aesthetic contemplation
had always been to transcend bodily reality, and this gustatory metaphor of
taste did not exist in classical aesthetics. Taste, symbolically connected as it
was to the guts, ranked low on the philosophical hierarchy of the senses.

It was only in the age of gastronomy, "when food was prepared and judged
as an aesthetic object, [that] the gastronome emerged as a guide and a
tastemaker, holding food to the same exacting standards of taste as the fine
arts." Gigante turns to the writings of Parisian cookbook author, William
Kitchiner, who in turn looked to Milton's conception of the aesthetics of
pleasure to articulate his theories of gastronomy. She argues that Milton
was a "gastronome *avant la lettre* who demonstrated the bon vivant's attitude toward good-living in the more comprehensive, philosophical sense
of goodness, which does not divide aesthetics from ethics." Her focus on
Kitchiner, Milton, and Milton's Comus, the ancient Greek god of cookery,
provides us with a fascinating study of early constructions of "foodie"
figures – masters in the arts of cookery-chicanery.

From Gigante's inquiry into the originary "who" figures of literary
food studies, we move to J. Michelle Coghlan's examination of the
"how to" genres in the field, specifically the recipe. In **"The Art of the
Recipe: American Food Writing Avant la Lettre,"** Coghlan begins with
a consideration of form:

> Is a recipe a list of ingredients and a formula of the steps to be taken in
> producing a given dish? If it comes to us in the form of a lyric could we
> call it a poem? If it is given to us, instead, in the form of an essay or in the
> midst of a memoir or dropped in as the supplement – or interruption – to
> a novel's narrative, can we think of the book it comes to us in as a kind of
> cookbook even if it would likely be more readily categorized, at least ini-
> tially, as something else?"

Coghlan's introductory questions lead her to an analysis of "Artful recipes –
or, recipes artfully merged into books we wouldn't immediately describe as
cookbooks." While M. F. K. Fisher's oeuvre and experimental cookbook-
cum-memoirs like *The Alice B. Toklas Cookbook* are well-known modern
literary forms of the artful recipe, Coghlan argues that far less attention
has been paid to the nineteenth-century American food writing that
anticipates and enriches our understanding of the aesthetic pleasures at the
heart of Fisher's essays and the modern recipistolary canon of which they
are part. Her chapter takes up the matter of American food writing "avant

la lettre" by turning to the exuberant – and now largely forgotten – food essays of expat American writer Elizabeth Robins Pennell.

Robert Appelbaum's chapter brings Part I to a close by offering us a philosophical consideration of what food is. He opens **"Existential Disgust and the Food of the Philosopher"** with a taxonomy of food. "Food, so far as it appears as an object in literary discourse, can be categorized as any of a number of things – 'things' in the sense of objects of experience, cognition, and inquiry." Appelbaum offers six of these "things" for us to consider: (1) food as material object; (2) food as an occasion of gustatory and olfactory sensation; (3) food as a historical phenomenon; (4) relatedly, food as a sociocultural phenomenon, at once material and symbolic; (5) food as the object of a practice; and (6) what might be thought of as the metaphysical identity of food, which can take two antithetical forms. On the one hand, (6a) food can be identified as pure nutrition, an element in the dynamic order of being, the being of living (and dying) things; on the other, (6b) food can be identified as an existent with irreducible qualities over and above its nutritional character; it can be identified as a characteristic or index of an order of being itself. It is the sixth, double-sensed meaning that Appelbaum takes up with a particular focus on Sartre's *Nausea*.

Collectively, these chapters are concerned with different points of origins in our study of food, whether in their consideration of commensality, foodscapes, dietary choices, taste, food genres, or food as object of philosophical inquiry in literature. While I have outlined the central question in each, they overlap in their shared concerns with the "why we eat," "what we eat," "how we eat," "where we eat," and "how we write about what we eat" questions that animate literary texts from a range of global literary traditions and time periods.

Developments

Part II takes Rabelais' ode to Master Belly as its guiding principle: "Master Belly is the true master of all the arts ... The whole world is busy serving him, everyone working. And in return he brings all sorts of good things to the world, inventing all the arts, every engine known, all trades and crafts, all machines and subtleties."[80] The act of eating, even as it is basic and necessary, is an act that affords boundless artistic and intellectual possibilities. If all arts and crafts and trades are the inventions of Master Belly, we might develop a critical practice in relation to our acts of feeding

---

[80] Rabelais, *Gargantua and Pantagruel*, 571.

him. Bakhtin, in his analysis of Rabelais, describes the act of eating as one that facilitates the body's interaction with the world: "The encounter of man with the world, which takes place inside the open, biting, rending, chewing mouth, is one of the most ancient, and most important objects of human thought and imagery. Here man tastes the world, introduces it into his body, makes it part of himself."[81] Such an image of man, eating and experiencing the world around him with his biting, chewing, rending mouth, provides us a useful analogy for the methods in this section. We might think of the developments in the field of food studies as the development of a way of experiencing and analyzing the world through food and its ingestion. The chapters in this part of the volume develop a critical approach grounded in an alimentary framework. They look at the development of food studies in relation to work that has particularly gained from an alimentary approach, whether in postcolonial studies, critical race studies, or gender and sexuality studies. These chapters can be seen as collectively tracing and examining the imperatives of Master Belly in different intellectual and artistic texts and contexts, where such imperatives are frequently complex, troubled, or historically noteworthy.

Catherine Keyser's chapter opens Part II by drawing on an alimentary approach in her reading of race in twentieth-century US literature. In **"Visceral Encounters: Critical Race Studies and Modern Food Literature,"** Keyser argues that in the literature of this period, food-related plots and recurring oral images express anxieties and ambivalences surrounding Jim Crow and its fetishization of light skin and supposedly pure white bodies. Beginning with structural anthropologists of the 1960s, moving through black studies of the 1980s, and into hemispheric American studies of the 1990s and 2000s, her chapter explores the critical approaches that scholars have used to interrogate this dynamic. Her analysis builds on bell hooks' argument that eating can be an appropriative act, in which the ethnic other is absorbed by white consumers as an exotic spice, and yet at the same time, eating is an intimate encounter that demonstrates the permeability of the body.

In the next chapter, Valérie Loichot revisits her own seminal work in food studies and postcolonial studies in *The Tropics Bite Back*. **"The Ethics of Eating Together: The Case of French Postcolonial Literature"** pairs well with Chapter 1, particularly analyzing commensality from a postcolonial perspective. Loichot looks at the ethics of eating together in the literature of a variety of writers born in France's colonies or postcolonies,

---

[81] Bakhtin, *Rabelais and His World*, 280.

including Aimé Césaire, Suzanne Césaire, Maryse Condé, Jacques Derrida, Michel Houellebecq, and Simone Schwarz-Bart. Her chapter ponders the fate of commensality when human communities are disrupted by slavery, colonialism, hyper-nationalism, or contemporary identity crises in Fortress Europe. Condé, Derrida, Schwarz-Bart, and Suzanne Césaire develop an ethics and practice of eating well together as an antidote to colonial or nationalist politics of discrimination. By contrast, François in Houellebecq's novel *Soumission*, who hopelessly eats alone, signals the fragility of a France desperately clinging to an illusory purity.

Like Loichot in the previous chapter, Elspeth Probyn's chapter develops arguments that appeared in her earlier monograph, *Carnal Appetites*. In **"Eating Athwart, and Queering Food Writing,"** Probyn seeks to queer the genre of food writing, to render it "athwart." According to Probyn, M. F. K. Fisher lets us see how food writing reveals and produces the full force of what Gilles Deleuze and Felix Guattari call "the obligatory, necessary, or permitted interminglings of bodies." These bodies – texts, descriptions of food, feeding, and eating, render messy any distinction between and among them. This calls forth a style of writing that seeks not the comfort of an identity in food but rather revels in what food can unleash. Drawing on Eve Sedgwick's understanding of queer as athwart, she argues that food writing has the potential to make present the materiality of eating, writing, and food and exemplify the always attendant "cruel optimism" (to use Lauren Berlant's words) of those pairings.[82]

In **"Utilizing Food Studies with Children's Literature and its Scholarship,"** Kara K. Keeling and Scott T. Pollard open by reflecting on their own trajectories as writers and editors of work in children's literature and food studies, as well as that of other early practitioners in the field. They go on to map these intersections in the work of Laura Ingalls Wilder. Wilder's *Little House* books demonstrate the overlooked but fundamental role that food can play in the ideological controversies current in American western frontier studies. They demonstrate how, ideologically, Wilder agrees with Frederick Jackson Turner's traditional view of western expansion as a predominantly white, male arena; nonetheless her novels inherently complicate and challenge his monolithic view of settlement through her focus on women's experiences on the frontier.

While the first four chapters in Part II trace the development of food studies in particular theoretical fields and literary disciplines, the last two chapters in this section examine its development in artistic movements

---

[82] Lauren Berlant, *Cruel Optimism* (Durham, NC: Duke University Press, 2011).

and epistemic paradigms like modernism and postmodernism. Both chapters suggest important ways in which the figure of the celebrity chef shapes the artistic landscape of food studies. In "**Avant-Garde Food Writing, Modernist Cuisine**," Allison Carruth examines the current culinary movement labeled "molecular gastronomy," contesting the vision of it as an extension of modernism. This twenty-first-century culinary trend exemplifies a wider pattern in innovation-driven industries of laying claim to literary and artistic traditions of aesthetic and sociocultural experimentation. In developing this argument, Carruth employs the term "culinary lab" to describe restaurant incubators such as Catalan chef Ferran Adrià's now shuttered elBulli and to apprehend interconnections between the rhetoric of *modernist cuisine* and tropes of prototyping, entrepreneurship, and invention in engineering writ large. Comparing modernist cuisine to alimentary texts penned by avant-garde artists and writers, her essay historicizes not only the chefs, restaurants, and cuisines but also the engineers, biochemists, designers, and venture capitalists who are collectively imagining and monetizing culinary innovation in the contemporary period.

Rohit Chopra turns to "**Comic Books and the Culinary Logic of Late Capitalism**" in the concluding chapter of this section. His work examines the relationship between food, violence, and capitalism in three comic book series on food, *Get Jiro!* and *Get Jiro! Blood and Sushi*, *Starve*, and *Chew*. Chopra argues that, in these series, food as the symbol of nature, unsullied human existence, and truth becomes a way to countenance the corrupting violence of capitalism. Food also serves as a symbol of an authentic human bond, one that is prior to and beyond capital. It stands as the basis of a critique of the violence of the contractual reason that is essential to capitalism. The world of food in these works embodies the contradictory logic of late capitalism, in which food culture and the chefs are both hyper-commodified and hyper-mediated yet are the source of critique and opposition to the very culture that produces them. Situating the food comic subgenre of comic books in the context of the recent global surge of interest in food culture and at the juncture of several traditions of representation, Chopra considers the political implications of the critique that it offers about present-day market-mediated representations of food.

Concluding Part II with Chopra's chapter, we also witness exciting new possibilities for the analysis of new food genres, a development that itself results from our late capitalist preoccupation with food. In their respective chapters, the contributors to this part of the volume offer a trajectory of literary food studies as it has evolved, in relation to fields by which it has been shaped, and that it continues to shape, in turn.

Applications

The final part of this volume follows Roland Barthes' imperative: "Information about food must be gathered wherever it can be
found: by direct ... and by indirect observation in the mental life of a
given society."[83] The chapters in Part III apply Barthes' method of direct
and indirect observation to a range of texts and contexts. They look at the
semiotic power of food in literature and culture. What do foodstuffs and
foodways in the text signify? How do writers develop what Barthes called
"a system of communication, a body of images, a protocol of usages" with
regard to food? We might think of these chapters as revisiting foundational ideas in food studies and applying them to literary texts in new
and interesting ways. In a sense, Part III is a culmination of the two parts
that have charted the origins and development of the field of literary food
studies and its intersections with related fields. It is a collection of what
we might call culinary close readings. It demonstrates how books are to
be tasted and chewed and digested, drawing on methods that have been
posited throughout the volume.

Sandra Gilbert, whose corpus of writing has shaped literary food studies
in profound ways, opens Part III with "**Inebriation: The Poetics of Drink**."
As with *The Culinary Imagination*, here Gilbert uses her "eating words"
to analyze the poetry of drink. Carl Jung, who explains that "'alcohol'
in Latin is *spiritus*, and one uses the same word for the highest religious
experience as well as for the most depraving poison," provides Gilbert
with a starting point for an exploration of poetic inspiration and intoxication. "The confusion of spirit as alcohol with spirit as soul or breath
helps explain why a poetics of drink seems to have shaped or shadowed
the poetry – and fiction – of so many writers," Gilbert argues. Her analysis includes "alcoholic writers" from a long list of Nobel prize winners
(Sinclair Lewis, Eugene O'Neill, Ernest Hemingway, William Faulkner)
and beyond the Nobel winners, Hart Crane, F. Scott Fitzgerald, Louise
Bogan, Dylan Thomas, Delmore Schwartz, Philip Larkin, Robert Lowell,
John Berryman, Edna St. Vincent Millay, Raymond Carver, Elizabeth
Bishop, John Cheever, and Dorothy Parker, among others.

Jennifer Park's chapter continues to explore drink, but we move to
the macabre here, from spirits to blood. In "**Vampires, Alterity, and
Strange Eating**," Park examines blood drinking as a form of *strange eating*,
to argue that vampiric feeding, or the impulse to drink blood, manifests

---

[83] Barthes, "Psychosociology of Contemporary Food Consumption," 29.

from the intersection of medicine, myth, and ideas of human difference to produce a diet that pushes on the boundaries of what constitutes humanity in the literary imagination. Although the Victorianist vampire tends to serve as our reference point for vampiric feeding, Park's chapter provides another angle in our understanding of blood drinking in the context of food and literature. Her chapter highlights the more obscure – and thus more urgent – alternative or marginalized histories and afterlives of vampiric feeding, before and beyond the Victorian vampire: blood lust as infant nourishment, medicinal ingestion, or eating disorder with racial ramifications, from ancient epileptic blood drinking and early modern menstrual blood to the cross-pollination of blood drinking, disordered eating, and community building in the twenty-first century.

From the debauched world of intoxicated poets and blood-thirsty vampires, we move to a kind of innocent, domestic bliss in Frances E. Dolan's chapter, "**Toast and the Familiar in Children's Literature.**" Buttered toast, which appears frequently in Anglophone children's literature, is the subject of Dolan's essay. In its very familiarity, buttered toast might seem to be the perfect comestible to sum up the Golden Age of Children's Literature: it calls to mind the Victorian nursery, or at least a vision of that nursery that has been created precisely through such representations, yet it is recognizable to many a young reader today, creating another filament of connection between reader and characters and drawing the reader into the imagined world. Dolan makes the familiarity of toast a question rather than an assumption, focusing on toast in *The Wind in the Willows* (1908), *Mary Poppins* (1934), the *Harry Potter* series (1997–2007), and *A Series of Unfortunate Events* (1999–2006). To what extent does toast connect readers across time and place and to what extent is it becoming an exotic comestible, a food in need of a gloss, Dolan asks.

Tomoko Aoyama's chapter takes us beyond the Anglophone traditions of food writing to examine "**Food, Humor, and Gender in Ishigaki Rin's Poetry.**" Aoyama shows how food-related motifs permeate the works of the Japanese poet Ishigaki Rin (1920–2004). Ishigaki's working life coincided with Japan's military aggression, defeat, and postwar democracy, economic recovery, and expansionism, all deeply connected to the question of food production and consumption. She was involved in the bank workers' union movement, and published socially engaged poetry on topics ranging from atomic bombs and wars, to poverty and industrial accidents. Food and family in her works are often confrontational rather than comforting, associated with exhaustion, solitude, death, and the "abject." Aoyama identifies the links between Ishigaki's "written food" and other prominent examples of food in modern Japanese literature.

The last two chapters examine the poetics and politics of hunger, with Miriam O'Kane Mara looking to the Irish context and Deepika Bahri turning to postcolonial Zimbabwe. Both serve as important reminders that hunger, whether as a form of political protest or as a result of privation and shortage, falls as crucially within the domain of food studies as the work on food consumption. Bahri brings up Doris Lessing's overwhelming question in her last novel: "What will our descendants blame us for as we now blame the slave traders? Surely that is easy enough. They will say that one half of the world stuffed itself with food while the other half was hungry." How characters negotiate this hunger, how they find self-expression through it, and how they find the language to articulate it is the subject of these chapters.

In "**Food, Hunger, and Irish Identity: Self-Starvation in Colum McCann's 'Hunger Strike**,'" Mara investigates how Colum McCann's representation of self-starvation in "Hunger Strike" expands representations of anorexia nervosa, emphasizing the political nature of all self-starvation. The novella presents a child protagonist, who uses food behaviors to negotiate changing relationships with his body, his family, and his nation as he haltingly moves toward maturity. Mara argues that the historical traces of famine join the religious residue of the Catholic Eucharist and the sectarian political significance of food refusal, deepening the ways that food interpolates Irish culture. By highlighting the connections between language and food in identity building, the analysis reflects the complexity of McCann's characters' communication through food-related signifiers.

In the final chapter, Bahri explores the hunger narrative as a species of postcolonial literary and political enjambment, an intertextual phenomenon typified by different writers taking up a temporally discontinuous but thematically connected screed on postcolonial hungers. For Bahri, the tradition of the postcolonial hunger narrative points to the failure of history to meet humanity's most fundamental need. She begins "**Postcolonial Hungers**" with an analysis of Tsitsi Dangarembga's debut novel, *Nervous Conditions* and its sequel, *The Book of Not*. She then moves to a third novel, published more than a quarter century after *Nervous Conditions*, NoViolet Bulawayo's *We Need New Names*. Bahri contends that the escape artists of Dangarembga's and Bulawayo's novels and their anorexic female hunger artists ask for a reckoning with the politics of food, food distribution, and women's voluntary self-denial as signs of "the malign order

... of a disturbed universe."[84] She argues that "the postcolonial hunger narrative ultimately showcases the alignment of power and foodways by asking us to consider not only who eats, how much, and in what order, but also whether the pleasures of food and eating are distributed equally, especially for women, immigrants, and other alimentary sub-citizens in the gastropolitical order."

In the **Afterword**, Darra Goldstein, founding editor of *Gastronomica: The Journal of Food and Culture*, series editor of California Studies in Food and Culture, and author of five awardwinning cookbooks, reflects on her personal and professional trajectories in literary food studies. Goldstein, who was celebrating her retirement as this volume was going to press, reflects on the intellectual climate in the 1970s when she decided to write her dissertation on food in Russian literature. It is such "primal scenes" (my words, not hers) that made the field possible, laid the groundwork for future scholars, and inspired volumes such as this one.

Finally, as anyone familiar with food preparation is well aware, any given set of ingredients will end up differently in the hands of different cooks. The results will variously please and offend different palates. *Food and Literature* reflects the culinary imagination and tastes of those who've come together to create it. We worked with the ingredients we had. But these approaches, methods, and points of entry do not by any means exhaust the field. And thus, like Saleem Sinai, Rushdie's pickle connoisseur with whom I began this chapter, I will leave you with several chapters and one empty jar, for "the process of revision must be constant and endless." As for their reception, in Saleem's words:

> They may be too strong for some palates, their smell may be overpowering, tears may rise to eyes; I hope nevertheless that it will be possible to say of them that they possess the authentic taste of truth ... that they are, despite everything acts of love.[85]

BIBLIOGRAPHY

Albala, Ken. *Eating Right in the Renaissance.* Berkeley: University of California Press, 2002.
    "Shakespeare's Culinary Metaphors." *Shakespeare Studies* 42 (2014): 63–74.
Appelbaum, Robert. *Aguecheek's Beef, Belch's Hiccup, and Other Gastronomic Interjections.* Chicago: University of Chicago Press, 2006.

---

[84] Dambudzo Marechera, *The House of Hunger* (Oxford: Heinemann, 1978), 18.
[85] Rushdie, *Midnight's Children*, 530–31.

"Rhetoric and Epistemology in Early Printed Recipe Collections." *Journal for Early Modern Cultural Studies* 3.2 (Fall/Winter 2003): 1–35.

Bakhtin, Mikhail. *Rabelais and His World.* Translated by Helene Iswolsky. Cambridge, MA: MIT Press, 1968.

Barthes, Roland. "Toward a Psychosociology of Contemporary Food Consumption." In *Food and Culture: A Reader*, edited by Carole Counihan and Penny Van Esterik, 28–35. New York: Routledge, 2008.

Berlant, Lauren. *Cruel Optimism.* Durham, NC: Duke University Press, 2011.

Berry, Wendell. "What Are People For?" In *Eating Words: A Norton Anthology of Food Writing*, edited by Sandra M. Gilbert and Roger J. Porter, 382–85. New York: Norton, 2015.

Brillat-Savarin, Anthelme. *The Physiology of Taste; or, Meditations on Transcendental Gastronomy.* Translated by M. F. K. Fisher. New York: Heritage Press, 1949.

Brown, James W. *Fictional Meals and their Function in the French Novel 1789–1848.* Toronto: University of Toronto Press, 1984.

Carruth, Allison. *Global Appetites: American Power and the Literature of Food.* New York: Cambridge University Press, 2013.

Cochoy, Frank, and Catherine Grandclément-Chaffy. "Publicizing Goldilock's Choice at the Supermarket: The Political Work of Product Packs, Carts and Talk." In *Making Things Public: Atmospheres of Democracy*, edited by Bruno Latour and Peter Weibel, 646–59. Cambridge, MA: MIT Press, 2005.

Coles, Kimberly Ann, and Gitanjali Shahani. "Diet and Identity in Shakespeare's England." *Shakespeare Studies* 42 (2014): 21–31.

Counihan, Carole, and Penny Van Esterik, eds. *Food and Culture: A Reader.* New York: Routledge, 2008.

Daniel, Carolyn. *Voracious Children: Who Eats Whom in Children's Literature.* New York: Routledge, 2006.

De Silva, Cara, ed. *In Memory's Kitchen.* Northvale, NJ: Jason Aronson, 1996.

DiMeo, Michelle, and Sara Pennell, eds. *Reading and Writing Recipe Books 1550–1800.* Manchester: Manchester University Press, 2013.

Eagleton, Terry. "Edible Ecriture." *Times Higher Education*, October 24, 1997. www.timeshighereducation.com/features/edible-ecriture/104281.article.

Ehrhardt, Julia C. "Towards Queering Food Studies: Foodways, Heteronormativity, and Hungry Women in Chicana Lesbian Writing." *Food and Foodways* 14.2 (2006): 91–109.

Fitzpatrick, Joan, ed. *Food in Shakespeare: Early Modern Dietaries and the Plays.* London: Ashgate, 2007.

——— ed. *Renaissance Food from Rabelais to Shakespeare: Culinary Readings and Culinary Histories.* Aldershot: Ashgate, 2010.

Gifford, William, ed. *The Works of Ben Jonson with a Biographical Memoir.* New York: D. Appleton, 1879.

Gilbert, Sandra M. *The Culinary Imagination: From Myth to Modernity.* New York: Norton, 2014.

Goldstein, David B. *Eating and Ethics in Shakespeare's England.* Cambridge: Cambridge University Press, 2013.

"Woolley's Mouse: Early Modern Recipe Books and the Uses of Nature." In *Ecofeminist Approaches to Early Modernity*, edited by Jennifer Munroe and Rebecca Laroche, 105–28. New York: Palgrave Macmillan, 2011.

Goldstein, David B., and Amy L. Tigner, eds. *Culinary Shakespeare*. Pittsburgh, PA: Duquesne University Press, 2016.

Greenblatt, Stephen, Walter Cohen, Jean E. Howard, and Katherine Eisaman Maus, eds. *The Norton Shakespeare*. New York: Norton, 2008.

Hall, Kim F. "Culinary Spaces, Colonial Spaces: The Gendering of Sugar in the Seventeenth Century." In *Feminist Readings of Early Modern Culture: Emerging Subjects*, edited by Valerie Traub, M. Lindsay Kaplan, and Dympna Callaghan, 168–90. Cambridge: Cambridge University Press, 1996.

"'Extravagant Viciousness': Slavery and Gluttony in the Works of Thomas Tryon." In *Writing Race Across the Atlantic World: Medieval to Modern*, edited by Philip D. Beidler and Gary Taylor, 93–111. New York: Palgrave Macmillan, 2005.

Hickman, Trenton. "Coffee and Colonialism in Julia Alvarez's *A Cafecito Story*." In *Caribbean Literature and the Environment: Between Nature and Culture*, edited by Elizabeth M. DeLoughrey, Renée K. Gosson, and George B. Handley, 70–82. Charlottesville: University of Virginia Press, 2005.

hooks, bell. *Black Looks: Race and Representation*. Cambridge, MA: South End, 1999.

Huang, Eddie. *Fresh Off the Boat: A Memoir*. New York: Spiegel & Grau, 2013.

Huggan, Graham, and Helen Tiffin, *Postcolonial Ecocriticism: Literature, Animals, Environment*. London: Routledge, 2010.

Hutcheon, Linda. "Historiographic Metafiction Parody and the Intertextuality of History." In *Intertextuality and Contemporary American Fiction*, edited by Patrick O'Donnell and Robert Con Davis, 3–32. Baltimore: Johns Hopkins University Press, 1989.

Keeling, Kara K., and Scott T. Pollard, eds. *Critical Approaches to Food in Children's Literature*. New York: Routledge, 2009.

Kilgour, Maggie. *From Communion to Cannibalism: An Anatomy of Metaphors of Incorporation*. Princeton: Princeton University Press, 1990.

Lahiri, Jhumpa. *Interpreter of Maladies*. Boston: Houghton Mifflin Harcourt, 1999. *The Namesake*. New York: First Mariner Books, 2003.

Leonardi, Susan. "Recipes for Reading: Summer Pasta, Lobster à la Riseholme, and Key Lime Pie." *PMLA* 104.3 (1989): 340–47.

Levi-Strauss, Claude. "The Culinary Triangle." *Partisan Review* 33.4 (1966): 586–95.

Lindenfeld, Laura. "Women Who Eat Too Much: Femininity and Food in *Fried Green Tomatoes*." In *From Betty Crocker to Feminist Food Studies: Critical Perspectives on Women and Food*, edited by Arlene V. Avakian and Barbara Haber, 221–45. Amherst: University of Massachusetts Press, 2005.

Loichot, Valérie. *The Tropics Bite Back: Culinary Coups in Caribbean Literature*. Minneapolis: University of Minnesota Press, 2013.

Mannur, Anita. *Culinary Fictions: Food in South Asian Diasporic Culture*. Philadelphia: Temple University Press, 2010.

Marechera, Dambudzo. *The House of Hunger*. Oxford: Heinemann, 1978.

McLellan, David, ed. *Karl Marx: Selected Writings*. Oxford: Oxford University Press, 2000.

Miller, Daniel. *A Theory of Shopping*. Cambridge: Polity, 1998.

Morton, Timothy. *The Poetics of Spice: Romantic Consumerism and the Exotic*. Cambridge: Cambridge University Press, 2000.

Nicholson, Mervyn. "Food and Power: Homer, Carroll, Atwood and Others." *Mosaic* 20.3 (1987): 37–55.

Petrini, Carlo. "Slow Food Manifesto." In *Eating Words: A Norton Anthology of Food Writing*, edited by Sandra M. Gilbert and Roger J. Porter, 408–9. New York: Norton, 2015.

Probyn, Elspeth. *Carnal Appetites: FoodSexIdentities*. New York: Routledge, 2000.

Robbins, Bruce. "Commodity Histories." *PMLA* 120.2 (2005): 454–63.

Roy, Parama. *Alimentary Tracts: Appetites, Aversions, and the Postcolonial*. Durham, NC: Duke University Press, 2010.

Ruark, Jennifer K. "A Place at the Table." *Chronicle of Higher Education* 45.44 (1999): A17–A19.

Rushdie, Salman. *Midnight's Children*. New York: Random House, 2006.

Schlosser, Eric. "Fast Food Nation: The Dark Side of the All-American Meal." *New York Times*, 2000. www.nytimes.com/books/first/s/schlosser-fast.html.

Sebek, Barbara. "'More Natural to the Nation': Situating Shakespeare in the 'Querelle de Canary.'" *Shakespeare Studies* 42 (2014): 106–21.

Shahani, Gitanjali. "The Spicèd Indian Air in Early Modern England." *Shakespeare Studies* 42 (2014): 122–37.

Stuart, Tristram. *The Bloodless Revolution: A Cultural History of Vegetarianism from 1600 to Modern Times*. New York: Norton, 2007.

Thieme, John, and Ira Raja, eds. *The Table Is Laid: The Oxford Anthology of South Asian Food Writing*. New Delhi: Oxford University Press, 2009.

Tompkins, Kyla Wazana. *Racial Indigestion: Eating Bodies in the Nineteenth Century*. New York: New York University Press, 2012.

Watson, James I., and Melissa I. Caldwell, eds. *The Cultural Politics of Food and Eating: A Reader*. Malden, MA: Blackwell, 2005.

PART I

Origins

CHAPTER I

Commensality

David B. Goldstein

Food as Relationship

We are trained by the Western tradition to think of food as a thing, a discrete object that we can measure and absorb.[1] We talk calories, nutrients, ingredients. We discuss our culinary preferences and poisons in terms of the substances that comprise our food: vegan, gluten-free, organic. We learned this from, among other sources, Plato.[2] In the *Gorgias*, one of the founding texts for Western philosophy's attitudes toward food, Socrates describes eating and drinking as nothing more than satisfying a need, like "itching and scratching" or any other simple pleasure or requirement.[3] Food for Socrates is a matter of inputs and outputs, a basic biological function devoid of philosophical interest. In the *Phaedo*, considering the approaching end of his life, Socrates waves aside matters of consumption altogether, taking it as a given that the philosopher should not "concern himself with the so-called pleasures connected with food and drink."[4] Socrates arrives to Plato's *Symposium* late, about "half-way through dinner," and is indifferent to whether there will be drinking involved at what is expected to be a drinking party. It is conversation that nourishes him. He professes the wish that "wisdom were like water, and flowed by contact out of a person who has more into one who has less."[5] He is teasing his friend, Agathon, but beneath the metaphor lies the dream that philosophy could do away with the need for material sustenance altogether. If only we

---

[1] I would like to thank Liz Pentland and Kristen Smith for their invaluable contributions to this chapter. I am grateful for a research release from York University that provided time to write it.
[2] For accounts of the denigration of food in Plato and Western philosophy, see e.g., Carolyn Korsmeyer, *Making Sense of Taste: Food and Philosophy* (Ithaca, NY: Cornell University Press, 1999); Deane W. Curtin and Lisa M. Heldke, *Cooking, Eating, Thinking: Transformative Philosophies of Food* (Bloomington: Indiana University Press, 1992).
[3] Plato, *Gorgias*, translated by Robin Waterfield (Oxford: Oxford University Press, 1994), 82 (494c).
[4] Plato, "Phaedo," in *The Collected Dialogues of Plato*, edited by Edith Hamilton and Huntington Cairns, translated by Hugh Tredennick (Princeton: Princeton University Press, 1961), 47 (64d).
[5] Plato, *The Symposium*, translated by Walter Hamilton (London: Penguin, 1951), 37–38 (175c).

could just think and talk all day and not worry about constantly filling and refilling these leaky vessels we call our bodies!

Plato's vision of food as a physical thing has influenced Western culture in countless ways. Such suppositions are ubiquitous in today's attitudes toward eating. In the United States, where, as Claude Fischler has shown, "eating has become individualized and medicalized," our views have progressed even further along this path, to the point where diners are now most likely to describe their meals "in terms of nutrients (carbohydrates, fats, proteins), not foods."[6] Modern science has thus accelerated an atomization of Western eating that has progressed for centuries. Meanwhile, mounting evidence suggests that thinking about food exclusively as an object contributes to a range of unhealthy eating practices, including obesity and other forms of disregulation.[7] It is true that part of the problem of our current food system lies in the quality of the ingredients that make up much of the packaged food in our stores and eating establishments.[8] But as urgent a problem is that we consider food to be a thing made up of ingredients in the first place. Those packages list by law what each food is made of, but they do not indicate that *how* or *with whom* we consume each food is just as important.

Absent from this empirical model of food is the recognition that we do not just consume food, we *eat* it. And eating is not simply a biological phenomenon. It is also a social one, even if one is eating alone. Food is relational. It doesn't stay in one place, one form, or one body. It circulates, first through ecological transformations that start with soils, plants, and nonhuman animals, and then through relationships with other people. Food constitutes a material trace of the biological, ecological, social, and symbolic interactions that link eater, eaten, and the macrocosm that surrounds them.

Many of the relationships that food marks fall under the term "commensality." Derived from the Latin *commensalis*, "with the table," commensality means eating together. Narrowly, then, commensality refers

---

[6] Claude Fischler, "Commensality, Society and Culture," *Social Science Information* 50.3–4 (2011): 541, doi:10.1177/0539018411413963.

[7] Claude Fischler and Estelle Masson, *Manger: Français, Européens et Américains face à l'alimentation* (Paris: Odile Jacob, 2008); Boris Andersen, "Commensality between the Young," in *Commensality: From Everyday Food to Feast*, edited by Susanne Kerner, Cynthia Chou, and Morten Warmind (London: Bloomsbury, 2015), 43–50.

[8] See, e.g., Marion Nestle, *Food Politics: How the Food Industry Influences Nutrition and Health* (Berkeley: University of California Press, 2013); Michael Pollan, *The Omnivore's Dilemma: A Natural History of Four Meals* (New York: Penguin, 2006); Eric Schlosser, *Fast Food Nation: The Dark Side of the All-American Meal* (New York: Houghton Mifflin Harcourt, 2001).

to the social aspects of the meal. More broadly, however, commensality describes the range of relationships that emerge and are reified through the act of eating. These relationships, which Penny Van Esterik describes as "commensal circles," begin with the placental transfer of nutrients between mother and fetus, expanding steadily outward through ever-wider eating communities, whose largest circle is the nonhuman world that grows and becomes our food, and to which we return as food.[9] Commensality is food in its relational aspect; it is eating conceived as a network or as a principle of connectivity.

Literature has always been exquisitely attuned to commensality, even if Western philosophy notably has not.[10] This is because literature has always been concerned with social relationships and with larger webs of connection. In the same period that Plato was dismissing eating as mere biology, for example, Socrates' contemporary and *Symposium* interlocutor, the comic poet Aristophanes, was using food to frame his masterpiece of political satire, *The Knights*. The play, first performed in 424 BCE, is a vicious attack on the Athenian demagogue Cleon, who had recently ascended to power. Capitalizing on the vulgarity of Cleon's leadership style and heritage (he was the son of a tanner, a profession with little social status), Aristophanes stages a contest between "the Paphlagonian," a Cleon-like tanner, and a sausage-seller (whose profession carries even less prestige), who battle for the affections of an old man named Demos ("the people"). At the play's climax, both the Paphlagonian and the sausage-seller ply Demos with food and drink, but the Paphlagonian is exposed as a fraud at the end of the meal. Opening Cleon's basket, Demos reveals piles of food that Cleon has withheld from the people. "Good heavens," cries Demos, "it's full of goodies! Look at all those cakes he's stashed away,

[9] Penny Van Esterik, "Commensal Circles and the Common Pot," in *Commensality: From Everyday Food to Feast*, edited by Susanne Kerner, Cynthia Chou, and Morten Warmind (London: Bloomsbury, 2015), 31–42; Penny Van Esterik, "Care, Caregiving and Caretakers," *Food and Nutrition Bulletin* 16.4 (1995): 378–88.

[10] Recent philosophy has taken a strong interest in food, and occasionally in commensality; see Georges Bataille, *The Accursed Share: An Essay on General Economy*, translated by Robert Hurley, vol. 1 (New York: Zone Books, 1991); Jacques Derrida, "'Eating Well' or the Calculation of the Subject: An Interview with Jacques Derrida," in *Who Comes After the Subject?*, edited by Eduardo Cadava, Peter Connor, and Jean-Luc Nancy (New York: Routledge, 1991), 96–119; Lisa M. Heldke, "Foodmaking as Thoughtful Practice," in *Cooking, Eating, Thinking: Transformative Philosophies of Food*, edited by Deane W. Curtin and Lisa M. Heldke (Bloomington: Indiana University Press, 1992), 203–29; Korsmeyer, *Making Sense of Taste*; Emmanuel Levinas, *Otherwise than Being: Or, Beyond Essence*, translated by Alphonso Lingis (Pittsburgh, PA: Duquesne University Press, 1998); Fritz Allhoff and Dave Monroe, eds., *Food and Philosophy: Eat, Think, and Be Merry*, 1st ed. (London: Wiley-Blackwell, 2007); David M. Kaplan, *The Philosophy of Food* (Berkeley: University of California Press, 2012).

and he gave me a tiny tiny slice!"[11] This greedy hoarding of food by the ostensible leader of the Athenians constitutes a grave insult to good governance. Here Aristophanes imagines the civic body as a feast at which the good host shares all. If the host shortchanges or disrupts the commensal relationships that bind the polis to itself, he fails to conduct the affairs of state with virtue. Commensality thus becomes a metaphor for political organization. As the sausage-seller proclaims at the end of the play, "I'll cherish you and nourish you, the People."[12] The trope of the governor as mother or as head of household partly originates in these early commensal conceptions of civic community.

Commensality and Social Science

If literature has long attended to commensality, literary criticism, blinded by the biases of philosophy, has only recently begun to explore its importance. Just as criticism began to address the role of sexuality in imaginative writing only after Freud and others showed the way, literary critics are now following in the footsteps of the social scientists regarding food. Sociology and anthropology are founded in part on analyses of religious, ceremonial, and (to a lesser extent) everyday commensality.[13] Over the course of the past century, these disciplines have developed a nuanced vocabulary for examining commensal dynamics. But this vocabulary, as we shall see, is not always appropriate to the needs of literature. Literary critics need to forge ahead with our own taxonomies in order to more accurately explain how food works in and among texts, and therefore to contribute most fully to a broad understanding of eating relations. By the same token, social science perspectives are limited in their ability to take account of how eating relations function not just socially but intellectually, symbolically, imaginatively, and creatively to help constitute the human. By this I mean that our conceptions of ourselves and of our relationships to the

---

[11] Aristophanes, *The Birds and Other Plays* (London: Penguin, 2003), 81.

[12] Ibid., 83.

[13] The tradition begins with William Robertson Smith, *Lectures on the Religion of the Semites* (A. & C. Black, 1907). See also especially Pierre Bourdieu, *Distinction: A Social Critique of the Judgement of Taste* (Cambridge, MA: Harvard University Press, 1984); Mary Douglas, *Purity and Danger: An Analysis of the Concepts of Pollution and Taboo* (London: Routledge, 2004); Norbert Elias, *The Civilizing Process*, translated by Edmund Jephcott (Oxford: B. Blackwell, 1978); Claude Lévi-Strauss, *The Raw and the Cooked* (New York: Harper & Row, 1969); Marcel Mauss, *The Gift: The Form and Reason for Exchange in Archaic Societies*, translated by W. D. Halls (New York: Norton, 1990); Anna Meigs, "Food as a Cultural Construction," in *Food and Culture: A Reader*, edited by Carole Counihan and Penny Van Esterik (New York: Routledge, 1997).

nonhuman (or in Stacy Alaimo's terms the "more than human"[14]) world as expressed through food are undergirded by certain specific conceptions of language and the imagination. Literary studies is among the best equipped hermeneutics to uncover and articulate these conceptions. Thus commensality provides a key model for understanding eating relations in literature and other forms of imaginative writing, while literary criticism can bring to bear important insights upon how eating works both in social theory and in the praxis of lived experience.

Social science tends to categorize commensal events based on the sort of meal under study; for instance, an informal family meal is considered differently from a communal or religious feast. These categories, which the sociologist Tan Chee-Beng groups under the terms "domestic," "kin and communal," "ceremonial and religious," "political," and "hospitality," can help clarify the circumstances of commensality in a given text, but are ultimately of limited use for literary criticism.[15] This is because while literary commensality takes place, as in real life, in particular social contexts, literary scenes of meals and metaphors of food and drink are usually constructed in order to point beyond and beneath the particular to the symbolic and material foundations of human relations. From a writerly point of view, the correlations among different acts of commensality are usually at least as compelling as the conditions of a single food interaction. Thus any scene or mention of commensality articulates both a specific set of interactions and an insight into general or metaphorical connectivity.

For an illustration of this literary capaciousness, how might we categorize *The Knights* in sociological terms? Aristophanes presents a domestic feast that demands to be read as a political allegory, the intersection of which brings an ethical message to bear on the play's depictions of kin, community, and hospitality networks. Finally, the play was produced in a religious context: it was first performed at the Lenaia, a festival celebrated in honor of Dionysus that involved rituals of sacrifice and wine-mixing. It is less productive to categorize Aristophanes' play as one or another kind of commensality based on the particular situation of the central meal than it is to examine the way the play uses commensal ideologies to comment holistically upon domestic, communal, political, and religious facets of Athenian life, all in order to make a powerful point about how Athenians should

---

[14] Stacy Alaimo, *Bodily Natures: Science, Environment, and the Material Self* (Bloomington: Indiana University Press, 2010), 2.

[15] Tan Chee-Beng, "Commensality and the Organization of Social Relations," in *Commensality: From Everyday Food to Feast*, edited by Susanne Kerner, Cynthia Chou, and Morten Warmind (London: Bloomsbury, 2015), 13–30.

conduct themselves as citizens in the fullest sense of human relations. Literary commensality quickly leaks past its own locality to expose broader expanses. This, arguably, is why commensality appears in literature in the first place.

Literary commensality becomes even more complex when turning to an instance of language that does not denote a proper meal in any sociological sense. Let us consider Gertrude Stein's famously gnomic sentence, "Roast potatoes for," which itself takes up an entire section of *Tender Buttons*, and which describes the relationality of food with admirable economy.[16] Here we have no coherent depiction of a meal, just a fragment of one. Stein focuses our attention not on a particular set of relationships but on the role of language itself in forging and articulating those relationships. Roast potatoes, Stein's fragment suggests, are not only themselves. They are always "for" something and someone. They have a purpose, and the purpose is inherently social. They point beyond themselves: toward language (or are already language and point out to materiality), toward cultural and biological networks, toward people. The object presupposes a preposition, a grammatical term that *positions* objects in relation to each other. There are no roast potatoes without "for."

One might argue that roast potatoes can very well be "for" biological nourishment and may not necessarily indicate a social interaction at all. This is true, although as I will suggest, the distinction between the social and the biological breaks down at higher levels of commensal analysis. Nevertheless, the passage's larger context mitigates against such a bounded reading. The general rhetorical action of *Tender Buttons* tends toward the social and away from an exclusively biological conception of the self. The "Food" chapter begins by meditating on feeling, on the apportioning of the day into socially constructed segments, on recognition. "In the inside there is sleeping," the section "Roastbeef" begins, "in the outside there is reddening, in the morning there is meaning, in the evening there is feeling. In the evening there is feeling."[17] The section directly preceding "Roast Potatoes," "Potatoes," emphasizes meal preparation, for an orchestration of social interactions through food: "In the preparation of cheese, in the preparation of crackers, in the preparation of butter, in it."[18] The section that follows "Roast Potatoes," "Asparagus," likewise points us toward social and creative interaction: "Asparagus in a lean in a lean to hot. This makes

---

[16] Gertrude Stein, *Tender Buttons* (Mineola, NY: Dover, 1997), 33.
[17] Ibid., 21.
[18] Ibid., 33.

it art and it is wet wet weather wet weather wet."[19] While the paragraph describes a standard technique for cooking asparagus – steaming it upright in a pot – Stein's diction points that technique toward the social: toward the "lean to" of early human civilization and toward art, that quintessential invention of the human collective. Roast potatoes, in this context, do not primarily signify sustenance. As the philosopher Emmanuel Levinas (one of the few Western philosophers to take food seriously) writes, "Food is not the fuel necessary to the human machine; food is a meal."[20] Stein's potatoes are "for" the meal, for the generation of meaning, for commensality.

Scholars often distinguish the commensal from the culinary aspects of food. The historian Jordan Rosenblum refers to the culinary as the "what" and the commensal as the "how" of eating.[21] We might, with a nod to Stein, call it the "for" of eating, or eating in its prepositional mode. But while it may be useful, and in some circumstances accurate, to divide food into culinary and commensal categories, in practice the two are usually interwoven, and it is hard to understand the full range of meanings inherent in the material and symbolic encounter of eating without addressing both. One way to think about the relationship between the two terms is to think of the culinary as a sort of snapshot of the commensal, a reification of a particular node in the commensal network. It is the moment or frame in which food can be viewed *as if it were* a collection of objects, in the mode of objectification. Thus the culinary may be taken in a sense as a slice of the commensal: it is to commensality what a CAT scan is to neural activity.

Inclusion and Exclusion

Commensality is often equated with conviviality, but as Claude Grignon has demonstrated, they are not the same thing. Commensality is the simple fact of the relationships that connect eaters. Conviviality is the social pleasure of taking part in those relationships.[22] Commensality, as anyone who has participated in an uncomfortable holiday dinner can attest, does

---

[19] Ibid.

[20] Emmanuel Levinas, *Nine Talmudic Readings*, translated by Annette Aronowicz (Bloomington: Indiana University Press, 1990), 97. For further discussion of Levinas in relation to food, see David B. Goldstein, "Emmanuel Levinas and the Ontology of Eating," *Gastronomica* 10.3 (Summer 2010): 34–44.

[21] Jordan Rosenblum, *Food and Identity in Early Rabbinic Judaism* (Cambridge: Cambridge University Press, 2010), 3.

[22] Claude Grignon, "Commensality and Social Morphology: An Essay of Typology," in *Food, Drink and Identity: Cooking, Eating and Drinking in Europe since the Middle Ages*, edited by Peter Scholliers (Oxford: Berg, 2001), 23–33.

not always produce social pleasure. In fact, some of the most interesting meals in life and in literature are difficult, dangerous, even downright violent. The banquet scene in Act 3 of *Macbeth*, in which Macbeth continually witnesses the ghost of Banquo sitting in his seat while his wife frantically tries to reassure her guests that their king is not losing his mind, provides a case in point. The scene offers a study in the collapse of conviviality through the performance of commensality. It is the climax of the play's emotional arc, not a failure but a great tragic success. The scene reminds us that meals, speaking in evolutionary terms, are charged with risk – here is a group of people, often armed with knives, tearing into other organisms with their teeth. What holds them back from eating each other is only, in the final analysis, a delicate web of fellow feeling, social graces, taboos, and rules of etiquette that stretch back into our cannibal primate past.[23] Literature finds power in disjunction; the disjunction between eating a meal together and enjoying it, or between eating with the other and eating the other, is one of its great sources of lyric and narrative engagement.

A related truth of eating relations is that any meal integrates some people while excluding others. Most meals experienced in everyday life emphasize inclusion over exclusion: those sharing a family dinner typically do not call attention to the families who were not invited. But the boundary is always present, and literary accounts of eating tend to be strongly drawn to the contrast between those who partake and those who only peer in at the window or lie motionless in the snow. "It is disingenuous," writes Mary Douglas, "to pretend that food is not one of the media of social exclusion."[24] Literature does not pretend. It revels in the fact. This is perhaps literature's most striking insight into commensality. Whereas everyday life often ignores the role of eating in keeping the in-group in and the out-group out – in fact, is in some sense *predicated* upon the ignorance of this distinction – literature, with its bird's eye view of human interaction, is constantly reminding us of it. One of its chief ethical purposes is to do so.

---

[23] On the evolution of table fellowship, see Martin Jones, *Feast: Why Humans Share Food* (Oxford: Oxford University Press, 2007); Richard W. Wrangham, *Catching Fire: How Cooking Made Us Human* (New York: Basic Books, 2009). On cannibalism, see, e.g., Frank Lestringant, *Cannibals* (Berkeley: University of California Press, 1997); Maggie Kilgour, *From Communion to Cannibalism: An Anatomy of Metaphors of Incorporation* (Princeton: Princeton University Press, 1990); Francis Barker, Peter Hulme, and Margaret Iversen, *Cannibalism and the Colonial World* (Cambridge: Cambridge University Press, 1998); and Chapter 8 in this volume.

[24] Mary Douglas, "Standard Social Uses of Food: Introduction," in *Food in the Social Order: Studies of Food and Festivities in Three American Communities*, edited by Mary Douglas (New York: Russell Sage Foundation, 1984), 36.

One of the best-known and most fundamental expressions of the tension between exclusion and inclusion in eating relations is the kosher laws of the Hebrew Bible. (Another is the Hindu caste system.) The kosher laws (collectively called *kashrut*) serve many functions, one of which is to separate those who keep the laws from those who do not. While those who do not keep kosher are welcome to eat at a kosher table (provided they eat the host's food), the reverse is not true. In Shakespeare's *The Merchant of Venice*, Shylock rejects Bassanio's invitation to dinner on precisely these grounds: "I will buy with you, sell with you, talk with you, walk with you, and so following. But I will not eat with you, drink with you, nor pray with you."[25] Here Shylock evokes the exclusionary aspect of commensality in order to insulate himself from what he views as the conniving and generally repugnant society of the Christians who spit on him and call him "dog."[26] But later in the play he famously invokes the *inclusive* aspect of eating relations in order to establish a common unity and sympathy of humankind:

> Hath not a Jew eyes? Hath not a Jew hands, organs, dimensions, senses, affections, passions – fed with the same food, hurt with the same weapons, subject to the same diseases, healed by the same means, warmed and cooled by the same winter and summer, as a Christian is?[27]

The distance between these speeches – the one using food to separate, the other to unite – encapsulates the great paradox of commensality. Food brings people together in a shared experience of humanity. But every meal privileges some of those particular humans over others. The play heightens that paradox through its framing of the threat of Jewish violence – Shylock's insistence upon extracting a "pound of flesh" from his enemy Antonio – within a Christian context that rejects an eating community bound by the literal kosher laws in favor of the metaphorical communion of the Eucharist. The play's navigation of this complex system of analogies and conflicts reflects upon broader attitudes about the political, social, and religious issues surrounding questions of eating, and about the mechanisms of inclusion and exclusion, both in the period and beyond it.[28]

---

[25] William Shakespeare, *The Merchant of Venice: Authoritative Text, Sources and Contexts, Criticism, Rewritings and Appropriations*, edited by Leah S. Marcus (New York: Norton, 2005) 1.3.30–33.

[26] Ibid., 1.3.123–25.

[27] Ibid., 3.1.48–53.

[28] For further discussion of this passage, see David B. Goldstein, *Eating and Ethics in Shakespeare's England* (Cambridge: Cambridge University Press, 2013), Chapter 2.

Literature's fascination with the conceptual and literal boundaries of eating relations cannot be overstated. The boundaries may be drawn in a variety of ways – along lines of religion, class, race, sex, and gender, but also using myriad other demarcations that echo other boundaries in a given text. Often imaginative writing uses these boundaries to contrast the movement of characters through an arc from exclusion to inclusion or vice versa. In the first installment of the Harry Potter series, *Harry Potter and the Philosopher's Stone*, J. K. Rowling uses this technique to great effect. Our first encounter with the tweenage Harry is through the lens of exclusionary commensality. Dragged from his cupboard under the stairs on the morning of his hated cousin Dudley's birthday, he is put to work cooking eggs and bacon for a family meal of which he is only nominally a part. While grudgingly allowed a space at the table, he is in no way welcomed there: he is neither spoken to nor encouraged to speak. As the meal threatens to unravel due to one of Dudley's self-serving tantrums, Harry "began wolfing down his bacon as fast as possible in case Dudley turned the table over."[29] Commensality here shows itself as the bare fact of enforced togetherness; conviviality and inclusivity are absent.

The arc of the first few chapters of the book, from Harry's exclusion by the Muggle world to his inclusion by the wizarding one, may be traced through three meals: first, the giant Hagrid's sharing of sausages with Harry in a desolate island cabin (and excluding the Dursleys from that feast); second, Harry's sharing of the contents of the Hogwarts Express food trolley with Ron Weasley, who will become his best friend; and finally, Harry's first meal at Hogwarts, with its groaning piles of food and laughing, expansive table fellowship. By the third meal, the circle of Harry's commensality has expanded to include the community within which he will grow up, for better and worse, over the course of the succeeding books. Rowling shows quite concisely how individual maturation may intersect with communal dynamics. The Harry Potter books in fact include a wealth of culinary and commensal material, which is in keeping both with Rowling's fascination with embodied representations of community and conflict, and more broadly with the genre of children's literature, which historically highlights the outsized role of food and eating in child development.[30] The

[29] J. K. Rowling, *Harry Potter and the Philosopher's Stone* (London: Bloomsbury, 1997), 21.
[30] On food in the *Harry Potter* series, see Siân Harris, "Glorious Food? The Literary and Culinary Heritage of the Harry Potter Series," in *J. K. Rowling: Harry Potter*, edited by Cynthia J. Hallett and Peggy J. Huey (Basingstoke: Palgrave Macmillan, 2012), 8–21. On food in children's literature, begin with Kara K. Keeling and Scott T. Pollard, eds., *Critical Approaches to Food in Children's Literature* (New York: Routledge, 2009).

early elaboration in the opening book of these food-related issues primes us to see the importance of eating and drinking throughout the series.

Scenes of or references to commensality may act as gateways to the various networks of a literary text even when (unlike in *Harry Potter*) the text hardly contains any representations of food at all. Chaucer's *Canterbury Tales* begins with a passing reference to the commensal origin of the pilgrimage that frames the narrative: the impromptu gathering of several pilgrims at a tavern in Southwark. Although the tavern meal is not discussed, it becomes the unspoken ground for the "felawshipe" that glues the disparate collection of characters together.[31] Mary Shelley's *Frankenstein*, a text that barely mentions food and whose central character hardly needs to consume it, nevertheless pivots upon a commensal scene: having taken up residence in a pigsty abutting the cottage of the De Lacey family, Frankenstein's creature begins to understand human relationships by watching the family interact in a domestic setting. Although the first meal the creature sees them share is "quickly dispatched" (on account of the family's poverty), the family's domestic rhythms take shape around the gathering of food and fuel as well as the table-fellowship of song and conversation that lingers after their meager meals.[32] It is their rejection of him, and the denial of hospitality and the "kindness and sympathy" that hospitality entails, that launches him upon his murderous path.[33]

If in Rowling's books, meals shape and reflect the relationship of the individual to the whole, in other instances the boundaries of inclusion can shift during the course of the meal itself. Such is the case in the "boeuf en daube" scene that takes up much of the first part of Virginia Woolf's *To the Lighthouse*.[34] This famous dinner functions as a cathecting point for numerous narrative strands, tying together the lives of the characters and the themes of the book in one long, interweaving series of thoughts and movements. Strangely, the different characters organize and dissolve the boundaries of in-groups and out-groups as the meal progresses. At

---

[31] Geoffrey Chaucer, *The Riverside Chaucer*, edited by Larry Dean Benson, 3rd ed. (Boston: Houghton Mifflin, 1987), General Prologue, ll.20–32.

[32] Mary Shelley, *Frankenstein*, edited by J. Paul Hunter (New York: Norton, 2012), 75. See Toby Benis, *Romantic Diasporas: French Émigrés, British Convicts, and Jews* (New York: Palgrave, 2009), 81. I am grateful to Ksenia Jourova for directing me to this passage.

[33] Shelley, *Frankenstein*, 92.

[34] On commensality in this scene, see especially Lisa Angelella, "The Meat of the Movement: Food and Feminism in Woolf," *Woolf Studies Annual* 17 (2011): 173–95; Diane McGee, *Writing the Meal: Dinner in the Fiction of Early Twentieth-Century Women Writers* (Toronto: University of Toronto Press, 2002), 143–46; Amy L. Tigner and Allison Carruth, *Literature and Food Studies* (New York: Routledge, 2018), 122–26.

first, commensality fails, at least in Mrs. Ramsay's mind, to take hold. Or rather, the commensality is circumstantially enforced but not viscerally experienced: "Nothing seemed to have merged. They all sat separate. And the whole of the effort of merging and flowing and creating rested on her."[35] But as the scene develops, this arid metonymy of bodies gives way to a nuanced pattern of shifting alliances. Mrs. Ramsay's sense of fellow feeling drives her to draw William Bankes into the commensal circle. Meanwhile, Charles Tansley, stereotyping the theater of cuisine as one ruled (threateningly) by women, tries to relinquish any role he might have in the meal: "They did nothing but talk, talk, talk, eat, eat, eat. It was the women's fault. Women made civilisation impossible with all their 'charm,' all their silliness."[36] But eventually a positive, inclusive commensality takes almost magical hold. "Some change at once went through them all ..." Woolf writes, "and they were all conscious of making a party together in a hollow, on an island; had their common cause against that fluidity out there."[37] As the dinner flows to its close, Mrs. Ramsay articulates one of the most finely tuned descriptions of inclusive commensality in Western literature. Her feeling of perfect harmony

> arose, she thought, looking at them all eating there, from husband and children and friends; all of which rising in this profound stillness (she was helping William Bankes to one very small piece more, and peered into the depths of the earthenware pot) seemed now for no special reason to stay there like a smoke, like a fume rising upwards, holding them safe together. Nothing need be said; nothing could be said. There it was, all round them ... Of such moments, she thought, the thing is made that endures.[38]

When the dinner ends, so does the real sense of immutability that has settled upon its hostess. As she leaves the room, the dinner "had become, she knew, giving one last look at it over her shoulder, already the past."[39] Commensal bonds, like the foods one eats, emerge, transform, and vanish, to recombine later, both as substance and memory. *To the Lighthouse* presents a meal that addresses human connectivity in all its ephemeral beauty and loss.

Commensal relationships inform much of Woolf's work. She demonstrates in *A Room of One's Own* a consideration for the culinary aspects of eating, but characteristically that consideration is immediately

[35] Virginia Woolf, *To the Lighthouse* (New York: Harcourt Brace, 1981), 83.
[36] Ibid., 85.
[37] Ibid., 97.
[38] Ibid., 105.
[39] Ibid., 111.

transferred to the commensal stakes of the food served. Novelists, she writes, "seldom spare a word for what was eaten" at some radiant luncheon party. "It is part of the novelist's convention," she continues,

> not to mention soup and salmon and ducklings, as if soup and salmon and ducklings were of no importance whatsoever, as if nobody ever smoked a cigar or drank a glass of wine. Here, however, I shall take the liberty to defy that convention.[40]

Woolf's uninterested novelist may remind us of Socrates' indifference to eating and drinking in the *Symposium*, a text that offers us commensality without the eating. Woolf's contributions to culinary literature force us to consider both at once. Rarely, if ever, does the food of her writings remain in an objectified state. It almost always functions to explore the network of human interaction. Immediately after the above passage in *A Room of One's Own*, for instance, Woolf embarks on a meticulous description of the opulent luncheon she is served at the Oxbridge college where she finds herself, which she then contrasts to clear effect with the paltry meals served in her own college, with its "plain gravy soup" and sad uncharitable prunes. She makes her point with a lurch of the stomach, and in a strange echo of Shylock's speech: "One cannot think well, love well, sleep well, if one has not dined well. The lamp in the spine does not light on beef and prunes."[41] The two meals serve to communicate several interlocking ideas about the ways in which meals create boundaries between those who have and those who have not (in this case along clear gender lines) and, further, how food as an object becomes transmuted into creativity, imaginative discourse, "the lamp in the spine" – how, in short, food becomes eating, and eating becomes living, and living becomes living *with*, living *for*.

Both Mrs. Ramsay's boeuf en daube and the two meals of *A Room of One's Own* remind us that there are always gender politics at work in commensal groupings. Here an understanding of hospitality theory is especially helpful, as in Tracy McNulty's argument about the division of hospitable labor in Western culture, in which the male host provides the conditions for hospitality and the hostess directs the material bodying forth of that hospitality.[42] Since hospitality is nearly always in some sense commensal (metaphorically in cases where food is not offered, literally in cases where it is), its structures and processes provide insight into how gender roles

---

[40] Virginia Woolf, *A Room of One's Own* (New York: Harcourt Brace, 1957), 10.
[41] Ibid., 18.
[42] Tracy McNulty, *The Hostess: Hospitality, Femininity, and the Expropriation of Identity* (Minneapolis: University of Minnesota Press, 2006).

operate in scenes of and references to literary commensality. Even in cases where women are nowhere present, such as the forest meal with which Duke Senior welcomes Orlando in Act 2, Scene 7 of Shakespeare's *As You Like It*, the metaphorical or political dynamics often point toward the silent labor or exclusion of women from the scene. At that luncheon, for example, Orlando takes on the role of Eve, caring for his servant, Adam, going "like a doe to find my fawn/ And give it food."[43]

Race and class dynamics feature prominently in the commensal politics of inclusion and exclusion. In nineteenth-century American literature, as Kyla Wazana Tompkins has shown, the black body is often depicted as itself a site of consumption. Eating, in Tompkins' view, becomes "a trope and technology of racial formation during the first 130 years of the US republic."[44] Class-based analysis of meals in British nineteenth-century fiction demonstrates the ways in which meals readily expose economic and moral fault lines, and often both at once, as is perhaps most obvious in the sentimental contrast between the wealthy Ebenezer Scrooge's "melancholy dinner in his usual melancholy tavern," and the Cratchits' poor but convivial Christmas feast.[45]

Cross-Cultural Commensality

This chapter has focused largely on the commensality tradition in Western literature. If anything, depictions and developments of eating relations are more pronounced in other national and regional literatures, and in diasporic narratives of migration and hybridity, especially those from cultures with more robust philosophical and religious attention to foodways than those of Britain and Caucasian North America.[46] Anita Desai's postcolonial novel *Fasting, Feasting* offers a striking account of cross-cultural commensality, in that it constructs a sort of split-screen approach to the question of how eating relations work in India and North America. Although the book presents an exercise in contrasts between cultural approaches to eating, the contrasts are neither simple nor sentimental. The first section of the novel is set within the household of a provincial Indian family, and is told through the eyes of the family's eldest daughter, Uma. Unmarried and

---

[43] William Shakespeare, *As You Like It*, edited by Juliet Dusinberre (London: Arden Shakespeare, 2006), 2.7.129–30.

[44] Kyla Wazana Tompkins, *Racial Indigestion: Eating Bodies in the Nineteenth Century* (New York: New York University Press, 2012), 2.

[45] Charles Dickens, *A Christmas Carol and other Christmas Books* (Oxford: Oxford University Press, 2006), 16.

[46] See e.g., Chapter 8 in the present volume.

developmentally delayed in a world in which daughters must be married off and in which difference is equated with insufficiency, Uma is routinely failed by her family unit and by the larger society through which she makes her way. The Indian meals and discussions of food explored in the first part of Desai's novel are characterized by concerns about dearth, by issues of class and caste hierarchy, by repressive gender norms, and by rigid notions of hospitality, all of which in turn express themselves as obstacles in the lives of Uma and her relatives.

The second part of *Fasting, Feasting* follows the family's youngest child and only son, Arun, to the University of Massachusetts for a semester abroad. Alienated by the foodways of his temporary adopted home, Arun (who, much to his parents' chagrin, is a vegetarian) struggles to cope with a world dominated by gleaming white supermarkets and backyard grills loaded with hamburgers, a world in which "there are so many objects, so rarely any people."[47] The suburban host family he stays with, though outwardly well off, also seems at a loss as to how to function in a society that privileges the objectification of food over traditional bonds, however stultifying, of hospitality and nourishment. Melanie, the daughter of Arun's host family, refuses to join the family for meals and hides her struggle with bulimia. Her eating disorder becomes a trope for the costs of the noncommensal relationship to eating that Arun witnesses in America, just as Uma's cousin Anamika, who dies a horrible death after she is forced into an abusive marriage, suffers the tragic costs of a society overly attached to demarcating its own boundaries. The novel's willingness to analyze commensality and conviviality as separate phenomena makes it a cogent primer for the cross-cultural issues at stake in eating relations.

Table Ecology

Social science, as I've noted, by definition concerns itself with commensality as a phenomenon of social circulation. A more capacious interpretation of the term opens the question of relationship not just to other humans, but to the entire ecological system of which humans and our food are both a part. Donna Haraway's "messmate," Michel Serres' "parasite," Wendell Berry's "pleasures of eating," Stacy Alaimo's "trans-corporeality," Anna Tsing's adage that "human nature is an interspecies relationship," and Timothy Morton's "ecological thought," with its vision of a "society of hospitality and responsibility" composed of all organisms, all point in various

[47] Anita Desai, *Fasting, Feasting* (New York: Houghton Mifflin, 2000), 160.

ways to a commensal understanding of the system in which humans are an inextricable part of organic life.[48] In the ecological sense, food once again unlatches itself from any objective status, becoming instead a metaphor for and momentary coagulation of coexistence – an animal, a plant, a conduit for sunlight and oxygen, a nodal point of circulating matter and energy, as are the humans who consume them and who are eventually consumed, as is Polonius by Hamlet's "convocation of politic worms" after he has killed him.[49] As Julian Yates, discussing both Hamlet and Haraway, puts it:

> From the perspective of such a general ecology, human foodways describe an interface between the boundaries of the household or collective (writ large or small) and the world, the kitchen a portal through which streams of animals, plants, and fungus are transformed into what is said to be that most human of things, a cuisine.[50]

The ecological understanding of commensality is ancient. Yates finds it in Shakespeare, but we can go back at least to the *Tattiriya Upanishad*, composed around the sixth century BCE, which maintains, "Food is Spirit. From food all things are born, by food they live, towards food they move, into food they return."[51] One astonishing textual evocation of this interconnectedness, in which multiple understandings of commensality are explored and layered upon one another, is the medieval English poem *Sir Gawain and the Green Knight*. Its narrative begins with a Christmas feast at King Arthur's court, a splendid meal replete with "Twelve dishes before each pair: / Good beer and bright wine both."[52] The gathering is interrupted by the appearance of a magical green knight who, having allowed Sir Gawain to slice off his head, exacts the promise that he will be allowed to treat Gawain in similar fashion in a year's time. The meal combines political, communal, religious, and social dynamics, providing a case study in the dangerous politics of medieval hospitality and commensality.

---

[48] Donna Jeanne Haraway, *When Species Meet* (Minneapolis: University of Minnesota Press, 2008); Michel Serres, *The Parasite*, translated by Lawrence R. Schehr (Minneapolis: University of Minnesota Press, 2007); Wendell Berry, "The Pleasures of Eating," in *The Art of the Commonplace: The Agrarian Essays of Wendell Berry*, edited by Norman Wirzba (Washington, DC: Shoemaker & Hoard, 2002), 321–27; Alaimo, *Bodily Natures*; Anna Tsing, "Unruly Edges: Mushrooms as Companion Species," *Environmental Humanities* 1 (2012): 144; Timothy Morton, *The Ecological Thought* (Cambridge, MA: Harvard University Press, 2012), 105.

[49] William Shakespeare, *Hamlet*, edited by A. R. Braunmuller (New York: Penguin, 2001), 4.3.19–20.

[50] Julian Yates, "Shakespeare's Messmates," in *Culinary Shakespeare*, edited by David B. Goldstein and Amy L. Tigner (Pittsburgh, PA: Duquesne University Press, 2016), 180. Yates' use of the term "general ecology" refers to Georges Bataille.

[51] Swami Shree Purohit and W. B. Yeats, trans., *The Ten Principal Upanishads* (London: Faber and Faber, 1970), 74.

[52] Marie Borroff, trans., *Sir Gawain and the Green Knight* (New York: Norton, 1967), 1.128–29.

In Part III of the poem, Sir Gawain ventures upon a castle in the western wilds, where he finds a recapitulation of the hospitality he enjoyed at Arthur's court. Here the social dynamics become even more complex, because in addition to being plied with food and drink for four days, Gawain also becomes the unwitting object of his hostess's sexual attentions. Meanwhile, the scenes of Gawain's attempted seduction are interleaved with descriptions of the animals who are hunted for each evening's meal. The purpose of these hunting scenes, each of which ends with a meticulous and spine-curling description of the animal's death and dismemberment, have perplexed scholars. But from a commensal perspective the hunting scenes make perfect sense. If the green knight of the poem, who is also Bertilak, Gawain's host in this second series of meals, stands in some way for a principle of natural generation and of the connection between humans and the green world, then it stands to reason that the commensal relationships at his castle include not only humans but the entire eco-system of which Bertilak is a part. The poem ultimately considers humans as deeply imbricated beings, both socially, religiously, and ecologically. *Sir Gawain and the Green Knight* demonstrates the power of literature to show us our multiple orientations in a world where we are eater, eaten, and the web that connects them.

BIBLIOGRAPHY

Alaimo, Stacy. *Bodily Natures: Science, Environment, and the Material Self.* Bloomington: Indiana University Press, 2010.

Allhoff, Fritz, and Dave Monroe, eds. *Food and Philosophy: Eat, Think, and Be Merry.* 1st ed. London: Wiley-Blackwell, 2007.

Andersen, Boris. "Commensality between the Young." In *Commensality: From Everyday Food to Feast*, edited by Susanne Kerner, Cynthia Chou, and Morten Warmind, 43–50. London: Bloomsbury, 2015.

Angelella, Lisa. "The Meat of the Movement: Food and Feminism in Woolf." *Woolf Studies Annual* 17 (2011): 173–95.

Aristophanes. *The Birds and Other Plays.* London: Penguin, 2003.

Barker, Francis, Peter Hulme, and Margaret Iversen. *Cannibalism and the Colonial World.* Cambridge: Cambridge University Press, 1998.

Bataille, Georges. *The Accursed Share: An Essay on General Economy.* Translated by Robert Hurley. Vol. 1. New York: Zone Books, 1991.

Benis, Toby. *Romantic Diasporas: French Émigrés, British Convicts, and Jews.* New York: Palgrave, 2009.

Berry, Wendell. "The Pleasures of Eating." In *The Art of the Commonplace: The Agrarian Essays of Wendell Berry*, edited by Norman Wirzba, 321–27. Washington, DC: Shoemaker & Hoard, 2002.

Borroff, Marie, trans. *Sir Gawain and the Green Knight*. New York: Norton, 1967.

Bourdieu, Pierre. *Distinction: A Social Critique of the Judgement of Taste*. Cambridge, MA: Harvard University Press, 1984.

Chaucer, Geoffrey. *The Riverside Chaucer*. Edited by Larry Dean Benson. 3rd ed. Boston: Houghton Mifflin, 1987.

Chee-Beng, Tan. "Commensality and the Organization of Social Relations." In *Commensality: From Everyday Food to Feast*, edited by Susanne Kerner, Cynthia Chou, and Morten Warmind, 13–30. London: Bloomsbury, 2015.

Curtin, Deane W., and Lisa M. Heldke. *Cooking, Eating, Thinking: Transformative Philosophies of Food*. Bloomington: Indiana University Press, 1992.

Derrida, Jacques. "'Eating Well' or the Calculation of the Subject: An Interview with Jacques Derrida." In *Who Comes After the Subject?*, edited by Eduardo Cadava, Peter Connor, and Jean-Luc Nancy, 96–119. New York: Routledge, 1991.

Desai, Anita. *Fasting, Feasting*. New York: Houghton Mifflin, 2000.

Dickens, Charles. *A Christmas Carol and other Christmas Books*. Oxford: Oxford University Press, 2006.

Douglas, Mary. *Purity and Danger: An Analysis of the Concepts of Pollution and Taboo*. London: Routledge, 2004.

"Standard Social Uses of Food: Introduction." In *Food in the Social Order: Studies of Food and Festivities in Three American Communities*, edited by Mary Douglas, 1–39. New York: Russell Sage Foundation, 1984.

Elias, Norbert. *The Civilizing Process*. Translated by Edmund Jephcott. Oxford: B. Blackwell, 1978.

Fischler, Claude. "Commensality, Society and Culture." *Social Science Information* 50.3–4 (2011): 528–48. doi:10.1177/0539018411413963.

Fischler, Claude, and Estelle Masson. *Manger: Français, Européens et Américains face à l'alimentation*. Paris: Odile Jacob, 2008.

Goldstein, David B. *Eating and Ethics in Shakespeare's England*. Cambridge: Cambridge University Press, 2013.

"Emmanuel Levinas and the Ontology of Eating." *Gastronomica* 10.3 (Summer 2010): 34–44.

Grignon, Claude. "Commensality and Social Morphology: An Essay of Typology." In *Food, Drink and Identity: Cooking, Eating and Drinking in Europe since the Middle Ages*, edited by Peter Scholliers, 23–33. Oxford: Berg, 2001.

Haraway, Donna Jeanne. *When Species Meet*. Minneapolis: University of Minnesota Press, 2008.

Harris, Siân. "Glorious Food? The Literary and Culinary Heritage of the Harry Potter Series." In *J. K. Rowling: Harry Potter*, edited by Cynthia J. Hallett and Peggy J. Huey, 8–21. Basingstoke: Palgrave Macmillan, 2012.

Heldke, Lisa M. "Foodmaking as Thoughtful Practice." In *Cooking, Eating, Thinking: Transformative Philosophies of Food*, edited by Deane W. Curtin and Lisa M. Heldke, 203–29. Bloomington: Indiana University Press, 1992.

Jones, Martin. *Feast: Why Humans Share Food*. Oxford: Oxford University Press, 2007.

Kaplan, David M. *The Philosophy of Food*. Berkeley: University of California Press, 2012.

Keeling, Kara K., and Scott T. Pollard, eds. *Critical Approaches to Food in Children's Literature*. New York: Routledge, 2009.

Kilgour, Maggie. *From Communion to Cannibalism: An Anatomy of Metaphors of Incorporation*. Princeton: Princeton University Press, 1990.

Korsmeyer, Carolyn. *Making Sense of Taste: Food and Philosophy*. Ithaca, NY: Cornell University Press, 1999.

Lestringant, Frank. *Cannibals*. Berkeley: University of California Press, 1997.

Levinas, Emmanuel. *Nine Talmudic Readings*. Translated by Annette Aronowicz. Bloomington: Indiana University Press, 1990.

  Otherwise than Being: Or, Beyond Essence. Translated by Alphonso Lingis. Pittsburgh, PA: Duquesne University Press, 1998.

Lévi-Strauss, Claude. *The Raw and the Cooked*. New York: Harper & Row, 1969.

Mauss, Marcel. *The Gift: The Form and Reason for Exchange in Archaic Societies*. Translated by W. D. Halls. New York: Norton, 1990.

McGee, Diane. *Writing the Meal: Dinner in the Fiction of Early Twentieth-Century Women Writers*. Toronto: University of Toronto Press, 2002.

McNulty, Tracy. *The Hostess: Hospitality, Femininity, and the Expropriation of Identity*. Minneapolis: University of Minnesota Press, 2006.

Meigs, Anna. "Food as a Cultural Construction." In *Food and Culture: A Reader*, edited by Carole Counihan and Penny Van Esterik. New York: Routledge, 1997.

Morton, Timothy. *The Ecological Thought*. Cambridge, MA: Harvard University Press, 2012.

Nestle, Marion. *Food Politics: How the Food Industry Influences Nutrition and Health*. Berkeley: University of California Press, 2013.

Plato. *Gorgias*. Translated by Robin Waterfield. Oxford: Oxford University Press, 1994.

  "Phaedo." In *The Collected Dialogues of Plato*, edited by Edith Hamilton and Huntington Cairns, translated by Hugh Tredennick. Princeton: Princeton University Press, 1961.

  The Symposium. Translated by Walter Hamilton. London: Penguin, 1951.

Pollan, Michael. *The Omnivore's Dilemma: A Natural History of Four Meals*. New York: Penguin, 2006.

Purohit, Swami Shree, and W. B. Yeats, trans. *The Ten Principal Upanishads*. London: Faber and Faber, 1970.

Rosenblum, Jordan. *Food and Identity in Early Rabbinic Judaism*. Cambridge: Cambridge University Press, 2010.

Rowling, J. K. *Harry Potter and the Philosopher's Stone*. London: Bloomsbury, 1997.

Schlosser, Eric. *Fast Food Nation: The Dark Side of the All-American Meal*. New York: Houghton Mifflin Harcourt, 2001.

Serres, Michel. *The Parasite*. Translated by Lawrence R. Schehr. Minneapolis: University of Minnesota Press, 2007.

Shakespeare, William. *As You Like It*. Edited by Juliet Dusinberre. London: Arden Shakespeare, 2006.

  Hamlet. Edited by A. R. Braunmuller. New York: Penguin, 2001.

The Merchant of Venice: Authoritative Text, Sources and Contexts, Criticism, Rewritings and Appropriations. Edited by Leah S. Marcus. New York: Norton, 2005.

Shelley, Mary. *Frankenstein.* Edited by J. Paul Hunter. New York: Norton, 2012.

Smith, William Robertson. *Lectures on the Religion of the Semites.* A. & C. Black, 1907.

Stein, Gertrude. *Tender Buttons.* Mineola, NY: Dover, 1997.

Tigner, Amy L., and Allison Carruth. *Literature and Food Studies.* New York: Routledge, 2018.

Tompkins, Kyla Wazana. *Racial Indigestion: Eating Bodies in the Nineteenth Century.* New York: New York University Press, 2012.

Tsing, Anna. "Unruly Edges: Mushrooms as Companion Species." *Environmental Humanities* 1 (2012): 141–54.

Van Esterik, Penny. "Care, Caregiving and Caretakers." *Food and Nutrition Bulletin* 16.4 (1995): 378–88.

"Commensal Circles and the Common Pot." In *Commensality: From Everyday Food to Feast,* edited by Susanne Kerner, Cynthia Chou, and Morten Warmind, 31–42. London: Bloomsbury, 2015.

Woolf, Virginia. *A Room of One's Own.* New York: Harcourt Brace, 1957.

To the Lighthouse. New York: Harcourt Brace, 1981.

Wrangham, Richard W. *Catching Fire: How Cooking Made Us Human.* New York: Basic Books, 2009.

Yates, Julian. "Shakespeare's Messmates." In *Culinary Shakespeare,* edited by David B. Goldstein and Amy L. Tigner, 179–98. Pittsburgh, PA: Duquesne University Press, 2016.

CHAPTER 2

The Drive-Thru Supermarket
Shopping Carts and the Foodscapes of American Literature

Andrew Warnes

This chapter considers the new foodscape of the supermarket as it appears in key writings of the postwar US canon.[1] It builds on critical works on this subject recently published by Tracey Deutsch, Frank Cochoy, and Catherine Grandclément-Chaffy. Above all it draws upon David J. Alworth's important *Site Reading: Fiction, Art, Social Form* (2016), sharing its hopes that a new sociology might "be found in the way literature itself grounds social experience, the way it imagines sociality in situ."[2] With *Site Reading* I find in the supermarket an exemplary instance of such imagined sociality: a foodscape which US writers have never just stumbled upon, but which their work has actively reshaped, remodeled, and rethought.

On these common grounds I offer a single modification. *Site Reading*'s view of the supermarket, I suggest, follows that of its major intellectual influence, Bruno Latour. Alworth emphasizes the technological sophistication of such stores, uncovering the Latourian "flux of interactions" that they create not just between humans and commodities but among such objects themselves.[3] In this chapter I agree that US literature often evokes such "flux," confirming Latour's belief that supermarkets "preformat" us into calculating, consuming actors.[4] But I add that these literary works also place so much emphasis on the glitches and tensions in the supermarket's system that what appears a smooth and masterful assemblage in Latour and Alworth alike begins to seem, instead, the ideal that the industry has set for itself and against which most of its actual stores fall short.[5] Works of

---

[1] This chapter draws upon archival research at the National Museum of American History. I would like to thank Trina Brown, Alison Oswald, Jim Roan, and Tracy Shaw for their expertise in guiding me through this rich resource.

[2] David J. Alworth, *Site Reading: Fiction, Art, Social Form* (Princeton: Princeton University Press, 2016), 11.

[3] Ibid., 33.

[4] Bruno Latour, *Reassembling the Social: An Introduction to Actor-Network Theory* (Oxford: Oxford University Press, 2005), 65.

[5] Alworth, *Site Reading*, 34.

US literature, if often recognising in the supermarket a "semiautonomous nonhuman sphere," also call attention to the new contradictions it puts into play, revealing the problematics embedded in its operation of "nonhuman agency."[6]

Of these problematics, moreover, such literary works cast light on the supermarket's long flirtation with the automobile above all. Often they evoke a foodscape which has virtually dragged car culture indoors, flooding the grocery store with scaled-down versions of its bright advertising, its lanes, junctions, and jams, and its sense of time being measured and weighed and always slipping away. They lament or at least worry about this transformation, wondering at the costs we incur when supermarkets become a quite different kind of "store you can drive through," to adapt Richard Longstreth's phrase.[7] And so they suggest that *Site Reading* might also consider what Grandclément-Chaffy and others see as the most important object of all: the shopping cart, the simple machine which urges us to wheel as we shop, "preformatting" us as supermarket shoppers as soon as we step outside our cars.[8]

Ginsberg and the Drive-Thru Supermarket

The US writers who, from about 1940, witnessed the first craze for the supermarket and all things self-service never seemed especially honored to find themselves on this particular historical vanguard. Supermarkets sometimes seem quite invisible in their work, and in a number of novels, from Walker Percy's *The Moviegoer* (1960) to Elizabeth Spencer's *The Snare* (1972), the suburban home overflows with packaged goods – milk comes in cartons and detergent comes in boxes and breakfast is eaten from a bowl – yet no one visits the source of this bright and stackable plenty. In such stories the supermarket acts as a kind of offstage power supply, too banal for words; food shopping, routine and feminine, only haunts the extraordinary happenings of the book. But a similar disinterest often hangs

---

[6] Ibid., 39.

[7] Richard Longstreth, *The Drive-In, the Supermarket, and the Transformation of Commercial Space in Los Angeles, 1914–1941* (Cambridge, MA: MIT Press, 1999), 142.

[8] See Frank Cochoy and Catherine Grandclément-Chaffy, "Publicizing Goldilocks' Choice at the Supermarket: The Political Work of Shopping Packs, Carts and Talk," in *Making Things Public: Atmospheres of Democracy*, edited by Bruno Latour and Peter Weibel (Cambridge, MA: MIT Press, 2005), 646–57; Catherine Grandclément-Chaffy, "Wheeling One's Groceries around the Store: The Invention of the Shopping Cart, 1936–1953," in *Food Chains: From Farmyard to Shopping Cart*, edited by Warren Belasco and Roger Horowitz (Philadelphia: University of Pennsylvania Press, 2008), 233–52.

over those works of the period which do attend to the supermarket and its reordering of consumerist experience; these direct engagements, too, can seem unsure whether to respond to such stores with boredom, wonder, or both. As they "voyage into the ordinary," in Michel de Certeau's phrase, they become arch and even mischievous in tone, still pushing upon us the unliterary nature of their setting.[9] Such a shuffling from boredom to wonder becomes clear in the lines Allen Ginsberg famously addressed to Walt Whitman early on in his debut collection *Howl* (1956):

> In my hungry fatigue, and shopping for images, I went into the
> neon fruit supermarket, dreaming of your enumerations!
> What peaches and what penumbras! Whole families shopping at
> night! Aisles full of husbands! Wives in the avocados, babies in the
> tomatoes! – and you, García Lorca, what were you doing down by
> the watermelons?
>
> I saw you, Walt Whitman, childless, lonely old grubber, poking
> among the meats in the refrigerator and eyeing the grocery boys.
> I heard you asking questions of each: Who killed the pork chops?
> What price bananas? Are you my Angel?
> I wandered in and out of the brilliant stacks of cans following you,
> and followed in my imagination by the store detective.
> We strode down the open corridors together in our solitary fancy
> tasting artichokes, possessing every frozen delicacy, and never
> passing the cashier.
>
> Where are we going, Walt Whitman? The doors close in an hour.
> Which way does your beard point tonight?
> (I touch your book and dream of our odyssey in the supermarket
> and feel absurd.)
> Will we walk all night through solitary streets? The trees add shade
> to shade, lights out in the houses, we'll both be lonely.
> Will we stroll dreaming of the lost America of love past blue
> automobiles in driveways, home to our silent cottage?[10]

Mock epic poems usually involve a careful negotiation of wonder. In the high burlesque, their commonest English form, they often begin by establishing a contrast between their low subject and the elevated manner in which they are treating it; but soon they then strain against this contrast, feigning surprise as they stumble upon the new fascinations to be had amid the base and the banal. In its extended description of London's Fleet

---

[9] Michel De Certeau, *The Practice of Everyday Life*, translated by Steven Rendall (Berkeley: University of California Press, 1988), 26.
[10] Allen Ginsberg, *Howl and Other Poems* (San Francisco: City Lights, 1956), 23–24.

Ditch, for example, Ben Jonson's "On the Famous Voyage" (c. 1610) begins in an inapposite Homeric register but is soon swept up in the effluvia's "merd-urinous load[s]" and roasted cats, its "cataplasms, suppositories, and lotions," regaining an epic scale of description through the accumulation of disgust.[11] Although it focuses on the opposite end of the digestive cycle, "A Supermarket in California" is another mock epic which gives "prominence to basic physical needs," telling "truths that epic cannot accommodate," as Ritchie Robertson puts it.[12] If read in *Howl* itself, it feels calm enough, a bit of a joint break Ginsberg is taking after his breathless title poem. Even amid its silence, however, the poem soon enters a state of radical indecision. On the face of it Ginsberg aims at irony. His celebrated compounds, his "neon fruit" and "brilliant cans," his "supermarket odyssey" overall, all dabble in disdain, and in every exclamation mark we can perhaps hear the voice of the jaded New York bohemian spluttering at the thought that a mere grocery store might invite the awe and wonder one would more properly feel before some masterpiece at the Met or when crossing the George Washington Bridge. Still, as in Jonson's sordid quest, there is a sense that Ginsberg's poem cannot quite seal the deal. As he faces the wide linoleum aisles, open fridges, and self-service displays that the commercial literature of the time associated with the latest Californian supermarkets, he cannot quite rid himself of wonder. His joy at the tilted Technicolor displays of "peaches" and "penumbras," if extravagant, is also ambivalent, and self-deprecatory perhaps, neither sincere nor insincere. Uncertainty of tone adds to the suspicion that Ginsberg's lyric is not leaving the mock epic behind but beginning to worry, on the contrary, whether all the old tools of rhetoric and poetry, from apostrophe to wordplay, will be any match for a coming consumerist world that now seems, not too banal for words, but too insistently seductive, and too adept at placing cornucopia within reach, to yield before such literary mediation.

This, though, is not the only mode of communication that fails in Ginsberg's store. His own stabs at bathos might falter, and the certainties of the mock epic might cede ground to the "ugly feelings" of stupefaction that for Sianne Ngai seize us when we face the immense variety of postmodern life.[13] But other utterances also miss their mark. Lorca hides, dumbstruck; Whitman proves hesitant, too timid to cruise, asking only

---

[11] Ben Jonson, "On the Famous Voyage," in *Ben Jonson: Oxford Poetry Library*, edited by Ian Donaldson (Oxford: Oxford University Press, 1995), 62.

[12] Ritchie Robertson, *Mock-Epic Poetry from Pope to Heine* (Oxford: Oxford University Press, 2009), 59.

[13] Sianne Ngai, *Ugly Feelings* (Cambridge, MA: Harvard University Press, 2007), 270–71.

rhetorical questions. Indeed, given the shadow he casts over the whole scene, it can come as a surprise to remember just how little Whitman is permitted to say in the poem – and to realize that what he does say falls so flat. Senile and befuddled, his final question ("Are you my Angel?") in fact confirms what his later description as a "graybeard" suggests: that "A Supermarket in California," though often read as a queer fantasy, has actually resurrected not the antebellum Whitman – not the unbuttoned beefcake of *Leaves of Grass*'s first frontispiece – but a septuagenarian Whitman, a Whitman of failing powers, a Whitman whose great "enumerations" remain trapped inside the poem's pre-supermarket past, far beyond its powers of revivification.[14] ("Who killed the pork chops?," meanwhile, might seem punchy enough, a half vegetarian half Marxist exposé of the violence harbored within the supermarket's dazzling displays; but it is radically unlike anything Whitman himself ever wrote.) Others experience the supermarket alone. Husbands are left marooned in its aisles; and while the "wives in the tomatoes" and the "babies in the avocadoes" might well allude to the smiling cartoons and speech bubbles which manufacturers were beginning to place in the heart of their product displays, they also suggest identities lost in desire, adding to an atmosphere of mutual atomization. Even as he continues philosophizing, Ginsberg himself gets caught in this web of disconnection. His initial rapture at the supermarket's offerings drains away, and he directs toward Whitman a series of worried questions that might be fuller and less cryptic but which otherwise mirror those of his fellow poet insofar as they too go unanswered.

As it falls into Ginsberg's hands, then, the supermarket becomes at once beautiful and fraught. It seduces and it isolates, pulling people ever deeper into their own consumer needs, and labeling them much as it does the items on its shelves. Leading US innovators of advertising and packaging design of the 1950s sought to optimize "impulse" purchases above all. The packaging maestro Walter Landor and other innovative designers wanted to magnify the supermarket's ability to lure passing shoppers into reaching out and grabbing various products over and over again, and without thinking much about it. Ginsberg's poem offers a literary attestation to

---

[14] In the 1855 frontispiece of *Leaves of Grass,* as Alan Trachtenberg notes, Whitman appears as "a standing workingman-poet … touching his own body," his beard emphatically dark. Trachtenberg, *Reading American Photographs: Images as History, Mathew Brady to Walker Evans* (New York: Hill and Wang, 1989), 63. Frank Kearful reads the poem as a fantasy of "gay male bonding" in "Alimentary Poetics: Robert Lowell and Allen Ginsberg," *Partial Answers: Journal of Literature and the History of Ideas* 11.1 (2013): 94–96. David J. Alworth agrees that this is a "homoerotic fantasy" while recognizing that Whitman is "wizened" in "Supermarket Sociology," *New Literary History* 41.2 (2010): 306.

the new world such pioneering figures created, consolidating a foodscape in which "brilliant" commodities have now begun to "speak" to women but only as cartoons, hailing them as childish mothers shopping for children's sugary snacks, or urging them to scoop up pre-wrapped meats or multipack beers to keep their husbands happy.[15] (And if "shopping for images" seems a doubtful alibi, and Ginsberg really went to the supermarket because of his "hungry fatigue," then the thought of him joining Whitman in "poking" around for food might remind us that these stores were starting to hail such men too, and were doing so under the vague but effective "admass" *bachelor*.) In other words, fifty years before Bruno Latour invoked the supermarket to show how "social links weave their way through non-social objects" in *Reassembling the Social* (2005) – and fifty-one years before he justified this choice by noting that "the supermarket is the place you hate most of all," and simply because it is "all about manipulation" – Ginsberg had already dramatized the rising agency objects hold over this new foodscape.[16] He reinforces many of the ideas Alworth explores in his Latourian reading of Don DeLillo's *White Noise* (1985):

> It is difficult ... to think of the social as a network comprising both humans and nonhumans as fully agential actors or actants.
>
> Unless we stroll through the supermarket. Latour himself heads there when he needs a familiar environment in which to situate his defamiliarizing claims. What Latour calls the "metaphor of the supermarket" ... serves to distance ANT [actor–network theory] from traditional sociology ... In the ANT supermarket, the human subject is not only one of the many actants constituting the network but is itself constituted by the nonhuman objects in its environment, the "bewildering array of devices" that buzz and jingle and flash in every aisle and on every shelf ... Thus, it makes no sense

[15] In the 1950s Landor Associates and other major packaging and advertising firms focused on giving their commissioned products instant appeal, and utilized new dyes and new moldable and squeezable plastics in order to maximize such "impulse" purchases. Walter Landor himself was interested in how "average" housewives moved through the supermarket, and for his firm's San Francisco headquarters he commissioned a replica store to study their behavior. In advertorials and interviews in the late 1940s he aired his discoveries. Supermarket packages, he emphasized, needed to be "catchy" if they were to distract the housewife without quite stopping her in her tracks. As a *Seattle Times* reporter put it in November 1955, Landor believed "not only in better mousetraps but better-looking ones," likening his designs to people in that "they should dress becomingly if they want to make a good impression." His focus remained on the housewife who, "pushing her cart through a supermarket," could take "only a fraction of a second over several brands." See "All Products Should 'Smile,' Says Experts on Packaging," *Seattle Times,* November 22, 1955.

[16] Latour, *Reassembling the Social*, 83; Christian S. G. Katti and Bruno Latour, "Mediating Political 'Things,' and the Forked Tongue of Modern Culture: A Conversation with Bruno Latour," *Art Journal* 65.1 (Spring 2006): 110.

to polarize subject and object in the ANT supermarket, just as it would be impossible to restrict agency in this site to the human particular.[17]

The difference is that Ginsberg continues to rail against this loss of "the human particular," his poem "underscoring" what Alworth calls a certain "longing" and "lack."[18] That is to say, Alworth, Latour, and Ginsberg all agree that upon entering these stores we are absorbed into a network in which objects interact with each other but also act on us, and with such insidious power, and at such a quickfire pace, that we must abandon any illusion of them being "female-controlled pleasure palaces," in Tracey Deutsch's phrase.[19] Ginsberg's poem never contradicts Alworth's and Latour's belief that such stores confront us with a commodity parade – a swift procession of goods that "buzz and jingle and flash in every aisle," each of which "keeps folded" within it a "flux of possibilities" as potent and determining as those Latour found in a single simple hammer.[20] But while Alworth offers a settled judgment on the equivalence between human and nonhuman all three intuit in the scene, even accepting it as a demystifying move away from the anthropocentric, Ginsberg laments the fading human bonds he finds.[21] The familiar hatred of the supermarket that Latour mentions in passing becomes for him the grounds of a passionate protest. As he shuttles from epic to mock epic his supermarket transpires as a foodscape where shoppers experience their isolation in close proximity to others. It sees them as strangers, never expecting them to "pay … attention to one another," as Grandclément-Chaffy puts it, and only recognizing them as social types no matter how resonant their name.[22] It even casts conversation itself as a source of congestion prone to disturb the movement of others. But it also brings these strangers closer together,

---

[17] Alworth, *Site Reading*, 29.

[18] Ibid., 33.

[19] Tracey Deutsch, *Building a Housewife's Paradise: Gender, Politics, and American Grocery Stores in the Twentieth Century* (Chapel Hill: University of North Carolina Press, 2010), 200.

[20] As Latour suggests, "There is nothing less local, less contemporary, less brutal than a hammer, as soon as one begins to unfold what it sets in motion; there is nothing more local, more brutal and more durable than this same hammer as soon as one folds everything implicated in it." Alworth makes clear that the heterogeneous temporalities *and* possibilities of the Latourian hammer (temporalities which would include the forest, the factory, the shop, and the workshop; possibilities which would include the opposition of construction and destruction) might also be folded out of each item in the supermarket's stunning range of commodities. Bruno Latour, "Morality and Technology: The End of the Means," *Theory, Culture and Society* 19.5/6 (2002), 249–50.

[21] Although even "demystification," as Jane Bennett notes, "tends to screen from view the vitality of matter and to reduce *political* agency to *human* agency." Bennett, *Vibrant Matter: A Political Ecology of Things* (Durham, NC: Duke University Press, 2010), xv.

[22] Cochoy and Grandclément-Chaffy, "Publicizing Goldilocks' Choice," 652.

leading them to cross paths and wait while each other shop, and generally eating into the feelings of personal space that John Fruin called the "body ellipse."[23] As such, alongside Latour's ANT analyses, Ginsberg's poem also looks ahead to landmark writings of the 1970s, and not only to Fruin's *Pedestrian Planning and Design* (1971) but also Lyn Lofland's *A World of Strangers* (1973) and its account of the innumerable Americans who had retreated "to the suburbs, ostensibly to escape the crowding and ano-nymity of the city," only to find themselves, "in the great shopping centers which dot their landscapes, confronted by as many strange faces as they ever confronted in the city."[24] As they turn into types and join this field of anonymity – a field into which Whitman and Ginsberg then project one unanswerable question after another – so Ginsberg's shoppers might seem, in Latour's language, not "preformatted" already but in the throes of *being* "preformatted." Their recognizability and silence performs a loss of control ordained in their encounter with Alworth's "agential" goods.

This subtle shift extends to Ginsberg's and Alworth's variations on the verb *to stroll*. Across *Site Reading*'s explorations this term, with its flaneurial overtones, emerges as Alworth's preferred way of describing movement in the store. Indeed, if we accept his invitation and "stroll" inside, we find ourselves walking around just like Durkheim and *White Noise*'s protag-onist do elsewhere in *Site Reading* – and just like Ginsberg himself does in Alworth's earlier *New Literary History* essay, all of us together "strolling the aisles" like we had nowhere else to go.[25] But Ginsberg remains open to other ways of describing movement in the supermarket. Against Alworth's *strolling* he lists sundry alternatives, and as he shuffles between them he covers the simple act of walking in doubt. He himself *went* into the store and, on noticing its "brilliant" commodities, settled into a Wordsworthian *wander* something like a stroll. But this aroused suspicions, at least in his own "imagination," so he and Whitman *strode* (the verb, though almost a homophone of *strolled,* of course means a much faster kind of walk) without *passing* the cashier. *Stroll* thus joins these synonyms only after the poem has left the supermarket behind. Ginsberg instead associates the verb with "a lost America of love," weaving it into his nostalgic fantasy of a future when he and Whitman, having got "past blue automobiles in driveways," might "stroll dreaming" together. A somewhat default term

---

[23] John T. Fruin, *Pedestrian Planning and Design* (Mobile, AL: Elevator World, 1987), 19.
[24] Lyn H. Lofland, *A World of Strangers: Order and Action in Urban Public Space* (New York: Basic Books, 1973), 179.
[25] Alworth, "Supermarket Sociology," 306.

in *Site Reading* thus becomes elusive, the object of an irrecuperable bond born in easy movement. *To stroll*, in Ginsberg, no longer names how we walk. It names how he would walk with Whitman, and how we would walk together, if only our yearning for some lost home or love came true.

This is a small difference, perhaps. But Site Reading's decision to treat these terms as interchangeable and synonymous is important because it encourages Alworth to go on and isolate the commodity and inspect it at length. *Stroll*, semantically, suggests a paced and uninterrupted zooming in on such items, granting them a starring role in the equalization of human and nonhuman that the supermarket performs. Its recurrence in turn helps Alworth carry off his brilliant Latourian riff on Vance Packard's *The Hidden Persuaders* (1957), allowing him to linger on *White Noise*'s luxuriant supermarket and to show how its "package[s]" all supplant "the salesperson," themselves "enticing, persuading and ultimately overpowering the customer."[26] Arguably, however, *Site Reading*'s preference for *stroll* carries costs as well as gains. Its connotations of leisurely urban spectatorship, of *noctambulisme* and the *flâneur,* lead Alworth to characterize the supermarket as a logical development and even a consummation of the privileges of choice first promised in the opulent arcades and department stores of late Victorian modernity.[27] What gets overlooked is the new temporal modality in which the supermarket operates: its pursuit of optimum flow. Once the *flâneur* sought stasis, and hoped to stand as still as "a paralytic," in Richard Sennett's phrase, pouring all his energies into the "art of seeing" whichever modern spectacle he happened upon.[28] The ordinary shopper, too, often found herself the target of window displays and other commercial vistas which held her captive as long as they could. If you stroll around staring at stuff like that in a supermarket, however, you turn yourself into a tractor on a freeway. Traffic gathers behind you, and people mutter and moan while they wait for you to move. Or, as DeLillo put it in his earlier *Americana* (1971), the supermarket might still place visual wonder before us – its gondolas might resemble a "spangled ark," full of "thunderbolts" and "rectangles of evangelistic writ" – but all such spectacles we must now forget or pre-emptively banalize, for fear that others will start "testing and prodding" us, "our cart nudging" theirs.[29] Old commercial imperatives of spectacle survive here, but only after being pressed into a tense, volatile

---

[26] Alworth, *Site Reading*, 39.
[27] Walter Benjamin, *Charles Baudelaire: A Lyric Poet in the Era of High Capitalism*, translated by Harry Zohn (London: Verso, 1992), 50.
[28] Richard Sennett, *The Fall of Public Man* (London: Penguin, 1976), 213.
[29] Don DeLillo, *Americana* (London: Penguin, 1990), 206.

equation with the supermarket's countervailing commitment to keep goods
and people on the move. The supermarket can only maintain such a flow
if its customers agree (perhaps on pain of their Latourian "preformatting")
to regulate and even curb their consumerist habits, never quite allowing
its distractions to distract them. The verb *stroll* is perhaps too redolent
of an earlier moment of modernity to help us navigate such paradoxical
demands.

Ginsberg's miscellaneous verbs for walking, on the other hand, at least
remind us that other nonhuman actants are lurking in this foodscape.
Like his sophomoric pleasure at "never passing the cashier," his encounters
with "wives" and "whole families" all acknowledge that others in the store
are not just "shopping for images," but are time and again reaching into
its "neon" displays, are "poking" around its "brilliant cans," and are now
carrying all their accumulated purchases with them. Without mentioning
the cart by name, Ginsberg's way of shopping "wrong" in the supermarket – his raptures, his apostrophes, his obstruction of its aisles – does
evoke the presence of all those who shop "right," the silent marginal mass
forever wheeling their groceries around. Yet insofar as he thus suggests the
cart's capacity to "channel ... lines of vision and gestures into the supermarket aisles," as Cochoy and Grandclément-Chaffy put it, Ginsberg also
links such "aisles" with the "blue automobiles" outside, expressing a desire,
ultimately, to find his way back "past" both.[30] In a state then known for
various imaginative applications of automobility, from drive-in restaurants
to a variety of new Park and Shop possibilities, Ginsberg thus finds in
the supermarket another "direct spatial tie between indoors and out," in
Richard Longstreth's phrase: a foodscape that invites its clientele to push
their carts around just as though they had never left the road.[31] Certainly
his fellow customers shop like others drive: in silence, with one eye on the
time, and without hearing others speak. Ginsberg's hope of communing
with Whitman is always in vain; but he can only dream of it after both
have left car and supermarket behind.

The Pause that Refreshes

Ginsberg, then, revels in the delights of the supermarket but soon longs to
abandon it. His poem arrives at a kind of future nostalgia which at once
looks before and beyond car culture toward some impossible renewal of the

---

[30] Cochoy and Grandclément-Chaffy, "Publicizing Goldilocks' Choice," 652.
[31] Longstreth, *The Drive-In*, 156.

fraternal bonds between poets. Other US texts move straight toward this bleak conclusion without bothering too much with Ginsberg's preliminary rapture. In 1963, for example, soon after he returned to the University of North Carolina at Greensboro following his Library of Congress laureateship, Randall Jarrell completed a lyric that found in such stores only barren ground, and not just for poetry but human understanding itself:

> Moving from Cheer to Joy, from Joy to All,
> I take a box
> And add it to my wild rice, my Cornish game hens.
> The slacked or shorted, basketed, identical
> Food-gathering flocks
> Are selves I overlook. Wisdom, said William James,
>
> Is learning what to overlook. And I am wise
> If that is wisdom.
> Yet somehow, as I buy All from these shelves
> And the boy takes it to my station wagon,
> What I've become
> Troubles me even if I shut my eyes.
>
> … Now that I'm old, my wish
> Is womanish:
> That the boy putting groceries in my car
> See me. It bewilders me he doesn't see me.[32]

On first impression "Next Day" can seem strikingly reminiscent of the first color photograph that William Eggleston felt happy with: his untitled image of a grocery boy outside a Memphis supermarket one sunny evening in 1965. The literary and visual texts are close not just in time period but also mood. In Randall's poem and Eggleston's photograph alike, the supermarket promises human encounter only to deny it, and in both an exception to the intimate isolations of the foodscape emerges as an older female shopper notices a younger male employee.

On further inspection, however, these scenes turn out to be somewhat different. In the shadow he casts upon the ground we can see that Eggleston is actually focusing on the line of telescoping carts. In "Next Day," by contrast, all the shoppers remain, in Jarrell's makeshift adjective, "basketed." This detail alone prises photo and poem apart, in effect pushing the setting of the latter all the way back to the time before *Life* magazine's famous cover of January 1955 announced the supermarket cart's ubiquity in US

---

[32] Randall Jarrell, "Next Day," in *The Lost World* (London: Eyre and Spottiswood, 1966), 4.

life. The conspicuous absence of these contraptions in the poem might even suggest the existing environment of "the immaculate Piggly Wiggly interior," as Marcie Ferris has described it, which Clarence Saunders based around "The Aristocracy of the Piggly Wiggly Basket," where "fashionable white women shoppers" were enjoined to "take what you please from the shelves" and "make your own decisions, leisurely."[33]

As such details accumulate, confirming the gap between the poem's setting and composition, supermarket carts loom up on its approaching horizon. Their future appearance, over the coming years that are also those of the poem's gestation, can seem to herald a rupture of some kind, perhaps signaling the coming moment when the last traces of face-to-face encounter, already faint in the scene, will disappear completely. The silence that the boy maintains in the poem in turn grows not just "bewildering" but uncanny, a sign that he might even be peering into his own impendent obsolescence. His youth alone returns attention to that contemporary phase of composition which the poem would rather escape, framing 1963 as a moment when supermarket carts have lost newsworthiness, checkout counters run beside rather than sit before customers, and only the most old-fashioned would expect to look anyone other than their own children in the eye.

Both Ginsberg's and Jarrell's poems, then, express wariness about the rise of the supermarket and its impact on face-to-face encounter. Whereas *Life* magazine's coverage in January 1955 fell in line with a host of industry specialists and trade journalists in celebrating supermarkets for offering such rapid improvements in efficiency and access to an unprecedented range of foods, Ginsberg and Jarrell seem determined to implicate these stores in the creeping erosion of community ties. Moreover, as walking grows contentious in Ginsberg and baskets become anachronistic in Jarrell, both seem indirectly to associate this erosion with the increased ubiquity of the cart. Issuing from them is a simple, subtle implication: that these contraptions might be efficient and accessible and ingeniously simple, but they also get in the way, being so big and bulky as to discourage interaction between us.

Similar tensions become apparent in *The Road* (2006). No longer a conspicuous absence, the supermarket cart becomes an object of sustained interest throughout Cormac McCarthy's novel, and not least because it has withstood apocalypse far better than a host of other, more sophisticated,

---

[33] Marcie Cohen Ferris, *The Edible South: The Power of Food and the Making of an American Region* (Chapel Hill: University of North Carolina Press, 2010), 192–93.

machines. Indeed, amid what Alworth calls the novel's portrait of "starkly inhuman activity and radical antisociality," the supermarket cart's endurance provides McCarthy's father with surprising grounds on which to claw back some fragile agency.[34] Because it has outlived car culture and supermarket alike, the cart can no longer act upon him – can no longer hope to "preformat" him into a calculating, consuming shopper. But it can be acted upon, and it can become an aid to his and his son's survival, and a surrogate car for their all too hopeful journey South. Its new identity seems both potent and permanent. Indeed, when he stumbles upon the ruins of an old supermarket, *The Road*'s father is at pains to keep the redefined cart away from it:

> On the outskirts of the city they came to a supermarket … They left their cart in the lot and walked the littered aisles. In the produce section in the bottom of the bins they found a few ancient runner beans and what looked to have once been apricots, long dried to wrinkled effigies of themselves. The boy followed behind. They pushed out through the rear door. In the alleyway behind the store a few shopping carts, all badly rusted. They went back through the store again looking for another cart but there were none. By the door there were two softdrink machines that had been tilted over into the floor and opened with a prybar. Coins everywhere in the ash. He sat and ran his hand around in the works of the gutted machines and in the second one it closed over a cold metal cylinder. He withdrew his hand slowly and sat looking at a Coca Cola.
>
> What is it, Papa?
> It's a treat. For you.
> What is it?
> Here. Sit down …
> The boy took the can. It's bubbly, he said.
> Go ahead.
> He looked at his father and then tilted the can and drank.
> He sat there thinking about it. It's really good, he said.
> Yes. It is.[35]

Suffering and alienation in *The Road* coexist with signs of God's design. To some extent it is when happening upon this unnamed Coke that the novel initiates this typological interest. Here, for the first time, McCarthy first suggests that his father – who has always found proof of God's grace in the sight of his son's face – might find it elsewhere too. The drink he offers his

[34] Alworth, *Site Reading*, 155.
[35] Cormac McCarthy, *The Road* (New York: Alfred Knopf, 2006), 19–20.

son here, after all, could have been a Mountain Dew or Doctor Pepper, and it could have been a Seven Up or Fanta. That it is instead a Coca Cola, and a commodity whose global mythologies all but exceed its contents, guarantees that its appearance in the ruins of the supermarket seems not just fortunate but providential, and altogether too pregnant with meaning to belong to the unplanned happenings on which novelistic reality normally depends.

Certainly, Coke is so intimately connected to the global expansion of US consumer culture that it can be difficult *not* to critique it, and lots of critics have been tempted to do so. Slavoj Žižek performed one of the most memorable of these critiques for his 2012 film *The Pervert's Guide to Ideology*. Here he suggests, in a riff he develops from *The Fragile Absolute* (2000), that Coke "always reflects an invisible transcendence."[36] Under postmodern conditions, Žižek adds, we "are obliged to enjoy, and enjoyment becomes a kind of weird, perverted duty." Coke fuels this perpetual obligation because, "as everyone knows, the more you drink it, the more thirsty you get." As such – although originally marketed for offering a "pause that refreshes" – it now feeds only our postmodern "desire for desire itself," our "desire to continue to desire."[37] On these grounds Žižek casts Coke as the "perfect commodity." For him it has become a drink which averts the total satisfaction we would understand as a melancholic "loss of desire." Instead it perpetually offers us access to the "real thing," or even "it," while perpetually withholding "it" from us.

Like much in *The Pervert's Guide to Ideology* this might seem a trap. Žižek delights in goading the rational into complaint, always seeking in such disruption some new dialectical path. The obvious response, in consequence, becomes unreliable. It becomes a little too easy to observe that McCarthy's young hero, after finishing his first Coke, does not say "can I have another one?" but "it's good." And it can feel simplistic to note that his refreshment includes no melancholic downside, or to conclude from this that *The Pervert's Guide to Ideology* and *The Road* are, therefore, at odds. Such a conclusion would certainly overlook the fact that *The Road* has only completed this return to authentic refreshment after it has comprehensively dismantled all the scenes and settings of commodity consumption familiar to us now. It would forget that McCarthy has only brought about this sensual redemption of Coke after his novel

---

[36] Slavoj Žižek, *The Fragile Absolute: Or, Why Is the Christian Legacy Worth Fighting For?* (London: Verso, 2001), 23.
[37] *The Pervert's Guide to Ideology*, directed by Sophie Fiennes (New York: Zeitgeist, 2012).

has stripped all commercial trappings from the drink; and it would elide, too, the novel's double annihilation, its staged apocalyptic burning of cars from the road and carts from the supermarket. In its dual rejection of car-centered consumer culture, indeed, *The Road* offers a rejection of the entire culture Žižek holds responsible for satisfaction's reconstitution as the melancholic loss of desire. He, like Ginsberg and Jarrell, suggests that pleasure and communication alike only become possible once we leave automobility behind.

BIBLIOGRAPHY

Alworth, David J. *Site Reading: Fiction, Art, Social Form.* Princeton: Princeton University Press, 2016.

"Supermarket Sociology." *New Literary History* 41.2 (2010): 301–27.

Benjamin, Walter. *Charles Baudelaire: A Lyric Poet in the Era of High Capitalism.* Translated by Harry Zohn. London: Verso, 1992.

Bennett, Jane. *Vibrant Matter: A Political Ecology of Things.* Durham, NC: Duke University Press, 2010.

Cochoy, Frank, and Catherine Grandclément-Chaffy. "Publicizing Goldilocks' Choice at the Supermarket: The Political Work of Shopping Packs, Carts and Talk." In *Making Things Public: Atmospheres of Democracy*, edited by Bruno Latour and Peter Weibel, 646–57. Cambridge, MA: MIT Press, 2005.

De Certeau, Michel. *The Practice of Everyday Life.* Translated by Steven Rendall Berkeley: University of California Press, 1988.

DeLillo, Don. *Americana.* London: Penguin, 1990.

White Noise. London: Picador, 2011.

Deutsch, Tracey. *Building a Housewife's Paradise: Gender, Politics, and American Grocery Stores in the Twentieth Century.* Chapel Hill: University of North Carolina Press, 2010.

Ferris, Marcie Cohen. *The Edible South: The Power of Food and the Making of an American Region.* Chapel Hill: University of North Carolina Press, 2014.

Fruin, John T. *Pedestrian Planning and Design.* Mobile, AL: Elevator World, 1987.

Ginsberg, Allen. *Howl and Other Poems.* San Francisco: City Lights, 1956.

Grandclément-Chaffy, Catherine. "Wheeling One's Groceries Around the Store: The Invention of the Shopping Cart, 1936–1953." In *Food Chains: From Farmyard to Shopping Cart*, edited by Warren Belasco and Roger Horowitz, 233–52. Philadelphia: University of Pennsylvania Press, 2008.

Jarrell, Randall. "Next Day." In *The Lost World*, 3–4. London: Eyre and Spottiswood, 1966.

Jonson, Ben. "On the Famous Voyage." In *Ben Jonson: Oxford Poetry Library*, edited by Ian Donaldson, 61–66. Oxford: Oxford University Press, 1995.

Katti, Christian S. G., and Bruno Latour. "Mediating Political 'Things,' and the Forked Tongue of Modern Culture: A Conversation with Bruno Latour." *Art Journal* 65.1 (Spring 2006): 94–115.

Kearful, Frank. "Alimentary Poetics: Robert Lowell and Allen Ginsberg." *Partial Answers: Journal of Literature and the History of Ideas* 11.1 (2013): 87–108.

Latour, Bruno. "Morality and Technology: The End of the Means." *Theory, Culture and Society* 19.5/6 (2002): 247–60.

Reassembling the Social: An Introduction to Actor-Network Theory. Oxford: Oxford University Press, 2005.

Lofland, Lyn H. *A World of Strangers: Order and Action in Urban Public Space*. New York: Basic Books, 1973.

Longstreth, Richard. *The Drive-In, the Supermarket, and the Transformation of Commercial Space in Los Angeles, 1914–1941*. Cambridge, MA: MIT Press, 1999.

McCarthy, Cormac. *The Road*. New York: Alfred Knopf, 2006.

Ngai, Sianne. *Ugly Feelings*. Cambridge, MA: Harvard University Press, 2007.

Packard, Vance. *The Hidden Persuaders*. New York: David McKay, 1957.

Percy, Walker. *The Moviegoer*. York: Methuen, 2013.

The Pervert's Guide to Ideology. Directed by Sophie Fiennes. New York: Zeitgeist, 2012.

Robertson, Ritchie. *Mock-Epic Poetry from Pope to Heine*. Oxford: Oxford University Press, 2009.

Sennett, Richard. *The Fall of Public Man*. London: Penguin, 1976.

Spencer, Elizabeth. *The Snare*. Jackson, MI: Banner Books, 1993.

Trachtenberg, Alan. *Reading American Photographs: Images as History, Mathew Brady to Walker Evans*. New York: Hill and Wang, 1989.

Žižek, Slavoj. *The Fragile Absolute: Or, Why Is the Christian Legacy Worth Fighting For?* London: Verso, 2001.

CHAPTER 3

Gothic Vegetarianism

Parama Roy

Vegetarians

In any global history of vegetarianism, most roads lead to the Indian subcontinent at some point or another. When Alexander reached India in 326 BCE as part of his project of world conquest, he knew already of its naked vegetarian philosophers, the gymnosophists. The story of his encounter with ten of them, one of the best-known elements of the Alexander legend, was commemorated in a number of Greek Indographic accounts of different periods, including ones by Plutarch, Arrian, and Strabo. The story of the great conqueror's encounter with these figures, whether identified as *brachmani* (Brahmins), *samanaei* (Shramana or Jain ascetics), or as gymnosophists, stresses their intellectual agility in response to his questions – an intellectual agility inseparable from their dietary norms, their bodily discipline, and their philosophical indifference to death. This conjunction of the territory called India to vegetarian and austere practice was to persist for a considerable duration, certainly into the nineteenth century.[1] In the early centuries of the Christian era some patristic literature, indebted as it was to Roman sources that were obsessively concerned with the ascetic dimensions of Indian religions, sought to highlight the continuities between the practices of early Church fathers and

---

[1] What counted as India, though, did not always correspond to a clearly delimited positive geography. "Although certainly indicating from European antiquity a loosely defined region of Asia somewhere between the Levant and China, 'India' equally marked the site of a series of allegorical operations, which impressed upon an ill-defined space an imagined content." Shankar Raman, *Framing "India": The Colonial Imaginary in Early Modern Culture* (Stanford: Stanford University Press, 2001), 2. For the early modern European voyager, he notes, "the figure of 'India' … functions as a boundary condition: the transgression of this hitherto unreachable limit transforms the very nature of the world that had partly constituted itself in relation to that limit" (ibid., 36). Also see Jonathan Gil Harris, "Introduction: Forms of Indography," and Jyotsna G. Singh, "Naming and Un-naming 'All the Indies': How India Became Hindustan," in *Indography: Writing the "Indian" in Early Modern England*, edited by J. Gil Harris (New York: Palgrave Macmillan, 2012), 1–20, 249–55.

the teachings of scriptural and Indic sources on abstinence, especially vegetarianism.[2] And, as Thomas Hahn has established, from the twelfth to the
fourteenth centuries these Indian gymnosophists or Brahmins enjoyed the
status of the best of the virtuous heathen, commendable for their simple,
devout behavior and for their adherence to the law of nature, which made
them apt models for Christian imitation.[3] This was to undergo some revision in the following centuries.

The accounts of late medieval and early modern travelers, merchants,
migrants, and other sojourners in the subcontinent added ethnographic
details to the extant vision of the religion and diet of these virtuous
primitives made famous by the Alexander Romance.[4] Tristram Stuart has
detailed a widespread European fascination from the seventeenth century on with the religious practices of the subcontinent's non-Islamic
populations, including their religiously mandated dietary restrictions, and
their ethical or cultic stance with respect to nonhuman life and nonhuman
death.[5] (Before the term "vegetarian" appeared in print in 1847, those
who abjured animal flesh and fish were often referred to as Brahmins, as
Timothy Morton reminds us.[6])

Given the importance of the trading cities of coastal Gujarat in western
India in the international trade of the Arabian Sea, this was the region
that saw a great influx of visitors from foreign parts. As a result, the vegetarian populations who drew the attention of British, French, Portuguese,
Dutch, Venetian, Roman, and German commentators from the late sixteenth century onwards often tended to be residents of these cities, though
several writers ranged significantly beyond this region. These chroniclers
distinguished between the Muslim populations they called "Moors" and the
non-Muslim and non-Christian peoples described variously as Gentiles or
Gentoos, sometimes Gentives; the latter terms derived from "a corruption
of the Portuguese *Gentio*, a 'Gentile' or heathen," which [was] applied to

---

[2] Nathan J. Ristuccia, "Eastern Religions and the West: The Making of an Image," *History of Religions*
53.2 (November 2013): 174. But while patristic and later medieval authors celebrate certain Eastern
religious figures whose practices resemble those of Christian ascetics, they reject as idolatrous the
popular forms of Indic religious practice (ibid., 201).

[3] Thomas Hahn, "The Indian Tradition in Western Intellectual History," *Viator* 9 (1978): 213–34.

[4] See John Michael Archer's *Old Worlds: Egypt, Southwest Asia, India, and Russia in Early Modern
English Writing* (Stanford: Stanford University Press, 2001), chapter 4, for a useful summary of the
classical knowledge of India that European travelers brought with them when they arrived there in
the fourteenth century.

[5] Tristram Stuart, *The Bloodless Revolution: A Cultural History of Vegetarianism from 1600 to Modern
Times* (New York: Norton, 2007), 39–40.

[6] Timothy Morton, *Shelley and the Revolution in Taste: The Body and the Natural World* (Cambridge:
Cambridge University Press, 1994), 16.

the Hindus in contradistinction to the Moros or 'Moors,' " according to *Hobson-Jobson*, the historical dictionary of terms in use in Anglo-India.[7] Moors were understood to be both carnivorous and warlike. Gentiles or Gentoos on the other hand were generally presumed to comprise three major castes or clusters, distinguishable from one another through occupation and diet. Thus Duarte Barbosa, among others, describes the Gentiles as consisting of *Resbutos* (Rajputs), *Bramenes* (Brahmins), and *Baneanes* (Banias).[8] The first are distinguished by military pursuits and carnivory (though not beef-eating); they are "the only idolaters who are brave," notes Jean-Baptiste Tavernier.[9] The latter two on the other hand are known for their scrupulous avoidance of "flesh ... fish, ... [and] anything subject to death."[10]

In seeking to establish themselves profitably on the west coast of India, and negotiate favorable terms with the Mughal state and its local satraps, European factors and travelers used the services of bankers, brokers, accountants, and interpreters, who were commonly designated as Banias.[11] European accounts were therefore replete with references to them. In addition to underlining Bania business acumen and acquisition of wealth, these accounts stressed the vegetarianism of this community as one of its most distinctive ethnographic characteristics. Banias were almost invariably members of both Hindu and Jain trading communities, though Jain principles of nonviolence were binding on both. The distinctions between Hindus and Jains were obvious to few European travelers, the French missionary J. A. Dubois being among the exceptions. In any event, several of the elements of western Indian vegetarianism were observed by Brahmins as well, and in other parts of India, and broadly classified under the rubric of a Gentile vegetarianism. So normative was vegetarianism,

---

[7] Henry Yule and A. C. Burnell, *Hobson-Jobson: A Glossary of Colloquial Anglo-Indian Words and Phrases, and of Kindred Terms, Etymological, Historical, Geographical, and Discursive*, edited by William Crooke (London: John Murray, 1903), 237. A few travel accounts focused on western India also paid attention to the small community of "Persies" (Parsis/Zoroastrians), who could not be identified as either "moors" or "Gentiles/Gentoos."

[8] Duarte Barbosa, *The Book of Duarte Barbosa*, vol. 1, translated by Mansel Longworth Dames (1516; London: Hakluyt Society, 1918), 109–17.

[9] Jean Baptiste Tavernier, *Travels in India*, vol. 2, translated by Valentine Ball (1676; London: Macmillan, 1889), 182.

[10] Barbosa, *Book of Duarte Barbosa*, 111.

[11] See Balkrishna Govind Gokhale, *Surat in the Seventeenth Century* (London: Curzon Press, 1979); Ashin Dasgupta, *Indian Merchants and the Decline of Surat, 1700–1750* (Wiesbaden: Franz Steiner Verlag, 1979); Lakshmi Subramaniam, "Banias and the British," *Modern Asian Studies* 21.3 (1987): 473–510. Though there were Muslim and Parsi merchants in Gujarat and elsewhere on the western coast of India, the caste designation of Bania was reserved for Hindus and Jains alone.

says Dubois, that even those Hindus who did not practice it were generally careful not to eat meat or serve it to others openly.[12]

European writers produced a fairly exhaustive inventory of the principles and practices of Gentile vegetarianism: a strong commitment to alimentary abstinence that entailed abjuring the flesh of any living (or potentially living) creature; the avoidance of many vegetables, including onion, garlic, and root vegetables; strict limits on commensality outside one's caste; the sacralization of the cow and the worship of zoomorphic gods; the use of cow dung and cow's urine for ritual and medicinal purposes; an active and outspoken commitment to the preservation of nonhuman life, even in its meanest forms; a belief in the transmigration of souls, glossed as a variety of Pythagoreanism; and the establishment of animal hospitals dedicated to the nurture and preservation of aged, diseased, injured, or otherwise economically non-viable animal life, including, perhaps most strikingly, the life of vermin such as snakes, rats, worms, fleas, and lice.

Through the seventeenth and eighteenth centuries, some observers were favorably impressed with what they described as the gentleness and compassion of these vegetarian populations, or at least largely neutral in their accounts of what a rigorously practiced vegetarianism entailed. (The most famous fictional treatment of this was Phoebe Gibbes' *Hartly House, Calcutta* [1789].) The clergyman John Ovington, who is often given to a hyperbolic praise of the alimentary exotics of western India that barely keeps from tipping over into the satiric, avows, in 1696, that

> India, of all the Regions of the Earth, is the only publick Theatre of Justice and Tenderness to Brutes, and all living Creatures; for not confining Murther to the killing of a Man, they Religiously abstain from taking away the Life of the meanest Animal, Mite, or Flea; any of which if they chance wilfully to destroy, nothing less than a very considerable Expiation must Atone for the Offence.[13]

More unconditionally, John Oswald speaks a century later of the way the "merciful Hindoo" "beholds, in every creature, a kinsman: he rejoices in the welfare of every animal, and compassionates his pains; for he knows, and is convinced, that of all creatures the essence is the same, and that one

[12] Abbe J. A. Dubois, *Hindu Manners, Customs and Ceremonies*, translated by Henry K. Beauchamp, 3rd ed. (Oxford: Clarendon Press, 1906), 188–90. Outside the pale of caste Hindu, Jain, or respectable Muslim society were outcasts who performed the most ritually polluting offices like the removal of excrement, the handling of animal carcasses, and the execution of criminals. They were bound by none of the dietary proscriptions of Hindus, Jains, and Muslims, and were designated, euphemistically, as *halalcores* (*halalkhors*) – those for whom every kind of food was lawful.

[13] John Ovington, *A Voyage to Suratt, in the Year 1689* (London: Jacob Tonson, 1696), 296.

eternal first cause is the father of us all."[14] Many spoke of the exertions of these vegetarians to redeem animals destined for religious sacrifice or for human tables (and, on far rarer occasions, of human criminals destined for execution).

If the vegetarian communities of the subcontinent were characterized by practices of dietary self-denial, Europeans resident there seemed to act on entirely contrary principles, partaking prodigiously of flesh and fish, and drinking inordinately. In the estimate of many European writers, vegetarianism (and its cognate, teetotalism) became something of a shorthand for moderation and an adherence to the dictates of nature, while carnivory and alcoholism were proxies for reckless abandon, luxurious appetite, and sexual incontinence. Edward Terry, chaplain to Sir Thomas Roe, James I's ambassador to the court of the Mughal emperor Jahangir, commented that the inhabitants of India enjoyed great longevity in consequence of their fidelity to principles "founded on the book of nature." Christians on the other hand brought themselves, and Christianity, into disrepute through their drunkenness and other misdeeds.[15] Ovington uses the satirical trope of the eastern observer to defamiliarize the normative status of carnivory among Britons, whether at home or abroad, and to comment scathingly on the plethoric excesses of their modes of consumption. The self-denying and nonviolent Banias, he says, "are astonished at Christians, who heap whole Bisks of Fish upon their Tables, and sacrifice whole Hecatombs of Animals to their Gluttony." They cannot be tempted away from their "innocent" and "lawful" vegetarian diet – the diet of "the original Inhabitants of the World, whom Antiquity supposes not to have been Carnivorous" – for reasons of mere appetite or even as a stay against sickness and death. The strictest of the Brahmin ascetics of Surat trust to providence for their sustenance, "as if they had been intimately acquainted with our Saviour's Rule, *Take no thought for tomorrow.*" Such habits conduce to longevity, mental acuity, and equanimity in the face of death. Moreover, in an echo of ongoing theological debates in Britain about the lawfulness of hematophagy, he notes that the Bania avoidance of blood is in conformity with the biblical prohibition against its consumption.[16] In this, as in other matters, Gentile vegetarians constitute a model of a lost Edenic or antediluvian paradise of harmonious coexistence

---

[14] John Oswald, *The Cry of Nature* (London: J. Johnson, 1791), 5–6.
[15] Edward Terry, *A Voyage to East India* (1655; London: J. Wilkie, 1777), 230, 461, 239–41.
[16] For an account of British theological debates in the sixteenth and seventeenth centuries about the consumption of blood, see Stuart, *Bloodless Revolution*, 102–8.

with nonhuman animals against which the fallenness of the British may be measured.[17] Were they to be transported to "the Tempestuous Regions, and Northerly Air of Europe," where carnivory is allied with the inclemencies of the northern climate, they would find confirmation of their Pythagoreanism by encountering the ferocious souls of tigers, bears, and wolves in the form of European humans.[18]

Even among writers less disposed to take a charitable view of the disposition of the vegetarians of western India, a vegetarian diet – or at least a significant curtailment of carnivory and alcoholic consumption – was believed to be a commonsensical adaptation to life in the tropics. Before the mid-nineteenth century, when the category of the "tropical" changed from being a descriptive climatic category to a marker for backwardness and civilizational inferiority, it was believed that people could adapt to the ecologies in which they found themselves, primarily through adopting local sartorial and dietary practices.[19] Meat was considered particularly hard to digest in India, where the heat was said to slow the process of digestion. Physicians such as Francois Bernier, the French physician to the Mughal emperor Aurangzeb, and John Fryer, otherwise contemptuous of the mores of vegetarian communities (including their bans on dissection and vivisection), cautioned against the indiscriminate consumption of flesh, fish, and alcohol. The sovereign remedy of abstinence in the case of sickness, and the avoidance of meat broth as a therapeutic had observable curative effects in Hindustan (the Gangetic plain), Bernier noted, and Fryer conceded that eating large quantities of roasted meat was a tax upon the Englishman's stomach in hot countries.[20] Dubois cautioned especially against the consumption of beef; forswearing it and other meats, as he did himself, would improve the health of Europeans resident in India, in addition to winning

[17] Ovington, *Voyage to Suratt*, 302–3, 335, 316–17. See Robert N. Watson on the conversations among sixteenth- and seventeenth-century English Puritan theologians about kinship with and sympathy for nonhuman animals. Watson, "Protestant Animals: Puritan Sects and English Animal-Protection Sentiment, 1550–1650," *ELH* 81.4 (Winter 2014), 1111–48. It should be conceded in fairness that Ovington's views are not consistently maintained over the course of his narrative; elsewhere he describes local non-Christian susceptibility to epidemics which leave Europeans in Surat unscathed, but attributes this not to diet or bodily heath but to their being outside the ambit of a Christian god's protective care.

[18] Ovington, *Voyage to Suratt*, 276–77.

[19] See Mark Harrison, *Climates and Constitutions: Health, Race, Environment and British Imperialism in India 1600–1850* (New York: Oxford University Press, 1999). Also see Jonathan Gil Harris, *The First Firangis* (New Delhi: Aleph, 2015) for an account of the ways in which migrants in the pre-British Raj era acclimated themselves to the subcontinent and made it their home.

[20] Francois Bernier, *Travels in the Mogul Empire, AD 1656–1668*, translated by Archibald Constable (London: Oxford University Press, 1916), 338; John Fryer, *Travels in India in the Seventeenth Century by Sir Thomas Roe and Dr. John Fryer* (1698; London: John Trubner, 1873), 263–64.

them friends among a population that reverenced cows and considered the consumption of beef indistinguishable from cannibalism.[21]

At the same time, even those who advocated carnivorous restraint, especially in torrid zones, noted that vegetarianism, especially in conjunction with the weather, made for slothfulness, military incapacity, and timorousness. "They want nothing but courage," observes Thomas Bowrey of Gentile males, a lack that leaves them susceptible to severe exactions from their warlike Muslim (and, needless to say, carnivorous) overlords.[22] (In this respect at least they are a far cry from the fearless gymnosophists who resisted the great Alexander through the sheer moral force of their abstinence.) Ovington accedes to the then commonplace notion that vegetarian diet, combined with the experience of living with so-called Oriental despotism, has made its practitioners feeble and pusillanimous and unable to resist tyranny, though he simultaneously takes pains to underline the absence of crime in Surat and the gentleness of the manners of the local vegetarians. The rare verbal quarrel among them or "Tongue-Tempest," he notes, "is term'd there a Bannian Fight, for it never rises to Blows or Bloodshed"; an almost comical hyper-sensitivity to violence makes them unable to bear even so much as "hot Words" from Europeans.[23] In fact, the aversion for violence that provided a philosophical and practical scaffolding for their meatless ways often made them figures of fun, ripe for exploitation. Sometimes, it was noted that, notwithstanding their shrewdness in worldly affairs, pious Gentiles could be tricked through their tenderness for physical suffering into ransoming animals supposedly intended for extermination or humans seeking to harm themselves. Moorish mendicants make a show of injuring themselves with stones and knives to extort large sums of money from the devotees of nonviolence, says Barbosa, while others are paid off to refrain from killing rats and snakes in their homes. "Thus they are much esteemed by the Moors!" he concludes caustically.[24] This tradition of exploitation was to find favor with young English employees of the English factory at Surat. On occasion, they would make the Banias the butt of profitable jests, making a show of targeting birds in the vicinity

---

[21] Dubois, *Hindu Manners*, 191–93, 201, 305–6. E. M. Collingham's account of the repasts of Anglo-Indians in the less gluttonous nineteenth century demonstrates that they were still ostentatious and elaborate. Collingham, *Imperial Bodies: The Physical Experience of the Raj, c. 1800–1947* (Cambridge: Polity Press, 2001).

[22] Thomas Bowrey, *A Geographical Account of Countries Round the Bay of Bengal, 1669 to 1679*, edited by Richard Carnac Temple (Cambridge: Hakluyt Society, 1905), 10. This became one of the dominant tropes of Indography, persisting well into the nineteenth century.

[23] Ovington, *Voyage to Suratt*, 275–77.

[24] Barbosa, *Book of Duarte Barbosa*, 111–12.

of their residences so as to extract bribes to desist from the projected slaughter.[25] These acts of extortion were given a keener edge no doubt by the widespread reputation of the merchants for sharp dealing and parsimoniousness; they were almost invariably compared to European Jews, whom they were said to outdo in craftiness and dishonesty.[26]

Vermin

In the centuries before colonization, Europeans often encountered popular opposition to hunting in a land teeming with unusual game, generally because of the interference of these theriophiles. The German traveler John Albert de Mandelso found himself compelled to give up hunting when his traveling companions objected strenuously to his slaughter of snakes, leopards, roebucks, and other animals and birds on the way from Agra to Surat.[27] The shooting of a monkey by a young Dutchman showing off his skill with a gun prompted outrage and the mass resignation of the Banias in the service of the Dutch East India Company.[28] But the prohibition against animal killing extended considerably beyond the slaughter of animals for food or sport. Writer after writer noted the prodigious size, quantity, and noxiousness of beasts of prey and other vermin, which were nonetheless exempt from check or harm. Birds wreak havoc among rice fields and fruit trees in Amadabat (Ahmadabad), notes Mandelslo wonderingly, but they neither can be killed nor even hindered from eating the crops. The rivers are full of crocodiles that prey upon cattle and humans on a daily basis, but the vegetarians will not permit their destruction, believing that being eaten by a crocodile assures entrance to felicity in the next world.[29]

All Gentiles, regardless of caste, demonstrated an inordinate reverence for the cow. Some commentators found the ban against bovine slaughter and consumption to be rationally founded, given the animal's ostensible

[25] Ovington, *Voyage to Suratt*, 298–99.
[26] See, for instance, Tavernier, *Travels in India*, vol. I, 29, 91, 136; Horton Ryley, *Ralph Fitch, England's Pioneer to India and Burma* (London: T. Fisher Unwin, 1899), 101; John Albert del Mandelslo, *Mandelslo's Travels into the Indies, the First Book*, translated by John Davies (1642; repr., London: John Starkey and Thomas Basset, 1669), 231, 252; Fryer, *Travels in India*, 266–67, 445–46; Bowrey, *Geographical Account*, 27–29.
[27] Mandelslo, *Travels into the Indies*, 45.
[28] Tavernier, *Travels in India*, vol. I, 78–79.
[29] Mandelslo, *Travels into the Indies*, 26–27. Even in the nineteenth century, Mark Twain suggests – with his tongue only slightly in cheek – that India is "by an unapproachable supremacy – the Land of Murderous Wild Creatures," and that it remains so because of the passivity of its populace. Twain, *Following the Equator, and Anti-Imperialist Essays*, edited by Shelley Fisher Fishkin (New York: Oxford University Press, 1996), 544.

utility and the inedibility of its flesh in hot climes; Pietro della Valle even commends the common practice of scouring floors with a mixture of cow dung and water as making for cleanliness and brightness.[30] But the veneration that was manifested in the consumption of bovine dung and urine, especially for purposes of religious purgation or penance, was not easily explicable either in terms of utility or of compassion for nonhuman life. Countless writers described – sometimes with a certain blandness and sometimes with outright horror and disgust – the ritualized consumption of the *panchagavya*, the five products of the cow, including dung and urine, as well as forms of asceticism that involved eating the undigested grain from the droppings of oxen, cows, and buffaloes.[31]

Perhaps even more astonishingly, Gentile vegetarianism entailed a tenderness for the lives of the meanest and minutest of creatures. Roe noted that Banias "will not kyll the Vermyne that bytes them."[32] Other writers took repeated note of some distinctive practices of the nonviolent: the feeding of ants, flies, and birds at home and outside it; the abstention from lighting candles or eating after dark lest insects be destroyed or ingested unawares; the offloading of lice to hermits who volunteer to house them; the payment to poor hirelings to offer up their bodies to satisfy the appetite of bloodsucking insects; and the refusal to injure household insects and other creatures customarily regarded as annoying or dangerous. Ascetics and members of monastic orders (sometimes designated, not necessarily correctly, as Brahmins) were subject to still more stringent regulations, and accounts of subcontinental life were full of the arresting and sometimes harrowing details that their bodily austerities assumed.

On occasion, Gentile merchants were seen as so promiscuous in their intimacy with animal life that vermin such as insects, snakes, and rats who took up habitation in their homes were not only not banished or killed but reverenced and offered hospitality, being seen as spirits of dead ancestors. Indeed, notes Kate Teltscher, "the idea that a Banian wouldn't even kill a fly (or louse, or flea) for fear of unhousing a relative's soul had by this

[30] Pietro della Valle, *The Travels of Pietro della Valle in India*, 2 vols., translated by George Havers and edited by Edward Grey (London: Hakluyt Society, 1892), 87–88.
[31] Tavernier, *Travels in India*, vol. 2, 210–11, 217. Also see (among others) Niccolao Manucci, *Storia do Mogor, or Mogul India 1653–1708*, translated and edited by William Irvine (London: John Murray, 1907), vol. 1, 155–157, and vol. 3, 41; Mandelslo, *Travels into the Indies*, 57; Ovington, *Voyage to Suratt*, 315.
[32] Sir Thomas Roe, *The Embassy of Sir Thomas Roe to the Court of the Great Mogul, 1615–1619, as Narrated in his Journal and Correspondence*, edited by William Foster, vol. 1 (London: Hakluyt Society, 1899), 123–24.

time entered the travel writer's lexicon of stock sayings."[33] For Fryer, Bania parsimony and joint family conditions were inseparable from vegetarianism and a loathsome proximity to animal life. Speaking of the perverse pleasures generated from the strange conjuncture of abstemiousness and profuse, filthy carnality, he notes of the rich merchants:

> They stew themselves out of a penurious humour, crowding Three or Four Families together into an Hovel, with Goats, Cows, and Calves, all Chamber fellows, that they are almost poysoned with Vermin and Nastiness; but surely they take delight in it, for they will fresh and fasting besprinkle themselves with the Stale of a Cow, as you behold a good Christian with Holy water, or a Moorman slabber his Beard with Rosewater. Nay more, they use it as a Potion, or Philter, and bid the Devil do his worst after it; so stupid that notwitstanding Chints, Fleas, and Muskeeto's, torment them every Minute, dare not presume to scratch where it itches, lest some Relation should be untenanted its miserable abode.[34]

In Fryer's narrative, as in that of many others, the vegetarian merchant lives meanly despite his great wealth, in a habitation scarcely distinguishable from one that houses animals. He is a grasping, covetous, usurious sort, a virtuoso of sharp practice given to affecting poverty in the midst of stupendous wealth. Here his commercial practice is crosshatched with the practice of joint family living and with the near proximity of goats, cows, and calves. This, like the practice of usury, produces its own series of unnatural begettings in the shape of vermin, who are also, given the belief in metempsychosis, relations. For the observing doctor there is thus in Surat a distinctive nexus of commerce, contagion, and false faith. It is worth noting that verminous life here is also a monetized domain, inseparable from the usurer-merchant's penny-pinching ways. In fact the grasping economy he practices eventuates logically in a life in the midst of vermin that he must then nurture. Even his proximity to domesticated animals is not for utilitarian or companionable purposes, nor is it a matter of poverty; the animals rather are a source of waste matter necessary for idolatrous worship and consumption. What one has here is something worse than filth; it is filth made sacred, and it stands in ironic counterpoint to the constant ablutions that European observers noticed as a feature of Indic religions.

This filth is no mere inert matter out of place but is alive with the horror generated by the unclean creeping things that one is forbidden to touch or

---

[33] Kate Teltscher, "'Maidenly and Well Nigh Effeminate': Constructions of Hindu Masculinity and Religion in Seventeenth-Century English Texts," *Postcolonial Studies* 3.2 (2000), 161.

[34] Fryer, *Travels in India*, 278.

to take into one's body. Not only does the Gentile vegetarian lack the appropriate mechanisms of disgust – hence he confuses the sacred and the polluted, humans and animals, food and excrement, circulation and arrest – but the scandalous excesses of false religion, false economy, false alimentation, and false hospitality lead him actually to delight in this dirty, sacrilegious carnality. Given Fryer's status as a surgeon it is perhaps unsurprising that he reads value and circulation in terms of disease and contagion, or medical and sanitary details, in other words. In an interesting variant on the common anti-semitic trope, the Bania is rapacious in his extortion of money but (a willing) prey to the vermin who both feast upon him and are likely kin. This, it should be noted, is more than an anthropology of vegetarian domestic life. It is a *zooanthropology*, an anatomization of an "animal-man" that, more than any mere animal, no matter how verminous, is the true source of contagion.[35] If Fryer had famously observed that in coastal western India there were "two sorts of Vermin, the Fleas and the Banyans,"[36] he demonstrates here that the loathsome habitus of the flea-ridden merchant is the gothic terminus of a vegetarianism run amuck.

Perhaps the most anthropologically curious instance, for European observers, of Indian nonviolence toward animals was the institution of the animal hospital or the *pinjrapole* – an institution that betrays some continuities with the domestic arrangements noted with such intense repugnance by Fryer. They noted that in the towns of western India there were hospitals for the refuge and care of birds (*parabdis*) and injured animals or working animals past their productive years (*pinjrapoles*). Della Valle, who had made it a point to visit Cambaia [Cambay/Khambhat] precisely to witness for himself the extreme forms of the "vain superstitions" of the Gentiles, noted with astonishment the tender care extended to some baby mice by an old man at one of the establishments there.[37] But by far the

---

[35] The term "animal-man" is Roberto Esposito's. Writing of Nazi eugenics in the 1930s, he says, "He who was the object of persecution and extreme violence wasn't simply an animal (which indeed was respected and protected as such by one of the most advanced pieces of legislation of the entire world), but was an animal-man: man in the animal and animal in the man." Esposito, *Bios: Biopolitics and Philosophy*, translated by Timothy Campbell (Minneapolis: University of Minnesota Press, 2008), 130. Fryer's zooanthropology precedes the eugenicist language by two and a half centuries, but the indebtedness of both to powerful anti-semitic tropes of long standing is clear.

[36] Fryer, *Travels in India*, 266.

[37] Della Valle, *Travels*, 68. He also saw in this animal hospital a Muslim thief with an amputated hand being cared for by "compassionate Gentiles." As Hannah Chapelle Wojciehowski notes of this detail, "What separates humans from animals, and which aspects of identity do they share? Moreover, how might the valuing of animal life entail a different set of moral obligations toward humans, as well as animals?" Wojciehowski, *Group Identity in the Renaissance World* (Cambridge: Cambridge University Press, 2011), 282.

most remarkable feature of these institutions, for most observers, was the existence in many of them, of rooms called the *jivat khana* (or, less commonly, a *jiva kothi*, literally an abode for the living) or insect rooms. Into these rooms, which were refuges for insects of various kinds, were housed the weevils and other insects found in grain. The inmates were supplied with a quantity of grain and, once they had filled up, the rooms were locked for several years, after which the life within had presumably reached its natural terminus.[38]

Writing of his visit in 1823 to the pinjrapole, Lieutenant Alexander Burnes of the Bombay military establishment wrote one of the most detailed descriptions of the institution. His report begins innocuously enough, with an account of domesticated vertebrates – mammals and poultry – walking about, and being fed and sheltered "without molestation." Established in a city suburb by Hindu Banias for animals of every description, it seems at first a hospitable institution, designed to increase "the general happiness, and [the philanthropists'] own reputation." It appears – as pinjrapoles described elsewhere over the course of the century would not be – spacious, open, and reasonably well provided with food and bedding for its animal objects of charity. But before long the narrative proceeds to "the most remarkable object in this singular establishment," a house with a depository underneath which is accessed through holes in the floor boards. This is the sanctuary for insect life, a sanctuary that poses a strong challenge to Burnes' sense of normative animality and induces a distinct perspectival shift as he views or senses "a depository where the deluded Banians throw in quantities of grain which gives life to and feeds a host of vermin, as dense as the sands on the sea-shore, and consisting of all the various genera usually found in the abodes of squalid misery."[39] Looking through the holes in this depository, Burnes examines a handful of erstwhile grain that has become "a moving mass," a circumstance that "hasten[s] [his] retreat" from the pinjrapole. The transit from the open, welcoming, transparent, familiar, self-evidently humanitarian and even hygienic space of the animal shelter without scarcely prepares us for the gothicism of the insect sanctuary, with its subterranean setting, its labyrinthine folds, its darkness and gloom, and its generally fantastic character.

---

[38] *Selections from the Records of the Bombay Government* (Bombay: Bombay Education Society's Press, 1856), 345. For a description of modern-day *jivat khanas*, see Deryck O. Lodrick, *Sacred Cows, Sacred Places: Origins and Survivals of Animal Homes in India* (Berkeley: University of California Press, 1981), 19–22.

[39] Alexander Burnes, "Notice of a Remarkable Hospital for Animals at Surat," *Journal of the Royal Asiatic Society of Great Britain and Ireland* 1.1 (1834), 96.

Not much is visible in this space, and what can be perceived by the author is some kind of undifferentiated but seething mass: "I examined a handful ... which had lost all the appearance of grain: it was a moving mass, and some of the pampered creatures which fed upon it were crawling about on the floor – a circumstance which hastened my retreat from the house in which this nest of vermin is deposited." It also has, we soon learn, "a most disagreeable closeness" from being the recipient of "the refuse of all the Banians' granaries in the town." Space itself is remade and rendered both disorienting and devouring in a manner that echoes the surrealist and social theorist Roger Caillois' description of "legendary psychasthenia." Callois was, as we know, fascinated by the capacity of some animals, especially insects, to camouflage their appearance and blend with their physical environment. Working against a utilitarian or functionalist reading of such mimicry, he noted that homomorphy or homochromy – this meshing of body and environment – did not purchase any indemnity against devourment but often the reverse and therefore must be seen not as a useful evolutionary adaptation but as a disturbance in spatial orientation, "a dangerous luxury." Linking anthropos and the entomonous, Caillois invites us to see the insect's wanton and often even suicidal mimicry as a condition described by Pierre Janet as "legendary psychasthenia," in which schizophrenics come to be captivated by space, unable to sustain a sense of distinctness from their surroundings. "To these dispossessed souls," says Caillois, "space seems to be a devouring force. Space pursues them, encircles them, digests them in a giant phagocytosis. It ends by replacing them. Then the body separates itself from thought, the individual breaks the boundary of his skin and occupies the other side of his skin. He feels himself becoming space, *dark space where things cannot be put*."[40] This devoured or digested subject exists in the condition of perilous, fearful "dark space" – the term is a psychiatric coinage (of Eugene Minkowski's), used to describe the schizophrenic's permeability to his surroundings – for the latter dark space has a depth unavailable to "light space" and the capacity to melt boundaries.[41] The very building assumes a biomorphic character, as its insectile inhabitants become ambulatory, numberless, and seething. The dark space militates against optical clarity and Burnes has to

[40] Roger Caillois, "Mimicry and Legendary Psychasthenia," translated by John Shepley, *October* 31 (1984): 30.
[41] " 'Dark space envelops me on all sides and penetrates me much deeper than light space; the distinction between inside and outside and consequently the sense organs as well, insofar as they are designed for external perception, here play only a totally modest role.' " Eugene Minkowski, quoted in ibid., 30.

examine a "handful" of what lies inside. He does not directly say that he feels the swarming verminous life upon his skin, but the references to the moving and crawling mass suggest the intimacy of touch, as some kind of haptic ooze comes to stand in place of less proximate ocularity. This is uncleanness or putrefaction in its most prodigal form, overspilling its boundaries and threatening the bourgeois protagonist in its midst with most vile contamination. Predictably it induces dread and disgust – and hasty flight. This is a significant amplification of the affect produced by Fryer's ethnography of the Bania *oikos*.

From the density of insectile life we move almost without interruption to the density of human populations. The pinjrapole, we are told, is in the very heart of one of the most densely populated cities in Asia, and is to be found in other large western cities of western India with populations of Banias or Jains. A passage of anthropological explanation follows:

> They have their origin, it is well known, in the great desire which possesses the minds of these people to preserve animal life; and though it is comprehensible to a native of Europe why aged cows and horses are preserved, from the circumstance of their having done their owners some service, still there can be no stronger instance of human caprice than to nurture a noxious and offensive mass of vermin, which every other race but themselves are anxious to extirpate and destroy. The great body of Hindus do not protect and preserve animal life as the Banians do; but it is a very common practice among them to feed with regularity pigeons, and even the fish in rivers. I have seen too, at Anjár, in Cutch, an establishment of rats, conjectured to exceed five thousand in number, which were kept in a temple, and daily fed with flour, which was procured by a tax on the inhabitants of the town!![42]

The avoidance of injury to animal life is by the nineteenth century understood to be a cultural touchstone for these populations, and no longer a characteristic that excites remark. Some versions of this practice can be fathomed by Europeans as a generous supplement to self-interest with respect to domesticated animals, especially in the context of domestic efforts to take up anti-cruelty as a cause, whether at the level of legislation or of social activism. The nurture of vermin, on the other hand, is the strongest possible instance of "human caprice," one that sets the protectors apart from the instincts and practices of humanity at large. Burnes goes on to note the singularity of Bania practice, distinct from what seems at first to be the relatively benign Hindu practice of feeding of pigeons and fish in rivers. Yet the next sentence – the capstone of Burnes' account – moves through a grammatical logic of continuity and amplification ("I have seen,

---

[42] Burnes, "Notice of a Remarkable Hospital," 97.

too") to another form of animal protection and worship which is indistinguishable from the protection of vermin with which the paragraph begins. As in the case of insectile life, the number of rats is sensational, beyond number, "conjectured to exceed five thousand in number." Like the insects, the rats are fed on grain of some form, procured through a city tax. It is "an establishment of rats," echoing the language of the "establishment" of the pinjrapole. Ending in a specific place – Anjār, in Cutch – it completes the circuit begun in Surat. What was true of Banias alone seems to be true of Gentiles or Hindus at large. What is also suggested is that the feeding of pigeons and fish leads without much interruption to the feeding and worship of rodents. The difference between Fryer's seventeenth-century account and Burnes' early nineteenth-century one is that the scale of the infestation has changed. What was domestic squalor in the first has transmogrified into the sheer uncountable, swarming excess of loathsome vitality that suffuses urban public space; it suggests something about the character of zooanthropic life that inhabits, nay overruns, a now colonial earth.

Widows and Other Sacrificial Offerings

These forms of nonviolence to nonhuman life were thought to constitute an unusual non-sacrificial economy, one that extended beyond a more familiar care of domesticated and wild animals to include forms of life well below the threshold of normative animality. This dilation of nonviolent obligation could be glossed as an extreme form of charity or hospitality to nonhuman animal life, turning the living human body into a source of nourishment for verminous forms of being. This fostering of noxious beings – on human flesh and blood, no less – was for most observers a clear limit case for thinking about the care of, or cruelty to, animals. It was seen almost invariably as the most preposterous and, simultaneously, the most gothic extension of subcontinental vegetarianism. Many, and especially the clergymen, reprobated this reversal of what was reckoned to be not just natural animal–human hierarchies but a human sovereignty established by a Christian deity. Henry Lord, chaplain to the East India Company in Surat in the 1620s, thought it absurd "in these better knowing times" to claim that nonhuman animals had immortal souls, and he sought to refute a Gentile gospel of vegetarianism with evidence from the Christian Bible.[43] The more tolerantly inclined Terry struggled strenuously to reconcile his admiration for the temperance of the Indians (both Gentile and Muslim) and his sense

---

[43] Henry Lord, *A Discoverie of the Sect of the Banians* (London: Constable, 1630), 55–56.

of the benevolence of some of the principles guiding the actions of the vegetarians ("having the impression of God upon them") with their theological error regarding the transcendent value of a human being:

> that scruple they make in forbearing the lives of the creatures made for men's use, shews how they have their dwelling in the dark, which makes them, by reason of their blindness, to deny unto themselves that liberty and sovereignty which Almighty God has given unto man over the beasts of the field, the fowls of the air, and the fishes of the sea, appointed for his food, given unto him for his service and his sustenance, to serve him, and to feed him, but not to make havoc and spoil of them.[44]

For Europeans who were familiar with campaigns at home to protect threatened food supplies from the depredations of rats, birds, insects, and other creatures, and who had experienced animal trials and extermination campaigns, any kind of interspecies community that included vermin was difficult to fathom. Vermin, moreover, had at best a doubtful and at worst a baneful theological status. As Lucinda Cole notes, they were regarded by many early modern writers as "zoological outcasts" not part of the first creation of all creatures and without a place on Noah's Ark. Moreover, witches and demons often assumed the form of creatures like toads, salamanders, and rats.[45] Hence many visitors to Indian shores felt that the nurture of noxious and verminous animals in particular showed local vegetarians, in Dubois' words, as "incapable of regulating their conduct with due regard to what is right and proper from a human point of view."[46] This was fully established even in scholarship by the end of the nineteenth century, so that the eminent Oxford Sanskritist Monier Monier-Williams could speak of the Jain respect for animal life as being carried "to a preposterous extreme."[47] Edward Washburn Hopkins, the American scholar of the religions of India, could pronounce more dismissively still: "A religion in which the chief points insisted upon are that one should deny God, worship man, and nourish vermin, has … no right to exist."[48]

Of a piece, for many, with the feeding of vermin on human blood was the fact that the partially burnt or even unburnt bodies of the dead were frequently left to be consumed by carrion animals and birds of prey like crocodiles, vultures, dogs, and jackals. (The dog at the burning ghat,

---

[44] Terry, *Voyage to East India*, 310.
[45] Lucinda Cole, *Imperfect Creatures: Vermin, Literature, and the Sciences of Life, 1600–1740* (Ann Arbor: University of Michigan Press, 2016), 1–23.
[46] Dubois, *Hindu Manners*, 643.
[47] Monier Williams, *Modern India and the Indians* (London: Trubner, 1878), 94.
[48] Edward Washburn Hopkins, *The Religions of India* (Boston: Ginn, 1895), 296–97.

feasting upon human remains, was a common trope of travel writing well into the twentieth century; it features in Katherine Mayo's 1927 volume, *Mother India*.) Sometimes, Ovington noted, there was a haste to proceed with cremation before actual expiration; and he tells the story of a Bania saved from the flames by a passing English surgeon.[49] The small non-Gentile and non-Muslim sect of "Persies" (Parsees) of western India engaged in an even more unusual form of funerary practice; they practiced excarnation of their dead by leaving them to be consumed by birds of prey. The urbane cultural relativist Ovington notes that inhumation in animal bodies is not uncommon in the east, but even he cannot contain his revulsion at the grossness of the burial place, "more frightful than a field of slaughtered men."[50]

Of course classical, medieval, and early modern Christian writers were entirely familiar with the notion of human flesh as food for animals large and small. From their readings of Herodotus and Mandeville, early modern writers had some prior familiarity with funerary practices called "sky burial," practiced by Magians/Zoroastrians (or, as they were known in the subcontinent, Persies), Tibetans, and Scythians. Medieval funerary art and poetry, fascinated with the phenomenon of human putrefaction, loved to horrify its living human viewers with reminders that they were food for worms, as Karl Steel notes.[51] But the eating of unburied human corpses by carrion animals and birds of prey was a fate contemplated for the most part with horror, whether in the *Iliad* or in the *Song of Roland* or in Montaigne's essay on cannibals; it was seen either as part of the terrible toll of war or, as in the instance of Homer, as a device for visiting dishonor on fallen foes. Being openly devoured by carrion animals or birds of prey (or devils in the afterlife) was the worst-case post-death scenario, an unbearable offense against human dignity. Hence the force of a centuries-long Christian literary and visual tradition of seeing hell as a giant mouth or kitchen and chewing, digestion, and regurgitation as its punishments for the damned, as Marina Warner notes.[52]

[49] Ovington, *Voyage to Suratt*, 341.
[50] Ibid., 376–81. On sky burial, also see Henry Lord, *The Religion of the Persees* (London: Constable, 1630), 40–52.
[51] Karl Steel, "Abyss: Everything is Food," *Postmedieval* 4.1, 93–104. Also see his blog posts, especially "Man is the Pasture of Being, Part 2: Sky Burial, Mostly Persian," July 26, 2015, and "Man is the Pasture of Being 3: Mandeville in Tibet, at Long Last," August 8, 2015, for a comprehensive account of medieval European knowledge about sky burial, https://medievalkarl.com/tag/ecology.
[52] Marina Warner, "Fee Fi Fo Fum: The Child in the Jaws of the Story," *Cannibalism and the Colonial World*, edited by Francis Barker, Peter Hulme, and Margaret Iversen (Cambridge: Cambridge University Press, 1998), 158–82.

All these instances of human putrefaction or offenses against bodily integrity, though, were visited upon the bodies of the dead. But the Gentile combination of abstinence from carnivory, exposure of the *living* human body to predation by verminous creatures, and indifference to the consumption of human corpses by larger creatures seemed to many early modern European observers a violation of what Derrida has designated the carnivorous foundation of human subjectivity, given its confusion of the distinctions between the categories of eater (human) and eaten (nonhuman).[53] Eating was meant to proceed in a single, non-reversible direction, with the human at the head of the food chain; the maintenance of an alimentary apartheid between predator and prey, edibility and non-edibility was crucial to human exceptionalism, or sovereignty over the nonhuman world. What the Gentile example of vegetarianism/non-violence seemed to offer instead was a model of trans-species sympathy in which each living being was capable of being the subject of harm and suffering and was bound to the others in a relation of radical equivalence, so that no being's body – or at least no human's body – could be understood ethically as her own peculiar or inviolable property. This not infrequently entailed abjuring any right to abstain from injuring or sacrificing this human body in favor of the nonhuman creature – including, quite often, the most insignificant, noisome, and worthless of all nonhuman creatures, the very opposite of the companion species or the charismatic megafauna for whom one could imagine sacrificing a human life. Hence writers return repeatedly to the macabre (and occasionally comic) fascination of these forms of self-sacrifice and their perversity.

Excesses of hospitality toward and clemency for animal life, moreover, were seen by some to generate unresolved antinomies and in fact their own forms of cruelty. Those who slew animals in the territories of vegetarian extremists were liable to legal as well as extra-judicial punishment by those enraged at such acts, and sensational tales were told of the vengeance wreaked upon them in the name of justice. While many writers avow that Gentile vegetarians would rather die than deprive an animal of life, Fryer insists on a threatening dimension to such abstinence, maintaining that the local vegetarians would "rather kill a man than suffer a beast to be led to the Stall."[54] As if in confirmation of this, Tavernier narrates with some glee what is in effect a crucifixion story of a rich Persian merchant

---

[53] Jacques Derrida, "'Eating Well,' or the Calculation of the Subject: An Interview with Jacques Derrida," in *Who Comes After the Subject?*, edited by Eduardo Cadava, Peter Connor, and Jean-Luc Nancy (New York: Routledge, 1991).
[54] Fryer, *Travels in India*, 383.

who purportedly was stripped of his wealth, tied to a tree, and whipped to death over three days by Banias enraged at his shooting of a peacock.[55]

So, almost as often as Banias or Gentiles were esteemed as exemplars of kindness to all living forms, they were reprobated for unusual and perverse forms of cruelty. Both Dubois and Niccolao Manucci manifested an explicitly Christian horror at abortions in the face of the relative moral indifference evinced by Gentile and Muslim. But above all European sojourners sought to situate *sati* or widow sacrifice (or *suttee*, as British texts of the period rendered the term) within a Gentile economy of kindness, cruelty, and the preservation of life. As many scholars have noted, the description (and occasional illustration) of a sati, often complete with the European male's conversation with the would-be victim, was a staple of the travel narrative of the seventeenth and eighteenth centuries. Few sights were as repulsive – or as mesmerizing – for the combination they offered of quasi-erotic female vulnerability and monstrous physical suffering. The event was viewed in a number of different and ambiguous – indeed, often incommensurable – ways, often by the same person: it was a display of female self-sacrificing valor; it was a superb instantiation of wifely devotion; it was an instance of fanatical and self-deluded self-destruction; it was the result of the scheming of Brahmins, who stood to profit from it; and it was an example of the ways in which cruel and irrational belief could override any natural instincts of compassion and justice.[56]

Sati narratives featured as routinely in travel writing as the descriptions of theriophily and vegetarian diet; indeed, for many writers, the practices were difficult to disaggregate. For the sixteenth-century merchant-traveler Ralph Fitch, bovine worship, protection of verminous life, the establishment of animal hospitals, and the burning of widows belonged to a single, coherent ethnographic continuum:

> They haue a very strange order among them, they worshippe a cowe, and esteeme much of the cowes doung to paint the walles of their houses. They will kill nothing not so much as a louse: for they holde it a sinne to kille anything. They eate no flesh, but live by rootes, and ryce, and milke. And when the husbande dieth his wife is burned with him, if shee be aliue: if she will not, her head is shauen, and then is neuer any account made of her after. They say if they should be buried, it were a great sinne, for of their bodies there would come many wormes and other vermine, and when their

[55] Tavernier, *Travels in India*, vol. 2, 70–71.
[56] Notably, the travel narratives averred that Muslim rulers in the subcontinent detested sati unreservedly and that, even though it was politically hazardous to forbid it outright, they sought to discourage the practice.

bodies were consumed, those wormes would lacke sustenance, which were a sinne, therefore they will be burned. In Cambaia they will kill nothing, nor haue anything killed: in the towne they haue hospitals to keepe lame dogs and cats, and for birds. They will giue meat to the Ants.[57]

India had long been seen in any case as a territory where the fanaticism of religion held a despotic sway, and it was therefore a showcase of sorts for the expression of excesses in their most heightened form. That this holy violence was presided over and abetted by those exemplars of holy abstinence, the Brahmins, spoke to the moral contradictions with a Brahminical or Gentile moral totalitarianism, directed against those subjects (vulnerable, widowed women in this case) believed to lie outside an ethics of hospitality or neighborliness or care routinely and even aggressively extended to the nonhuman. The burning of the widow was thus a noncriminal putting to death in a way that the animal's sacrifice was not. Dubois noted bitterly that vegetarian Brahmins who were horrified at the destruction of the minutest insect life, not to mention cows, could nonetheless tolerate the barbaric practice of sati; others spoke of the ways in which widows were compelled to their place of sacrifice by drugs, physical violence, and social pressure.[58] Such a conjunction in so many seventeenth-century narratives of the malevolence of sati with an inordinate vegetarian care for the nonhuman seemed to suggest, albeit indirectly, that a logic of human sacrifice linked these two seemingly discrepant acts together.[59] Sacrificing one kind of sacrifice – that of the nonhuman animal – does not place one outside a sacrificial economy or allow one to surmount it, these writers suggest. Someone – and something – is invariably sacrificed, actually or symbolically, whether in a vegetarian or a carnivorous economy. In sacrificing animal sacrifice, Gentile vegetarians are not freed of the guilt of sacrifice. Reversing the usual logic of sacrifice, in which an animal victim substitutes for the human sacrificer, Gentile vegetarians may think they are sacrificing themselves; but this cannot be done without also outlawing humans – widows in this case – from moral and physical protection. The staging of the scene of verminous protection cheek by jowl with the spectacle of the burning widow ensures that Gentile vegetarianism remains firmly ensconced within the violent logic of sacrifice – and, indeed, might have perfected its most baroque and pitiless forms.

---

57 Ryley, *Ralph Fitch*, 60–61.
58 Dubois, *Hindu Manners*, 366.
59 For a twentieth-century reading of Jain nonviolence that reproduces this logic, see Philip Roth, *American Pastoral* (Boston: Houghton Mifflin, 1997), in which Merry Levov's turn to Jainism is both suicidal and an extension of her murderous radical politics.

BIBLIOGRAPHY

Archer, John Michael. *Old Worlds: Egypt, Southwest Asia, India, and Russia in Early Modern English Writing.* Stanford: Stanford University Press, 2001.

Barbosa, Duarte. *The Book of Duarte Barbosa.* Vol. 1. Translated by Mansel Longworth Dames. 1516. Reprint, London: Hakluyt Society, 1918.

Bernier, Francois. *Travels in the Mogul Empire, AD 1656–1668.* Translated by Archibald Constable. London: Oxford University Press, 1916.

Bowrey, Thomas. *A Geographical Account of Countries Round the Bay of Bengal, 1669 to 1679.* Edited by Richard Carnac Temple. Cambridge: Hakluyt Society, 1905.

Burnes, Alexander. "Notice of a Remarkable Hospital for Animals at Surat." *Journal of the Royal Asiatic Society of Great Britain and Ireland* 1.1 (1834): 96–97.

Caillois, Roger. "Mimicry and Legendary Psychasthenia." Translated by John Shepley. *October* 31 (1984): 16–32.

Cole, Lucinda. *Imperfect Creatures: Vermin, Literature, and the Sciences of Life, 1600–1740.* Ann Arbor: University of Michigan Press, 2016.

Collingham, E. M. *Imperial Bodies: The Physical Experience of the Raj, c. 1800–1947.* Cambridge: Polity Press, 2001.

Dasgupta, Ashin. *Indian Merchants and the Decline of Surat, 1700–1750.* Wiesbaden: Franz Steiner Verlag, 1979.

Della Valle, Pietro. *The Travels of Pietro della Valle in India.* 2 vols. Translated by George Havers and edited by Edward Grey. London: Hakluyt Society, 1892.

Derrida, Jacques. " 'Eating Well,' or the Calculation of the Subject: An Interview with Jacques Derrida." In *Who Comes After the Subject?*, edited by Eduardo Cadava, Peter Connor, and Jean-Luc Nancy, 96–119. New York: Routledge, 1991.

Dubois, Abbe J. A. *Hindu Manners, Customs and Ceremonies.* Translated by Henry K. Beauchamp. 3rd ed. Oxford: Clarendon Press, 1906.

Esposito, Roberto. *Bios: Biopolitics and Philosophy.* Translated by Timothy Campbell. Minneapolis: University of Minnesota Press, 2008.

Fryer, John. *Travels in India in the Seventeenth Century by Sir Thomas Roe and Dr. John Fryer.* 1698. Reprint, London: John Trubner, 1873.

Gokhale, Balkrishna Govind. *Surat in the Seventeenth Century.* London: Curzon Press, 1979.

Hahn, Thomas. "The Indian Tradition in Western Intellectual History." *Viator* 9 (1978): 213–34.

Harris, Jonathan Gil. *The First Firangis.* New Delhi: Aleph, 2015.

    "Introduction: Forms of Indography." In *Indography: Writing the "Indian" in Early Modern England*, edited by J. Gil Harris, 1–20. New York: Palgrave Macmillan, 2012.

Harrison, Mark. *Climates and Constitutions: Health, Race, Environment and British Imperialism in India 1600–1850.* New York: Oxford University Press, 1999.

Hopkins, Edward Washburn. *The Religions of India.* Boston: Ginn, 1895.

Lodrick, Deryck O. *Sacred Cows, Sacred Places: Origins and Survivals of Animal Homes in India.* Berkeley: University of California Press, 1981.

Lord, Henry. *A Discoverie of the Sect of the Banians*. London: Constable, 1630.
The Religion of the Persees. London: Constable, 1630.

del Mandelslo, John Albert. *Mandelslo's Travels into the Indies, the First Book*. Translated by John Davies. 1642. Reprint, London: John Starkey and Thomas Basset, 1669.

Manucci, Niccolao. *Storia do Mogor, or Mogul India 1653–1708*. Translated and edited by William Irvine. London: John Murray, 1907.

Morton, Timothy. *Shelley and the Revolution in Taste: The Body and the Natural World*. Cambridge: Cambridge University Press, 1994.

Oswald, John. *The Cry of Nature*. London: J. Johnson, 1791.

Ovington, John. *A Voyage to Suratt, in the Year 1689*. London: Jacob Tonson, 1696.

Raman, Shankar. *Framing "India": The Colonial Imaginary in Early Modern Culture*. Stanford: Stanford University Press, 2001.

Ristuccia, Nathan J. "Eastern Religions and the West: The Making of an Image." *History of Religions* 53.2 (November 2013): 170–204.

Roe, Sir Thomas. *The Embassy of Sir Thomas Roe to the Court of the Great Mogul, 1615–1619, as Narrated in his Journal and Correspondence*. Edited by William Foster. Vol. 1. London: Hakluyt Society, 1899.

Roth, Philip. *American Pastoral*. Boston: Houghton Mifflin, 1997.

Ryley, Horton. *Ralph Fitch, England's Pioneer to India and Burma*. London: T. Fisher Unwin, 1899.

Selections from the Records of the Bombay Government. Bombay: Bombay Education Society's Press, 1856.

Singh, Jyotsna G. "Naming and Un-naming 'All the Indies': How India Became Hindustan." In *Indography: Writing the "Indian" in Early Modern England*, edited by J. Gil Harris, 249–55. New York: Palgrave Macmillan, 2012.

Steel, Karl. "Abyss: Everything is Food." *Postmedieval* 4.1 (2013): 93–104.

Stuart, Tristram. *The Bloodless Revolution: A Cultural History of Vegetarianism from 1600 to Modern Times*. New York: Norton, 2007.

Subramaniam, Lakshmi. "Banias and the British." *Modern Asian Studies* 21.3 (1987): 473–510.

Tavernier, Jean Baptiste. *Travels in India*. Vols. 1–2. Translated by Valentine Ball. 1676. Reprint, London: Macmillan, 1889.

Teltscher, Kate. " 'Maidenly and Well Nigh Effeminate': Constructions of Hindu Masculinity and Religion in Seventeenth-Century English Texts" *Postcolonial Studies* 3.2 (2000): 159–70.

Terry, Edward. *A Voyage to East India*. 1655. Reprint, London: J. Wilkie, 1777.

Twain, Mark. *Following the Equator, and Anti-Imperialist Essays*. Edited by Shelley Fisher Fishkin. New York: Oxford University Press, 1996.

Warner, Marina. "Fee Fi Fo Fum: The Child in the Jaws of the Story." In *Cannibalism and the Colonial World*, edited by Francis Barker, Peter Hulme, and Margaret Iversen, 158–82. Cambridge: Cambridge University Press, 1998.

Watson, Robert N. "Protestant Animals: Puritan Sects and English Animal-Protection Sentiment, 1550–1650." *ELH* 81.4 (Winter 2014): 1111–48.

Williams, Monier. *Modern India and the Indians*. London: Trubner, 1878.

Wojciehowski, Hannah Chapelle. *Group Identity in the Renaissance World.* Cambridge: Cambridge University Press, 2011.

Yule, Henry, and A. C. Burnell. *Hobson-Jobson: A Glossary of Colloquial Anglo-Indian Words and Phrases, and of Kindred Terms, Etymological, Historical, Geographical, and Discursive.* Edited by William Crooke. London: John Murray, 1903.

CHAPTER 4

Good Taste, Good Food, and the Gastronome

Denise Gigante

That which is not good, is not delicious
To a well govern'd and wise appetite.

Milton, *A Masque Presented at Ludlow Castle*[1]

In the years around the turn of the nineteenth century in Paris, good food and good taste came together in the figure of the gastronome. The term, etymologically derived from γαστερ (*gaster*: stomach) and νομος (*nomos*: mind), was devised at this time to indicate a sagacious eater. Prior to the advent of gastronomy, such a figure would have been a paradox. The Enlightenment discourse of aesthetic taste was, after all, predicated on the distancing of mental from bodily taste, privileging the former over the latter. Taste philosophers struggled with the metaphor (*goût*, *gusto*, taste) given by the modern languages to aesthetic experience. What could the intellectual activity of objective, disinterested judgment have to do with the salivary organs of the mouth – seat of instinctive, unthinking sensation? The purpose of aesthetic contemplation had always been to transcend bodily reality, and this gustatory metaphor of taste did not exist in classical aesthetics. Taste, symbolically connected as it was to the guts, ranked low on the philosophical hierarchy of the senses.[2] But in the age of gastronomy, when food was prepared and judged as an aesthetic object, the gastronome emerged as a guide and a tastemaker, holding food to the same exacting standards of taste as the fine arts. The restaurant, by putting culinary artistry on display, demanded connoisseurship, encouraging consumers to develop critical sensibilities worthy of the chef, an artist of nouvelle cuisine.

---

[1] This and all subsequent quotations from Milton's poetry refer to the edition of his *Complete Poems and Major Prose*, edited by Merritt Y. Hughes (New York: Odyssey, 1957), hereafter cited parenthetically in the text by line number, according to the following scheme: *M* for *A Masque*, *PL* for *Paradise Lost*, *PR* for *Paradise Regained*, and *S* for *Samson Agonistes*. Here, (*M* 704–5).

[2] Carolyn Korsmeyer, *Making Sense of Taste: Food and Philosophy* (Ithaca, NY: Cornell University Press, 1999).

The Parisian restaurants of post-revolutionary France, as venues of *discretionary* dining, differed from earlier eating establishments in catering to the cultivated tastes of consumers.[3] They differed in this respect from the early French *tables d'hôte,* or the equivalent English ordinaries across the channel, which served a communal meal. There, consumers partook of the same fare, at the same table, at the same time, for the same price. There was little room for distinction among diners, and hence choice, that prerogative of the connoisseur, did not figure into the dining experience. By contrast, diners in the Parisian restaurants confronted a dizzying array of options. As dishes shrunk into à la carte portions, the fixed bill of fare expanded into an extravagant, folio-sized menu. The restaurants also privatized the public dining experience, isolating diners at separate tables where, cordoned off from the crowd, one could be as discriminating as one chose. But with this newfound freedom of choice came the responsibility to live up to the gastronomical standards of the connoisseur and eat sagaciously, rather than gluttonously. Appetite needed to be controlled, not because eating is bad or morally opposed to virtuous spirituality, but because intemperance leads to surfeit, the *loss* of appetite. The goal of the gastronome was to keep on eating, to prolong the taste experience.

The pages that follow take a cue from an early nineteenth-century gastronome and cook, the aptly named William Kitchiner. In his best-selling gastronomical cookbook of 1817, *The Cook's Oracle,* Kitchiner adopts the poet John Milton's view of the "good" life as "a perpetual feast of nectar'd sweets, / Where no crude surfeit reigns."[4] Miltonic taste represents a divinely sanctioned, full-bodied form of pleasure that even angels, those spiritually transcendent beings, experience. I have elsewhere argued that Milton's epic exploration of the metaphor of taste in *Paradise Lost* and *Paradise Regained* was foundational for British empirical aesthetic taste theory.[5] Here I want to argue that Milton was also a gastronome *avant la lettre* who demonstrated the bon vivant's attitude toward good living in the more comprehensive, philosophical sense of goodness, which does not divide aesthetics from ethics.

By pushing back the Miltonic frame of reference to the beginning of the poet's career, specifically to the masque known as *Comus* presented at Ludlow Castle in 1634, we find, in the title character, Milton's portrayal of

[3] Rebecca L. Spang, *The Invention of the Restaurant: Paris and Modern Gastronomic Culture* (Cambridge: Harvard University Press, 2000).

[4] Quoted from Milton's *Masque Presented at Ludlow Castle* in William Kitchiner, *The Cook's Oracle* (London: Whittaker, Treacher, and Co., 1831), 5.

[5] Denise Gigante, *Taste: A Literary History* (New Haven: Yale University Press, 2005).

the Ancient Greek god of cookery (κωμος: Komos). The masque is a celebration of temperance, but from a gastronomical perspective the epigraph
to this chapter can be turned around. For if it is true that what is not good,
is not delicious, as Comus' dinner guest claims, it is equally true that what
is not delicious, is not good. Deliciousness here is a form of beauty, and
Milton, a pivot between ancient and modern aesthetics, had not let go of
the ancient trinity of the true, the beautiful, and the good. More than a
good liver or bon vivant, Milton's Comus, the brainchild of a gastronome
and a sadly misunderstood figure, is in point of fact the world's first restaurateur. We might call him the "foodie" precursor of Milton's Satan (who
coming before human culture knew little about cooking), for he is master
of that cookery-chicanery now known as culinary artistry.

Culinary Ancestry

When we first encounter Comus in Milton's *Masque*, he is involved in
apparently bacchanalian festivities with a group of animal-headed, yet
otherwise human, companions. A young Lady, lost in the woods nearby,
attracts Comus' attention when she cries out for her two brothers, who
have gone in quest of food and left her alone. Comus approaches her in the
guise of a shepherd and claims to have seen her brothers gathering fruit,
but at some distance. He invites her to his cottage for some refreshment.
When she arrives, however, rather than the humble rustic abode she had
been led to expect, she finds "a stately Palace, set out with all manners
of deliciousness" and "tables spread with all dainties."[6] Mistrusting such
culinary lavishness, she refuses everything Comus offers her, including
what appears to be his signature concoction, an "orient liquor in a crystal
glass" (*M* 65). The Lady threatens to leave the table, but Comus charms
her so that she cannot move. Her brothers suddenly arrive on the scene,
grab Comus' glass, and smash it to the ground. He departs and Sabrina,
a naiad, arrives to release the Lady from her spell. The *Masque* ends with
a dance performed by the children as a triumph over "sensual Folly, and
Intemperance" (*M* 974). The Spirit of the masque, in epilogue, exults in
his liberation from watching over the children in much the same manner
(and in the exact same meter) as Shakespeare's spirit Ariel at the end of *The
Tempest*.
　　There is, in fact, much in Milton's debut drama that echoes Shakespeare's
farewell to the stage – as if Milton were picking up where Shakespeare

---

[6] The stage direction follows line 657 in Milton's *A Masque Presented at Ludlow Castle*.

left off, as a dramatist self-conscious of his own artistry. The feast that Prospero conjures for the shipwrecked mariners on his island resonates in the one that Comus causes to appear before the young Lady as a spectacle that appeals to all the senses. Both are Magian-artists, stand-ins for the playwrights, both of whom are concerned with the ethical and aesthetic implications of conjuring airy nothings for the delectation of an audience. Prospero compares his theatrical illusions to "subtleties," referring to those spectacular sugary sculptures that adorned the Renaissance banquet table and that dissolved or melted in the mouth when touched or tasted.[7] He calls Ariel "my dainty," and he is addressed in turn as "an enchanted trifle," another light and airy dessert.[8] His island is full of "sweet airs that give delight and hurt not," and the sweetness here as elsewhere is synesthetic, musical as well as tasty.[9] Ariel claims to "drink the air,"[10] and the Spirit of Milton's *Masque* echoes him: "I suck the liquid air" (*M* 980). Here Milton also echoes Ariel's song in praise of honeyed, aesthetic delight: "Where the bee sucks, there suck I."[11] The insubstantial delicacies sprinkled throughout Shakespeare's play are a fit model for Comus' since such foodstuffs have everything to do with the taste, and little to do with appetite.

If Milton's *Masque* constitutes a polemic in favor of temperance, it would be a mistake to characterize that temperance as monkish austerity, a bitter and "crabbed" asceticism, or even abstinence (*M* 477). Milton was temperate in his habits, but he was by no means opposed to pleasure. His biographers note his exacting standards of taste at table, and the fact that what he ate had to be "of the best" with ingredients "most in season."[12] Comus, although typically seen as a personification of intemperance, shows no evidence of this himself. It is true that he is descended from an intemperate father, Bacchus (βάκχος), otherwise known as Dionysus (Διόνυσος), who presides over grape harvests, wine pressing, merrymaking, and naturally, theater. But Milton has Comus run away from home. He renounces his Dionysian paternity by wandering out of Arcadia, and northwest across continental Europe. The Celtic and Iberian fields do not suit him, so he crosses the English Channel and settles in the woods surrounding Ludlow Castle. The Lady imagines that she has seen him reveling with hinds and

---

7 William Shakespeare, *The Tempest*, edited by Robert Langbaum, revised ed. (New York: Signet, 1998), 5.1.124.
8 Ibid., 5.1.95, 112.
9 Ibid., 3.2.141.
10 Ibid., 5.1.101.
11 Ibid., 5.1.88.
12 Barbara Lewalski, *The Life of John Milton: A Critical Biography* (Malden, MA: Wiley-Blackwell, 2000), 12.

shepherds to thank "the bounteous Pan" for "their teeming Flocks and grange full" (*M* 175–76). But such a pastoral idyll seems incompatible with the "ominous Wood" that the Spirit describes as being "in the thick shelter of black shades imbowr'd" (*M* 61–62). The Lady herself complains of "the blind mazes of this tangl'd Wood" (*M* 180).

The reason the Lady is alone in the dark labyrinth of the wood in the first place is that the path she has traveled with her brothers has been anything but "bounteous." It is barren of food, and the Lady explains to Comus that her brothers have gone to look for "Berries, or such cooling fruit / As the kind hospitable Woods provide" (*M* 185–86). She seems mentally trapped in a Golden Age of innocence, for the woods are about as hospitable as a "Thicket" can be (*M* 192). Her brothers have had to wander out of eyesight and out of earshot in their possibly fruitless quest. "I saw them under a green mantling vine / That crawls along the side of yon small hill," Comus says, but he is too artful to be trusted when he adds what they were doing: "Plucking ripe clusters from the tender shoots" (*M* 294–96). The woods are dark, not only because it is evening, and it does not take a vintner to know that grapes and berries in order to ripen need sun. The spot where the Lady encounters Comus is shadowed by a canopy of pines, an arboreal genre one does not associate with Bacchus. Milton's Comus, albeit the son of Bacchus, has left his ancestral fields, ripe with abundantly clustering grapes, far behind.

Milton describes Bacchus as he who "first from out the purple Grape, / Crusht the sweet poison of misused Wine" (*M* 46–47). Wine becomes "poison" when it is "misused." Bacchus presses the grapes, but the responsibility for their goodness lies less with the provider than the consumer: it has deleterious effects when imbibed intemperately. The Spirit of the masque confirms that "most do taste" Comus' liquor "through fond intemperate thirst" (*M* 67). As a result, their animality becomes apparent, as they transform into so many human monsters. Their countenances assume "some brutish form of Woolf, or Bear, / Or Ounce, or Tiger, Hog, or bearded Goat," and their higher faculties of intellection, sensibility, and judgment become obscured (*M* 70–71). We might, with the young Lady, blame their fates on Comus, assuming that "none / but such as a good man can give good things" (*M* 702–3). But the brute features seem merely to reflect the brute natures of those who greedily quaff Comus' liquor. Besides, we must ask, when did such pat morality as this ever apply to artists, or artistry? Shakespeare knew better in his dark portrait of Prospero, and Milton's Satan, the most artful character of *Paradise Lost*, steals that show, leading many to believe that Milton was of the devil's party.

Comus is, in any event, less his father's child than his mother's. "Much like his Father," the Spirit describes him, "but his Mother more" (*M* 57). This is striking because, for one thing, the Comus of classical mythology did not have a mother. Milton makes Circe, a hostess with a bad reputation if ever there was one, his parent. We associate her with the "charmed Cup" that turns Odysseus' men into pigs in Homer's *Odyssey* (*M* 50). "Whoever tasted" from the cup, the Miltonic Spirit relates, "lost his upright shape, / And downward fell into groveling Swine" (*M* 51–52). But like the thirsty travelers in Comus' wood, Odysseus' men are famished and give into their cravings without restraint. They gobble up the oxen of the sun god Helios when they know they shouldn't, and they become gluttons at Circe's board. They, like Comus' guests, forget their higher human natures and "roll with pleasure in a sensual sty" (*M* 76). Comus recalls his mother "Amidst the flowry-kirtl'd *Naiades* / Culling their Potent herbs, and baleful drugs," but we do not know whether Circe's herbs – like Bacchus' wine – are baleful because they are misused (*M* 252–53). Comus' concoction represents an advance in culinary chemistry, for we are told that he "Excells his Mother at her mighty Art" (*M* 63).

Manipulating "nature" in any way through culinary chemistry, whether it be boiling vegetables, roasting flesh, distilling fruit, grain, tea leaves, coffee beans, herbs, or what have you, involves the contamination we call culture. This artful transfiguration of products of nature is also the condition of possibility for nouvelle cuisine, which turns food into a fine art (*haute cuisine*). Before the revolution in cookery that resulted in French nouvelle cuisine, the epitome of culture was a courtly table heaped high with the results of the hunt. Abundant, communal dishes were spread across the table *à la française* in several removes, and meat was ostentatious in its animality. Game, livestock, and fish were, to the degree possible, dressed and served up whole. The aristocratic art of carving figured into the dining experience, as guests performed the honors at table. Norbert Elias and Stephen Mennell have narrated the story of how the "civilizing process" intended to produce tasteful subjects gradually made animals disappear from the table.[13] Roasts were relegated to a side table for carving, and ultimately disappeared behind the closed doors of the kitchen, to lose the shape of the animals they once were before ever appearing at the table. As Rebecca Spang explains, "nature needed to be

---

[13] Norbert Elias, *The Civilizing Process: The History of Manners*, translated by Edmund Jephcott (New York: Urizen Books, 1978); Stephen Mennell, *All Manners of Food: Eating and Taste in England and France from the Middle Ages to the Present*, 2nd ed. (Urbana: University of Illinois Press, 1996).

cleansed in order to be fit for human consumption; cookery, by civilizing the raw materials of human diet, could propel humanity from its brutish origin."[14] A correspondent change in service patterns, whereby single portions prearranged on a plate followed each other sequentially (*à la russe*) to the table for individual delectation and judgment, carries over into restaurant practice today.

A diet weighed down by large cuts of meat had bred a host of distempers, from indigestion to gout (a bad form of *goût*), and the central tenet of the nouvelle cuisine that emerged in early eighteenth-century France held that good food ought to be good *for* you. The nouvelle cuisine was lighter, like the preparations of Milton's Comus and his mother Circe, consisting only of the chemically distilled essences of food. Delicacy, the metric of the connoisseur, became the standard by which such refined food would be judged. The bible of French nouvelle cuisine, titled *Gifts of Comus* (*Les dons de Comus*) and prepared by the Parisian chef François Marin, remarks: "Cookery, like all the other arts invented for need or pleasure, is perfected with the genius of a people, and becomes more delicate to the same degree that they become more polished."[15] Delicacy was the chief gift of the modern Comus to a culture of taste. In this respect, Milton's Comus is more in step with the culinary chemistry that made possible nouvelle cuisine, and in turn the modern institution of the restaurant, than the early-modern version of the feast.

The Gifts of Comus

In cataloguing the various soups, consommés, ragoûts, fricassees, and other fluid mixtures of the nouvelle cuisine in *The Gifts of Comus*, Marin puts the emphasis on the most delicate, the bouillon, which he calls *l'âme de la cuisine*, the soul, spirit, or vital principle of cookery.[16] "The science of cooking consists today in composing, in making digestible and quintessencing food [*quintessencier des viands*]," he instructs, "of extracting their nourishing and light juices, in mixing and confounding them together, in such a way that none dominate and that all are able to be perceived."[17] Just as a man of fine taste in writing can pick out literary beauties from a work, only a man with a refined palate can discern nicely between the finely blended flavors of

[14] Spang, *Invention of the Restaurant*, 41.
[15] [François Marin,] *Les Dons de Comus, ou l'Art de la Cuisine, Réduit en practique*, 2nd ed. (Paris: Pissot, 1758), xxviii; my translations.
[16] Ibid., 1.
[17] Ibid., xxii.

nouvelle cuisine. In a famous *Spectator* paper from 1712 (no. 409) on taste, Joseph Addison used this same analogy to compare the literary critic to a tea connoisseur:

> after having tasted ten different kinds of tea … [the connoisseur] would distinguish, without seeing the colour of it, the particular sort which was offered him; and not only so, but any two sorts of them that were mixt together in an equal proportion; nay, he has carried the experiment so far, as upon tasting the composition of three different sorts, to name the parcels from whence the three several ingredients were taken.[18]

The food of nouvelle cuisine was spiritualized, and delicacy guided the art of judgment in corporeal as in mental, or aesthetic, taste.

The quintessence dubbed the "soul of cuisine" in *The Gifts of Comus* would come to be known – for its goodness – as a *restaurant* (restorative). Milton's Comus offers his distillation to the Lady in Milton's masque as just such a restorative, suggesting that she is laboring under a digestive distemper. Her frowns are symptoms of poorly concocted food. Bad digestion has caused an imbalance in her bodily fluids (humors), and her blood is clotted down with black bile, her spleen swollen with that same brownish sediment: "the lees / And settlings of a melancholy blood" (*M* 809–10). What she needs is something light and medicinal. Comus offers his glass, promising that its contents "will cure all straight, one sip of this / Will bathe the drooping spirits" (*M* 811–12). But he makes the mistake of slipping from the rhetoric of dietary health into the more alarming arena of gastronomical pleasure when he adds, in the line immediately following, "in delight / Beyond the bliss of dreams" (*M* 813). The Lady, who associates pleasure with sin, rejects his brew, convinced as she is that since Comus is not "good," he cannot produce good food, despite whether it tastes good or is good for her.

The dialectic between Comus and the Lady leading up to this point constitutes a debate over the ontology of food – its ethical, epistemological, and aesthetic dimensions – in which Miltonic ideas are bandied about and something like a Miltonic perspective can only be distilled by the reader. Kitchiner quotes the Lady's own words ("That which is not good, is not delicious / To a well-govern'd and wise appetite") against her, so to speak, as evidence that Milton did not make one of those "gloomy philosophers (uninitiated in Culinary Science)," who "have tried to make the world believe – who seem to have delighted

---

[18] Joseph Addison, Richard Steele et al. *The Spectator*, 8 vols. (London: J. and R. Tonson, 1749), vol. 6, 53.

in persuading you, that every thing that is Nice must be noxious; –
and that everything that is Nasty is wholesome."[19] How appetite is to
be governed, and to what end, is the central question of *Comus*. Seen
from a gastronomical perspective, the question turns out to be more
interesting than an allegorical interpretation of good and evil might have
it. Kitchiner claims to have based the recipes in *The Cook's Oracle* on the
principles of nouvelle cuisine, or "the purest Epicurean principles of
indulging the Palate as far as it can be done without injury or offense to
the Stomach, and forbidding nothing but what is absolutely unfriendly
to Health."[20] Milton's own epicurean philosophy – sweetened, as in
Epicurus, by being rendered in verse – is then invoked as an authority
by Kitchiner: a "perpetual feast of nectar'd sweets, / Where no crude
surfeit reigns" (*M* 479–80).

   This appeal to dietary health by the artists of nouvelle cuisine was used to
advertise the first restaurants in Paris in the 1760s. Jean François Vacossin
opened a restaurant on the rue-de-Grenelle shortly after Mathurin Roze
de Chantoiseau led the way with the first restaurant of record. Vacossin
offered *restaurants* to the public under a sign in Latin saying, "Run to me
all you whose stomachs labor and I will restore you" (*Accurite ad me omnes
qui stomach laboratis et ego vos restaurabo*).[21] While taste could be cultivated,
without a healthy appetite no progress could be made. The quintessence
known as the *restaurant* was the first step in a culinary advance that would
come to fruition in the nouvelle cuisine of the grand Parisian restaurants of
the Napoleonic era. The slogan was a cheeky adaptation of Christ's words
as recorded by Matthew: "Come to me, all ye that labor and are heavy
laden, and I shall give you rest."[22] In Vacossin's version, the restaurateur
appears as a savior of appetite. He relieves the sins of intemperate eating
and counters the heavy, indelicate fare of contemporary bon vivants with
delicate preparations that did not require the same kind of digestive labor.
Proponents of the nouvelle cuisine, to quote Spang, "contrasted the old-
fashioned eater, weighed down with extraneous and heavy, earthy foods,
with a modern eater, released from corporeality by his subsistence on
'essences.' "[23] The new cookery, in accord with the new science, intended to
lead culture back through empirical experience to Paradise, with the abundant recompense of good taste.

---

[19] Kitchiner, *Cook's Oracle*, 5.
[20] Ibid., 4–5.
[21] Spang, *Invention of the Restaurant*, 28
[22] Matthew, 11:29. Holy Bible, King James Version.
[23] Spang, *Invention of the Restaurant*, 48.

Comus' Restaurant

Comus emphasizes the "dainty limbs" and "soft delicacy" of his guest in Milton's *Masque*, and in offering her the contents of his glass, assures her that it "will restore all soon" (*M* 687–90). He points out that she has "been tir'd all day without repast" (*M* 688). He has in fact offered his *restaurant* "to every weary Traveller," with the promise that it will provide "Refreshment after toil" and "ease after pain" (*M* 64–65). *Accurite ad me*, he might have said, *et ego vos restaurabo*. What he does say, in his last words of the play, is: "Be wise, and taste. –" (*M* 813). It is important to note that he does *not* say, like Satan more than once in *Paradise Regained*, "sit and *eat*" (*PR* 2.336, 368, my emphasis). He rather uses the same language as Adam, who invites his angelic guest to "sit and taste" the good things prepared by Eve from the garden of Eden (*PL* 5.368–69). A good chef requires a good critic. "The most skillful of cooks will soon lapse into mediocrity, if in the service of a careless master, who has neither the feeling, nor the taste, nor the judgment, nor the experience that true *gourmandise* requires," insists the father of French gastronomy, Alexandre Balthasar Laurent Grimod de la Reynière.[24] Milton's Comus has yet to find such an appropriate patron with experience, sensibility, and judgment. It is a theme in Milton that to taste intemperately is not to taste, but to gluttonously devour, as Eve does for example when she eats the forbidden fruit: "Greedily she ingorg'd without restraint" (*PL* 9.791). Those who have partaken of Comus' concoction have done so greedily and *un*wisely, as we have seen, through "fond intemperate thirst." An epicure in a puritanical land, Comus is a chef in search of a connoisseur.

We cannot venture to say whether Milton would have gone so far as to espouse the gastronomical maxim that one may live to eat, rather than merely eating to live, but it is hard to believe that for an aesthete like Milton the latter would qualify as good living. The poet's happiest marriage seems to have been bound by a culinary contract. "God have mercy, Betty," he exclaimed once to his third wife, "I see thou wilt perform according to thy promise in providing me such dishes as I think fit whilst I live; and, when I die, thou knowest that I have left thee all."[25] Like Milton's wife Elizabeth,

---

[24] Alexandre Balthasar Laurent Grimod de la Reynière, *Manuel des Amphitryons, Contenant un traité de la dissection des viandes à table, la nomenclature des menus les plus nouveaux pour chaque saison, et les elemens de politesse gourmande* (Paris: Capelle et Renand, 1808), as translated by Michael Garval and excerpted in Denise Gigante, ed., *Gusto: Essential Writings in Nineteenth-Century Gastronomy* (New York: Routledge, 2005), 51.

[25] Quoted in David Masson, *The Life of John Milton: Narrated in Connexion with the Political, Ecclesiastical, and Literary History of his Time*, 7 vols. (Gloucester, MA: Peter Smith, 1965), vol. 6, 728.

Eve worries about preparing food to her husband's satisfaction in *Paradise Lost*. We see her in a veritable agony of decision as she inspects the fruits and vegetables of the garden:

> on hospitable thoughts intent
> What choice to choose for delicacy best,
> What order, so contriv'd as not to mix
> Tastes, not well joyn'd, inelegant, but bring
> Taste after taste upheld with kindliest change;
>   (*PL* 5.332–36)

In planning her menu, Eve is concerned not only with the quality of ingredients, but with the way the different dishes will harmonize sequentially in the meal to best effect. Invoking Comus as an authority, Grimod de la Reynière states that, "pretty much the same is true of a Menu as of a sonnet. Comus 'Forbade a weak *dish* ever to appear, / Nor a *delicacy*, once served, to reappear.' "[26] Grimod adapts these lines from Nicolas Boileau's *The Art of Poetry* (*L'art poétique*). This was a neoclassical version of the Horatian *Art of Poetry* (*Ars poetica*), which points out which defects a poet ought to avoid. The central Horatian faux pas, however, was not a weak phrase or the repetition of a fine one, but that monstrosity, the mixed metaphor. In culinary terms, this becomes the tasteless mixture of flavors that Eve, in composing her meal, strives to avoid: "Tastes, not well joyn'd, inelegant."

The Miltonic pleasures of the table, even in prelapsarian Paradise, are hardly puritanical. Adam and Eve's lunch guest, the archangel Raphael, declares that God has caused the earth to be fruitful and multiply, "for food and for delight" (*PL* 5.400). This is another culinary adaptation of the Horatian *Ars poetica*, which famously defines the purpose of art as *dulce et utile*, pleasing and useful, or in culinary terms, tasty (sweet) and nutritive.[27] Eve seems to know what the young Lady of Milton's *Masque* does not, namely that Milton's "holy dictate of spare Temperance" does not mean self-denial (*M* 765). It is instead the well-govern'd appetite that will allow one to taste, and to taste again to the power of infinitude the gustatory delights provided by one's maker. Miltonic philosophy expresses the bon vivant's version of the good life as a neverending feast of nectared sweets, and, had Milton stepped into his own *Masque*, he might have shown

---

[26] Grimod de la Reynière, *Manuel des Amphitryons*, as translated by Michael Garval and excerpted in Gigante, *Gusto*, 51.

[27] Horace, *Satires, Epistles, and Ars Poetica*, translated by H. Rushton Fairclough (Cambridge, MA: Harvard University Press, 1926), 443.

the experience, perhaps also the sensibility and judgment, that the Lady lacks – and that Comus needs in the form of a food critic. He might have shown that one can taste with "Sapience," to use his own double entendre from *Paradise Lost*, from the Latin *sapore* which combines both flavor and wisdom, the taste of the palate and the mental taste called judgment (*PL* 9.1018). The goal of every gastronome was to become, as Adam puts it, "exact of taste" (*PL* 9.1017).

God the "Nourisher" in *Paradise Lost* provides more food than necessary for bodily sustenance. He pours his "bounties ... unmeasur'd out" for Eve to gather, which she does and then "on the board / Heaps with unsparing hand" (*PL* 5.398–99, 343–44). As the cornucopia spills over, Eve spreads her table with the best of what India, the Middle East, and the Mediterranean have to offer (*PL* 5.338–41). She does not serve her produce in crude form, but crushes, presses, and tempers it into liquids, "dulcet creams," which she pours into vessels carved from gourds (*PL* 5.345–48). Her tempering is a kind of tampering that softens and harmonizes flavors tastefully like the artistry of nouvelle cuisine. Given the quantity of imported luxury goods, her meal is not only cultured, but Orientalized. "Luxury and delicateness at the table, had their birth in Asia, with the Assyriens and the Persians," we learn in *The Gifts of Comus*, "and the quality of the climate did not contribute little, without doubt, to render those people so voluptuous."[28] Voluptuousness is a feature of Orientalism, as Edward Said has shown, a celebration of sensual pleasure associated with the moral corruption of an indolent East.[29] But in *The Gifts of Comus*, luxury was born as the twin of delicacy at the Oriental tables of the East.

The coffeehouses of the Enlightenment culture of taste originated in the East, and a form of Orientalized exoticism characterized the culture of gastronomy as an extension of that culture. According to Grimod de la Reynière, one can be a refined gourmand or, to put it the other way around, a sensual man of taste, for, "one may eat much, and for a long time, without becoming indisposed; this is what a Gourmand desires above all."[30] Immediately following this gastronomical vision of the good life, he adds: "what an existence is that of a true Gourmand! – the very image of Mohammed's paradise!"[31] If culinary delicacy originates in the Orient, it would make sense that the gastronomical version of Paradise is Oriental.

[28] Marin, *Les Dons de Comus*, xxviii–xix.
[29] Edward Said, *Orientalism* (London: Pantheon, 1978).
[30] Alexandre Balthasar Laurent Grimod de la Reynière, *Almanach des Gourmands, servant de guide dans les moyens de faire excellente chère* (Paris: Périgord, Maradon, 1803–12), 12, my translation.
[31] Ibid.

Luxuriousness is a form of goodness for the gastronome, whose philosophy insists that one can indulge epicurean principles of pleasure tastefully.

Although we do not know what exactly is in Comus' glass, the Spirit labels it an "orient liquor." If the Orient is associated with an anti-puritanical luxuriousness that even the Lady of Milton's *Masque* admits has the power to "charm" her eyes, it would make sense that Said should choose the illustration of a snake charmer for the cover of *Orientalism* (*M* 758). Artifice can be interpreted with the Lady as a morally suspect corruption of natural innocence. Metaphorical language is a form of fabrication, which is a form of lying, or as Kant puts it, "consciously representing the false as true."[32] Milton's subtle serpent is dangerous because of his forked double-speech. Yet, Satan's artistry, which makes him charming to Eve, turns out to be no less suspect than the culinary subtleties of nouvelle cuisine. "Rejecting any possibility of artistic genius in the kitchen," Spang explains, its early critics "presented cooks as masters of deception."[33] Cookery, to the Lady in *Comus*, means only falsification (as in "cooking" the evidence). But fictionalizing is the poet's job, as much as the chef's. If Shakespeare is Prospero, as the epilogue to *The Tempest* suggests, Milton is Comus.

Another Amphitryon

Once food has been transformed from its natural state through *L'Art de la Cuisine*, as the art of cookery is called in the title of the second edition of *The Gifts of Comus*, it takes not only a refined but a curious consumer to discern what went into the composition. The first edition of 1739 addressed itself to those curious (*curieuses*) consumers "who are desirous of knowing what they are given to eat (*donner à manger*)."[34] Comus' gifts, his *dons* (a noun derived from the French verb for hospitality), are intended for the curious. Eve's curiosity is what made her take the plunge into culture that the Lady in *Comus* resists, for the latter is not in the least curious to try what is in Comus' glass, or prove her "judicious" palate (*PL* 9.1017). As Eve knew, one must taste, or test, the thing oneself in order to judge. Milton leans upon this contemporary meaning of taste in *Samson Agonistes* when

---

[32] Immanuel Kant, *Anthropology from a Pragmatic Point of View*, translated by Victor Lyle Dowdell (Carbondale: Southern Illinois University Press, 1978), 150.

[33] Spang, *Invention of the Restaurant*, 49.

[34] The full title published in Paris by Prault & Sons in 1739 reads: *Les dons de Comus, ou Les delices de la table. Ouvrage non-seulement utile aux officiers de bouche pour ce qui concerne leur art, mais principalement à l'usage des personnes que sont curieuses de sçavoir donner à manger, & d'être servies délicatement, tan en gras qu'en maigre, suivant les saisons, & dans le goût le plus nouveau.*

the protagonist challenges his opponent to test his strength: "The way to know were not to see but taste" (*S* 1091). In refusing to taste, the Lady in *Comus* refuses to leave innocence, for knowledge (*conaissance*), if it come at all, must come through empirical probation. "Prove all things," Milton would argue in the first edition of *Areopagitica* ten years after *Comus*, but "hold fast that which is good."[35]

The Lady will only allow one meaning of good when she calls nature a "good cateress," who "Means her provision only to the good / That live according to her sober laws" (*M* 764–65). But in her abstinence, she takes the "holy dictate of spare Temperance" to an un-Miltonic extreme. "Wherefore did Nature pour her bounties forth," Comus asks the Lady, only to follow his question up with an answer that goes some way to explain the problem he is having: "But all to please and sate the curious taste" (*M* 710–14). A culinary art that alters food through artifice into objects of cultural consumption necessarily involves some moral ambivalence. To this degree, the Lady is right. Taste is a mark of culture and intellectual distinction, which entails a sense of moral superiority, but it is also a sign of cultural sophistication at odds with innocence, nature, and hence, moral purity. But with her straitened notion of goodness, we must wonder whether she is philosophically equipped to judge or appreciate any of Comus' gifts.

The gift he seems the most proud of – dramatic as any flambé made to dazzle diners in the best restaurants – "flames and dances in his crystal bounds / With spirits of balm and fragrant Syrups mixt" (*M* 673–74). Syrups that are fragrant are by definition flavorful, and these "spirits of balm," to the degree that they are balmy, are also Oriental. But the Lady announces that she will not let Comus "charm" her judgment with his "orient liquor" (*M* 758, 65). She seems to see herself only as a character in a morality play, a personification of Virtue struggling against the Vice cast as Comus. She rejects his glass "and goes about to rise."[36] Perhaps forgetting that taste cannot be compelled, Comus demands that she remain seated, threatening to chain up her nerves and deaden her sensibility by freezing her into alabaster (*M* 658–60). But to numb her is to give up on her as someone who can taste his "cordial Julep" correctly (*M* 672). "Corporeal taste and spiritual taste depend equally on the conformation of the nerves," *The Gifts of Comus* instructs, "with the organs of sensation."[37] Without

[35] John Milton, *Areopagitica: A Speech of Mr. John Milton for the Liberty of Unlicensed Printing, to the Parliament of England* (London, 1644), 11.

[36] From the stage direction immediately above *M* 658.

[37] Marin, *Les dons de Comus*, xxvii.

the nervous tentacles of perception, she can taste neither physically nor mentally. Yet, if the punishment fits the crime, such that the intemperate consumers of *Comus* are reduced to their own base animality, the Lady's insentient condition would seem a more appropriate result of not tasting – not testing, not being curious to know, good food or bad, or just *what* is in Comus' cup.

The last words we hear Comus say are these: "Be wise, and taste. –" The stage direction immediately following informs us that the Lady's brothers make this impossible by rushing in and destroying his elegant glass. Sabrina then arrives from the court of the sea goddess Amphitrite and uses her own knowledge of culinary chemistry to reduce the tackiness of the gums that Comus has heated to affix the Lady to her seat, thus freeing her from his "clasping charm" and "numbing spell" (*M* 853). This watery spirit of Amphitrite is a spirit of hospitality, insofar as the name *Amphitrite* phonetically echoes *Amphitryon*, associated with an ancient myth of hospitality that reverberates in the literature of gastronomy. Jupiter assumes the shape of the Theban General Amphitryon in that myth and hosts a lavish banquet at the latter's villa. When Amphitryon returns home, the guests do not acknowledge him, caring only for the "Amphitryon" who has wined and dined them. Molière's comedy *Amphitryon* culminates in the line: "The true Amphitryon is the Amphitryon who entertains."[38] In the age of gastronomy Amphitryon would become synonymous with host. Grimod de la Reynière calls his 1805 etiquette book, *Manuel des Amphitryons*. Milton would not have known Molière's comedy, for it was first performed in the court of Louis XIV in 1668, but the Roman comedian Plautus had staged it as a burlesque.

Milton points out in his masque that naiads waited on Circe when she prepared for her feast, and Sabrina informs the Lady that she must return "To wait in *Amphitrite's* bow'r" (*M* 921). When imagining "the sort of banquet which might have served for the marriage feast of Neptune and Amphitrite," Benjamin Disraeli writes that it "ought to have been administered by the Neireids and the Naiads; terrines of turtle, pools of water souchee, flounders of every hue, and eels in every shape, cutlets of salmon, salmis of carp, ortolans represented by whitebait, and huge roasts carved out of the sturgeon."[39] Perhaps, in the end, the gastromedicinal

---

[38] Molière [Jean-Baptiste Poquelin], *Amphitryon*, edited by Pierre Mélèse (Lille: Librairie Giard, 1950), 98; my translation.

[39] Benjamin Disraeli, *Wit and Wisdom of Benjamin Disraeli, Earl of Beaconsfield, Collected from His Writings and Speeches* (London: Longmans, Green, and Co., 1881), 103.

restaurant Comus peddles in the wilds of Britain is eclipsed by the more Mediterranean "restaurant" of Amphitrite, a female Amphitryon who sends her waitress Sabrina with a vial of healing "liquors" to the Lady seated at Comus' table, on a mission to restore her (*M* 847). While there is plenty of moralizing at the end of the masque on the part of the children and their attendant Spirit about virtue and chastity, Milton believed as little in the latter as a "cloistered virtue" as he did in a beadle's sense of the good.[40] In the end, Comus' meal may have been fit only for a connoisseur like Milton – tried through experience, perfected through practice, prophetic of finer things to come in the form of that grand gastronomical theater, the gourmet restaurant.

BIBLIOGRAPHY

Addison, Joseph, Richard Steele, et al. *The Spectator.* 8 vols. London: J. and R. Tonson, 1749.

Disraeli, Benjamin. *Wit and Wisdom of Benjamin Disraeli, Earl of Beaconsfield, Collected from His Writings and Speeches.* London: Longmans, Green, and Co., 1881.

Elias, Norbert. *The Civilizing Process: The History of Manners.* Translated by Edmund Jephcott. New York: Urizen Books, 1978.

Gigante, Denise, ed. *Gusto: Essential Writings in Nineteenth-Century Gastronomy.* New York: Routledge, 2005.

   Taste: A Literary History. New Haven: Yale University Press, 2005.

Grimod de la Reynière, Alexandre Balthasar Laurent. *Manuel des Amphitryons, Contenant un traité de la dissection des viandes à table, la nomenclature des menus les plus nouveaux pour chaque saison, et les elemens de politesse gourmande.* Paris: Capelle et Renand, 1808.

   Almanach des Gourmands, servant de guide dans les moyens de faire excellente chère. Paris: Périgord, Maradon, 1803–12.

Horace, *Satires, Epistles, and Ars Poetica.* Translated by H. Rushton Fairclough. Cambridge, MA: Harvard University Press, 1926.

Kant, Immanuel. *Anthropology from a Pragmatic Point of View.* Translated by Victor Lyle Dowdell. Carbondale: Southern Illinois University Press, 1978.

Kitchiner, William. *The Cook's Oracle.* London: Whittaker, Treacher, and Co., 1831.

Korsmeyer, Carolyn. *Making Sense of Taste: Food and Philosophy.* Ithaca, NY: Cornell University Press, 1999.

Lewalski, Barbara. *The Life of John Milton: A Critical Biography.* Malden, MA: Wiley-Blackwell, 2000.

[Marin, François]. *Les Dons de Comus, ou l'Art de la Cuisine, Réduit en practique.* 2nd ed. Paris: Pissot, 1758.

---

[40] This phrase was added after the first edition of *Areopagitica*; see Milton, *Complete Poems*, 728.

Masson, David. *The Life of John Milton: Narrated in Connexion with the Political, Ecclesiastical, and Literary History of His Time.* 7 vols. 1877–96. Reprint, Gloucester, MA: Peter Smith, 1965.

Mennell, Stephen. *All Manners of Food: Eating and Taste in England and France from the Middle Ages to the Present.* 2nd ed. Urbana: University of Illinois Press, 1996.

Milton, John. *Complete Poems and Major Prose.* Edited by Merritt Y. Hughes. New York: Odyssey, 1957.

Areopagitica: A Speech of Mr. John Milton for the Liberty of Unlicensed Printing, to the Parliament of England. London, 1644.

Molière [Jean-Baptiste Poquelin]. *Amphitryon.* Edited by Pierre Mélèse. Lille: Librairie Giard, 1950.

Said, Edward. *Orientalism.* London: Pantheon, 1978.

Shakespeare, William. *The Tempest.* Edited by Robert Langbaum. Revised ed. New York: Signet, 1998.

Spang, Rebecca L. *The Invention of the Restaurant: Paris and Modern Gastronomic Culture.* Cambridge, MA: Harvard University Press, 2000.

CHAPTER 5

The Art of the Recipe
American Food Writing Avant la Lettre

J. Michelle Coghlan

Is a recipe a list of ingredients and a formula of the steps to be taken in producing a given dish? If it comes to us in the form of a lyric could we call it a poem? If it is given to us, instead, in the form of an essay or in the midst of a memoir or dropped in as the supplement – or interruption – to a novel's narrative, can we think of the book it comes to us in as a kind of cookbook even if it would likely be more readily categorized, at least initially, as something else? And, finally, could cookbooks be read – even savored – for something beyond themselves, or rather, for a pleasure in the form their recipes take rather than simply the foods they instruct us to prepare?

Artful recipes – or, recipes artfully merged into books we wouldn't immediately describe as cookbooks – have long been regarded as a modern literary creation, originating in the twentieth century with the exquisite gastronomical essays of M. F. K. Fisher in *Serve It Forth* (1937), *Consider the Oyster* (1941), and *How to Cook a Wolf* (1942); the publication of experimental cookbook-cum-memoirs like *The Alice B. Toklas Cookbook* (1954); and, at least since the 1980s, the emergence of a veritable cornucopia of novels and memoirs which ingeniously embed recipes for the dishes cooked up in their pages, including Nzotake Shange's *Sassafrass, Cypress and Indigo* (1982), Nora Ephron's *Heartburn* (1983), Leslie Li's *Daughter of Heaven: A Memoir with Earthly Recipes* (2013), and recent bestselling detective series like Cleo Coyle's Coffee House Mysteries. Literary scholar Doris Witt coined the term for this emergent culinary-narrative form, "recipistolary" in her seminal reading of Shange's novel, and influential food studies scholars such as Kyla Wazana Tompkins continue to identify it as a uniquely contemporary genre: "We might argue that recipes, so often considered marginal to the literary archive and historical record, consistently reference what we might call micro-theories and micro-performances of time, exhibiting a now-ness that might explain the vogue for recipes in twentieth-century literature, a century in which the sense of time has been under constant assault".[1]

Yet far less attention has been paid to the nineteenth-century American food writing that anticipates and enriches our understanding of the aesthetic pleasures at the heart of Fisher's essays and the modern recipistolary canon of which they are part. This chapter takes up the matter of American food writing "avant la lettre" by turning to the exuberant – and now largely forgotten – food essays of expat American writer Elizabeth Robins Pennell, originally penned for the *Pall Mall Gazette* and recirculated, on both sides of the Atlantic, in her 1896 collection *The Feasts of Autolycus: Or, the Diary of a Greedy Woman*.[2] Although Pennell made her name as both a New Art Critic and a celebrated food columnist in fin-de-siècle London, her contributions to American food writing have so far gone largely unexamined. In taking seriously the hybrid, proto-modern form of her recipistolary essays, I aim to recover the formal innovation of Pennell's radical celebration of women's right to unbridled gastronomical pleasure, or as Pennell herself puts it, "the virtue of gluttony," as well as rethink at once the art of writing and reading recipes.[3]

Literary Cookery

In his 1942 *New York Times* review of *How to Cook a Wolf*, Orville Prescott sets the scene for his thoughts on Fisher's book by first conjuring the image of an ever-expanding sea of American cookbooks rising to meet the demands of a seemingly limitlessly increasing market, running the gamut from "lordly and expensive tomes invoking the honored names of Escoffier, Vatel and Brillat-Savarin to cute and coy brides' companions designed to aid in holding a husband's love and winning a mother-in-law's respect."[4] Yet he raises the specter of the cookbook as too-easy-bestseller precisely to distinguish Fisher's now-classic work from the rest:

---

[1] Doris Witt, *Black Hunger: Food and the Politics of US Identity* (New York: Oxford University Press, 1999); Kyla Wazana Tompkins, "Consider the Recipe," *J19: Journal of Nineteenth-Century Americanists* 1.2 (2013): 443. Tompkins rightly points out that this form has most often emerged in women's literature. Tompkins, "Consider the Recipe," 442. A number of male novelists who lavish attention on a particular dish, such as Ian McEwan in *Saturday*, do not provide the recipes for said dish within the pages of the text itself, though McEwan did bow to reader pressure and eventually provide the fish stew recipe on his website after the book's publication. Ian McEwan, *Saturday* (New York: Knopf Doubleday, 2006).

[2] Elizabeth Robins Pennell, *The Feasts of Autolycus: Or, the Diary of a Greedy Woman* (London: Merriam, 1896).

[3] Ibid., 16.

[4] Orville Prescott, review of *How to Cook a Wolf* by M. F. K. Fisher, *New York Times*, May 22, 1942.

Few indeed have any claims to literary merit. At least, few did until a knowing lady who signs herself austerely M. F. K. Fisher began conducting her *one-woman revolution in the field of literary cookery*. Mrs. Fisher writes about food with such relish and enthusiasm that the mere *reading* of her books creates a clamorous appetite. She also writes with a robust sense of humor and a nice capacity for a neatly turned phrase.[5]

Prescott's judgment of Fisher – that most of all her work represented a significant turning point *"in the field of literary cookery"* – has certainly held up against the test of time. While it has taken literary studies a bit longer to recognize her literary merit, she is nevertheless now held up as the paragon of American food writing by contemporary American food writers and literary critics alike.

Writing in *Raritan*, Library of America publisher Max Rudin puts it this way: "Fisher had discovered that in writing about food she could at the same time be writing about the human heart, and with this discovery *she introduced gastronomy to American literature*" and adds decidedly that while she was "never a cookbook writer or culinary professional like her friends Julia Child and James Beard, Fisher's reputation as the preeminent American food writer is based primarily on personal essays and memoir."[6] But even in praising Fisher for single-handedly revolutionizing American food writing, Rudin points us to the difficulty of pinning her down. For *How to Cook A Wolf*, though initially reviewed as a cookbook, is now quite often considered to be something else we don't quite have a term for, with "a collection of gastronomical essays" our closest approximation.

Tamar Adler, in the introduction to her own recent not-quite-cookbook, *An Everlasting Meal*, thus begins her book by relaying what Fisher's text is not – *"How to Cook a Wolf is not* a cookbook or a memoir or a story about one person or one thing. It is a book about cooking defiantly, amid the mess of war and the pains of bare pantries"– and signals in turn that her own collection of gastronomical essays aims to follow Fisher's lead.[7] And yet literary critic and food studies scholar Allison Carruth, examining Fisher's writing in the context of the transatlantic food politics of late modernism, describes *How to Cook a Wolf* as a "cookbook" without qualification and argues quite compellingly that we ought to read it as both an inflection and a re-articulation of modernist aesthetic form, wedding "nonlinear narrative, montage, and irony ... with journalistic

---

[5] Ibid. (emphasis mine).
[6] Max Rudin, "M. F. K. Fisher and the Consolations of Food," *Raritan Quarterly Review* 21.2 (2001): 129 (emphasis mine).
[7] Tamar Adler, *An Everlasting Meal: Cooking with Economy and Grace* (New York: Scribner, 2011), 1.

commentary on overconsumption and government rations" in a way that "redirect[s] modernist techniques to the material (and often banal) history of war rationing, middle-class appetites, and the agricultural industries that underlie them."[8]

But if Fisher has consistently been heralded as the exemplar of a new phase in both culinary literature and American modernism, and continues to offer a model for contemporary food writers because she so flagrantly pushed the boundaries of the cookbook, the memoir, and the personal essay in her work, she also provides us with an oft-overlooked *alternate* chronology for the rise of such modern American food writing, another entry point into what we might call American food writing *avant la lettre*, in *An Alphabet for Gourmets,* the column she penned for *Gourmet Magazine* in 1948 and later republished as a collection of the same name. In her opening essay, "A is for Dining Alone," she celebrates the joys of solitary eating when she can't be with that rare dining companion whose company rivals her own, but to get us there she makes an extravagant, we might even say an altogether extraneous, *detour.* She writes:

> There is always the prospect to cheer us of a quiet or giddy or warmly somber or lightly notable meal with "One" as Elizabeth Robins Pennell refers to him or her in *The Feasts of Autolycus,* "... one sits feasting in silent sympathy," this lady wrote at the end of the last century, in her mannered and delightful book. She was, just there on the page, thinking of eating an orange in southern France, but any kind of food will do, in any clime, so long as One is there.[9]

And, Fisher goes on to posit, if such a one isn't there, it isn't worth the bother.

Fisher's passing mention here of Elizabeth Robins Pennell remarkably invokes but notably *does* and *does not* situate this fin-de-siècle expatriate American writer. We are told she wrote a "delightful book" in the nineteenth century but nothing more – and the affectionate if gratuitous nod to her collection of essays at the start of Fisher's own suggests Fisher's familiarity with this earlier gastronomical text even as it also seems to suggest we *should* but likely *don't* already know it. Some sixty years later, Jeanette Winterson, after reading contemporary domestic goddess Nigella Lawson's *own* tattered copy of Pennell's 1896 collection, would trace yet another lineage between Pennell and modernist food writing, insisting after reading

[8] Alison Carruth, "War Rations and the Food Politics of Late Modernism," Modernism/modernity 16.4 (2009): 777.
[9] M. F. K. Fisher, *An Alphabet for Gourmets* (New York: Viking Press, 1949), 1.

Pennell alongside *The Alice B. Toklas Cookbook* that she was certain "Toklas had been influenced by this pioneering writer. The same excess and recklessness is present in the writing of both of them."[10] This recent return to Pennell was inspired in part by Adam Gopnik's decision to craft his 2011 collection of essays on contemporary food culture, *The Table Comes First*, around a set of "emails" directed to this still mostly forgotten nineteenth-century American woman author – though it is perhaps worth noting that Gopnik initially introduces her as an "English" rather than an American one.[11] Which brings us, finally, to the question of Pennell herself, and the alternate temporal trajectory of modern American food writing that this chapter argues she represents.

Not unlike Fisher, or, for that matter, many nineteenth-century American cookery writers, Pennell was a prolific author who tried her hand at a variety of different genres in addition to gastronomical essays.[12] A Philadelphian by birth, she began writing topical essays for high-brow American periodicals in her twenties and first made a name for herself by authoring a biography of Mary Wollstonecraft. In 1881 she met her husband, celebrated American illustrator Joseph Pennell, who was three years her junior, while collaborating on a piece about Philadelphia for *Scribner's Monthly*, and two years later, at twenty-nine, she married him. Their honeymoon tour took them across France – a not altogether surprising nineteenth-century destination, but one they traversed entirely by way of tandem bicycle, publishing travel sketches of the journey written by Elizabeth and illustrated by Joseph, first in *The Century* magazine and later collected in a series of popular books (among them, *Our Sentimental Journey across England and France*). Later that year, they settled in London where they soon counted James McNeill Whistler, Oscar Wilde, George Bernard Shaw, Max Beerbohm, and Henry James among their circle. (Pennell once lamented of this nocturnal set: "How, if I did not get to bed until two or three or four o'clock on Friday morning, was I to sit down

---

[10] Jeanette Winterson, "Greedy Women," *Stylist Magazine*, 2012, www.stylist.co.uk/life/greedy-women.

[11] Adam Gopnik, *The Table Comes First: Family, France, and the Meaning of Food* (New York: Alfred A. Knopf, 2011). The tendency to treat Pennell as English rather than American is not Gopnik's alone: Talia Schaffer's fascinating reading of *The Feasts of Autolycus* similarly sidesteps Pennell's expatriate status. Talia Schaffer, "The Importance of Being Greedy: Connoisseurship and Domesticity in the Writings of Elizabeth Robins Pennell," in *The Recipe Reader: Narratives, Contexts, Traditions*, edited by Janet Floyd and Laural Foster (2003; Lincoln: University of Nebraska, 2010), 105–26.

[12] Take, for example, Metta Victoria Victor, who wrote *The Dime Cook Book*, an early detective novel, and some hundred dime novels (among other things), Eliza Leslie, who initially published her cookbook so she could publish other things, and Sarah Josepha Hale, who published novels and edited *Godeys* in addition to her career as the writer of household manuals.

at my desk at nine and be the brilliant authority on Eating that I thought I was?"[13])

As the Pennells settled into their life in London, Joseph continued his work as an illustrator but also embarked on a new career as an art critic; by the late 1880s, he had succeeded George Bernard Shaw as critic for the London *Star*, though he also wrote regularly for *The Century*. Elizabeth took over this art column whenever art or other journalism commitments took Joseph away from London, but she soon began authoring an increasing number of art essays in her own right for the *Daily Chronicle* and the *Pall Mall Gazette*. From this forum, the Pennells were among the group of fin-de-siècle "New Critics" who championed radical new art, Whistler's most of all. But Pennell's prolific writings about art did not keep her from continuing to publish articles on a variety of other subjects – from sociology and architecture to the London underground and French literature – for prominent periodicals on both sides of the Atlantic.[14] At the same time, she began writing a regular culinary column called "The Wares of Autolycus" for the *Pall Mall Gazette,* later collected in *The Feasts of Autolycus,* an experience that led her, in turn, to develop a near-mania for cookbook collecting.[15]

Perhaps in part because of the sheer *volume* of her writing, but also because of a continued scholarly reluctance to examine the literary aspirations of pre-twentieth-century food writing, the last decade's critical revival of interest in Pennell has most often turned to her contributions to New Journalism and fin-de-siècle art criticism, largely passing over her gastronomical essays much in the same way that her entry in the encyclopedia of *Notable American Women* many decades earlier noted only that she had a "lesser interest in the field of cookery"– Fisher's and Gopnik's nods to her notwithstanding.[16] But, as I will argue, Pennell's New Critical

---

[13] Quoted in Jacqueline Williams, "Elizabeth Robins Pennell," *Quarterly Book Club of Washington Newsletter* 10.4 (Winter 1992): 8.

[14] Jane S. Gabin, *American Expatriate Women in Gilded Age London: Expatriates Rediscovered* (Tallahassee: University Press of Florida, 2006), 124–25.

[15] Pennell's cookery collection, later donated to the Library of Congress, eventually comprised over 400 limited, rare, and first edition cookbooks dating from the fifteenth century through the nineteenth century.

[16] Edward T. James, Janet Wilson James, and Paul S. Boyer, eds., *Notable American Women, 1607–1950,* vol. 3 (Cambridge: Belknap Press, 1971), 49. Art historian Meaghan Clarke, in her study of New Woman art journalists, celebrates, for example, the way that Pennell's art criticism "makes visible a diversity of visions of modernity both inside and outside metropolitan London." Clarke, "New Woman on Grub Street: Art in the City," in *Gissing and the City: Cultural Crisis and the Making of Books in Late Victorian England,* edited by John Spiers (London: Palgrave, 2006), 39. Kimberly Morse Jones, another art historian who has done much to recover Pennell's unsigned art columns, helpfully reminds us that Pennell "was amongst a new breed of professional art critics who possessed

tendency to attend to the formal characteristics of an artwork surfaces not only in the way that she crafts the recipes she offers but also in the meals she writes about in *Feasts*.

Recent work by Talia Schaffer and Jamie Horrocks on *The Feasts of Autolycus* present two important exceptions to the trend of recovering Pennell only for the sake of her art criticism. Yet in both their readings, *Feasts* emerges as a queer, or rather not-quite, cookbook: Schaffer identifies it, in fact, as "the strangest book to appear during what was admittedly a decade of unusual publications."[17] In particular, Pennell's refusal to adopt the voice of a domestic authority, and her repeated reluctance to offer precise recipes, emerges in these accounts as a kind of "trick," an overturning of the cookbook or household manual genre. Notes Horrocks: "Pennell's instructions often culminate in a rejection of the idea of the list itself as insufficiently adaptable to the impressions of the culinary artist – a habit that makes following any of her recipes an exercise in frustration, as I know from personal experience."[18] (Gopnik, on the other hand, goes into near-rhapsodies over Pennell's recipes, insisting that "there is nothing on Pennell's menus that is not delicious ... Reading Pennell's recipes makes you think of what you'd want *your* last meal to be.")[19]

Pennell's repurposing of aestheticism for the kitchen might then be taken to be, first and foremost, deeply parodic – as Horrocks argues, even campy – in nature, using food primarily as a vehicle to camp aestheticism itself. From this vantage point, Pennell's meandering meditations on delightful meals that she's eaten or invites us to try anticipate not so much the hybridity of Fisher's food writing as the modern disavowal of gustatory matters by those who seem most invested in reading them, an avoidance that literary critic Jennifer Fleissner argues is the curious hallmark of so much recent work in food studies: "To be sure, unlike nearly all their scholarly predecessors, the food studies writers do consider scenes of literal tasting. Yet the point of these, over and over, is to elevate eating by showing

---

critical expertise" and argues that she "strategically used her journalistic platform to encourage her readership to change their view of art, *by considering form above content.*" Jones, " 'Making a Name for Whistler': Elizabeth Robins Pennell as a New Art Critic," in *Women in Journalism at the Fin de Siecle: Making a Name for Herself*, edited by F. Elizabeth Gray (London: Palgrave, 2012), 129 (emphasis mine).

[17] Schaffer, "Importance of Being Greedy," 105.

[18] Jamie Horrocks, "Camping Out in the Kitchen: Locating Culinary Authority in Elizabeth Robins Pennell's Delights of Delicate Eating," Nineteenth-Century Gender Studies 3.2 (Summer 2007), www.ncgsjournal.com/issue32/horrocks.htm.

[19] Gopnik, *Table Comes First*, 70.

that its occasions reach for something far more transcendent – and specif-ically human – than the satisfaction of bestial hunger."[20]

But I wonder if Pennell's paeans to artful eating and her clarion call for a woman's right to indulge in gastronomic pleasure might be read otherwise, and – in turn – if reading her "diary of a greedy woman" as if it were a kind of cookbook might in fact help us to reconsider whether cookery books and the recipes they offer us must function as they are often suggested to do? Let us take, for example, the generic definition offered by literary scholars Janet Floyd and Laurel Foster in their groundbreaking 2003 collection *The Recipe Reader*, "Recipe books [by nature] retain an element of interpol-ation and assume that readers will perform the instructions they catalog, becoming cooperative participants in the literal re-creation of dishes."[21] Yet in seemingly refusing to so function, Pennell's exquisitely modern recipe-essays at once look forward to Fisher and backwards to older receipt books that offered their readers far less accurate – or rather, less exactly reprodu-cible – receipts. For as Tompkins has recently reminded us, the precise, prescriptive recipe form aimed at allowing for a "literal re-creation" by the reader is a relatively recent invention, emerging in the late nineteenth and early twentieth century from, as she points out, "the home economics movement, which sought to rationalize domestic labor by borrowing from science to rationalize the recipe form."[22]

Consider, for example, Pennell's recipe for "Gaspacho," which she offers in her rhapsodic chapter on "The Salads of Spain." Before offering any instruction whatsoever on how the dish is made, she first evocatively invokes its origins: "But once, in sheer levity of spirit and indolence, the gay Andalusian determined to invent a salad that, to the world beyond his snowy Sierras, would seem wildest jest, but to himself would answer for food and drink … And so, to the strumming of guitars and click of castanets … gaspacho appeared."[23] She thus signals an awareness that readers accustomed to hotels where "butter comes out of tins and salad is garlicless" might be imagined to shrink from gazpacho's charms, but she

[20] Jennifer Fleissner, "Henry James's Art of Eating," *ELH* 75.1 (2008): 28–29.
[21] Floyd and Foster, *Recipe Reader*, 2.
[22] Tompkins, "Consider the Recipe," 442. For more on "scientific cookery" and the rise of the home economics movement in the US, see Laura Shapiro, *Perfection Salad: Women and Cooking at the Turn of the Century* (New York: Farrar, Straus, and Giroux, 1986); Megan J. Elias, *Stir It Up: Home Economics in American Culture* (Philadelphia: University of Pennsylvania Press, 2008). The exacting and reproducible recipes that emerge out of the turn to scientific cookery also reflect a shift in the technology of the kitchen, in particular the standardization of US measuring cups and utensils championed by Fannie Farmer in the late nineteenth century.
[23] Pennell, *Feasts of Autolycus*, 210.

nevertheless champions the dish and prepares us to arrive at the mechanics of its preparation awash in the sensations of its fabular genealogy, the music of Andalusia merging with the labor that produced the dish that is a salad that crosses the boundary of food and drink, a labor itself characterized as at once a kind of "jest" and a heroic act of languor rather than culinary exertion.[24]

The recipe itself thus comes to us, finally, as an aside, rather than the central focus, of this section of Pennell's book, and she further embeds it by framing its description of ingredients and indication of the steps to be taken in gazpacho's preparation as gems she has lifted from her own reading of cookery literature rather than as something she devised herself:

> To describe it, Gautier must have borrowed from … Never be guilty of any work when others may do it for you. Listen then to the considerate Gautier: "*Gaspacho* deserves a description to itself, and so we shall give here the recipe which would have made the late Brillat-Savarin's hair stand on end. You pour water into a soup tureen, to this water you add vinegar" (why omit the oil, you brilliant but not always reliable poet?), "shreds of garlic, onions cut in quarters, slices of cucumber, some pieces of pepper, a pinch of salt; then you add bits of bread, which are left to soak in this agreeable mess, and you serve cold." It should further be explained that, in the season, tomatoes are almost invariably introduced, and all the greens are chopped very fine.[25]

The Andalusian languor conjured in the recipe's preface thus gets reworked here in the act of conveying the recipe itself, with Pennell framing the choice to defer to Gautier's authority on the subject as a form of, shall we say, virtuous laziness. But the reference to French art critic and poet Théophile Gautier also underscores Pennell's work – implicitly within *Feasts*, explicitly within *My Cookery Books* – to gesture to and archive culinary literature as at once a canon of notable texts and an ongoing conversation between writers and cooks. She thus quotes Gautier, who in turn makes a nod to Brillat-Savarin, only to offer us a recipe for a dish that he suggests the famous French gastronome would have hated. Such a framing permits Pennell to allow Gautier to anticipate that some nineteenth-century Anglo-American readers may share Brillat-Savarin's imagined aversion to a dish that is both food and drink and not-quite a salad, not to mention to the idea of a soup laden with onions and garlic, and to follow his recipe with an itemization of its merits for any readers left unconvinced

---

24 Ibid.
25 Ibid., 211.

by Gautier's dish: "it is pleasant to the taste, piquant in its very absurdity; it is refreshing, better than richly spiced-sauces when the sun shines hot at mid-day."[26] But so too does this framing allow Pennell to position herself as capable of questioning exactly the culinary authority that she's seemingly deferring to, as when she interrupts Gautier's merged list of ingredients and actions to point out that the dish requires the reader to add in the olive oil which this "unreliable poet" has neglected to mention, and goes on to add that the vegetables Gautier mentioned should be "chopped very fine." In turn, that the quantities of the ingredients the reader would need to produce this dish are left entirely to the reader's discretion, and also that the reader is set up here to fall in love with a dish she is expected not to particularly want to make before this moment, and perhaps even to make her own additions to it, demonstrate a hallmark of the recipe form however much they might now seem a departure from it. For as Tompkins has recently argued, regardless of their precision, recipes always already trade upon "a field of embodied knowledges, movements, flavors, smells, gestures, and habits that is only hinted at by [their] own textual remains."[27] Your gazpacho may not taste, in other words, the way that Pennell's did, but her aim is to get you past any aversions that might have kept you from tasting it, and ultimately for you to make what you will of it.

Perhaps unsurprisingly, there is evidence to suggest that earlier readers treated Pennell's collection of gastronomical essays, for all their imprecision and digressions, as a cookbook rather than as the something else it now might more immediately seem to be. For example, on the flyleaf of my very worn 1896 edition of *Feasts*, picked up some years back at Bonnie Slotnick's West Village bookshop, which is devoted entirely to vintage cookbooks, there are handwritten notes left by a previous owner directing herself (and by extension, this later owner) to pages containing beloved recipes ("Gazpacho p. 211"; "Anchovie [sic] sandwich p. 220"), as well as itemizing instructions gleaned from Pennell on the proper method for preparing various dishes: "For salad in general, rub bowl with onion" (original emphasis); "For potato salad, small round potatoes" (original emphasis). Yet such directives to a future self (or indeed, for a future reader) signal an injunction as well as a conversation, with tips about the type rather than a list of ingredients gesturing to the conversational tone of Pennell's cookbook, and the way that all recipes, left to themselves, archive moments of repetition but also reinvention.

---

[26] Ibid., 212.
[27] Tompkins, "Consider the Recipe," 442.

Pennell notably opens *Feasts* with an introduction that suggests that what follows "does not pretend to be a 'Cook's Manual,' or a 'Housewife's Companion'… it is rather a guide to the Beauty, the Poetry, that exists in the perfect dish, even as in the masterpiece of a Titian or a Swinburne."[28] She makes clear, in other words, that the essays to come aim not so much to instruct as to indulge the senses and take eating seriously – and thus to refashion readerly palates as much as culinary *savoir-faire*. I think that Kimberly Morse Jones gets it right when she argues in passing that "employing aesthetic rhetoric in her discussions of food, [Pennell] described a meal *as one would* a painting."[29] But if *Feasts* therefore can be said to be a cookbook that takes art seriously, it takes eating to be no less an art. In the section entitled "A Perfect Dinner," Pennell thus takes fashionable hostesses to task for imagining the perfect meal can be built out of excess for its own sake – "dish follows dish, conceit is piled upon conceit."[30] And she offers an alternate vision of the perfect meal by way of art criticism:

> Art despises show, it disdains rivalry, and it knows not excess. A Velasquez or a Whistler never overloads his canvas for the sake of gorgeous detail … It matters not how many courses between oysters and coffee Fashion may decree, if, turning your back upon her and her silly pretensions, you devise a few that it will be a privilege for your guest to eat, a joy for them to remember.[31]

Her artistic commitments thus cross over into her food writing, allowing her to champion Whistler by linking him to Velasquez even as she criticizes those who serve overwrought, fashionable feasts rather than artfully "devise[d]" meals. And in her ode to the unappreciated vegetable in "The Incomparable Onion," she similarly treats culinary and artistic sensibilities on similar footing when she suggests "the plodding painter looks upon a nocturne by Whistler, and thinks how preposterously easy! A touch here, a stroke there, and the thing is done. But let him try! And so with *Sauce Soubise*," at once critiquing those who would fail to see the artfulness of Whistler's brushstrokes and drawing on her experiences reading canvas to shape her vision of a model meal that is no less aesthetically pleasing.[32]

But it would not do full justice to Pennell if we only consider the ways that her art criticism textures her food writing, for as we've seen she also

---

[28] Pennell, *Feasts of Autolycus*, 6.
[29] Jones, "Making a Name," 138 (emphasis mine).
[30] Pennell, *Feasts of Autolycus*, 44.
[31] Ibid., 45.
[32] Ibid., 164.

seamlessly (even proto-modernly) intermingles travel sketches, personal anecdotes, literary allusions, and recipes within the borders of her essays on artful eating. In her homage to soup she suggests that "magical, indeed, is the spell good soup can cast," acting as tonic for the sick but also conjuring travels through France and Pullman railway carriages.[33] But she also turns to the way that soup lingers in literary form, continuing to salivate the palate: "No wonder, then, that it has kindled even Mr. Henry James into *at least a show* of enthusiasm; his bowls of *bouillon* ever remain in the reader's memory, the most prominent pleasures of his *Little Tour in France*."[34] What interests me most about *Feasts* is, then, not just what it withholds from us – an exact recipe for the perfect sandwich, for example – but what she gives us instead: the way that her writing about food resists categorization and exceeds the cookbook form, crisscrossing a variety of genres, and in so doing produces a quintessentially modern gastronomical essay even as it points to the hybrid forms already latent in earlier cookery literature.

Artful Reading

In her essay "Recipes for Reading," literary critic Susan J. Leonardi famously offered us a strategy for taking recipes – and the cookbooks or memoirs they came in – seriously as complex narrative forms. Most crucially, she suggested that "a recipe is … an embedded discourse, and like other embedded discourses it can have a variety of relationships with its frame, or its bed."[35] Taking the 1951 *Joy of Cooking* as her initial test case, Leonardi attends to the ways that Irma Rombauer crafted a variety of "personas" for herself and her daughter, thus framing her recipes within a wider narrative by prefacing them with "dialogue" staged between herself and her daughter in the 1951 edition – dialogue her daughter notably cut from later editions – and embedding sections within asides laced with jokes, extravagant literary allusions, and references to the readers, neighbors, and friends who had contributed additions or emendations to the recipes that follow, even offering, on occasion, her own enthusiasm (or lack thereof) for particular dishes. In that sense, Leonardi found this earlier *Joy of Cooking* to be more "akin to literary discourse" – with Rombauer approaching "the first-person narrator of fiction or autobiography."[36]

---

[33] Ibid., 76.
[34] Ibid., 80 (emphasis mine).
[35] Susan J. Leonardi, "Recipes for Reading: Summer Pasta, Lobster à la Riseholme, and Key Lime Pie," *PMLA* 104.3 (1989): 340.
[36] Ibid., 342.

Pennell productively supplements this reading because she so resolutely reads cookery books not as a discourse with a *kinship* to literary forms but rather as embodying a distinctly recognizable *literary tradition*. In 1903, she published *My Cookery Books*, a gorgeous meditation on her extensive collection of cookbooks from the fifteenth through the nineteenth century, and dubbed it pointedly a survey of the "literature of the kitchen."[37] As in her art criticism, she examines her cookery books in a way that privileges form over content, and packages the volume so artfully – including reproductions of title pages and illustrations from many of the early cookbooks she discusses – that a *New York Times* review averred that "ignore or shun cookbooks though they may, the bibliophiles of the future can hardly afford to turn their backs upon [Pennell's book]."[38] And while said review acknowledges that the cookbooks in Pennell's collection would likely have been overlooked by other bibliophiles, falling beneath the purview of traditional book collecting, it nevertheless points out that Pennell writes about them with such "ardor" that she invests them with an unexpected canonicity, convincing the reader that "they form a library of undoubted usefulness."[39]

Even more suggestively, Pennell argues that to begin to study the *cookbook form* we must first turn to its unlikely *literary* progenitors:

> Man, the cooking animal, has had from the beginning a cooking literature. What are parts of the Old Testament, of the Vedas, but cookery books? You cannot dip into Athenaeus without realizing what an inspiration food and drink always were to the Greek poet … Early French and English historical manuscripts and records are full of cookery; and almost as soon as there was a printing press cookery books began to be printed, and they have kept on being printed ever since.[40]

What is perhaps most remarkable about Pennell's reading of the literature of the kitchen is, then, that it underscores that cookbooks have a far longer lineage than we might imagine, intermingling with literary and religious texts we wouldn't otherwise identify as cookery books, and that the taste for cookbooks which might now feel particularly modern hasn't abated since the technology for printing them emerged in the fifteenth century. But she also aims to reeducate our palate in another sense, asking readers to rethink the joys of devouring cookbooks for their own sake.

[37] Elizabeth Robins Pennell, *My Cookery Books* (Boston: Houghton Mifflin, 1903), 78.
[38] Review of *My Cookery Books* by Elizabeth Robins Pennell, *New York Times*, January 23, 1904, BR 51.
[39] Ibid.
[40] Pennell, *My Cookery Books*, 6.

In particular, she exhorts us to read them "not solely for information, but for pleasure."[41] In turn, she offers us a taxonomy of the ways that early cookbooks digested the literary forms of their day, dissecting the way that, for instance, seventeenth-century cookbooks dished up "brocaded language, full of extravagant conceits, full of artificial ornament; a lover writing to his mistress, you would say, rather than a cook or a housewife giving practical directions."[42] But most of all she calls on us as readers and as critics to always keep in mind that "the cookery book" – in all its hybrid forms – "can have every good quality that a book can have."[43] That some sixty years later Sylvia Plath would describe her experience of reading *The Joy of Cooking* in similar terms, suggesting in her diary that she found herself, almost in spite of herself, "reading it like a rare novel" is testament to the way that cookbooks – and the recipes they ostensibly contain – can by turns arrest and delight us regardless of the forms they take.[44]

BIBLIOGRAPHY

Adler, Tamar. *An Everlasting Meal: Cooking with Economy and Grace*. New York: Scribner, 2011.

Bundtzen, Lynda K. "Lucent Figs and Suave Veal Chops: Sylvia Plath and Food." *Gastronomica* 10.1 (2010): 79–90. www.jstor.org/stable/10.1525/gfc.2010.10.1.79.

Carruth, Allison. "War Rations and the Food Politics of Late Modernism." *Modernism/modernity* 16.4 (2009): 767–95.

Clarke, Meaghan. "New Woman on Grub Street: Art in the City." In *Gissing and the City: Cultural Crisis and the Making of Books in Late Victorian England*, edited by John Spiers, 31–40. London: Palgrave, 2006.

"Cookery Books." Review of *My Cookery Books* by Elizabeth Robins Pennell. *New York Times,* January 23, 1904.

Elias, Megan J. *Stir It Up: Home Economics in American Culture*. Philadelphia: University of Pennsylvania Press, 2008.

Ephron, Nora. *Heartburn*. 1983. Reprint, New York: Knopf Doubleday, 2011.

Fisher, M. F. K. *An Alphabet for Gourmets*. New York: Viking Press, 1949.
  Consider the Oyster. New York: Duell, Sloan and Pearce, 1941.
  How to Cook a Wolf. New York: Duell, Sloan and Pearce, 1942.
  Serve It Forth. New York: Farrar, Straus and Giroux, 1937.

Fleissner, Jennifer. "Henry James's Art of Eating." *ELH* 75.1 (2008): 27–62.

---

[41] Ibid., 9.
[42] Ibid., 10.
[43] Ibid., 5.
[44] Quoted in Lynda K. Bundtzen, "Lucent Figs and Suave Veal Chops: Sylvia Plath and Food," *Gastronomica* 10.1 (2010): 83, www.jstor.org/stable/10.1525/gfc.2010.10.1.79.

Floyd, Janet, and Laurel Foster. *The Recipe Reader: Narratives, Contexts, Traditions.* Lincoln: University of Nebraska, 2010.

Gabin, Jane S. *American Expatriate Women in Gilded Age London: Expatriates Rediscovered.* Tallahassee: University Press of Florida, 2006.

Gopnik, Adam. *The Table Comes First: Family, France, and the Meaning of Food.* New York: Alfred A. Knopf, 2011.

Horrocks, Jamie. "Camping Out in the Kitchen: Locating Culinary Authority in Elizabeth Robins Pennell's *Delights of Delicate Eating.*" *Nineteenth-Century Gender Studies* 3.2 (Summer 2007). www.ncgsjournal.com/issue32/horrocks.htm.

James, Edward T., Janet Wilson James, and Paul S. Boyer, eds., *Notable American Women, 1607–1950.* Vol. 3. Cambridge: Belknap Press, 1971.

Jones, Kimberly Morse. "'Making a Name for Whistler': Elizabeth Robins Pennell as a New Art Critic." In *Women in Journalism at the Fin de Siecle: Making a Name for Herself,* edited by F. Elizabeth Gray, 129–47. London: Palgrave, 2012.

Leonardi, Susan J. "Recipes for Reading: Summer Pasta, Lobster à la Riseholme, and Key Lime Pie." *PMLA* 104.3 (1989): 340–47.

Li, Leslie. *Daughter of Heaven: A Memoir with Earthly Recipes.* 2005. Reprint, New York: Arcade, 2013.

McEwan, Ian. *Saturday.* New York: Knopf Doubleday, 2006.

Pennell, Elizabeth Robins. *My Cookery Books.* Boston: Houghton Mifflin, 1903.
  The Feasts of Autolycus: Or, The Diary of a Greedy Woman. London: Merriam, 1896.

Prescott, Orville. Review of *How to Cook a Wolf,* by M. F. K. Fisher. *New York Times,* May 22, 1942.

Rudin, Max. "M. F. K. Fisher and the Consolations of Food." *Raritan Quarterly Review* 21.2 (2001): 127–38.

Schaffer, Talia. "The Importance of Being Greedy: Connoisseurship and Domesticity in the Writings of Elizabeth Robins Pennell." In *The Recipe Reader: Narratives, Contexts, Traditions*, edited by Janet Floyd and Laurel Foster, 105–26. 2003. Reprint, Lincoln: University of Nebraska, 2010.

Shange, Ntozake. *Sassafrass, Cypress & Indigo: A Novel.* New York: St. Martin's Press, 1982.

Shapiro, Laura. *Perfection Salad: Women and Cooking at the Turn of the Century.* New York: Farrar, Straus, and Giroux, 1986

Toklas, Alice B. *The Alice B. Toklas Cookbook.* 1954. Reprint, New York: HarperCollins, 2010.

Tompkins, Kyla Wazana. "Consider the Recipe." *J19: Journal of Nineteenth-Century Americanists* 1.2 (2013): 439–45.

Victor, Metta Victoria. *The Dime Cook Book: Embodying What Is Most Economic, Most Practical, Most Excellent.* New York: Irwin P. Beadle, 1859.

Williams, Jacqueline. "Elizabeth Robbins Pennell." *Quarterly Book Club of Washington Newsletter* 10.4 (Winter 1992): 6–10, 13.

Winterson, Jeanette. "Greedy Women." *Stylist Magazine.* 2012. www.stylist.co.uk/life/greedy-women.

Witt, Doris. *Black Hunger: Food and the Politics of US Identity.* New York: Oxford University Press, 1999.

CHAPTER 6

Existential Disgust and the Food of the Philosopher

Robert Appelbaum

On Nausea

Food, so far as it appears as an object in literary discourse, can be categorized as any of a number of things – "things" in the sense of objects of experience, cognition, and inquiry. Six of them seem especially important. (1) Food can be a material object, among other material objects. (2) Similarly (but this is not exactly the same, since a material object can be observed without being tasted and smelled) it can be an occasion of gustatory and olfactory sensation. (3) Food can be a historical phenomenon, as when it is observed that new products and technologies of trade and cookery have been discovered or developed, most famously in modern history such products as chocolate and sugar. Recipes, kitchen protocols, and regulations about taste and propriety are a part of this historicity of food. (4) Or, again which is not the same thing as the historicity of the phenomena of food, although it is related to it, food can be a sociocultural phenomenon, at once material and symbolic – material because food is part of the economic life of a society, symbolic because food also *means*; it is inevitably a sign, a signifier, or in special cases, as Barthes initially put it, a "myth."[1] (5) But food can also be not just a subject of meaning but also the object of a practice, or even of several practices, since cooking is not the same as eating, and exchanging food is not the same as taking it, or even of buying and selling it, and all these practices are socially regulated. Ritual practice comes under this category, as do social norms concerning such categories as status and habit. (6) And then there is what might be thought of as the metaphysical identity of food, which takes at least two antithetical forms. On the one hand, (6a) food can be identified as pure nutrition, an element in the dynamic order of being, the being of living (and dying) things; on the other, (6b) food can be identified as an existent with irreducible qualities over and

---

[1] Roland Barthes, *Mythologies*, translated by Annette Lavers (London: Vintage, 2009).

above its nutritional character; it can be identified as a characteristic or index of an order of being itself.

That sixth, double-sensed, and last quality of food may seem strange. That food is a nutrient metaphysically speaking may come as no surprise, although the very concept of nutrition is subject to considerable variation. What is nutrition in *Paradise Lost* is a lot different from what is nutrition in *The Atkins Diet*. In the former nutrition is a process enlivening the great chain of being, from maggots to angels; in the latter nutrition is a calculus of costs and benefits. But for food to be an index of "being itself" may be an unusual idea, especially if one is not familiar or comfortable with the language of twentieth-century continental philosophy, presided over by the spirits of Edmund Husserl and Martin Heidegger. But the idea that food is an index of being is central to a book that even the non-philosophically inclined have often found fascinating, Jean-Paul Sartre's *Nausea*. The title of the book would seem to give this away. Nausea is clinically associated with turbulence in the upper stomach. If Sartre's philosophical hero expresses an attitude toward the concept of his own being, he does so with respect to the experience of nausea. In fact, as I have observed before, the climax of the novel comes during a scene at a restaurant.[2] The main character, Antoine Roquentin, gets nauseated in the company of someone who has invited him to lunch, just as he bites into a piece of "chalky" Camembert cheese. His nausea triggers an epiphany, where Roquentin realizes the meaning, or rather what Sartre would later call the "facticity" of existence, beginning with his own facticity.

Roquentin's nausea does not come only from a metaphysical intuition, it must be observed; it also comes from his perception of the cheese in his mouth as a material object, as an occasion of sensation, as a historical and cultural phenomenon, as the object of a practice, and even as a form of nutrition. And his nausea in this respect is not unique. One does not have to be an existentialist to combine all these perceptions with metaphysical intuition and a sense of disgust. In a notorious scene in Dickens' *Great Expectations*, Pip is led by his patroness Miss Havisham into a dark and airless room, where he beholds the ruins of what had been intended many years ago to be her wedding cake.[3]

> [The room] was spacious, and I dare say had once been handsome, but every discernible thing in it was covered with dust and mold, and dropping to

[2] Robert Appelbaum, *Dishing It Out: In Search of the Restaurant Experience* (London: Reaktion, 2011), 75–102.
[3] See Nicola Humble, *Cake: A Global History* (London: Reaktion, 2010), 90–92.

pieces. The most prominent object was a long table with a tablecloth spread on it, as if a feast had been in preparation when the house and the clocks all stopped together. An epergne or centre-piece of some kind was in the middle of this cloth; it was so heavily overhung with cobwebs that its form was quite undistinguishable; and, as I looked along the yellow expanse out of which I remember its seeming to grow, like a black fungus, I saw speckle-legged spiders with blotchy bodies running home to it, and running out from it, as if some circumstances of the greatest public importance had just transpired in the spider community.

I heard the mice too, rattling behind the panels, as if the same occurrence were important to their interests. But the black beetles took no notice of the agitation, and groped about the hearth in a ponderous elderly way, as if they were short-sighted and hard of hearing, and not on terms with one another.

These crawling things had fascinated my attention, and I was watching them from a distance, when Miss Havisham laid a hand upon my shoulder. In her other hand she had a crutch-headed stick on which she leaned, and she looked like the Witch of the place. "This," said she, pointing to the long table with her stick, "is where I will be laid when I am dead. They shall come and look at me here."

With some vague misgiving that she might get upon the table then and there and die at once, the complete realization of the ghastly waxwork at the Fair, I shrank under her touch.

"What do you think that is?" she asked me, again pointing with her stick; "that, where those cobwebs are?"

"I can't guess what it is, ma'am."

"It's a great cake. A bride-cake. Mine!"[4]

Pip says nothing more about it. Miss Havisham leads him away. Pip after all is not a philosopher, and as a narrator he lets the details and the ironic surprise speak for themselves. But there is horror and disgust in his narrative, where a wedding cake is as it were married to death and decomposition and the flourishing of creepy crawlers and mold. And there is also, as we will see again in the case of Sartre, an association of the disgust with freedom. For if there is one thing that has to be done in response to the spectacle of the cake it is to escape – which Pip unfortunately is not for a long time allowed to do. In fact, it is noticeable that Pip claims to be "fascinated" at the spectacle rather than alarmed; he does not run away. It is one of the ironies of the book that the young Pip is so blasé about the ugliness of the world about him, and is as yet unfamiliar with the idea of his own freedom.

---

[4] Charles Dickens, *Great Expectations* (Harmondsworth: Penguin, 2012), 112–13.

But note in any case what is involved in this scene, in view of the distinctions I began with: (1) the material object, as Pip is exposed to a rotted cake; (2) an occasion of gustatory sensation, since what is most remarkable about this cake is that it was meant to be tasted, though now it has become an occasion of disgust; (3) a historical phenomenon, since cakes and wedding cakes have a history, the modern wedding cake not coming into existence, until the late eighteenth century;[5] (4) a social and cultural phenomenon, since the wedding cake obviously serves an important ritual function, both as an object of admiration and a substance to be consumed; (5) the object of practice, since there is art to making a wedding cake, as well as an art to serving it, and there is a practice of being a bride just as there is a practice of being a jilting groom or a loyal wedding guest; (6) a metaphysical index, as the image here so grotesquely juxtaposes life and death, nutrition and decay, time and space. There is probably an intentional reminder here of the scene in *Hamlet*, when Hamlet says that the dead Polonius is to be found "Not where he eats, but where he is eaten."

Miss Havisham in fact goes even further with the conceit, adding to it another idea of Shakespeare's (that living off the wealth of another is a way of "eating" a person) when she relates what will happen when her corpse will be laid on the table, along with the cake. All her relatives will finally be gathered around her, even one who has been ignoring her for years.

> "Matthew will come and see me at last," said Miss Havisham, sternly, "when I am laid on that table. That will be his place – there," striking the table with her stick, "at my head! And yours will be there! And your husband's there! And Sarah Pocket's there! And Georgiana's there! Now you all know where to take your stations when you come to feast upon me. And now go!"[6]

Luckily, for he is an orphan and not an heir, Pip does not have to imagine himself feasting on a corpse. But even if he is blasé he cannot help but place before his intended readers the horror of what it can mean to be one person too many, an outsider looking in, when what is being looked at is the way of the world, and the way of the world is abhorrent.

Poor Roquentin, the historian in a fictional town, Bouville, based on Le Havre, finds himself similarly confronted in *Nausea*. Roquentin is alienated – from himself, from his work, from society, and even (he suspects) from being itself:

---

[5] Humble, *Cake*.
[6] Dickens, *Great Expectations*, 116.

Something has happened to me …

For instance, there is something new about my hands, a certain way of picking up my pipe or fork. Or else it's the fork which now has a way of having itself picked up, I don't know. A little while ago, just as I was coming into my room, I stopped short because I felt in my hand a cold object which held my attention through a sort of personality. I opened my hand, looked: I was simply holding the door knob.[7]

Unlike Pip, Roquentin is neither poor nor helpless. But he is alone and alienated. One of the main signs of his alienation is that, no less than a helpless orphan, he cannot take life for granted. And then comes the climax, when he is seated in a restaurant across from someone he calls the "Self-Taught Man," a bailiff who frequently studies at the library where Roquentin conducts his research, and who has invited Roquentin to lunch in a gesture of friendship. The Self-Taught Man has been trying to impress Roquentin with his broadmindedness and his humanism as well as his hospitality. He keeps ordering things for Roquentin that Roquentin would rather not have, expensive items like oysters and *poulet chasseur* (a fricassee with chicken and mushrooms), all for the sake of displaying his generosity, and he keeps talking about his commitment to the good of humanity. As the dessert course comes, he goes on about his "deep love for people."

I keep quiet [Roquentin writes]. I smile constrainedly. The waitress puts a plate of chalky Camembert in front of me. I glance around the room and a violent disgust floods me. What am I doing here? Why did I get mixed up in a discussion on humanism? Why are all these people here? Why are they eating? It's true they don't know that they exist. I want to leave, go to some place where I will be really in my own niche, where I will fit in … But my place is nowhere; I am unwanted, *de trop*.[8]

The Self-Taught Man keeps talking, and keeps looking for a response. But Roquentin writes,

I can't speak anymore, I bow my head. The Self-Taught Man's face is close to mine. He smiles foolishly, all the while close to my face, like a nightmare. With difficulty I chew a piece of bread which I can't make up my mind to swallow. People. You must love people. Men are admirable. I want to vomit – and suddenly there it is: the Nausea.

A fine climax: it shakes me from top to bottom. I saw it coming more than an hour ago, only I didn't wish to admit it. This taste of cheese in my mouth …[9]

[7] Jean-Paul Sartre, *Nausea*, translated by Lloyd Alexander (New York : New Directions, 2007), 4.
[8] Ibid., 122.
[9] Ibid.

Recall one more time the six categories with which I began. The material object, the occasion of gustatory sensation, the historical phenomenon, the social and cultural phenomenon, the object of practice, and then the metaphysical index – they are all there in Roquentin's discomfort. But it is the metaphysical that is emphasized and expanded upon:

> So this is Nausea: this blinding evidence? I have scratched my head over it! I've written about it. Now I know: I exist – the world exists – and I know that the world exists.[10]

Roquentin is made to deliver what may be read as a parody of Descartes' *Discourse on Method*. "I vomit, therefore I am." Certainly he has been made to construct what is technically called an "ontological argument" on the basis of a point of "blinding evidence" that no philosopher before (so far as I know) took as such a point of departure. Roquentin is perhaps also being made to appear melodramatic, even inappropriately mystical, in his encounter with being. But there is evidence from Sartre's major philosophical work, *Being and Nothingness*, that Roquentin's "blinding evidence" is neither (in principle) parodic nor melodramatic.[11] For Sartre emphasizes the body as the beginning of philosophical speculation. The difference is that for Sartre the subject is the *situated* body, the body as a "project" of the self in a matrix of circumstances. Since Plato philosophers have asked, what do I perceive with my senses, and can I trust it? In Sartre the question is more like, what do I *feel* as I see, hear, touch, smell, and taste, and what do I feel in my situatedness? Can I trust my feelings? That is, can I trust them as *authentic* feelings, attuned to existence? Even Plato, to be sure, was aware of these kinds of questions, for whether a feeling is authentic or inauthentic (an illusion or a reality, appropriate or inappropriate, and so forth) is a problem that arises on the subjects of poetics, rhetoric, and psychology. But responding to what we now call the existentialist tradition, beginning with Kierkegaard and Nietzsche, Sartre pushes the concept to a limit. He makes feeling into a touchstone of both personal knowledge and general philosophical truth. One result of this approach is that people might really be able to come to terms with themselves and the beings they are by experiencing nausea. Another is that in experiencing that nausea, people may confront not just a metaphysical puzzle but also material objects, sensations, cultural formations, and social practices. Or to be more exact, they may experience a sense of the utter contingency of objects, sensation, formations and practices: that's what "facticity" is.

---

[10] Ibid.
[11] Jean-Paul Sartre, *Being and Nothingness*, translated by Hazel E. Barnes (London: Routledge, 2007).

In my previous article, focusing on the scene of the restaurant, I expanded on Sartre's concept of "bad faith." The restaurant is a scene, and all the people in it are players. The question that arises for Sartre is whether people who play a part in that scene are anything but players, following rules, enacting the roles assigned to them, and therefore persons in a condition of bad faith. The answer seems to be that they are nothing but players. They do not know that they exist. Eating in a restaurant, comporting themselves in socially expected ways, they live in bad faith. The experience of nausea, of being repelled to the core of one's body, therefore serves as repudiation. The good customer of the restaurant, like the good guest, can experience nothing but pleasure, however mild the pleasure is, or however tempered with other feelings. The bad customer, the customer who is repelled by the food, by the ambience, by fellow diners, by the whole situation, is either a cranky narcissist, an indignant gourmet, or else the one who just might realize he or she is "de trop," unneeded and unwanted: and therefore who just might touch upon authenticity.

Here I turn to the metaphysical itself: food as an index of "being," but this index encountered in an experience of disgust, and in particular, for Sartre's main character, "the Nausea."

On Disgust

The general concept of disgust has been a theoretical topic, as I have already hinted, for a great many philosophers, going back to Plato, who raises the issue, for example, in *The Republic*.[12] Aristotle discusses it in *Nichomachean Ethics*.[13] In recent times disgust has been discussed at length by such social thinkers and philosophers as Ian Miller, Carolyn Korsmeyer, Colin McGinn, and Deborah Durham.[14] Sartre was perhaps familiar with *On Disgust*, by Aurel Kolnai, originally published in 1927.[15] A problem comes up with the word, though, for not every language frames "disgust" primarily as a sensation rooted in the stomach. And Sartre himself, in his

[12] Rana Saadi Liebert, "Pity and Disgust in Plato's *Republic*: The Case of Leontius," *Classical Philology* 108.3 (2013): 179–201.

[13] Erik J. Wielenberg, *Robust Ethics: The Metaphysics and Epistemology of Godless Normative Realism* (Oxford: Oxford University Press, 2014), 117–19.

[14] William Ian Miller, *The Anatomy of Disgust* (Cambridge, MA: Harvard University Press, 1998); Carolyn Korsmeyer, *Savoring Disgust: The Foul and the Fair in Aesthetics* (New York: Oxford University Press, 2011); Colin McGinn, *The Meaning of Disgust* (Oxford: Oxford University Press, 2011); Deborah Durham, "Disgust and the Anthropological Imagination," *Ethnos: Journal of Anthropology* 76.2 (2011): 131–56.

[15] Aurel Kolnai, *On Disgust*, edited by Carolyn Korsmeyer and Barry Smith (Chicago: Open Court, 2003).

novel, uses several terms in association with the phenomena he addresses too: *dégoût*, of course, which is possibly the original source for the word in English, but also, as we have seen *écoeurement*, which has no English equivalent, and which refers metaphorically not to the stomach but the heart, and then, conversely, *vomir*, vomit, and inversely, *ennui*, which also has no equivalent in English. In German the word is *Ekel*, referring to repulsion. Kolnai argues that *Ekel* is a "defense reaction" or "mode of aversion" which responds to objects of the organic world, involves an intentional state that grips the "entire condition of the person," and includes a "linkage to the body."[16] Interestingly, Kolnai distinguishes sharply between disgust and nausea (*Übelkeit*). The latter is somatic only; disgust, however, can be moral or aesthetic, and is more likely to be linked with fear.

The question of disgust inevitably raises the question of cultural conditions. For what may disgust people in one culture (for example, eating insects) may cause pleasure in another. The landmark study is Mary Douglas' *Purity and Danger*.[17] Disgust and related emotions for Douglas are boundary markers, where societies protect themselves from the danger of perceived pollution and hence from threats of social dissolution from within. But in the discourse of German aesthetics, the concept of disgust refers to boundary markers of a rather different kind. The work of Winfried Menninghaus is especially thorough on this subject. Although disgust, or *Ekel*, can be said to typify responses of the most intense sort of revulsion, it can also be said to refer to cases of cloying satiation. That which is interesting in art, according to aestheticians like Moses Mendelssohn, is that which resists mere beautifulness, for in the end mere beautifulness becomes disgusting:

> What is merely pleasant soon produces satiation, and finally *Ekel* … By contrast, the unpleasant that is mixed with the pleasant seizes our attention, preventing all too early satiation. Daily experience with those tastes that are sensual shows that pure sweetness soon leads to *Ekel*.[18]

Sartre himself began working on the subject in a text published in 1939, *Sketch of a Theory of Emotions*.[19] Disgust would certainly have seemed to

---

[16] Ibid., 30–32.
[17] Mary Douglas, *Purity and Danger: An Analysis of the Concepts of Pollution and Taboo* (London: Ark, 1984).
[18] Moses Mendelssohn, "Rhapsodie oder Zusätze zu den Briefen über die Empfindungen" (1761). Cited in Winfried Menninghaus, *Disgust: Theory and History of a Strong Sensation*, translated by Howard Eiland and Joel Golb (Albany: SUNY Press, 2003), 26.
[19] Jean-Paul Sartre, *Sketch for a Theory of the Emotions*, translated by Philip Mairet (London: Routledge, 2002).

be categorized as an "emotion" in Sartre's sense, but Sartre does not discuss it, dwelling rather on anger, fear, and joy. All the same, what Sartre thinks about the emotions may be important for an understanding of "the Nausea." For Sartre insists that emotions are forms of behavior, involving a change in a state of being by a subject confronted with an unchangeable object. I get angry at a politician because there is nothing I can do about the politician objectively; I can only change my state of being with regard to him or her. I fear the wild animal rushing toward me not because I can do anything about the animal, but precisely because I cannot do anything about it. Emotions for Sartre are purposeful and meaningful; and for that reason individuals can be held responsible for them. Although classic psychology pitted reason against emotion, and held reason responsible for bridling the latter, Sartre's psychology, wedded in part to psychoanalysis, sees emotion as an autonomous signifying system, which is correlative and not subordinate to what is conventionally known as reason.[20] But the question of asserting conscious control over an emotion is in some respects irrelevant for Sartre, since having an emotion is already an attempt to exert conscious control over a situation. The problem is that emotion, being subjective only, is ineffective. It cannot change what it wants to control; it can only provide a kind of illusion, in Sartre's words a "magical consciousness," about a situation otherwise incontrollable. "Emotion may be called a sudden fall of consciousness into magic."[21] I ought to do something about that politician mouthing hateful ideas; instead I get angry, and there is a magical solution to the problem in that.

There is to my mind much to be said against Sartre's admittedly incomplete theory. It wants to be at once positive and negative. It imagines emotions as reactions, like Kolnai, but it also wants to say that "Emotion is not an accident; it is a mode of our conscious existence, one of the ways in which consciousness understands … its Being-in-the-World."[22] Sartre divides consciousness between instrumental awareness, where one can actually effect a change, and non-instrumental "magic." And yet we all know that anger and fear, for example, are prime motives behind violence, and provide the tone and machinery of violence too. The angry husband attacks his wife. The fearful mob attacks a foreigner. Emotions operate as tools for action – without emotion it is likely that there would be no action.

---

[20] Some neuroscientists are coming toward a similar point of view. See, e.g., Antonio Domasio, *Descartes' Error: Emotion, Reason and the Human Brain* (London: Vintage, 2006).
[21] Sartre, *Sketch*, 60.
[22] Ibid., 61.

Sartre's theory of the emotions may nevertheless help us understand at least one aspect of "the Nausea," its phenomenality. In Sartre's own terms it is a reaction against a situation that is outside the individual's control. Roquentin cannot change his world, but he can be nauseated by it. This is not, it is important to stress, a *satisfaction*. It is "magic." But then, too, it is more than magic. For emotions are media of consciousness, and they reveal structures of being-in-the-world to us. The magic, if attended to, is also a kind of numinous revelation – akin to mystical experience and hallucination. It tells me what I am, and what my being is.

In *Being and Nothingness*, when he comes close to explaining what he had written earlier in *Nausea*, Sartre is perhaps inconsistent. I earlier supposed there was a consistency in the last chapters of *Being and Nothingness*, and that Sartre presented a reliable key to the interpretation of his novel. I now suspect otherwise. For there is in the first place an effort, in *Being and Nothingness*, to reduce "the Nausea" to a sensual phenomena, even if sensuality has plenty of existential significance. And yet there is in the second place an effort to change the subject, and make the sensuality of emotions like disgust and nausea not into aspects of the subject, but into qualities of things themselves. The "taste of cheese in my mouth" – that is pure sensuality, and hence purely subjective: a matter for the "for-itself," the human subject. But cheese, with its qualities would seem, in keeping with the final arguments of the treatise, to belong to a category of things that *in themselves* harbor a meaning for the subject, the meaning of an "in-itself," and therefore of an objectivity.

Whether consistent or not, the analysis given at the end of *Being and Nothingness* illuminates *Nausea* even more than the earlier *Sketch*. There is first, again, a brief discussion of "the Nausea," couched in terms of sensuous self-awareness, and in particular of the sense of taste. Sartre notes that a part of self-awareness is located in the mouth and gullet. My awareness of myself is not just the experience of sensory input or the generation of thought; and, on the subject of taste (other senses could be submitted to similar analyses), it is not just having a mouth and a tongue; but it is precisely *this self*, this self I feel, my tongue against my palate and the inside of my cheeks, my saliva and mucous membrane. I am this person with this "taste" in my mouth – this *insipid* taste. I am. I am this insipidity. But also I am more than that. For to eat and drink, as I must, is to escape this insipidity. The main flavors of food, the sweet, the salty, the sour, the bitter, and the savory, are *not* insipid. And solid foods and liquid foods (although here I think the analysis is, as it were, on slippery ground) are not saliva- and mucous-like; they too escape the self-perceiving condition of the mouth.

When I choose what to eat and drink, I am producing the "project" that is myself, that freedom of self-creation out of which I emerge as the sensual, conscious, and self-conscious being that I am, the being I am *for myself*. In other words, in a quiescent state I am this insipid taste in my mouth. But in an active condition, I change that taste, I make myself a subject with flavor and texture in action. I have subscribed to this "project" of flavor and texture. Nausea is in this respect a passive condition; it comes to me without my willing it to come.

From Slime to Freedom

As for the object, however, there Sartre suggests, as I have said, that the aims of sensuous perception have a kind of quality in themselves. Toward the end of the treatise he calls for a "psychoanalysis of objects," expressing admiration for the work of Gaston Bachelard, and he develops his own notion of "the slimy." The slimy – of which saliva and mucous are precursors – becomes a theme of particular interest, presenting a peculiar challenge to the subject's consciousness, a challenge because slimy things are viscous, sticky, hard to appropriate: oysters, mushrooms, cheese, those foods Roquentin eats in succession, different though they are, are not quite solid or liquid, but something in between. Viscosity is a problem – indissolubility, stickiness, "a fluidity which holds me and which compromises me … it clings to me like a leech."[23] But a kind of horror at the contact with viscous entities is a problem too. Slime is "the revenge of the In-itself" even, though, correlatively, "the slimy is myself"; "to touch the slimy is to risk being dissolved in sliminess"; the slimy arouses "horror"; "the horror of the slimy is the horrible fear that time might become slimy"; when one tries to consume and appropriate the slimy, "the sliminess is revealed … as a symbol of an anti-value; it is a type of being not realized but threatening which will perpetually haunt consciousness as the constant danger it is fleeing, and hence will suddenly transform the project of appropriation into the project of flight."[24] Unlike, say, a radish or a piece of beef, slimy foodstuffs stick; they won't let me go, and yet they make me want to escape.

Stickiness is often considered to be a prime quality of that which is horrible in horror fiction, and one "philosophy of horror" approves of the tradition where horror and the sticky go together as a semiotic core.[25] Sartre

---

[23] Sartre, *Being and Nothingness*, 630.
[24] Ibid., 609–11. See Appelbaum, *Dishing It Out*, 95–97.
[25] Noël Carroll, *The Philosophy of Horror, or Paradoxes of the Heart* (New York: Routledge, 1990).

would not seem to contradict that idea. But the slimy is also "myself." What I taste when I taste slimy objects is on the one hand that which is not *for me*, that which is *in itself*, resisting my efforts of appropriation; but on the other hand, it is an index of my own being, for it tells me that I myself am not really *for me*.

On a purely speculative level, this idea makes little sense, and it seems all too culturally specific. My conscious "I" does not make judgments of this kind. I may recoil at the idea of eating a raw oyster, but I do not associate the oyster with "me." Moreover, the taste for slimy things, we know, is culturally variable. So some of Sartre's analysis may seem doubtful.

But Sartre also discusses a form of sensual self-awareness that seems to come when the "insipidity" of saliva and mucous is both connected to and pitted against the "horror" of the slimy: the one banal, the other extreme, the one emotionally neutral, and part of my "for-itself," the other charged with uncomfortable feelings, and yet also part of the "in-itself." As if to accentuate his inconsistency, Sartre makes the following statement, which is the only direct reference in his treatise to his earlier novel: "This perpetual apprehension on the part of my for-itself of an insipid taste which I cannot place, which accompanies me even in my efforts to get away from it, which is my taste – this is what we have described elsewhere under the name of Nausea."[26]

Insipidity is apparently the name of the game: or rather, a certain kind of insipidity which links Sartre's idea with that of German aesthetics: after the Self-Taught Man's sickly expressions of good will toward man, "this taste of cheese in my mouth." The experience as a whole is nightmarish. But what is Roquentin really rebelling against? He is rebelling not against a ghoulish monster, but a sticky insipidity. This whole experience, as it were, sticks in his mouth. But again, it is not the monstrous that appalls him; it is the insipid. It is the whole scene at the restaurant where people are routinely going through the business of their lives, more or less in bad faith, not being conscious of the fact that they "exist." It is this as it were sickly sweet scene that repels Roquentin. And that reminds us of what Mendelssohn said: "What is merely pleasant soon produces satiation, and finally *Ekel*."

But this *Ekel* gets transformed into something else. As Roquentin leaves the restaurant he hallucinates, and the sweet stickiness of the restaurant becomes a monstrous overwhelming slime. What is first a taste and

[26] Sartre, *Being and Nothingness*, 362.

intuition inspiring queasiness becomes a hallucination, inspiring revulsion, hatred, contempt:

> It was repugnant.
> Had I dreamed of this enormous presence? It was there, in the garden, toppled down into the trees, all soft, sticky, soiling everything, all thick, a jelly. And I was inside, I with the entire garden. I was frightened but above all furious, I thought it was so stupid, so out of place, I hated this ignoble jelly. It was there, it was there! ... I shouted "what filth, what filth!" and shook myself to get rid of this sticky filth, but it held fast and there was so much, tons and tons of existence, indefinitely.[27]

That which is merely too insipid turns into that which is much too gross, a "filth." And "the Nausea," a dizzy psychosomatic upheaval, turns into disgust, anger, contempt. An intuition of the contingency of being, including *my* being, and hence an intuition of my freedom – my not *having to be*, my not in other words having an essence – turns into an intuition of the inescapability of the contingent, the filthy hateful clinging jelly of existence.

More could be said on this subject. "This moment was extraordinary," writes Roquentin. "I was there, motionless and icy, plunged into a horrible ecstasy. But something fresh had just appeared in the very heart of this ecstasy; I understood the Nausea, I possessed it ... The essential thing is contingency."[28] But what we have seen so far is how Sartre turns experiences of disgust, from nauseous rebellion at insipidity to clamorous contempt for the filth of the world, into an index of what the world of eating and drinking and all those other things we do all the time really *is*, and really is *for us*.

And he is not alone. The scene from *Great Expectations* operates with much the same logic: the sticky sweetness of the wedding cake becomes a decrepit mound of mold, ash, and bugs. In popular novels like Fannie Flagg's *Fried Green Tomatoes* and John Lanchester's *The Debt to Pleasure*, food – metaphysically first of all nutrition, and psychologically and socially a source of immense satisfaction – becomes something monstrous and disgusting: in the first case, a tool of cannibalistic revenge, in the second, a lethal poison.[29] In some respects such representations of disgust at what is meant to be pleasant function as *momento mori*: today you may eat this wedding cake, a sign of fertility to come, but tomorrow you will die, and

---

[27] Sartre, *Nausea*, 129–30.
[28] Ibid., 127.
[29] Fannie Flagg, *Fried Green Tomatoes at the Whistle Stop Cafe* (New York: Vintage, 1992); John Lanchester, *The Debt to Pleasure* (London: Picador, 1997).

you too will be food for worms. But these writers are also saying something about the world of the living. After the pleasure comes disgust, and with disgust comes knowledge that the world as such is not "for us." That such an appreciation of the contingency of being means that we can go on to experience something like freedom may seem small consolation. But for writers like Sartre, even with all the other conditions of our situatedness, contingency is the only freedom we have – and we cannot have it and eat it too.

BIBLIOGRAPHY

Appelbaum, Robert. *Dishing It Out: In Search of the Restaurant Experience.* London: Reaktion, 2011.

Barthes, Roland. *Mythologies.* Translated by Annette Lavers. London: Vintage, 2009.

Carroll, Noël. *The Philosophy of Horror, or Paradoxes of the Heart.* New York: Routledge, 1990.

Dickens, Charles. *Great Expectations.* Harmondsworth: Penguin, 2012.

Domasio, Antonio. *Descartes' Error: Emotion, Reason and the Human Brain.* London: Vintage, 2006.

Douglas, Mary. *Purity and Danger: An Analysis of the Concepts of Pollution and Taboo.* London: Ark, 1984.

Durham, Deborah. "Disgust and the Anthropological Imagination." *Ethnos: Journal of Anthropology* 76.2 (2011): 131–56.

Flagg, Fannie. *Fried Green Tomatoes at the Whistle Stop Café.* New York: Vintage, 1992.

Humble, Nicola. *Cake: A Global History.* London: Reaktion, 2010.

Kolnai, Aurel. *On Disgust.* Edited by Carolyn Korsmeyer and Barry Smith. Chicago: Open Court, 2003.

Korsmeyer, Carolyn. *Savoring Disgust: The Foul and the Fair in Aesthetics.* New York: Oxford University Press, 2011.

Lanchester, John. *The Debt to Pleasure.* London: Picador, 1997.

Liebert, Rana Saadi. "Pity and Disgust in Plato's *Republic*: The Case of Leontius." *Classical Philology* 108.3 (2013): 179–201.

McGinn, Colin. *The Meaning of Disgust.* Oxford: Oxford University Press, 2011.

Menninghaus, Winfried. *Disgust: Theory and History of a Strong Sensation.* Translated by Howard Eiland and Joel Golb. Albany: SUNY Press, 2003.

Miller, William Ian. *The Anatomy of Disgust.* Cambridge, MA: Harvard University Press, 1998.

Sartre, Jean-Paul. *Being and Nothingness.* Translated by Hazel E. Barnes. London: Routledge, 2007.

   Nausea. Translated by Lloyd Alexander. New York: New Directions, 2007.

   Sketch for a Theory of the Emotions. Translated by Philip Mairet. London: Routledge, 2002.

Wielenberg, Erik J. *Robust Ethics: The Metaphysics and Epistemology of Godless Normative Realism.* Oxford: Oxford University Press, 2014.

PART II

Developments

CHAPTER 7

Visceral Encounters
Critical Race Studies and Modern Food Literature

Catherine Keyser

US literature of the twentieth century dramatizes the process of race-making through the mouth and the stomach. Appetite and disgust reinforced Jim Crow segregation. In *Home to Harlem* (1928), for example, Claude McKay depicts the Pullman train, in which the white consumer is kept carefully separate from the kitchen, which is staffed by black workers. In this kitchen, a chef renounces watermelon, fried chicken, and other black-coded foods, in the interest of associating his culinary arts with his patrons rather than his co-workers: "This heah white man's train service ain't no nigger picnic."[1] Enraged by his reluctant association with "nigger waiter[s]," the chef threatens their food: "I'll make you eat mah spittle. I done do it a'ready and I'll do it again. I'll spit in you' eats –."[2] In revenge, his rival the pantryman spirits away the eggs that the chef needed for meal service, and the chef is fired and cast out from the train. The train could have produced new affiliations because of its clear spatialization of racial and class hierarchies, but because the chef longs to ascend in that hierarchy – suggestively, he was flirting with a "yellow girl" when the pantryman made off with the eggs – he fails to "team together on the dining-car," a clear metaphor for diasporic black and working-class solidarity.[3] Food provides the chef's idiom both for abjection (spitting in the waiters' soup) and aspiration: he is "a splendid cook, an artist in creating palatable stuff."[4] This episode bears out Pierre Bourdieu's contention in *Distinction* (1979) that by "choosing and modifying everything that the body ingests and digests and assimilates, physiologically and psychologically," individuals shape the body "to reproduce in its specific logic the universe of the social

---

[1] Claude McKay, *Home to Harlem* (Boston: Northeastern University Press, 1987), 124.
[2] Ibid., 171, 172.
[3] Ibid., 180, 184.
[4] Ibid., 173.

structure."[5] Though Bourdieu focuses on the way that the consumer and corporeal choices reinforce class identity, his account is equally apt for the construction of racial hierarchies, as McKay's fiction reveals.

White writers have also registered the construction of race through fantasies of the body. In Flannery O'Connor's story "The Artificial Nigger" (1955), for example, two white Southerners, a grandfather and grandson, visit the city for the first time. The grandson has never seen a black person before: "'You said they were black,' he said in an angry voice. 'You never said they were tan.'"[6] A gap emerges between actual bodies and racial categories; cultural fantasy sutures this fissure with stereotype: on the train, they pass a sign advertising "Southern Mammy Cane Syrup!"[7] When they arrive in the city, they stumble into a black neighborhood, and their hunger and thirst leave them open to an unfamiliar environment: "the odor of dinners cooking" permeate the air. The boy runs into a black woman and "stood drinking in every detail of her."[8] This encounter exposes the white oral imaginary that treats black women as an emblem of maternity, nature, and body, in Eric Lott's words, "the black woman as the *world's mother*."[9] The materialization of that "Southern Mammy" advertised on the billboard, she even calls the boy "Sugar-pie."

Next to this oral bliss, whiteness offers cold comfort; in fact, when the grandson runs into a white woman on the city street and knocks over her groceries, his grandfather denies knowing him. The grandfather tries to make up for this failure with the promise of a "Co' Cola" – suggestively a sweet, brown beverage.[10] Ultimately, they stumble across a racist statue, a "plaster figure of a Negro" who "held a piece of brown watermelon."[11] This statue at once uncannily resembles the pair, as it looks both like a little old man and like a child; represents the hunger spurring the boy throughout the story; and allows them – even though they openly admit that it is an "artificial nigger" – to restore their connection by sharing racist feeling in response to the caricature: "They could both feel it dissolving their differences."[12] The boy has a "hungry need" for his grandfather to be an authority, and their

[5] Pierre Bourdieu, *Distinction: A Social Critique of the Judgement of Taste* (New York: Routledge, 2010), 188, 191.
[6] Flannery O'Connor, "The Artificial Nigger," in *A Good Man Is Hard to Find and Other Stories* (New York: Houghton Mifflin, 1983), 112.
[7] Ibid., 114.
[8] Ibid., 120, 121.
[9] Eric Lott, *Love and Theft: Blackface Minstrelsy and the American Working Class* (New York: Oxford University Press, 1993), 147.
[10] O'Connor, "Artificial Nigger," 128.
[11] Ibid., 130.
[12] Ibid.

shared racism provides the basis for this chimerical bond.[13] It is telling that they agree never to return to the city, where they must confront both the corporeality of black people and also the artificiality of racist projections.

As these two brief readings indicate, racial categories are both created through the modern food system (segregated dining cars, racist advertisements) and also undermined through the intimacies occasioned by the mouth and spit, the imperatives of hunger and thirst. Literary representations hold these paradoxes in suspension, as McKay and O'Connor describe both the social world and its symbolic substratum, both the process of seeking a literal meal and the deeper hungers answered by racial identification and even racist disgust. Critical race studies has infused literary food studies with these preoccupations, concluding that racialization occurs in an alimentary as well as a visual idiom.

Antecedents

Structural anthropologists of the 1960s argued that food played a central role in defining in-groups and tribal affiliation. Perhaps most famously, Claude Lévi-Strauss defined the raw and the cooked as a symbolic binary between nature and culture, wildness and civilization.[14] In *Purity and Danger* (1966), Mary Douglas argues that hygiene and diet attempt to cordon off the pure body and to enforce the boundaries between cultures. At the same time, Douglas suggests, "processes of ingestion portray political absorption. Sometimes bodily orifices seem to represent points of entry or exit to social units, or bodily perfection can symbolise an ideal theocracy."[15] Structural anthropologists recognized that cultures used food rituals to define and manage otherness but also that the act of eating breached the boundary between self and other in ways that were potentially threatening or dislocating. Their work is an important precursor to the theorization of eating and food that animates contemporary literary criticism about racialization. This critical race scholarship explores what Anne Anlin Cheng calls "the interstitial spaces between the binaries traditionally set up by structural anthropology."[16]

---

[13] Ibid., 131.

[14] Claude Lévi-Strauss, *The Raw and the Cooked,* translated by John and Doreen Weightman (New York: Harper & Row, 1969).

[15] Mary Douglas, *Purity and Danger: An Analysis of Concepts of Pollution and Taboo* (London: Routledge, 2002), 7.

[16] Anne Anlin Cheng, "Sushi, Otters, Mermaids: Race at the Intersection of Food and Animal; or, David Wong Louie's Sushi Principle," *Resilience: Journal of the Environmental Humanities* 2.1 (2014), https://muse.jhu.edu/article/583709.

Both Lévi-Strauss and Douglas were interested in premodern cultures and the hints that they might offer an anthropologist about universal mythologies. Black cultural critics of the 1990s exposed the persistence of an imperial imaginary in a corporate present. In "Old and New Identities" (1991), Stuart Hall memorably writes:

> I am the sugar at the bottom of the English cup of tea. I am the sweet tooth, the sugar plantations that rotted generations of English children's teeth. There are thousands of others beside me that are, you know, the cup of tea itself. Because they don't grow it in Lancashire, you know. Not a single tea plantation exists within the United Kingdom.[17]

When Hall follows the sugar and tea back to their colonial source, he demonstrates that the myth of whiteness – the "symbolization of English identity" – emerges from imperial appetites.[18] Hall proposes that narrative can illuminate these obscured relationships and the dependence of identity upon its other. In "Eating the Other" (1992), bell hooks argues that "within commodity culture, ethnicity becomes spice, seasoning that can liven up the dull dish that is mainstream white culture."[19] Hall and hooks both see globalized food as a key to recognizing imperial history and its afterlives in white nostalgia and racial exploitation, but in order for that recognition to destabilize racist cultural imaginaries, it must result in historiography and narrative, the thick contextualization that literature offers rather than the slick appeal of appetizing commodity.

As Hall and hook elucidate, the production of whiteness often depends upon the projection of corporeality onto blackness. In "National Brands/National Body: *Imitation of Life*" (1991), Lauren Berlant traces the anxious defense of whiteness in Fannie Hurst's 1934 novel.[20] The protagonist, a white woman running a pancake business, can negotiate the marketplace without compromising her "bourgeois female body" because she can hide behind the "overembodied, colonized" trademark of a black woman, Aunt Delilah.[21] This Aunt Jemima stereotype draws on a longer history of black stereotypes that embody orality. In *Love and Theft* (1993), Eric Lott points to the erotogenic role of the mouth in minstrelsy: "fat lips, gaping

[17] Stuart Hall, "Old and New Identities, Old and New Ethnicities," in *Culture, Globalization, and the World-System: Contemporary Conditions for the Representation of Identity*, edited by Anthony D. King (Minneapolis: University of Minnesota Press, 1997), 48–49.
[18] Ibid., 49.
[19] bell hooks, *Black Looks: Race and Representation* (New York: Routledge, 2015), 21.
[20] Lauren Berlant, "National Brands/National Body: *Imitation of Life*," in *Comparative American Identities: Race, Sex, and Nationality in the Modern Text*, edited by Hortense Spillers (New York: Routledge, 1991), 110–40.
[21] Ibid., 118, 122.

mouths, sucks on the sugarcane."²² The "oral bliss" attributed to the excessive black body became an escape for working-class white men, who were called upon in the new industrial economic order to discipline their bodies and restrain their appetites.²³

In *Racial Formations in the United States* (1994), sociologists Michael Omi and Howard Winant adopt the term "racialization" to describe "the extension of racial meaning to a previously racially unclassified relationship, social practice, or group."²⁴ Race, Omi and Winant underscore, "is not a fixed, static category rooted in some notion of innate biological differences," but rather a social construct that "varies according to time and place."²⁵ At the same time, Omi and Winant note, though racial affiliation does not derive from essential sameness, "the creation of social categories of difference" can support "resistance to such oppressive practices."²⁶ In other words, racial affiliation may be an imaginative act rather than a recovery of kin, but this community creation is no less powerful for that, as it troubles the terms of oppression. Omi and Winant point out that "there is a crucial *corporeal* dimension to the race-concept" because "such sociohistorical practices as conquest and enslavement classified human bodies for the purposes of domination."²⁷ Omi and Winant focus on the visual dimensions of racial phenotypes, while critical race scholars in food studies look to the processes of cooking, eating, digesting, and excreting that contribute to the creation of racial categories. This process of racialization invents whiteness as much as it produces others. In *White* (1997), Richard Dyer suggests that diet, exercise, and hygiene were all used to support the ideal of white mastery of the body in the service of the spirit.²⁸

Édouard Glissant and Paul Gilroy explore the invention of black diasporic culture as a creative response to the alienation and exile of plantation slavery. Glissant uses the term "creolization" both to describe the past conditions of plantation life and to evoke a rich, border-crossing goal for future, hybridized identity.²⁹ In "Peter's Pans: Eating in the Diaspora,"

²² Lott, *Love and Theft*, 143.
²³ Ibid., 147–48.
²⁴ Michael Omi and Howard Winant, *Racial Formation in the United States: From the 1960s to the 1990s*, 3rd ed. (New York: Routledge, 2014), 13.
²⁵ Ibid., 12–13.
²⁶ Ibid., 12.
²⁷ Ibid., 13.
²⁸ Richard Dyer, *White* (London: Routledge, 1997), 23–24.
²⁹ Édouard Glissant, *Poetics of Relation*, translated by Betsy Wing (Ann Arbor: University of Michigan Press, 1997), 33–34.

Hortense Spillers argues that food plays a special role in this process: "the arts of cuisine offer a central metaphor for the 'contact zone' and our pluralist possibilities."[30] Colonialism itself, Spillers contends, was spawned by an "*addictive* craving" that brought together racialized bodies: "At great human cost, this cuisinart of the modern has blood on its hands, as the pillage and enslavement of millions are implicated in its development."[31] In its wake, black diasporic cultures cook up local and global affiliation.[32]

While Spillers writes in an idiom of intermixture and abundance, the threat of hunger and starvation has been equally important in defining racial subjectivity. If blackness was produced through "brute force that brands, rapes, and tears open the flesh," as Saidiya Hartman writes in *Scenes of Subjection* (1997), slaves rewrote this category through "forms of pleasure that stand as figures of transformation."[33] This "counterinvestment" in the body expressed "a protest or rejection of the anatomo-politics that produces the black body as aberrant."[34] Black culture articulated "the unmet longings of the ravished and ravenous black body" and attested to exploitation and mistreatment.[35] As Hartman aptly puts it: "the art of need is nothing less than a politics of hunger."[36]

Literary Traditions and Culinary Communities

In the late 1990s and early 2000s, scholars brought together these fermenting ideas about racialization, orality and stereotype, slaves' starvation and diasporic cuisines, and applied them to African American foodways in literature and culture. In Rafia Zafar's essay "The Signifying Dish" (1999), she argues that by declaring themselves cooks, the contemporary black woman "must engage with the reigning ghosts of American racism; she must tackle literally visceral ideas with metaphor, individual agency, and historical memory."[37] In *Black Hunger* (1999), Doris Witt interrogates "how the concept of culinary authenticity operates in the

---

[30] Hortense Spillers, "Peter's Pans: Eating in the Diaspora," in *Black, White, and in Color: Essays on American Literature and Culture* (Chicago: University of Chicago Press, 2003), 42.

[31] Ibid., 43.

[32] Ibid., 42.

[33] Saidiya Hartman, *Scenes of Subjection: Terror, Slavery, and Self-Making in Nineteenth-Century America* (New York: Oxford University Press, 1997), 58.

[34] Ibid., 59.

[35] Ibid., 70.

[36] Ibid., 72.

[37] Rafia Zafar, "The Signifying Dish: Autobiography and History in Two Black Women's Cookbooks," *Feminist Studies* 25.2 (1999): 450.

construction of racialized subjectivities," particularly an overdetermined identification between black women and food.[38] She begins with the Aunt Jemima trademark and ends with Gloria Naylor's grotesque depiction of the "hyperbolized bingeing and purging" of Evelyn Creton in *Linden Hills* (1985).[39] In *Hunger Overcome* (2004), Andrew Warnes explores the association "between cooking and writing" in twentieth-century African American literature: "both processes [could] replenish two disabling voids – hunger and illiteracy – that external forces have invested with special prominence throughout African American history."[40] Psyche Williams-Forson investigates how black women wrote against the stereotype of the black mammy frying chicken in *Building Houses out of Chicken Legs* (2006).[41] These critics emphasize that the black literary tradition speaks back to a history of exploitation and stereotyping through culinary tradition and community affiliation.

Black people are, of course, not the only group in America or in the Americas racialized through their appetites and foodways. In *Hungering for America* (2001), historian Hasia Diner argues that Italian, Jewish, and Irish immigrant writers used literature to document their material need, the hunger they came to America to escape, but also to celebrate their homeland's cuisines and ingredients, which in turn created community in the new national context.[42] Food could, by contrast, represent class mobility, a betrayal of ethnic origins and even eating preferences. In James T. Farrell's *Studs Lonigan* (1932), for example, Old Man Lonigan "consumed [beef] to prove that he was no longer poor."[43] The home economics movement pressured early twentieth-century immigrants to shed their culinary traditions.[44] When they refuse to abandon recipes and rituals from home, the characters in immigrant literature make a political choice.

---

[38] Doris Witt, *Black Hunger: Soul Food and America* (Minneapolis: University of Minnesota, 2004), 13.

[39] Ibid., 207.

[40] Andrew Warnes, *Hunger Overcome?: Food and Resistance in Twentieth-Century African American Literature* (Athens: University of Georgia Press, 2004), 2.

[41] Psyche Williams-Forson, *Building Houses out of Chicken Legs: Black Women, Food, and Power* (Chapel Hill: University of North Carolina, 2006).

[42] Hasia Diner, *Hungering for America: Italian, Irish, and Jewish Foodways in the Age of Migration* (Cambridge, MA: Harvard University Press, 2001).

[43] Ibid., 124.

[44] As historian Harvey Levenstein observes: "the new professionals studied assiduously the food habits of the immigrants they confronted. But they sought not to learn from them but to learn how to change them … food preferences often became the touchstone of Americanization. 'Still eating spaghetti, not yet assimilated,' noted a social worker after visiting an Italian household." Levenstein, *Revolution at the Table: The Transformation of the American Diet* (New York: Oxford University Press, 1988), 103, 105.

Asian immigrants were often identified with exotic cuisines in the white cultural imaginary, but their own narratives of immigration and assimilation emphasized the threat of starvation and the glut of the new American context, as Sau-ling Cynthia Wong argues in *Reading Asian American Literature* (1993). Immigrant parents view food as a necessity, and their American-born children long for extravagance.[45] While food exposes the tensions between these generations, the dream of a shared meal also promises "a reordering of the entire American body politic."[46] Other scholars have followed Wong's lead in viewing food preparation as a potentially utopian medium for self-expression. As Laura Anh Williams argues of Jhumpa Lahiri's *The Interpreter of Maladies* (1999), food serves as "the means for characters to assert agency and subjectivity in ways that function as an alternative to the dominant culture."[47] Asian American literature both recognizes food as a medium for Orientalizing stereotype and a site of economic exploitation, and also articulates possible new relationships to food, sometimes embedded within the alienating ones. For example, Wenying Xu argues that John Okada's *No-No Boy* (1957) uses food to dramatize "the atrocious impact that institutional racism had on Japanese Americans in the 1940s and 1950s" by showing the "internaliz[ation of] repugnance toward forms of enjoyment specific to their ethnicity."[48] At the same time, Okada's novel treats Japanese dishes as "the very expressions of the maternal" and implies that these pleasures have "the power to sustain a community at a time of deep trouble and to nurture it back to health."[49] In *Culinary Fictions* (2010), Anita Mannur suggests that for South Asian writers food creates "defining moments in marking ethnicity for communities that live through and against the vagaries of diasporized realities" but also "strategically disrupt[s] the notion that cultural identity is always readily available for consumption and commodification."[50]

Recent scholarship about food in Asian American literature connects developments in ecocriticism and queer theory with the politics of antiracism. Jennifer Ho argues that in *Wrack and Ruin* (2008), a novel in which

---

[45] Sau-ling Cynthia Wong, *Reading Asian American Literature: From Necessity to Extravagance* (Princeton: Princeton University Press, 2001), 37.

[46] Ibid., 76.

[47] Laura Anh Williams, "Foodways and Subjectivity in Jhumpa Lahiri's *Interpreter of Maladies*," *MELUS* 32.4 (2007), 70.

[48] Wenying Xu, *Eating Identities: Reading Food in Asian American Literature* (Honolulu: University of Hawai'i Press, 2008), 27.

[49] Ibid.

[50] Anita Mannur, *Culinary Fictions: Food in South Asian Diasporic Culture* (Philadelphia: Temple University Press, 2010), 8.

an independent organic farmer refuses to sell out to agribusiness, Don Lee connects anti-racism with environmental justice and "complicate[s] our notion of affiliation and affinity."[51] In a more minor key, Monique Truong's *Book of Salt* (2003) juxtaposes exploitation and pleasure in the production of food and intimacy, as Denise Cruz observes: "*The Book of Salt* stresses that the most delicious recipes require some sort of sacrifice, from the death of a young animal to the realization that while the taste of a meal might linger on the tongue, the labor and sacrifice required to learn and master a dish often disappears once the results are consumed."[52] Class, racial, and even species hierarchies subtend these sacrifices, but at the same time, Cruz notes, the sensuousness of "the culinary also offers, at least for ephemeral moments, access to nonnormative communities and intimacies that work against imperial and heteropatriarchal structures."[53] Mannur expands upon the utopian promise of the "transnational queer kitchen" in South Asian fiction and film.[54]

Food has played an equally crucial role in the cultural imaginary of Latino/a/x writers. Mexican American and Chicano/a/x literature has long documented the ecological injuries and the deplorable working conditions of the modern food system, from María Amparo Ruiz de Burton's *The Squatter and the Don* (1885), a novel about the end of open grazing of livestock, to David Dominguez's *Work Done Right* (2003), a poetry collection about contemporary industrial food.[55] The plot of Helena María Viramontes' *Under the Feet of Jesus* (1995) centers on the agricultural industry, as it follows the coming-of-age story of teenage *piscadore* Estrella. Estrella wryly recognizes the distance between the "picture on the red raisin boxes [she] saw in the markets … [of] the woman wearing a fluffy bonnet, holding out the grapes with her smiling, ruby lips, the sun a flat orange behind her" and her own crushing experience of physical labor: "Estrella's eyes sting like an onion, and the baskets of grapes resisted

51 Jennifer Ho, "Acting Asian American, Eating Asian American: The Politics of Race and Food in Don Lee's *Wrack and Ruin*," in *Eating Asian America: A Food Studies Reader*, edited by Robert Ji-Song Ku, Martin F. Manalansan, and Anita Mannur (New York: New York University Press, 2013), 318.

52 Denise Cruz, "'Love is Not a Bowl of Quinces': Food, Desire, and the Queer Asian Body in Monique Truong's *The Book of Salt*," in *Eating Asian America*, edited by Ku, Manalansan, and Mannur, 359.

53 Ibid., 360.

54 Anita Mannur, "Perfection on a Plate: Readings in the South Asian Transnational Queer Kitchen," in *Eating Asian America*, edited by Ku, Manalansan, and Mannur, 392.

55 Meredith E. Abarca, "Culinary Encounters in Latino/a Literature," in *Routledge Companion to Latino/a Literature*, edited by Suzanne Bost and Francis R. Aparicio (New York: Routledge, 2013), 253–54.

her muscles, pulling their magnetic weight back to the earth."[56] As Janet Fiskio notes, "Industrial agriculture is … imagined as a sublimated form of cannibalism, and becoming one with the earth means being reduced to raw material in the system of capitalist production."[57] In the face of this devaluing, devouring force, Latino/a workers exchange peaches, tortillas, and pinto beans in "an informal gift economy" that both creates and reinforces community.[58]

Food provides a potent metaphor for the creation and circulation of "transcultural latinidad."[59] In *Borderlands/La Frontera* (1987), Gloria Anzaldúa calls for a queer *mestiza* identity under the sign of corn:

> Indigenous like corn, like corn, the mestiza is a product of crossbreeding, designed for preservation under a variety of conditions. Like an ear of corn – a female seed-bearing organ – the mestiza is tenacious, tightly wrapped in the husks of her culture. Like kernels she clings to the cob; with thick stalks and strong brace roots, she holds tight to the earth – she will survive the crossroads.[60]

In *Talking Back* (1992), Debra Castillo proposes that the recipe form could be a theoretical model for Latin American feminist cultural production, and Tey Diana Rebolledo follows up on this model in *Women Singing in the Snow* (1995), underscoring the importance of the "writer as cook" in the Mexican and Chicana literary traditions.[61] Food reflects women's prescribed role in the household and its patriarchal underpinnings, but it also provides a medium of protest. In Rosario Castellanos' "Lección de cocina" (1971), a burnt piece of meat displays a wife's resentment of her husband's adultery; in Edna Escamill's "The Pan Birote" (1993), two brothers devour a loaf of bread under a grandmother's condoning eyes while their sister screams: "'I want it! I want it! Give it to me!' demanding more from the world than just bread," as Meredith Abarca explains.[62] In Carla Trujillo's *What Night Brings* (2003), a preteen lesbian rebels against

[56] Helena María Viramontes, *Under the Feet of Jesus* (New York: Penguin, 1995), 49–50.
[57] Janet Fiskio, "Unsettling Ecocriticism: Rethinking Agrarianism, Place, and Citizenship," *American Literature: Journal of Literary History, Criticism, and Biography* 84.2 (2012), 312.
[58] Ibid., 311.
[59] Ibid., 251.
[60] Gloria Anzaldúa, *Borderlands/La Frontera: The New Mestiza* (San Francisco: Aunt Lute Books, 2007), 103.
[61] Debra A. Castillo, *Talking Back: Toward a Latin American Feminist Literary Criticism* (Ithaca, NY: Cornell University Press, 1992), 8; Tey Diana Rebolledo, *Women Singing in the Snow: A Cultural Analysis of Chicana Literature* (Tucson: University of Arizona Press, 1995), 130.
[62] Meredith E. Abarca, *Voices in the Kitchen: Views of Food and the World from Working-Class Mexican and Mexican American Women* (College Station: Texas A & M University Press, 2006), 149, 158.

patriarchal authority and heteronormative femininity by refusing her father's preferred foods.[63] Hunger itself can disrupt these hierarchies and prescriptions. In *Loving in the War Years* (2000), Cherríe Moraga takes up the Aztec myth of the "hungry woman" with "mouths in her wrists, mouths in her elbows, and mouths in her ankles and knees" as a "literary ancestor" for the Chicana lesbian.[64]

Contemporary Latino/a/x literature also emphasizes the construction of food communities across national and cultural boundaries. In Cristina García's *Monkey Hunting* (2003), a mixed-race former slave marries a Chinese immigrant in Cuba, and the novel celebrates the "*ajiaco* stew," "a mixture of many ingredients derived from Spain, Africa, and China."[65] In *Rethinking Chicana/o Literature through Food* (2013), Abarca and her coeditor Nieves Pascual Soler emphasize the importance of "cooking in the literature of those expropriated by the consuming narrative of the nation."[66] Writing across borders, Chicana/o writers create new transnational affiliations, Abarca and Soler argue, through "the creative practice of cooking based on reseasoning old dishes, creating new mestizo recipes, and using methods that surpass national food imperatives to foodways produced by the appetite for the desire for postnational subjectivities."[67] Even a broadly commodified and distributed food like tacos, Cristina Herrera argues, could become a literary emblem of cultural identity, political consciousness, and anti-racist epistemologies, as in Denise Chávez's memoir *A Taco Testimony* (2006).[68] Some contemporary writers take an ironic perspective on purported connection between the construction of Latino/a identity and the preparation of traditional foods. In Paul Martínez Pompa's "The Abuelita Poem" (2009), the poet-speaker compares his grandmother's skin to milk and corn: "Her brown skin glistens as the sun / Pours through the kitchen window / Like gold *leche* …," only to undermine the exotic racial fantasy of ancestry and authenticity: "I cannot remember / if she made corn tortillas from

[63] Julia C. Ehrhardt, "Towards Queering Food Studies: Foodways, Heteronormativity, and Hungry Women in Chicana Lesbian Writing," *Food and Foodways* 14.2 (2006): 91–109.

[64] Ibid., 96.

[65] Abarca, "Culinary Encounters," 256.

[66] Meredith E. Abarca and Nieves Pascual Soler, *Rethinking Chicana/o Literature: Postnational Appetites*, edited by Meredith E. Abarca and Nieves Pascual Soler (New York: Palgrave Macmillan, 2013), 3.

[67] Ibid., 8.

[68] Cristina Herrera, "Delfina, ¡más tacos!: Food, Culture, and Motherhood in Denise Chávez's *A Taco Testimony*," *Food, Culture, and Society: International Journal of Multidisciplinary Research* 13.2 (2010): 243.

scratch / but, O, how she'd flip the factory fresh / El Milagros (Quality Since 1950) / on the burner."[69]

Nationalism, Colonialism, Globalism

Each of these works addresses the literature of a racialized group in order to argue that while stereotype often objectifies and exoticizes otherness through food, the culinary idiom can produce political affiliation and articulate new subjectivities. Postcolonial and biopolitical theory takes center stage in the work of another set of food studies critics who focus on interracial imaginaries and cultural production across the putative color-line. In *Alimentary Tracts* (2010) Parama Roy argues that visceral disgust and nutritional ideals shape colonial subject *and* imperial subjugator: "This alimentary habitus, one that included not just the mouth but also skin, sinew, and gut, was the banal yet crisis-ridden theater for staging questions central to encounter and rule, questions of proximity, cathexis, consumption, incorporation, digestion, commensality, and purgation."[70] In *Racial Indigestion,* Kyla Wazana Tompkins contends that the nation-building US fictions of the nineteenth century attempt to consume and expel black bodies. The "constitution of whiteness," she argues, relies upon "the fantasy of a [racialized] body's edibility," but "black bodies and subjects stick in the throat of the (white) body politic."[71]

Roy and Tompkins teach us how to maintain a productive double-vision when we read texts through an alimentary lens. Both critics attend to the physical regimens of diet and exercise, the concrete details of commodity and cuisine, and also connect oral pleasures and taboos to national and imperial fantasies of the body politic. As Roy puts it, "The body was both a figurative reservoir, generating tropes of encounter – such as cannibalism or even caste – with abandon, and the materialist locus of transformation."[72] This approach unearths the internal contradictions of racial imaginaries manifested through and superimposed upon the processes of eating, digesting, and excreting. These contradictions often emerge in conflicting layers of narrative: imagery, characterization, and plot. In Upton

---

[69] Paul Martínez Pompa, "The Abuelita Poem," in *My Kill Adore Him* (Notre Dame: University of Notre Dame Press, 2009), 40–41, lines 1–3, 20–23. With thanks to Michael Dowdy for bringing this poem to my attention.

[70] Parama Roy, *Alimentary Tracts: Appetites, Aversions, and the Postcolonial* (Durham: Duke University Press, 2010), 7.

[71] Kyla Wazana Tompkins, *Racial Indigestion: Eating Bodies in the Nineteenth Century* (New York: New York University Press, 2012), 8.

[72] Roy, *Alimentary Tracts,* 7.

Sinclair's *The Jungle* (1905), for example, the "white," "black," and "brown" pigs, each with "an individuality of his own, a will of his own, a hope and a heart's desire," destined for the slaughter, stand in for the multiethnic meat-packing laborers, unwittingly united in their helplessness and victimization.[73] In spite of this message of unity, Sinclair mobilizes nativist fears to distinguish virtuous immigrants from dangerous others. When the protagonist Jurgis agrees to break a strike, he finds himself surrounded by "negroes and the lowest foreigners – Greeks, Roumanians, Sicilians, and Slovaks."[74] Sinclair underscores the threat of racial contamination with chemical adulteration; Jurgis accepts a beer "doctored … with chemicals" from a "negro" bartender who provides shelter for "a mass of degraded outcasts."[75] This approach, which Tompkins names "critical eating studies," helps us to see both the ideological projects that construct an idealized white body and also the circulation and consumption that dismantle it.[76] While Sinclair uses the threat of unregulated consumption to generate naturalist pathos – the noble white man Jurgis "degraded" – a reparative reading might follow the racial and ecological implications of toxicity as a challenge to the individualism and white purity explicitly championed in the novel.[77]

Incorporation metaphors support nationalist and imperialist projects, as recent work in transnational American studies makes clear. These cannibalistic fantasies, often invoked to rationalize imperial absorption, create an uncanny underbelly that enables imaginative resistance. Zita Nunes' *Cannibal Democracy* (2008) follows the ideal of "racial democracy" and the persistent metaphor of cannibalism to describe assimilation in US and Brazilian literatures.[78] Nunes argues that "the incorporation cannot be total; there must be a remainder, an excretion. This remainder can be seen as something that has been rejected from the body, but it can also be seen as something that refuses to be incorporated, as a sign of resistance."[79] In Nunes' readings, authors like Toni Morrison, Alejo Carpentier, and Wilson Harris exhume these remainders, expelled by the cannibalizing

---

[73] Upton Sinclair, *The Jungle*, edited by Russ Castronovo (New York: Oxford World Classics, 2010), 37.
[74] Ibid., 260.
[75] Ibid., 274.
[76] Tompkins, *Racial Indigestion*, 3.
[77] Mel Chen writes stirringly about the theoretical potential of thinking through toxicity: "How can we think more broadly about synthesis and symbiosis, including toxic vapors, interspersals, intrinsic mixings, and alterations, favoring interabsorption over corporeal exceptionalism?" Chen, *Animacies: Biopolitics, Racial Mattering, and Queer Affect* (Durham: Duke University Press, 2012), 197.
[78] Zita Nunes, *Cannibal Democracy: Race and Representation in the Literature of the Americas* (Minneapolis: University of Minnesota Press, 2008), 15
[79] Ibid., 39.

nation. In *The Tropics Bite Back* (2013), a study of Caribbean literature, Valérie Loichot concurs that the "confrontational trope of cannibalism" is recast and rejected by writers like Maryse Condé who instead adopt "a relational model of eating, cooking, writing, and speaking. It is no longer a matter of eating the other, but of eating with the other and of feeding the other," a utopian state that Loichot calls, quoting Derrida, "that law of infinite hospitality."[80] These Latin American and Caribbean writers repurpose a predatory idiom for anti-colonial ends.

This general sense that North America fed upon, or at least was fed by, South America and the Caribbean was of course no mere metaphor, as Catherine Cocks reminds us in *Tropical Whites* (2013): "Beginning in the 1880s, a network of fruit plantations, railroads, and steamships linked first Southern California and Florida to the rest of the United States and then Mexico and the Caribbean ever more closely to their northern neighbor."[81] In *Sugar and Civilization* (2015), April Merleaux argues that "categories of race, articulated through discourses of civilization and nationalism, provided a vocabulary through which people made sense of new geographies of sugar and empire after the turn of the twentieth century."[82] Merleaux follows the trope of sugar cane in works by "middle class African American and Asian American writers," Pauline Hopkins, Paul Laurence Dunbar, Claude McKay, and Edith Maude Eaton/Sui Sin Far, who "complicate the racial hierarchies articulated by white US consumers and racial theorists" and view "the Caribbean in particular" as "a regenerative space in which binaries of race and refinement were unstable and more easily rewritten."[83] In representing tropical food chains, modern fiction confronted the interdependence of the Americas and the production of race to support the plantation economy. This literary mapping of hemispheric circulation could serve starkly divergent political ends: in *Cabbages and Kings* (1904), O. Henry coins the phrase "banana republic" and laments the tropicalization of white bodies in hot climates; in *Tropic Death* (1926), Eric Walrond dramatizes the precarity of black lives in the West Indies and resurrects "rapacious Negro ghosts."[84]

---

[80] Valérie Loichot, *The Tropics Bite Back: Culinary Coups in Caribbean Literature* (Minneapolis: University of Minnesota Press, 2013), 176.

[81] Catherine Cocks, *Tropical Whites: The Rise of the Tourist South in the Americas* (Philadelphia: University of Pennsylvania Press, 2013), 5.

[82] April Merleaux, *Sugar and Civilization: American Empire and the Cultural Politics of Sweetness* (Chapel Hill: University of North Carolina Press, 2015), 2.

[83] Ibid., 77.

[84] O. Henry, *Cabbages and Kings* (New York: Doubleday, Page, 1904), 132; Eric Walrond, *Tropic Death* (New York: Norton, 2013), 159.

Recent poetry criticism by Sonya Posmentier and Erica Fretwell demonstrates the rich rewards of a critical approach grounded in this colonial frame, ever aware of the plantation economies that supported North American abundance.[85] In Posmentier's gorgeous rereading of Claude McKay's "The Tropics in New York," the space of the poem becomes a provision ground, "plots of land on plantation outskirts, which some Jamaican planters allotted to slaves for subsistence farming," which "tak[es] shape in relationship to colonial tradition while defining a black expressive form that resists its own utility within the postplantation aesthetic economy."[86] Fretwell parses Dickinson's appetite for exotic sweets and identification with rebellious, excessive black bodies: "Recipes and poems, cookbooks and fascicles, ingredients and fragments alike are formal structures that Dickinson used ... to transform sensory excess from a marker of racial inferiority into an experiment in poetical freedom and political freedom, respectively."[87] McKay and Dickinson take the perceived abjection of racial alterity and turn it into the race-affiliated liberation of poetic expressivity.

Contemporary fiction continues to map the US food chain and to expose its construction of racial hierarchies, "making visible," as Allison Carruth puts it, "both the multiple empires that have garnered food power in the Americas and the diasporic communities for whom access to the means of food production and to community food security have been central to decolonial resistance."[88] Carruth argues that Toni Morrison and Ruth Ozeki "narrat[e] the effects of globalization on women as both producers and consumers of food" and "rejoin established globalization discourses by representing trade liberalization as a threat to women's food sovereignty."[89] In Ruth Ozeki's *My Year of Meats* (1998), a corporate-sponsored reality show attempts to woo Japanese housewives to red meat. In Toni Morrison's *Tar Baby* (1981), a mixed-race model shops for chutney and olive oil at a supermarket in Paris. These novels expose a key component of rationalizing global trade, namely the racialization of gender roles: the woman of color as the vulnerable consumer who requires Americanization or as the spectacular trademark of global capital.

---

[85] Sonya Posmentier, "The Provision Ground in New York: Claude McKay and the Form of Memory," *American Literature* 84.2 (2012): 273–300; Erica Fretwell, "Emily Dickinson in Domingo," *J19: Journal of Nineteenth-Century Americanists* 1.1 (2013): 71–96.

[86] Posmentier, "Provision Ground in New York," 276.

[87] Fretwell, "Emily Dickinson in Domingo," 74.

[88] Allison Carruth, *Global Appetites: American Power and the Literature of Food* (New York: Cambridge University Press, 2013), 115.

[89] Ibid., 139.

Theoretical Horizons: New Materialisms, Animal Studies, Post- and Para-Humanism

Food studies exposes the way that objects cross into and become part of the body, as Tompkins observes: "Eating threatened the foundational fantasy of a contained autonomous self – the 'free' Liberal self – because as a function of its basic mechanics, eating transcended the gap between self and other, blurring the line between subject and object as food turned into tissue, muscle, and nerve and then provided the energy that drives them all."[90] This proximity between body and object is a particularly vexed one for the history of slavery and racialization, as Bill Brown argues in his important essay on racist kitsch, "Reification, Reanimation, and the American Uncanny" (2006).[91] Tompkins argues that Brown's set of examples – racist tchotchkes that represent a minstrelized black mouth – "requires us to think about those apertures where the object and the subject open up to the world *and to each other*, sometimes as mirror images of each other, sometimes so that the one may devour the other."[92] Tompkins thus draws upon object-oriented ontology and new materialisms but insists on their implication in a racially stratified social world: "Reading fictions of bodily essence and materiality through the mouth points to the ways that food and eating culture provide a metalanguage through which we tell stories about the materials that constitute both object *and* subject, flesh and food."[93]

Recent criticism draws upon this metalanguage to think through both the racialization of foodstuffs and the vibrant materials that, adopted as embodied trope, challenge and blur racial classification. In "Bottles, Bubbles, and Blood: Jean Toomer and the Limits of Racial Epidermalism" (2015), I argue that Toomer takes up the transmutations of sugar and the modern chemistry of soft drinks, their artificial colors and their carbonation, to refuse the one drop rule in favor of identity alchemy and to dramatize affects that bubble beyond the skin.[94] In "'Hearty and happy and with a lively, yeasty soul': Feeling Right in Louisa May Alcott's *The Candy Country*" (2015), Tompkins explores the lively trope of fermenting

---

[90] Tompkins, *Racial Indigestion*, 3.
[91] Bill Brown, "Reification, Reanimation, and the American Uncanny," *Critical Inquiry* 32 (2006): 175–207.
[92] Tompkins, *Racial Indigestion*, 194 note 20.
[93] Ibid., 7–8.
[94] Catherine Keyser, "Bottles, Bubbles, and Blood: Jean Toomer and the Limits of Racial Epidermalism," *Modernism/modernity* 22.2 (2015): 279–302.

yeast: "Alcott allows this classically rhizomatic substance – yeast – to catalyze a vision of chemical interconnection between radically disparate bodies" which are ultimately "contained within unsurprising and unimaginative racial regimes."[95]

Equally urgent are the interventions of animal studies in rethinking species difference and racial hierarchies. As Cheng puts it in "Sushi, Otters, and Mermaids," some literature "compels us to consider, first, how taxonomies of power (such as race and species) are imbricated and, second, what happens when we confront the collapse of their shared assumptions."[96] In the ontological confusion between eater and eaten, human and animal, Cheng sees the potential for a revised ethics: "Can there be kinship (what would it look like?) that is not human or blood-line based but structured along other networks of animated affinities?"[97] Staging the collapse between skin and meat, woman and fish, otter and mermaid under the sign of sushi, David Wong Louie's story "Bottles of Beaujoulais" offers "a meditation about what it means to be radically open to difference, what it means to live outside the boundary of taxonomy and in the interstitial spaces between the binaries traditionally set up by structural anthropology."[98] In this reading, Cheng draws upon Mel Chen's *Animacies* (2012), which draws attention to the blurred boundaries not only between animals and humans but between animate and inanimate objects. The shifting hierarchies of "animals, humans, and living and dead things," Chen opines, are "shaped by race and sexuality, mapping various biopolitical realizations of animacy."[99] Defining and ingesting food reveals the mutability of these supposedly stable hierarchies, from the unexpected animacy of the vegetable to the "enfacement" of animals.[100] Cheng's essay demonstrates the rich opportunities that Chen's theory affords literary scholars in parsing the paradoxes of edibility and objecthood upon which racialization so often depends.

Other critical race theorists emphasize both the precarity and posthuman potential of racialized bodies and their consuming practices. In *Ariel's Ecology* (2013), Monique Allewaert traces the disaggregation of the body in the colonial Atlantic World in what she calls "plantation zones": "a

---

[95] Kyla Wazana Tompkins, " 'Hearty and happy and with a lively, yeasty soul': Feeling Right in Louisa May Alcott's *The Candy Country*," *Women and Performance: A Journal of Feminist Theory* 24.2–3 (2014): 162.

[96] Cheng, "Sushi, Otters, and Mermaids," n.p.

[97] Ibid.

[98] Ibid.

[99] Chen, *Animacies*, 5.

[100] Ibid., 41, 124.

place that is tropical (or subtropical) and whose economy and political structures are shaped by the plantation form."[101] Allewaert observes that "colonial texts typically understood African-descended human beings as constituting a kind of interstitial life between humans, animals, objects and even plants," and she argues that Afro-Americans "who were excluded from the fold of the human and forced into the position of parahumanity" found ways to express the "knowledges and possibilities" made available by this ecological enmeshment.[102] Though Allewaert focuses on Anglo-American botany and African fetishism rather than food, her conclusions suggest a fruitful direction for critical eating studies: "the (para)human body and person, instead of being delimited by the skin-envelope, extends into the natural world, and ... consciousness, instead of being a power fundamentally distinct from materiality, emerges from extensions in space through which one body is brought into relation with other bodies and forces."[103] In *Habeas Viscus* (2014), Alexander Weheliye writes, "How do we describe the sweetness that reclines in the hunger of survival? How is the craving for life sweetened by the sugary textures, smells, and tastes of freedom? ... Will every cook finally be able to govern once we leave Man by the wayside?"[104] Weheliye reads C. L. R. James' account of his detainment and nausea in *Mariners* (1953) as a "visceral response to the food and a political stance that exorcizes the powers that be from his body."[105] Thus, Weheliye defends the political possibilities of what he calls "enfleshment."

These recent theoretical forays into enfleshment, para-humanity, and animacies offer a way into contemporary fiction of the modern food system that questions the primacy or even the desirability of individual subjecthood in the face of structural racism and systemic injustice. Chang-rae Lee's science fiction novel *On Such a Full Sea* (2014) speculates about a future in which Chinese immigrants occupy an abandoned Baltimore to work on indoor, industrial farms that supply food to affluent settlements elsewhere.[106] The narrator of this novel is a collective "we," who imagine the heroic story of a single girl, Fan, who killed all the fish in her tank and escaped from her settlement. In this collective voice, Lee mirrors the schooling of fish around Fan's lithe diver-body, and he charts the creation

---

[101] Monique Allewaert, *Ariel's Ecology: Plantations, Personhood, and Colonialism in the American Tropics* (Minneapolis: University of Minnesota Press, 2013), 30.
[102] Ibid., 6.
[103] Ibid., 126.
[104] Alexander Weheliye, *Habeas Viscus: Racializing Assemblages, Biopolitics, and Black Feminist Theories of the Human* (Durham, NC: Duke University Press, 2014), 114.
[105] Ibid., 116.
[106] Chang-rae Lee, *On Such a Full Sea* (New York: Riverhead Books, 2014).

of a mythology of racial and economic affiliation. In another novel that targets labor exploitation in the contemporary food system, James Hannaham's *Delicious Foods* (2015), inspired by a real case of inner-city addicts conscripted to work without pay on a Florida farm and fed a steady supply of drugs by their captors, is narrated in part by crack, destabilizing the convention of first-person narration reflecting autonomy and subjectivity.[107] His protagonist, Darlene, becomes addicted to drugs in part because of the violent death of her husband at the hands of white supremacists. Thus, Hannaham connects the injuries of racism with the agency of psychotropic substances and the continuing history of black enslavement. These writers begin to suggest that the fiction of whiteness as purity, autonomy, and non-corporeality is dangerously unsustainable.

BIBLIOGRAPHY

Abarca, Meredith E. "Culinary Encounters in Latino/a Literature." In *Routledge Companion to Latino/a Literature,* edited by Suzanne Bost and Francis R. Aparicio, 251–60. New York: Routledge, 2013.

Voices in the Kitchen: Views of Food and the World from Working-Class Mexican and Mexican American Women. College Station: Texas A & M University Press, 2006.

Abarca, Meredith E., and Nieves Pascual Soler. *Introduction to Rethinking Chicana/ o Literature: Postnational Appetites.* Edited by Meredith E. Abarca and Nieves Pascual Soler, 1–23. New York: Palgrave Macmillan, 2013.

Allewaert, Monique. *Ariel's Ecology: Plantations, Personhood, and Colonialism in the American Tropics.* Minneapolis: University of Minnesota Press, 2013.

Anzaldúa, Gloria. *Borderlands/La Frontera: The New Mestiza.* San Francisco: Aunt Lute Books, 2007.

Berlant, Lauren. "National Brands/National Body: *Imitation of Life.*" In *Comparative American Identities: Race, Sex, and Nationality in the Modern Text,* edited by Hortense Spillers, 110–40. New York: Routledge, 1991.

Bourdieu, Pierre. *Distinction: A Social Critique of the Judgement of Taste.* New York: Routledge, 2010.

Brown, Bill. "Reification, Reanimation, and the American Uncanny." *Critical Inquiry* 32 (2006): 175–207.

Carruth, Allison. *Global Appetites: American Power and the Literature of Food.* New York: Cambridge University Press, 2013.

Castillo, Debra A. *Talking Back: Toward a Latin American Feminist Literary Criticism.* Ithaca, NY: Cornell University Press, 1992.

Chen, Mel. *Animacies: Biopolitics, Racial Mattering, and Queer Affect.* Durham, NC: Duke University Press, 2012.

---

[107] James Hannaham, *Delicious Foods: A Novel* (New York: Little, Brown, 2015).

Cheng, Anne Anlin. "Sushi, Otters, Mermaids: Race at the Intersection of Food and Animal; or, David Wong Louie's Sushi Principle." *Resilience: Journal of the Environmental Humanities* 2.1 (2014). https://muse.jhu.edu/article/583709.

Cocks, Catherine. *Tropical Whites: The Rise of the Tourist South in the Americas.* Philadelphia: University of Pennsylvania Press, 2013.

Cruz, Denise. "'Love is Not a Bowl of Quinces': Food, Desire, and the Queer Asian Body in Monique Truong's *The Book of Salt*." In *Eating Asian America: A Food Studies Reader*, edited by Robert Ji-Song Ku, Martin F. Manalansan, and Anita Mannur 354–70. New York: New York University Press, 2013.

Diner, Hasia. *Hungering for America: Italian, Irish, and Jewish Foodways in the Age of Migration.* Cambridge, MA: Harvard University Press, 2001.

Douglas, Mary. *Purity and Danger: An Analysis of Concepts of Pollution and Taboo.* London: Routledge, 2002.

Dyer, Richard. *White.* London: Routledge, 1997.

Ehrhardt, Julia C. "Towards Queering Food Studies: Foodways, Heteronormativity, and Hungry Women in Chicana Lesbian Writing." *Food and Foodways* 14.2 (2006): 91–109.

Fiskio, Janet. "Unsettling Ecocriticism: Rethinking Agrarianism, Place, and Citizenship." *American Literature: Journal of Literary History, Criticism, and Biography* 84.2 (2012): 301–25.

Fretwell, Erica. "Emily Dickinson in Domingo." *J19: Journal of Nineteenth-Century Americanists* 1.1 (2013): 71–96.

Glissant, Édouard. *Poetics of Relation.* Translated by Betsy Wing. Ann Arbor: University of Michigan Press, 1997.

Hall, Stuart. "Old and New Identities, Old and New Ethnicities." In *Culture, Globalization, and the World-System: Contemporary Conditions for the Representation of Identity*, edited by Anthony D. King, 48–49. Minneapolis: University of Minnesota Press, 1997.

Hannaham, James. *Delicious Foods: A Novel.* New York: Little, Brown, 2015.

Hartman, Saidiya. *Scenes of Subjection: Terror, Slavery, and Self-Making in Nineteenth-Century America.* New York: Oxford University Press, 1997.

Henry, O. *Cabbages and Kings.* New York: Doubleday, Page, 1904.

Herrera, Cristina. "Delfina, ¡más tacos!: Food, Culture, and Motherhood in Denise Chávez's *A Taco Testimony*." *Food, Culture, and Society: International Journal of Multidisciplinary Research* 13.2 (2010): 241–56.

Ho, Jennifer. "Acting Asian American, Eating Asian American: The Politics of Race and Food in Don Lee's *Wrack and Ruin*." In *Eating Asian America: A Food Studies Reader*, edited by Robert Ji-Song Ku, Martin F. Manalansan, and Anita Mannur, 303–22. New York: New York University Press, 2013.

hooks, bell. *Black Looks: Race and Representation.* New York: Routledge, 2015.

Keyser, Catherine. "Bottles, Bubbles, and Blood: Jean Toomer and the Limits of Racial Epidermalism." *Modernism/modernity* 22.2 (2015): 279–302.

Lee, Chang-rae. *On Such a Full Sea.* New York: Riverhead Books, 2014.

Levenstein, Harvey. *Revolution at the Table: The Transformation of the American Diet*. New York: Oxford University Press, 1988.

Lévi-Strauss, Claude. *The Raw and the Cooked*. Translated by John and Doreen Weightman. New York: Harper & Row, 1969.

Loichot, Valérie. *The Tropics Bite Back: Culinary Coups in Caribbean Literature*. Minneapolis: University of Minnesota Press, 2013.

Lott, Eric. *Love and Theft: Blackface Minstrelsy and the American Working Class*. New York: Oxford University Press, 1993.

Mannur, Anita. *Culinary Fictions: Food in South Asian Diasporic Culture*. Philadelphia: Temple University Press, 2010.

"Perfection on a Plate: Readings in the South Asian Transnational Queer Kitchen." In *Eating Asian America: A Food Studies Reader*, edited by Robert Ji-Song Ku, Martin F. Manalansan, and Anita Mannur, 393–408. New York: New York University Press, 2013.

McKay, Claude. *Home to Harlem*. Boston: Northeastern University Press, 1987.

Merleaux, April. *Sugar and Civilization: American Empire and the Cultural Politics of Sweetness*. Chapel Hill: University of North Carolina Press, 2015.

Nunes, Zita. *Cannibal Democracy: Race and Representation in the Literature of the Americas*. Minneapolis: University of Minnesota Press, 2008.

O'Connor, Flannery. "The Artificial Nigger." In *A Good Man Is Hard to Find and Other Stories*, 103–32. New York: Houghton Mifflin, 1983.

Omi, Michael, and Howard Winant. *Racial Formation in the United States: From the 1960s to the 1990s*. 3rd ed. New York: Routledge/Taylor & Francis Group, 2014.

Pompa, Paul Martínez. "The Abuelita Poem." In *My Kill Adore Him*, 40–41. Notre Dame: University of Notre Dame Press, 2009.

Posmentier, Sonya. "The Provision Ground in New York: Claude McKay and the Form of Memory." *American Literature* 84.2 (2012): 273–300.

Rebolledo, Tey Diana. *Women Singing in the Snow: A Cultural Analysis of Chicana Literature*. Tucson: University of Arizona Press, 1995.

Roy, Parama. *Alimentary Tracts: Appetites, Aversions, and the Postcolonial*. Durham, NC: Duke University Press, 2010.

Sinclair, Upton. *The Jungle*. Edited by Russ Castronovo. New York: Oxford World Classics, 2010.

Spillers, Hortense. "Peter's Pans: Eating in the Diaspora." In *Black, White, and in Color: Essays on American Literature and Culture*. Chicago: University of Chicago Press, 2003.

Tompkins, Kyla Wazana. "'Hearty and happy and with a lively, yeasty soul': Feeling Right in Louisa May Alcott's *The Candy Country*." *Women and Performance: Journal of Feminist Theory* 24.2–3 (2014): 153–66.

Racial Indigestion: Eating Bodies in the Nineteenth Century. New York: New York University Press, 2012.

Viramontes, Helena María. *Under the Feet of Jesus*. New York: Penguin, 1995.

Walrond, Eric. *Tropic Death*. New York: Norton, 2013.

Warnes, Andrew. *Hunger Overcome?: Food and Resistance in Twentieth-Century African American Literature*. Athens: University of Georgia Press, 2004.

Weheliye, Alexander. *Habeas Viscus: Racializing Assemblages, Biopolitics, and Black Feminist Theories of the Human*. Durham, NC: Duke University Press, 2014.

Williams, Laura Anh. "Foodways and Subjectivity in Jhumpa Lahiri's *Interpreter of Maladies*." *MELUS* 32.4 (2007): 69–79.

Williams-Forson, Psyche. *Building Houses Out of Chicken Legs: Black Women, Food, and Power*. Chapel Hill: University of North Carolina, 2006.

Witt, Doris. *Black Hunger: Soul Food and America*. Minneapolis: University of Minnesota, 2004.

Wong, Sau-ling Cynthia. *Reading Asian American Literature: From Necessity to Extravagance*. Princeton: Princeton University Press, 2001.

Xu, Wenying. *Eating Identities: Reading Food in Asian American Literature*. Honolulu: University of Hawai'i Press, 2008.

Zafar, Rafia. "The Signifying Dish: Autobiography and History in Two Black Women's Cookbooks." *Feminist Studies* 25.2 (1999): 449–69.

CHAPTER 8

The Ethics of Eating Together
The Case of French Postcolonial Literature

Valérie Loichot

Novelist Simone Schwarz-Bart and philosopher Jacques Derrida spent their childhoods in two geographically, historically, culturally, linguistically distinct zones of the French colonial Empire, respectively Guadeloupe and Algeria. While their relationships to France and French colonialism seem dissimilar, they both belong to these colonial zones as a result of aleatory historical and familial paths. Schwarz-Bart descends from enslaved Africans who were brought to Guadeloupe by a tragic twist of fate and the steel hand of human traffickers. Derrida was born in Algiers, as he claims, due to a "final throw of the dice."[1] Both Schwarz-Bart and Derrida occupy a position of being "less French," albeit in different ways. While inhabitants from overseas departments such as Guadeloupe, Martinique, and the Reunion Island are politically French citizens, have been French citizens for longer than some European French, such as Alsatians, they are often culturally perceived as "Frenchness deficient" because of their religion, ethnicity, and, to be completely candid, the color of their skin.[2] The French state under the Vichy Régime of World War II stripped Jacques Derrida, like other famous Jews of Algeria such as Hélène Cixous, of their French citizenship through the revocation of the *Crémieux Decree* in 1940. They abruptly became stateless, *heimatlos*. Thus, Schwarz-Bart and Derrida are both crippled citizens of sorts.

I do not claim to reduce Schwarz-Bart's and Derrida's multivalent works and complex relationship toward the French Nation to autobiography.

---

[1] "Un coup de poker." Geoffrey Bennington and Jacques Derrida, *Jacques Derrida* (Paris: Seuil, 1991), 43. All translations are mine, unless listed otherwise in the bibliography.

[2] See French Guyanese poet Léon Gontran Damas' acute portrayal of the lack of Frenchness projected onto the language of black and mulatto subjects in his poem "Hoquet": "Le français de France, le français français, le français du français" [The French of France, the French French, the French of the French]. In the poem, a "deficiency" in speaking French is strongly associated with eating "French" improperly, and with practicing the wrong religion. Damas, *Pigments* (Paris: Présence africaine, 2001), 37.

Rather, I begin with these few apparently "simple" facts to introduce the enmeshment of self and politics during problematic, at times even tortured, relations to colonialism, empire, citizenship, and nation. But why begin with politics in a chapter devoted to the ethics of eating together? My main argument is that Schwarz-Bart and Derrida, as well as other authors faced with the daily and historical relation to colonialism, respond to political ostracism not with a parallel oppositional politics, but, rather, with an ethics. I mean ethics in its ancient Greek sense of that which is related to customs, the customary, the quotidian, and thus communal acts of living together. Such an ethics is specifically interested in commensality.[3] When the political hurts, the customary resists. The stronghold of customary resistance is culinary expression. The privileged site of ethical resistance is the scene of eating together. Thus, the two authors express their ethics of resistance in surprisingly similar terms: "Manger seul n'est pas manger" (Eating alone is not eating), declares Schwarz-Bart; "On ne mange jamais tout seul" (We never eat all alone), seconds Derrida.[4]

Eating is an essential function that qualifies us as basic living animals. Taken a step further, *eating together*, or commensality, when articulated as cooking and the sharing of food defines us as humans, members of families, social groups, religions, and nations, as many an anthropologist, theologian, philosopher, psychologist, and historian has discussed and theorized.[5] From the milk transmitted from mother to child to the couscous, apple pie, ajiaco, fufu, maqluba, röesti, gumbo, paella we share as immediately recognizable to our respective communities; to eating around a bowl with the right hand; to sitting straight at a table with forks and knives; to lifting dainty pinkies in tea ceremonies, our eating habits define us first as a child to its parent, then as a member to its community. Conversely, and as radically, our eating ways define us as uncouth or even "savage," in the eyes of others who do not share our ways: *frogs, Krauts, cannibals* aggressively define outsiders to a group.

Ideally, there is a smooth transition from milk transmission, to family meals, to eating properly in a cultural group. Ideally, there is a seamless

---

[3] See Chapter 1 in this volume.

[4] Simone Schwarz-Bart, "Du fond des casseroles," in *Nouvelles de Guadeloupe* (Paris: Miniatures, 2009), 80; Jacques Derrida, " 'Il faut bien manger' ou le calcul du sujet," in Points de suspension (Paris: Galilée, 1992), 297.

[5] To start with the basics, see Claude Lévi-Strauss, *The Raw and the Cooked: Introduction to a Science of Mythology* (New York: Harper & Row, 1969); Roland Barthes, *Mythologies*, selected and translated by Annette Lavers (New York: Hill and Wang, 1995); Maggie Kilgour, *From Communion to Cannibalism: An Anatomy of Metaphors of Incorporation* (Princeton: Princeton University Press, 1990); Sydney W. Mintz, *Tasting Food, Tasting Freedom* (Boston: Beacon Press, 1996).

passage between the ontogenic and the phylogenic. For Martinican psychiatrist Frantz Fanon, the situation in which "there's no disproportion between familial life and national life" constitutes the model for white European communities.[6] For Fanon, racism, enslavement, and colonialism sever these ties for subjects faced with and shaped by these controlling forces.[7]

There is a violent interruption when a mother's milk is made to deviate from its family flow, as the character Sethe, from Toni Morrison's *Beloved*, cries bitterly, " 'And they took my milk.' "[8] When a nursing mother becomes a feeding machine for the children of planters; when a human being is reduced to a commodity that feeds the machine of slavery; when a French president-to-be declares that food prepared by immigrants "smells";[9] when pronouncing food names with an imperfect accent becomes the pretext to decide who will live or die – as in *shibboleth* or *parajil*;[10] when *good* relations, ethical relations, in a group become interrupted, skewed, or invaded by the political: this is precisely when an ethics of eating together, such as that proposed by Derrida and Schwarz-Bart, matter.

The Cannibal and the Famished

My book, *The Tropics Bite Back*, analyzed tropes and customs of eating in the colonized Tropics, specifically the Caribbean.[11] I will not rehash my detailed arguments and will invite you to read the book as well as literary critic Njeri Githire's *Cannibal Writes*.[12] I will, however, give a quick summary of the main narratives that drove my argument. In my analysis, actions and representations of eating and cooking were polarized around two extreme positions: excessive and transgressive eating represented by

---

[6] Frantz Fanon, *Peau noire, masques blancs* (Paris: Seuil, 1952), 116.

[7] Ibid., 115–17.

[8] Toni Morrison, *Beloved* (New York: Knopf, 1987), 19.

[9] See Jacques Chirac's "Discours d'Orléans" (1991), in which the then Mayor of Paris denounced "le bruit et l'odeur" (the noise and stench) of ethnic minorities in France, www.ina.fr/video/ CAB91027484.

[10] At different times and in different spaces, the words *shibboleth* ("ear of corn") and *parajil* ("parsley") were used to segregate and eliminate those who were not part of a ruling group and failed to pronounce the word correctly, respectively in the massacre of Ephraimites by Gileadites and Haitians by Dominicans. See Book of Judges 12:4–6; Edwidge Danticat, *The Farming of Bones* (New York: Penguin, 1998), 193–94.

[11] Valérie Loichot, *The Tropics Bite Back: Culinary Coups in Caribbean Literature* (Minneapolis: University of Minnesota Press, 2013).

[12] Njeri Githire, *Cannibal Writes: Eating Others in Caribbean and Indian Ocean Women's Writing* (Urbana Champaign: University of Illinois Press, 2014).

the figures of the glutton and the cannibal, and dismal hunger represented by figures of the starved slave or citizen and the hulking zombie. From Columbus' journal to twenty-first century contemporary poetry and narrative, these two parallel narratives unfolded.

On one side runs the cannibal narrative. Indeed, the name and figure of the cannibal were born with the first European-Amerindian contact when, as I explained in *Tropics Bite Back*, Columbus resurrected, through a fantasist interpretation of the name of a nation, *caríba* ("Caribs") the tremendous figure of the caníbal (cannibal). Mishearing the consonants, Columbus' mind wandered into Greco-Latin mythology and its figure of the anthropophagous *canis*, the dog-headed man-eater, which quickly merged with the *cari* of *caríba*. Thus, the conqueror spat out the word that became the enduring stereotype of the cannibal.[13] Europeans consecutively applied the image of the cannibal to those they constructed as absolute others: first the Amerindians, then the Africans.[14] Reciprocally, albeit with less catastrophic consequences, enslaved Africans and pillaged Amerindians qualified the machine of slavery, slave ships, slave traders, and colonizers as absolute cannibals.[15] The trope of cannibalism became, for Renaissance thinker Michel de Montaigne, the epitome of cultural relativism. In his essay "Of Cannibals," which is actually a criticism of the French wars of religion under the guise of a narrative of the Brazilian *Tupi* or *Tupinamba*, Montaigne ironically implies that the cannibal is not the one we think, but that there is more savagery in the French wars of religions than in the highly codified *Tupinamba* ritual cannibalism. For Montaigne, Tupi cannibalism constitutes an integral part of an ethics of commensality, of memory transmission, of hospitality – in the sense of taking in the host's body, the enemy's body, into one's own physiological and cultural body – and is reciprocal: "For they will be eating at the same time their own fathers and grandfathers, who have served to feed and nourish [the enemy's] body ... Savor them well. You will find in them the taste of your own flesh."[16]

Significantly, from an intellectual history and aesthetics perspective, artists and writers from the Americas soon brandished the figure of the

---

[13] See Frank Lestringant's compelling history of the birth of the cannibal in European fictions. Lestringant, *Le Cannibale: Grandeur et décadence* (Paris: Perrin, 1994).

[14] See ibid., 28.

[15] See C. L. R. James, *Black Jacobins* (New York: Vintage, 1989), 7; Jack D. Forbes, *Columbus and Other Cannibals: The Wétiko Disease of Exploitation, Imperialism, and Terrorism* (New York: Seven Stories Press, 2008), 9–25.

[16] Michel de Montaigne, *The Complete Essays of Montaigne*, translated by Donald Frame (Stanford: Stanford University Press, 1958), 158.

cannibal as their own – the *Caníbal* being revived through its new association with the Carib. They used the aesthetic gesture of "eating the other" as a revenge against a cannibalistic colonialism that pillaged and obliterated. Brazilian modernist Oswald de Andrade's and Martinican essayist Suzanne Roussi Césaire's respective cries of war – "Tupi or not Tupi, that is the question" and "Martinican poetry will be cannibal or will not be"[17] – epitomize this extended movement of cultural and aesthetic cannibalism, which is, like Montaigne's, based on revenge, survival, and cultural reciprocity. The Brazilian writer who "eats" Shakespeare's words as revenge for the European pillage of Brazil also conserves the English dramaturge's text, and, in turn, inhabits the body of the English literary canon.[18]

The figure of the famished runs parallel to, yet in intricate relation with, the cannibal narrative. An estimated 15–20 percent of Africans deported from their native continent to the Americas perished in the hold of the cannibal slave ship, dying from disease, thirst, hunger, or drowning as a result of the inhuman economic motivation of lighting the ship of its cargo. On the plantation, legal slave codes such as the *Code noir* prescribed an economic formula in which enslaved humans were maintained in a constant state of hunger while eating just enough to produce.[19] Creole folktales told during slavery abounded with hulking starving figures, such as Yé, "Master of Famine," who was enchained by his stomach to the system of slavery.[20] Aimé Césaire in his poignant *Cahier d'un retour au pays natal* stages a personified hunger who smothers the Martinican subject. The hunger inhabiting Césaire's *Cahier* is abysmal, plunging into the bottomless swamps of hunger ("les marais de la faim").[21] Twenty-first-century writers and filmmakers such as Edwidge Danticat, Dany Laferrière, and Michelange Quay linger on starving Haitian citizens and a nation depleted again and again of food and natural resources.[22]

---

[17] Oswald de Andrade, "Cannibalist Manifesto" (1928), translated by Leslie Bary, Latin American Literary Review 19.38 (1991): 38; Suzanne Césaire, Le grand camouflage: Écrits de dissidence (1941–1945) (Paris: Seuil, 2009), 66.

[18] See Luís Madureira, Cannibal Modernities: Postcoloniality and the Avant-Garde in Caribbean and Brazilian Literature (Charlottesville: University of Virginia Press, 2005).

[19] Le Code noir (Paris: L'Esprit frappeur, 1998).

[20] See "Yé, Master of Famine," in Patrick Chamoiseau, Creole Folktales (New York: New Press, 1994), 75–84.

[21] Aimé Césaire, Cahier d'un retour au pays natal (Paris: Présence africaine, 1983), 12.

[22] See Danticat, Farming of Bones; Mange, Ceci est mon corps, directed by Michelange Quay (Paris: Cinéma de Facto, 2007); Dany Laferrière, Pays sans chapeau (Paris: Le Serpent à plumes, 1999).

The cannibal narrative and the famished narrative constitute two sides of one coin. Aimé Césaire stages the rum factory workers' hulking hunger as a direct consequence of the sugar-production machine that is described as "vomiting its exhaustions of men."[23] The acute confusion between the starved enslaved and the cannibal eater is caused by an enormous irony: that those in an extreme state of vulnerability, hunger, and depravation were represented in fiction and colonial discourses as the threatening figure of the monstrous cannibal. *The Tropics Bite Back*, as its title indicates, scrutinizes the productive revenge of *eating* the colonial other in constructive acts of literary and culinary creations.

A Symposium

The coda to *Tropics Bite Back*, in contrast with the body of the book, turned to a non-antagonistic relation to food in the postcolonial context: that of eating together. My book dealt with reestablishing balance between the disproportionate objectification of the Caribbean subjects as cannibals, and the agency of Caribbean writers to use precisely the trope of the cannibalism to perform an act of legitimate revenge against the colonizer's discourse.[24] I realized, nonetheless, that the focus on this antagonistic relationship to eating overshadowed the importance of community-building acts of eating together omnipresent in Caribbean literature. Commensality and cannibalism are often evoked with a passion in the works of a single author. For instance, Guadeloupean novelist Maryse Condé champions "literary cannibalism" in her Caribbean rewriting of Emily Brontë's *Wuthering Heights* (1847), *La Migration des cœurs*.[25] She also wrote *Histoire de la femme cannibale*, a highly ironic novel on the hypertrophic representation of black women as cannibals in post-Apartheid South-Africa.[26] Three years later, Condé published *Victoire, la saveur et les mots*, a homage to her grandmother Victoire Élodie Quidal, a domestic cook, whose meals consolidate generations, like a writer's words would: "Lost in deep thoughts in front of her stove like a writer in front of her computer."[27] Culinary

---

[23] Césaire, *Cahier*, 11.

[24] Similarly to Peter Hulme, who worked to demonstrate the disproportion between representations of the cannibal and actual acts of cannibalism. Hulme, "Introduction: The Cannibal Scene," in *Cannibalism and the Colonial World*, edited by Francis Barker, Peter Hulme, and Margaret Iversen (Cambridge: Cambridge University Press, 1998), 3–5.

[25] Maryse Condé, *La Migration des cœurs* (Paris: Robert Laffont, 1994), published in English as *Windward Heights* in 2003.

[26] Maryse Condé, *Histoire de la femme cannibale* (Paris: Mercure de France, 2005), published in English as *The Story of the Cannibal Woman* in 2008.

[27] Maryse Condé, *Victoire, les saveurs et les mots* (Paris: Mercure de France, 2006), 85.

creation abolishes the distance between cook grandmother and writer granddaughter, separated by time, social class, and level of education. In Condé's novel, food does not only bite back, does not only cut, but also consolidates communities across time.

The most striking example of the coincidence of the passion for eating together and the cannibal trope is perhaps best illustrated in the seven published essays by Roussi Césaire, published in the Martinican review *Tropiques* (1941–45) and collected in *The Great Camouflage*. Recall, Roussi Césaire is the author who, in October 1941, screamed her cannibal scream: "Martinican poetry will be cannibal or will not be." In *Tropics Bite Back*, I analyzed in depth Roussi Césaire's practice of literary cannibalism, and her complex relation of eating/eater, and relations of power – sexual, generational, colonial – with French leader of surrealism, André Breton. However, I did not get a chance to focus much on the trope of "eating together" in her essay, which we could call "Suzanne Roussi Césaire's symposium." I mean "symposium" in the Greek sense of the term, derived from *sympotein*, which means, literally, "to drink together." My question about her work is: can we offer food and libations to one's hosts while devouring them? Can commensality and cannibalism coincide? One could reply that it is one of the principle rules of cannibalism. According to early accounts such as Montaigne's, and more contemporary ones such as the Brazilian film *How Tasty Was My Little Frenchman*, cannibalism goes hand in hand with hospitality. Not only is the French "guest" well fed for practical reasons (provide a fleshier meal), but he is also given a woman as well as luxurious accommodations. We could even go further by associating cannibalism, as the act of taking the other inside oneself, with the Eucharist and communion. After all, as etymology shows and as Derrida has articulated, hospitality, the host, and *hostia* are imbricated.[28] Hence hospitality, hostility, the hospital, and *hostia* refer to ambivalent relations to the other which are both antagonistic and communal, in that they blur the differences between self and other.[29] Such is the case of Roussi Césaire's symposium, in which the receiving host, Suzanne, simultaneously feeds (symbolically as well as literally) and devours her guests (symbolically but not literally). The interchangeability of host and guest is even more compelling in French since the word "hôte" defines both.

Roussi Césaire's seven essays indeed function like a banquet or symposium à la Plato, in which the hosts are conveyed to share the author's

[28] See Jacques Derrida and Anne Dufourmantelle, *De l'hospitalité* (Paris: Calmann-Lévy, 1997).
[29] See Kilgour, *From Communion to Cannibalism*.

literary table in order to expose their ideas in the form of a dialogue. Césaire's textual literary guests include André Breton, the Bible, Sigmund Freud, Leo Frobénius, Friedrich Nietzsche, and William Shakespeare, among many others. Roussi Césaire ingests bits and pieces of their words, transforms, and subverts them. For instance, her cannibal motto is a performative act of cannibalism since she ingests and regurgitates in a new form Breton's surrealist definition of beauty from his novel *Nadja*: "Beauty will be convulsive or will not be."[30] The hosts turn into *hostia*, in the sense that their words become something sacred that transforms both the eater and the eaten. The "Pope of surrealism," Breton, in particular, is simultaneously hosted in Césaire's textual body (he is the most cited, ingested author in her essays),[31] and he is also a guest in the flesh at Suzanne and Aimé Césaire's table. During his brief, forced stopover in Martinique during World War II, Breton joins the Césaires' dinner table, spends evenings on their balcony, and visits the island with them. It is thus not only literary cannibalism, but also a lived experience of receiving hospitality.

Plato's *Symposium* provides further insight into this specific situation of commensality, where an ethical relationship is invaded by the political, as evoked earlier, and further complicates this relation of hospitality with a visit from Eros. Apollodorus, who crashed the party, delivers the main speech that he collected from Aristodemus, a disciple of Socrates.[32] Aristodemus also attends the banquet without having been invited.[33] From its prologue, Plato's text complicates the rules of narrative transmission, as well as those of hospitality. It also troubles the very etymology of the banquet as *sympotein*, or "drinking together," since the hungover guests, head heavy from yesterday's libations, decide not to drink or to drink only a little.[34] To complicate things, the slaves serving at the banquet are asked to serve as house hosts. The philosophers will not be "masters" but "dinnerguests."[35] Plato's narrative, not unlike Roussi Césaire's practice, undergoes destabilizing since the narrative is told from intermediary to intermediary and they often forget what had been said in the first place. More crucially, the master–slave relation is turned on its head since the slaves become hosts in a position of offering hospitality. Roussi Césaire's banquet is similarly invaded by the political since, on many levels, Breton is in a position

---

[30] André Breton, *Nadja* (Paris: Gallimard, 1964), 91
[31] See Loichot, *Tropics Bite Back*.
[32] Plato, *Symposium*, translated by Robin Waterfield (Oxford: Oxford University Press, 1994), 174A.
[33] Ibid., 174B.
[34] Ibid., 176a.
[35] Ibid., 175c.

of power in relation to the young Césaire couple. He is the leading figure of surrealism. He cultivates a paternalistic, albeit protective, stance toward the Césaires, and visits an old colony of France and its colonial subjects, the Césaires, from the French capital or *Métropole*. The problematics expressed in Plato return in the Martinican banquet: the slaves are asked to serve as masters of the house. However, they still do so under command, and are thus still enslaved in an intersecting web of power dynamics. Equally, Roussi Césaire is in a similar precarious relation to a limited power, which is further complicated by Eros. Just like Plato's *Symposium*'s main subject is not drinking or eating but love, Breton's imperial stance over Roussi Césaire is reinforced in the love poems he writes to her on postcards,[36] turning a powerful writer in her own right into an emblematic muse who, as I show in *Tropics Bite Back*, both conveys in her symposium the surrealist writer and takes revenge by cannibalizing his words in her essays.

Eating Together

In her autobiographically inspired essay "Du Fond des casseroles" (From the bottom of the pans), Schwarz-Bart recalls that her grandfather, when he plucked fruit from the trees or picked vegetables from his garden "would leave part of it on the side of the road." The grandfather's gesture, she adds "had a double meaning: to give back to nature a part of its due, and to share ahead all the meals from his crops."[37] This circular and reciprocal transaction of taking and giving back to the land is particularly significant in the Martinican context in which the forced labor of the enslaved dominated the economy between the sixteenth and late nineteenth century (if not for longer). For the enslaved women and men working in the fields in particular, their relationship to food was an interrupted, tortured one, in which humans worked the land for a profit that escaped them completely. While mass-produced cash crops such as sugar, indigo, coffee, and bananas were exported, the product of the sales reserved to the Béké ethnoclass, the enslaved complemented their meager food allowance with small garden plots that they could cultivate in the little time left free from the legal dawn-to-dusk work time imposed by slave codes. Similarly, the land was exploited, exhausted, deforested, and weakened by the extensive production of cash crops, and deprived of its minerals as well as the roots

---

[36] See André Breton, *Martinique Snake Charmer*, translated by David Seaman and introduced by Franklin Rosemont (Austin: University of Texas Press, 2008).

[37] Schwarz-Bart, "Du fond des casseroles," 80.

that maintained its stability. Schwartz-Bart's grandfather's early twentieth century was thus a time of reestablishing reciprocal connections of nourishment between land and humans. Thus, the grandfather farmer gave back to nature "a part of its due" and also ensured a connection between his generation and the next by "sharing ahead."

While not explicitly expressed in Schwartz-Bart's essay, leaving fruit and vegetables on the side of the road has a sure agricultural composting function, but also a sacred one. The land is indeed strongly connected to the presence of ancestors in Caribbean sacred practices, which are shaped by African-derived religions. For example, the placenta of a child is buried with the roots of a newly planted tree in a process called "twinning." The two then grow intricately connected and look alike.[38] The yams, growing deep roots, strongly connect to the departed of a community.[39] In Nigerian novelist Chinua Achebe's *Things Fall Apart*, sharing food carries the same triple function of consolidation: reinforcing links between community members in the present time; establishing continuity between past, present, and future; and ensuring a sacred connection between the villagers and their dear departed. A community elder in Achebe's novel presages that ceasing to eat together would have dramatic consequences for the community:

> A man who calls his kinsmen to a feast does not do so to save them from starving. They all have food in their own homes ... We come together because it is good for kinsmen to do so. You may ask why I am saying all this. I say this because I fear for the younger generation, for you people.[40]

Achebe's notion of "eating together" clearly carries an ethics: "we come together because it is *good*" (my emphasis). This "good" or "bien" similarly feeds Derrida's reflection on eating together. Let's specify first that Derrida builds his discourse on a French pun or multiple-entendre. "Il faut bien manger" refers to an imperative of life.[41] In the first interpretation, "bien" simply has an emphatic function: "one must eat," "il faut bien manger," implicitly, in order to survive. This basic physiological imperative is complicated by the casual, quotidian pleasure associated with eating. "Il faut bien manger" also means "one must eat healthily," as the mother would tell her child in order to go to school with a belly full of a balanced

[38] See ibid., 175.
[39] See Mintz, *Tasting Food, Tasting Freedom*; Ntozake Shange, *If I Can Cook/You Know God Can* (Boston: Beacon Press, 1998).
[40] Chinua Achebe, *Things Fall Apart* (London: Heinemann, 1958), 155.
[41] Derrida, "Il faut bien manger," 269–301.

meal. "Bien manger" also refers to the quotidian, culinary pleasure linked to an aesthetic experience, as in "I ate well in this fantastic restaurant." Finally, and philosophically, like Achebe, Derrida refers to the philosophical *good* or *bien* implied in an ethical practice. Derrida's deceptively simple quotidian expression shelters a host of characteristics of what constitutes life, and, crucially, what constitutes a good life, living well, including physiology, health, pleasure, aesthetics, and ethics.

Like in Schwartz-Bart and Achebe, "bien manger," "eating well," or should we use the colloquium expression "eating good," which could also refer to the ethical good, is inseparable from the good of eating with a community. Schwartz-Bart's "Eating alone is not eating," echoes in Derrida's ethics of eating:

> The question of the "we must eat well' can't only be nourishing to myself, for a myself, who would then eat badly ... We must eat well does not primarily mean to take and to comprehend within oneself but to learn to feed, to learn-to-feed-the-other. We never eat all alone, this is the rule of the "we must eat well." It is a law of infinite hospitality.[42]

While Derrida's ethical imperative of "learning-to-feed-the-other" is undeniably metaphorical, as in exchanging language, it must also be taken quite literally in considering that food exchange and circulation has crucial implications for living together in ethical good and in a political balance. "You know that, against all appearance, I now speak of very 'concrete' and 'timely' issues," Derrida interjects.[43] In this model, one doesn't devour or assimilate the other in a flattening-difference bulldozing but, instead, learns to feed the other. In our very contemporary time, this practice of infinite and reciprocal hospitality seems to be, to say the least, interrupted, if not violated, by politics. In order to receive and to give hospitality, one needs a home. If we shift the individual relations of hospitality to the level of state relations, and if states are increasingly homeless, *unheimlich*, if national homes become fortresses, then we increasingly eat alone.

Eating Alone

Colonial politics disturbs and ultimately threatens this good, ethical way of being together as a community. Schwarz-Bart and Achebe both describe this nurturing and ethical eating together nostalgically as a thing of the

[42] Ibid., 296–97.
[43] Ibid., 299.

past. Achebe's elder prophesizes the downfall of the community when the "younger generation" will cease to eat together. Things fall apart when missionaries and colonists break the village's basic epistemic, religious, and social structures. Schwarz-Bart's grandfather lived at a time when "the Antillean way of life was still intact for the people."[44] We can venture that the intact "Antillean way of life" was disrupted by the 1948 Law of Departmentalization, which turned Martinique into a "French Overseas Department" with all the economic, social, and political consequences that Martinican philosopher Édouard Glissant scrutinizes in depth and breadth in his 1981 *Discours antillais*.[45]

In fresh memory and in our lived contemporaneity, a new type of colonial interruption of the ethics of living together, and living well together, has shaken the former center of the French Empire. Notably, in Nice, July 2016, a terrorist, a madman, massacred indiscriminately with his truck nearly one hundred people, including Catholics, Muslims, Jews, agnostics, and laicists; women, children, and men; French citizens and foreign nationals. A few weeks later, *The Guardian* reported that the police ordered a woman to remove her head scarf and shirt on the beach of the Promenade des Anglais, a few feet away from the stage of the July 14, 2016 massacre. Sunbathers in bikinis shouted at her to go back home.[46]

Contemporary French novelist Michel Houellebecq, known for his provocative ways and distasteful misogyny is also arguably one of the most influential French writers of the twenty-first century. His dystopian – yet close to home, some will say prophetic – 2015 novel *Soumission* describes the manifestation of the French fear of Islam consolidated in an extreme faith in *laïcité* or secularism. In a novel full of misogyny, gender, racial stereotyping (including French white men), and aggression, French politics is now dominated by fictional politician Mohammed Ben Abbes, candidate of the fictional party "La Fraternité Musulmane" (Muslim Brotherhood).[47] Ben Abbes' sole opponent is politician Marine Le Pen, current head of the Front National in real life. The two mainstream parties of the traditional right and left have lost their footing, and the political

[44] Schwarz-Bart, "Du fond des casseroles," 80.
[45] Édouard Glissant, *Caribbean Discourse: Selected Essays*, translated by Michael J. Dash (Charlottesville: University Press of Virginia, 1989).
[46] Ben Quinn, "French Police Make Woman Remove Clothing on Nice Beach Following Burkini Ban," *Guardian*, August 23, 2016, www.theguardian.com/world/2016/aug/24/french-police-make-woman-remove-burkini-on-nice-beach.
[47] I thank literary critic Nicolas Rémy for his insights on Houellebecq and masculinity.

forces now concentrate in these two extremes, constituting a "symmetrical schismogenesis," to use anthropologist Gregory Bateson's concept.[48]

In a French society fractured by insidious religious and political factions, food is omnipresent in the life of the main protagonist, François, aptly named after the moribund fictional French nation. The middle-aged university literature professor, severely bored and blasé, attains rare titillation, not from sex with multiple multiethnic "call girls," but, rather, from eating. The food, painted in minute detail, is extremely varied and includes "exotic" global meals such as "chicken tikka masala," Moroccan dishes such as tagine, and hearty classics of French cuisine such as "pot-au-feu."[49] Significantly for this discussion on eating together in the French (post)colonial situation, Houellebecq was born in the French Overseas Department of Reunion Island, and then spent his early boyhood with his maternal grandparents in Algiers during the transition between a war-torn Algeria and the new independent nation. This autobiographical detour shows us that Houellebecq, too, who is a "very French"[50] writer at least in the eyes of his readership, is also directly shaped by a (post)colonial childhood, agglutinating origins, not unlike the meals his character favors.

Literary critic Jean-Marc Quaranta devoted a critical monograph and cookbook, *Houellebecq aux fourneaux*, to cooking in the contemporary writer's novels. As Quaranta astutely remarks, the story told by food in *Soumission* provides a counter-narrative of a "multiculturalist integration" in sharp contrast with the novel's setting of an antagonistically polarized society: "The most spectacular fact in *Soumission* is that the culinary subtext seems to say the opposite of what the text pretends to be saying."[51] For Quaranta, the fact that Mediterranean delicacies such as baklava and fava beans are served in the same meal with "croustade landaise aux pommes," southwestern France's equivalent of a Pennsylvania apple pie, provides a counter-narrative not of "invasion" but of eating well together. I was left with the same opinion as Quaranta upon my first reading of *Soumission*, interpreting the following description as praise for harmonious diversity: "de la blanquette de veau, du colin au cerfeuil, de la

[48] Gregory Bateson, "Culture Contact and Schismogenesis," *Man* 35 (December 1935): 178–83.

[49] Late eighteenth-century gastronome and philosopher of taste Brillat-Savarin describes *pot-au-feu* as the "basic broth of French national diet, which century-long experience helped bring to perfection." Jean Anthelme Brillat-Savarin, *Physiologie du goût* (Paris: Flammarion, 1982), 82.

[50] I use this formula to approximate the untranslatable term "*Français de souche*" or "French from the roots."

[51] Jean-Marc Quaranta, "Toute l'œuvre de Michel Houellebecq décortiquée par le menu," *Munchies*, June 23, 2016, https://munchies.vice.com/fr/articles/toute-loeuvre-de-michel-houellebecq-decortiquee-par-le-menu.

moussaka berbère."⁵² *Blanquette de veau* represents the hearty, working-class, French-French meal, *colin au cerfeuil* a nouvelle cuisine and upper-class, health-conscious dish, and the puzzling "Berber Musaka," a strange amalgam of Mediterranean cuisine conflating Greece and North Africa in one made-up meal absent from cookbooks, which seems to be an entirely houellebecquian creation since all Google hits for the dish refer to his novel.

However, if we shift the question from the "what of eating" to "how of eating," as David Goldstein puts it in the opening chapter of this volume and in his book, our understanding starts to shift. We take an even sharper turn when we question the "with whom of eating." We then get a dent in our optimism about the ability to eat together, to eat well, and to eat together well. With the exception of one pleasurable moment of commensality, the decadent French professor eats desperately alone. For Schwarz-Bart, if "eating alone is not eating," then the François character does not eat at all.

Smack in the middle of the novel, François is invited for dinner over at his university colleague (a Balzac specialist) and her husband's home. Marie-Françoise (also aptly named after the vulnerable nation – Françoise – and Catholicism – Marie), is a refined French cook, a chef *cuisinière*: "Elle avait préparé des tartelettes au cou de canard et aux échalotes délicieuses."⁵³ The dish, involving pies with duck necks, evokes the gastronomy of an aristocrat medieval and feudal past. After the shared meal, the narrator exclaims: "It had been a while since I had eaten that well."⁵⁴ "Eating well," "bien manger," happens in rare temporal oasis ("it had been a while"). "Eating well" also resides in the nostalgic space of François' pet author, the decadent turn-of-the-century novelist Joris-Karl Huysmans. According to the narrator, absolute happiness for Huysmans is "bourgeoisie happiness" epitomized in "honest home-cooking" and represented by "a merry meal shared amongst friends and artists, a pot-au-feu with its raifort sauce, served with an 'honest' wine."⁵⁵ This is a true scene of commensality since the guests are a comfortable community of "artists and friends." The recurrence of the adjective "honest," in the sense of "good," associated with French bourgeois cuisine may imply that other types of cuisine are dishonest.

"Honest" also points to an ordinariness leaning toward mediocrity: not too luxurious a wine, yet drinkable and good enough. This averageness

---

⁵² Michel Houellebecq, *Soumission* (Paris: Flammerion, 2015), 120–21.
⁵³ Ibid., 151.
⁵⁴ Ibid., 159.
⁵⁵ Ibid., 281.

resembles the French, white, mediocre man with whom François identifies: "As an average Occidental man ... I was unable to live for myself, and for whom else would I have lived?"[56] The "how of eating" in the novel corroborates François' absolute loneliness and barred relations not only with others, but also with himself. Numerous scenes in the novel present him reheating his packaged Very French and exotic meals, ordering from "Rapid'Sushi," and eating in front of the TV.[57] The "ethnic" dishes on his plate are microwaved meals, whose neat packaging indicates an absolute isolation from their context. They are ready to be consumed, submitted to the palate, as dead. If *Soumission*, the novel's title, can be interpreted as the submission of "Western men" to growing Islamist and Nationalist extremisms, and of women to men, it can also be applied to the tamed microwaved food, packaged and swallowed easily, and, by extension, to the eater, himself packaged as the average white, occidental French man. As François mindlessly teaches his literature seminar, his thought can only weakly wander between the false choices facing him that night: "Which Indian dish could I reheat in the microwave tonight? Chicken Biryani? Chicken Tikka Masala? Chicken Rogan Josh?"[58]

François has one semi-serious romantic relationship in the novel. His "copine" (girlfriend) Myriam, a former student of his, is about to relocate to Israel with her family to escape anti-Semitism in France. Myriam's love for France is comically reduced to her infatuation for French cheese: "[Myriam:] 'I love France! ... I love ... I don't know ... I love cheese! ... [François:] 'I do have cheese! I do!' ... Saint Marcellin, Comté, and blue cheese from the Causses. I had also bought a nice bottle of white wine. She couldn't have cared less."[59] Myriam's words contradict her actions since she ignores the food and wine and neglects to eat it. Her attachment to the country is only putative. For a variety of circumstances, such as sushi delivered too late, she never eats with François, thus putting into question their very togetherness. Conversely, François is irked by, even jealous of, Myriam's commensality: "Myriam, at over twenty, still ate with her family every night ... They were a tribe, a tightly knit family tribe, and in light of what I'd gone through, I had to refrain from sobbing."[60] The family tribe, as a distinct part of a larger group, no longer functions for the average very-French man François who has lost allegiance to nation,

---

[56] Ibid., 207.
[57] Ibid., 44.
[58] Ibid., 37.
[59] Ibid., 104.
[60] Ibid., 111.

religion, family. When François receives the official written news that his mother was dead and buried in a pauper's grave ("le carré des indigents") he feels slightly irritated but can't be bothered to give her a proper grave.[61] This isolation from family goes hand in hand with the relation to France, the *Mère-Patrie*, for which François only feels annoyance. Myriam's familial commensality continues in their embracing a nation as shelter. François' farewell words to Myriam are: "'Il n'y a pas d'Israël pour moi.'" (For me, there's no Israel).[62] At the opening of this chapter, we saw that an incomplete Frenchness, a crippled Frenchness imposed on the colonized, the enslaved, ethnic and religious minorities, and migrants, facilitated ethical ways of eating together. In contrast, François' very-Frenchness, and the desperate desire for a nation to remain very-French, forbid functional relations and the *good* of eating together. Politics trump the ethics of eating together.

BIBLIOGRAPHY

Achebe, Chinua. *Things Fall Apart*. London: Heinemann, 1958.
Andrade, Oswald de. "Cannibalist Manifesto." 1928. Translated by Leslie Bary. *Latin American Literary Review* 19.38 (1991): 38–47.
Barthes, Roland. *Mythologies*. Selected and translated by Annette Lavers. New York: Hill and Wang, 1995.
Bateson, Gregory. "Culture Contact and Schismogenesis." *Man* 35 (December 1935): 178–83.
Bennington, Geoffrey, and Jacques Derrida. *Jacques Derrida*. Paris: Seuil, 1991.
Breton, André. *Nadja*. Paris: Gallimard, 1964.
    Martinique Snake Charmer. Translated by David Seaman. Introduced by Franklin Rosemont. Austin: University of Texas Press, 2008.
Brillat-Savarin, Jean Anthelme. *Physiologie du goût*. Paris: Flammarion, 1982.
Césaire, Aimé. *Cahier d'un retour au pays natal*. Paris: Présence africaine, 1983.
Césaire, Suzanne. *Le grand camouflage: Écrits de dissidence (1941–1945)*. Paris: Seuil, 2009.
Chamoiseau, Patrick. *Creole Folktales*. New York: New Press, 1994.
Condé, Maryse. *Histoire de la femme cannibale*. Paris: Mercure de France, 2005.
    La migration des cœurs. Paris: Robert Laffont, 1994.
    Victoire, les saveurs et les mots. Paris: Mercure de France, 2006.
Damas, Léon-Gontran. *Pigments*. Paris: Présence africaine, 2001.
Danticat, Edwidge. *The Farming of Bones*. New York: Penguin, 1998.
Derrida, Jacques. "Il faut bien manger ou le calcul du sujet." In *Points de suspension*, 269–301. Paris: Galilée, 1992.

---

[61] Ibid., 174–75.
[62] Ibid., 112.

Derrida, Jacques, and Anne Dufourmantelle. *De l'hospitalité*. Paris: Calmann-Lévy, 1997.

Fanon, Frantz. *Peau noire, masques blancs*. Paris: Seuil, 1952.

Forbes, Jack D. *Columbus and Other Cannibals: The Wétiko Disease of Exploitation, Imperialism, and Terrorism*. New York: Seven Stories Press, 2008.

Githire, Njeri. *Cannibal Writes: Eating Others in Caribbean and Indian Ocean Women's Writing*, Urbana Champaign: University of Illinois Press, 2014.

Glissant, Édouard. *Caribbean Discourse: Selected Essays*. Translated by Michael J. Dash. Charlottesville: University Press of Virginia, 1989.

Houellebecq, Michel. *Soumission*. Paris: Flammarion, 2015.

How Tasty Was My Little Frenchman [Motion picture]. Directed by Nelson Pereira dos Santos. Rio de Janeiro: Condor filmes, 1971.

Hulme, Peter. "Introduction: The Cannibal Scene." In *Cannibalism and the Colonial World*, edited by Francis Barker, Peter Hulme, and Margaret Iversen, 1–38. Cambridge: Cambridge University Press, 1998.

James, C. L. R. *The Black Jacobins*. New York: Vintage, 1989.

Kilgour, Maggie. *From Communion to Cannibalism: An Anatomy of Metaphors of Incorporation*. Princeton: Princeton University Press, 1990.

Laferrière, Dany. *Pays sans chapeau*. Paris: Le Serpent à plumes, 1999.

Le Code noir. Paris: L'Esprit frappeur, 1998.

Lestringant, Frank. *Le Cannibale: Grandeur et décadence*. Paris: Perrin, 1994.

Lévi-Strauss, Claude. *The Raw and the Cooked: Introduction to a Science of Mythology*. New York: Harper & Row, 1969.

Loichot, Valérie. *The Tropics Bite Back: Culinary Coups in Caribbean Literature*. Minneapolis: University of Minnesota Press, 2013.

Madureira, Luís. *Cannibal Modernities: Postcoloniality and the Avant-Garde in Caribbean and Brazilian Literature*. Charlottesville: University of Virginia Press, 2005.

Mange, Ceci est mon corps [Motion picture]. Directed by Michelange Quay. Paris: Cinéma de Facto, 2007.

Mintz, Sidney W. *Tasting Food, Tasting Freedom*. Boston: Beacon Press, 1996.

Montaigne, Michel de. *The Complete Essays of Montaigne*. Translated by Donald Frame. Stanford: Stanford University Press, 1958.

Morrison, Toni. *Beloved*. New York: Knopf, 1987.

Plato. *Symposium*. Translated by Robin Waterfield. Oxford: Oxford University Press, 1994.

Quaranta, Jean-Marc. *Houellebecq aux fourneaux*. Paris: Plein jour, 2016.

"Toute l'œuvre de Michel Houellebecq décortiquée par le menu." *Munchies*, June 23, 2016. https://munchies.vice.com/fr/articles/toute-loeuvre-de-michel-houellebecq-decortiquee-par-le-menu.

Quinn, Ben. "French Police Make Woman Remove Clothing on Nice Beach Following Burkini Ban." *Guardian*, August 23, 2016. www.theguardian.com/world/2016/aug/24/french-police-make-woman-remove-burkini-on-nice-beach.

Shange, Ntozake. *If I Can Cook/You Know God Can*. Boston: Beacon Press, 1998.

Schwarz-Bart, Simone. "Du fond des casseroles." In *Nouvelles de Guadeloupe*, 78–81. Paris: Miniatures, 2009.

CHAPTER 9

Eating Athwart and Queering Food Writing

Elspeth Probyn

On the move again: we are on our fifth or sixth temporary accommodation in as many months. This is not a tragic tale of displacement, just the banal machinations of urban life. But each move strips my dwindling hoarding of spices – smoked ancho Mexican chilies that are hard to source in Sydney; my bay tree, the lime tree that rarely produced much fruit but was still a thrill for a former Montrealer, and all my herbs are long gone. At first there was the glee of living in what Sydney tries to pass off as its "Paris" quartier, Potts Point. The joy of good coffee and croissants, a decent butcher, a proper Italian deli with great wines, and walking to restaurants purveying the best vitello tonnato, or outstanding saganaki, was enough to soothe my displaced soul. The next apartment was a soulless box in inner city Darlinghurst, the previous beating heart of queer Sydney that is now stilled to a comatose state. And now we have descended to the nadir – an apartment building seemingly totally comprised of AirBnB transient bodies, as of course we are too. No smiles in the elevator. A dark, mean kitchen, and nowhere to buy anything to cook. Situated next to the main Central station, it's all buses, trains, grime, and dust and really bad takeaway joints. Depression sets in. I feel malnourished in so many ways.

Reading the great American (food) writer M. F. K. Fisher helps in an odd way. She understands that "our three basic needs, for food and security and love, are so mixed and mingled and entwined that we cannot straightly think of one without the others."[1] But she doesn't give us a saccharine version of food as easy comfort. This framing has become legion. If I had to read Elizabeth Gilbert's horrendously successful *Pray, Eat, Love* in my current state, I'd vomit.[2] No, the comfort of and from food is hard won. Fisher brings an edge even if at times her descriptions of food, the space

---

[1] M. F. K. Fisher, *The Gastronomical Me* (New York: North Point Press 1934/1954), 353.
[2] Elizabeth Gilbert, *Eat, Pray, Love: One Woman's Search for Everything Across Italy, India and Indonesia* (New York: Penguin, 2006).

it forms and the milieu in which it is found, are excessive. But that's the point. While Fisher was the original from which many have deviated, in this chapter I argue that Fisher's writing queers that realm. Fisher had a distinct style that pushed at the genre even as she was making it up. That style is more than just a way of writing. It can be understood in a Deleuzian vein as that which "makes the writer change the world at large through microperceptions that become translated into a style."[3] Her detours, her close-up descriptions, and manner of assembling and disassembling so many objects made her books vibrate. This is what Eve Sedgwick would characterize as queer: "continuing moment, movement, motive – recurrent, eddying, *troublant*."[4]

There is, I think, a difference between writing through food, and food writing. The former is now quite a well-trodden object in queer, feminist, and cultural and literary studies. For instance, Jaime Cantrell charts how American Southern writers such as Dorothy Allison and Minnie Bruce Pratt "celebrated their lesbianism through love of food and love of region, creating a sense of unity and sociality over the most mundane and routine of southern foods: tomatoes, peaches, blackberries, and biscuits."[5] As Cantrell points out, food and eating offers the writer an optic through which to depict and convey the sensuality and mundane nature of bodies that eat – to coin a phrase of mine from *Carnal Appetites*.[6] In that long ago book I sought to bring an extended Deleuzian frame, including feminist and queer articulations, to explore whether food had become the new sex. By this somewhat provocative phrase, I meant to interrogate how food and eating acted as vectors of power, and as a regime of truth. Across media and other texts, it seemed that food had become porn and a form of self-abjection.[7] Certainly, as I argued in the final chapter, eating had become a site of shame, and shaming, as well as disgust. Of course, this affective thrust was focused on some bodies – often fat, female, queer, and raced bodies – and not on others: white, middle-class, and heteronormative. This interest in bodies and shame became the subject of my next book,

---

[3] Tom Conley, "Singularity", in *The Deleuze Dictionary* edited by Adrian Parr (Edinburgh: Edinburgh University Press, 2010), 256. I have discussed at length Deleuze's idea of style in relation to queer writing in Elspeth Probyn, *Outside Belongings* (London: Routledge, 1996).
[4] Eve Kosofsky Sedgwick, *Tendencies* (Durham, NC: Duke University Press, 1993), 12.
[5] Jaime Cantrell, "Put a Taste of the South in Your Mouth: Carnal Appetites and Intersextionality," *Study the South*, September 10, 2015, southernstudies.olemiss.edu/study-the-south/put-a-taste-of-the-south-in-your-mouth.
[6] Elspeth Probyn, *Carnal Appetites: FoodSexIdentity* (London: Routledge, 2000).
[7] At the time of writing that book in the late 1990s, food porn etc. had yet to become quite the overwhelming avalanche that it now has become.

Blush: Faces of Shame.[8] Since then I have become much more deeply involved with ethnographic research focused on what I call more-than-human communities of fish/people. Through detailed case studies (of oysters, Bluefin tuna, anchovies, and many other marine lives), my most recent book, *Eating the Ocean*, considers how an ethics of taste and place might allow us to eat the ocean better.[9]

All of which is quite different from the focus in this chapter – food writing.[10] Food writing is notoriously difficult to pin down. But in relation to the feminist and queer writing *with* food, the negative distinctions include: food writers as professionals, at the edge of journalism, and published in lifestyle magazines and with specialized presses – to put it bluntly, not academics. As we will see, there are many critics of the genre of food writing as it is practiced today. But as I will argue, in the case of Fisher we find a particular food writer who let us see how food writing reveals and produces the full force of "the obligatory, necessary, or permitted interminglings of bodies."[11] These bodies – texts, descriptions of food, feeding, and eating – render messy any distinction between and among them. For Gilles Deleuze and Feliz Guattari these interminglings are regulated by "above all an alimentary regime and a sexual regime."[12] This calls forth a style of writing that seeks not the comfort of an identity in food but rather revels in what food can unleash.

The Singular Mrs. Fisher

The mention of Fisher's name either draws exclamations of joy from her fans, or people confess they don't really know who she is. For the ignorant, I mention that W. H. Auden said of Fisher, "I do not know of anyone in the United States today who writes better prose."[13] Then there are those who hate her, and her writing. The late food writer and blogger Josh

---

[8] Elspeth Probyn, *Blush: Faces of Shame* (Minneapolis: University of Minnesota Press, 2005).
[9] Elspeth Probyn, *Eating the Ocean* (Durham, NC: Duke University Press, 2016).
[10] I am highly influenced and helped in this consideration by my student Helen Greenwood's thesis, "Turning the Tables: How Women Invented Food Writing" (forthcoming), on women food writers, including Fisher. In addition to fleshing out individual women food writers, Greenwood explores the genealogy that allowed for the modern food writer.
[11] Gilles Deleuze and Félix Guattari, *A Thousand Plateaus*, translated by Brian Massumi (London: Athlone Press, 1988), 90.
[12] Ibid.
[13] Quoted in J. Reardon and M. F. K. Fisher, "M. F. K. Fisher: A Celebration," in *The Art Of Eating*, by M. F. K. Fisher, 50th anniversary ed. (New Jersey: Wiley, 2004), xiv.

Ozersky blames her writing and the model she set for the state of food writing today:

> I personally find her work to be dull, monotonous, and eventually stupe-fying, like the endless chatter of some lady you sit next to on a bus. Fisher belongs, I think, to that cold class of mid-century authors whose voices, once thought profound, have now receded into an indistinct din: Edmund Wilson, V. S. Naipaul, Susan Sontag, Paul Goodman, et al.[14]

Fisher epitomizes for him all that is wrong with the food writing scene: dominated by upper-class, beautiful white women who are and were unaware of the realities of food and eating for many if not most Americans. Ozersky has a point about exclusions in foodie media. His list of what is never mentioned in food writing includes:

> Compulsive overeating, obesity, diabetes, GI problems outside of designer allergies; Hunger; the interaction of food with alcohol, cocaine, marijuana, amphetamines, hallucinogens, narcotics, or prescription medications; junk food, fast food, fried food, supermarkets, food courts, non-Neapolitan pizza, convenience stores, diners, chain restaurants, boxed food, canned food, frozen food, and cheap Chinese of the non-nostalgic kind.[15]

It seems a little unfair to ask of Fisher to address what are relatively new food-related aspects of life – real and terrible as they are. As Lauren Berlant writes, the American scene of food prohibition, morality, and celebration constitutes one of the twenty-first century's most notable cases of "cruel optimism."[16] In her own way, however, Fisher tried to burst that bubble of optimism – she cruels it – in her scathing, off-hand remarks about the monotony of 1950s American familial mealtimes. Fisher was certainly not about happy families around the 5.00 pm dinner table. While she lauded and practiced different forms of commensality, the image and, in her time, the widespread practice of enforced, formalized, and familiarized eating was abhorrent. The little wife bringing a steaming casserole to hubby just back from work and kids was a thing of horror. Of course, I may be freighting this with my own affective reaction but the 5.00 pm dinner table is such an arresting image of, especially, American heteronormativity. Perversely while the practice of eating together – especially at such a bizarre time – has become very hard to practice, it is an ideal that is often waved in front of mothers whose lack of "home-cooking" and getting the family

---

[14] Josh Ozersky, "Consider the Food Writer," *Medium*, October 7, 2014, https://medium.com/@ozerskytv/m-f-k-fishers-invisible-empire-b7df8755e1a4#.j467f7cot.
[15] Ibid.
[16] Lauren Berlant, *Cruel Optimism* (Durham, NC: Duke University Press, 2011).

around the table all together is fingered as the cause of childhood obesity and other afflictions. My reaction to the early family dinner may sound elitist, and certainly my predilection for eating at 8.30 pm comes from a habitus that harbors no children. However, the women who are routinely blamed for the death of home cooking tend to be working class and poor, while those who frolic in designer kitchens, testing out their *Master Chef* recipes are not.

In her self-presentation Fisher was neither of these extremes though she came from an affluent and somewhat bohemian family. They lived in style in Whittier, California, where her father owned a newspaper. It was a small Quaker community, and Fisher's family were Episcopalians. This set them apart though perhaps not as much as Fisher recounts: "Episcopalians were the third world in Whittier."[17] The details of her life are well known to her fans but perhaps not to all. To briefly summarize, she was a prolific writer, and published twenty-seven books, including novels, collections of her essays, and countless articles for publications including the *New Yorker* and *Vogue*. She was a stunning dark-haired young woman. Man Ray captured her in his usual fashion – dark hair flowing over a pillow with closed darkened eyes caught from the camera hovering overhead, eyebrows perfectly shaped, her mouth unsmiling yet hinting at some pleasure that only MFK knows. She retained her striking looks into old age. As Betty Fussell recalls, "in 1978, she was 70. But the image she presented was in a time warp, as familiar to me as all those movie heroines on the big screen of the '30s and '40s."[18] Ozersky somewhat snarkily writes, "Fisher had it all, and she knew it."[19] (His account of Fisher and food writers in general oozes with disdain for women.) Fisher's take was different: "I wasn't so pretty that I didn't have to do something else."[20]

While it is important to note that her writing queered the genre of food writing just as she invented it, I make no causal connection to what her sexuality might have been. Nonetheless, her life bled into her writing, and her life was long and bumpy. She left her first husband, Al Fisher, who in her account was obsessed with the working girls who hung out at a café near where they lived in Dijon. Fisher describes the Café de Paris as "Al's

[17] Interview with M. F. K Fisher quoted in Kelly Alexander, "The Daily Meal Hall of Fame: M. F. K. Fisher," *Daily Meal*, March 31, 2015, www.thedailymeal.com/eat/daily-meal-hall-fame-mfk-fisher.

[18] Betty Fussell, "She Spoke in Paragraphs," *Food Arts*, September 13, 2013, http://foodarts.com/news/views/28442/she-spoke-in-paragraphs.

[19] Ozersky, "Consider the Food Writer."

[20] M. F. K. Fisher quoted in Robert McCrum, "The Best 100 Nonfiction Books," *Guardian*, October 10, 2016, www.theguardian.com/books/2016/oct/10/110-best-nonfiction-37-how-to-cook-a-wolf-mfk-fisher.

first love, and a faithful one."[21] Later in *Long Ago in France*, she reflects on this:

> He loved the prostitutes, as I was soon to learn. He loved to talk with them. I do not think he ever went with one to her chambers, partly because he was horrified by social diseases, but he asked all of them very intimate brotherly, fatherly probing questions.[22]

You get the sense that Al was a manipulative sort who liked to withhold sex. As Julie Campbell notes, "Thanks to this same fear of 'social diseases', Fisher recalls that Al 'was afraid to sleep with me for a month' after her first visit to a public bath."[23] This description makes Al sound quite vile – incestuous relationships with sex workers combined with a refusal of his wife. No wonder she dumped him for her great love, Dillwyn Parrish. Perversely she set up "an uneasy ménage à trois with Parrish" and Al for a time.[24] When she finally severed ties with Al she reflects on her time with him: "it took me a long time to get used to living side by side with a man whom I still loved passionately and who was almost sickened at the thought of being with me."[25]

Parrish, who Fisher called Chexbres after the area in Switzerland where they lived for some time, was to contract Buerger's disease. This caused the amputation of his leg. In pain and fearing the loss of more limbs, he killed himself in 1941 just as the book she had written to divert him, *Consider the Oyster*, was published. His suicide caused her much pain, and in 1986, not long before she died, she wrote of it in an essay that was published posthumously in the *Paris Review*: "there are many evil things that lurk in the minds of all people who are left after the suicide of somebody they love."[26] She went on to marry another man whom she also subsequently left. She sounds like a bit of a "bolter," but it's not clear from what or whom she was bolting.

---

[21] M. F. K. Fisher, *Long Ago in France: The Years in Dijon* (Englewood Cliffs, NJ: Prentice-Hall, 1991), 30.

[22] Ibid., 40.

[23] J. D. Campbell, "M. F. K. Fisher and the Embodiment of Desire: A Study in Autobiography and Food as Metaphor," *Biography* 20.2 (1997), 186; Fisher, *Long Ago in France*, 26.

[24] Corby Kummer, " 'The Theoretical Foot' and 'The Arrangement,' " Sunday Book Review, *New York Times,* February 19, 2016, www.nytimes.com/2016/02/21/books/review/the-theoretical-foot-and-the-arrangement.html?_r=0.

[25] M. F. K. Fisher, *The Gastronomical Me*, reprinted in *The Art of Eating* (New York: Vintage, 1976), quoted in Campbell, "M. F. K. Fisher," 201.

[26] M. F. K. Fisher, "Jumping from Bridges," *Paris Review*, May 26, 2016, www.theparisreview.org/blog/2016/05/26/jumping-from-bridges.

If Ozersky blames Fisher for the now dominant form of food writing, Sandra Gilbert argues that M. F. K. Fisher stands out from the genre of "foodoir." "Foodoir" consists of "one part chick lit mixed with one part chicken lit."[27] For Gilbert there is grit that lurks in Fisher's writing, against which her style is honed. As Gilbert writes, "for Fisher the 'dread fact' of eating is the ontological fact of primal hunger and of the food chain in which we too are mortal links, dining on mortality and in the end destined to become dinner ourselves, whether for worms or flames or vultures."[28] In sociological terms, Fisher's "dread fact" that we have to eat meets with George Simmel's formulation of eating as the fundamental quandary of human social life: "what the individual eats, no one else can eat under any circumstance."[29] Eating for Simmel is what we all share as humans but equally is an act of such individuality that it forms an absolute limit of commonality, or indeed commensality. In this sense, eating is as individual as dying – a universal experience that is lived in profound aloneness. Gilbert catches at this when she describes how Fisher's "art is everywhere darkened by dread, it's not so much energised by the force of gastronomic desire as it is by the memories that flavour past appetites."[30] Gilbert gestures here to two quite different and conflicting temporalities. The memories of the past overlap with dread – a feeling mobilized by a feared future.

Athwart

This movement across memory and the apprehension of the future troubles Fisher's writing – it queers it in Sedgwick's precise yet expansive understanding of the word. " 'Queer' itself means *across* – it comes from the Indo-European root *-twerkw*, which also yields the German *quer* (transverse), Latin *torquere* (to twist), English *athwart*".[31] To work athwart is for Sedgwick to be within the spheres of "continuing moment, movement, motive – recurrent, eddying, *troublant.*" In *Eating the Ocean*, I use Sedgwick's sense of queer as athwart as a way of deepening the shallow debates about sustainability. Given the focus on the marine, I pair Sedgwick's sense of queer as athwart with the nautical understanding that

[27] C. Muhlke, "Kiss the Cook," *New York Times*, December 6, 1999, quoted in Sandra M. Gilbert, "Feeding the Foodoir: Hunger Artistry", *Gastronomica: Journal of Food and Culture* 14.3 (2014): 74.
[28] Ibid., 74.
[29] Georg Simmel, "The Sociology of the Meal," translated by Michael Symons, *Food and Foodways* 5.4 (1994): 346.
[30] Gilbert, "Feeding the Foodoir," 80.
[31] Sedgwick, *Tendencies*, 12.

Stefan Helmreich brings to "athwart theory" in his *Alien Ocean*.[32] This he describes as

> An empirical itinerary of associations and relations, a travelogue which, to draw on the nautical meaning of *athwart*, moves sidewise, tracing the contingent, drifting and bobbing, real-time, and often unexpected connections of which social action is constituted, which mixes up things and their descriptions.[33]

If Sedgwick's understanding gives us a way of seeing the twistedness, the queerness of life's entanglements, Helmreich's use of athwart brings to the surface how reading athwart focuses us on the "unexpected connections" which mix up things. For me, this going across is deeply caught up in how we relate – bring together and narrate – different dimensions of the social. This is then a method of reading, and an ontology of how that reading relates in and to the world.

Athwart captures the many aspects of Fisher's writing. It certainly describes how she writes sideways from memory to meal to personal reflection. Julie Campbell and others focus on the supposed autobiographical nature of Fisher's work. Campbell calls Fisher's *The Gastronomical Me* "her autobiography of her palate."[34] Fisher's is certainly not a typical autobiography but more a use of the self where she is sometimes foregrounded but then steps back.[35] As Fisher states: "I made myself disappear. This is something that takes practice … It is mainly a question of withdrawing to the vanishing point from the consciousness of the people one is with, before one actually leaves."[36] This spectral self is of course seductive. As Elizabeth Tamny writes, "Fisher's greatest appeal was her oblique style." Her many fans were "frustrated by Fisher's ability to both seduce them and keep them at arm's length."[37] Joan Reardon has done the most to flesh out the detail that Fisher seemingly wanted hidden – the parts of her life when she withdrew "to a vanishing point."[38] Laura Shapiro, in her review

---

[32] Stefan Helmreich, *Alien Ocean: Anthropological Voyages in Microbial Seas* (Berkeley: University of California Press, 2009), 23.

[33] Ibid.

[34] Campbell, "M. F. K. Fisher," 182.

[35] In *Sexing the Self*, I called this a use of the self as form – a form or a problematization that twists, renders athwart, any causal connection with the autobiographical. Elspeth Probyn, *Sexing the Self: Gendered Positions in Cultural Studies* (London: Routledge, 1993).

[36] M. F. K. Fisher, *A Map of Another Town* (1964; reprinted in *Two Towns in Provence*, New York: Vintage, 1983) quoted in Campbell, "M. F. K. Fisher," 199.

[37] Elizabeth Tamny, "Secret Recipe," *Chicago Reader*, May 15, 2003, www.chicagoreader.com/chicago/secret-recipe/Content?oid=912078 15/5/2003.

[38] Reardon and Fisher, "M. F. K. Fisher: A Celebration."

of Reardon's *Poet of the Appetites* (the title was John Updike's assessment of Fisher), mentions that among the many parts of Fisher hidden from view "there was, for example, a significant romance that was never mentioned in print – a secret liaison with Marietta Voorhees, a drama teacher in St. Helena, in the late 1950's."[39] And of course her writing was within the bounds of the travelogue. In her introduction to Fisher's *Long Ago in France*, the eminent (travel) writer Jan Morris describes how Fisher – in this case – made Dijon into a character in her Bildungs-essays:

> In *Long Ago in France* Mrs. Fisher recalls, with an intimacy that is always self-amused, her growing up in the old city. She learns to speak French there. She learns to understand French ways and prejudices. She tries her hand at the journal, the essay, and the short story. The marvels of the French cuisine are gradually revealed to her and she begins to sense (one reads between the lines) the first traumas of marriage.[40]

If, as Elizabeth Moulton reports in her obituary, Fisher spoke of how "I write as I talk,"[41] she also ate as she wrote and as she traveled. Growing up grounded in "the country outside a very small Californian town", she "had never travelled more than a twelve-hour trip home from school for vacations."[42] On her first real trip – a train to Chicago in her youth – she learned a vital lesson: a meal is not to be trifled with. Under her uncle's tutelage a young Mary Frances Kennedy learnt to never "say, or even think, 'Oh anything', about a meal, even if I had to eat it alone, with death in the house or in my heart."[43]

Fisher's writing travels across, transverses, and twists, and this passage demonstrates her awareness of the necessity of also being singular – of stopping. The choosing of a meal requires absolute attention. Another way of thinking about how Fisher articulates movement and stillness is through Deleuze's notion of "singularity." Tom Conley describes both the concept and also how for Deleuze, like Fisher, movement and fixed points are inherent to style.

> As a philosopher he embraces the idea of virtual travel, along infinite tra-jectories or lines of flight that lead the thinker anywhere about the world, but first and foremost among and between conceptual islands or points of

---

[39] Laura Shapiro, " 'Poet of the Appetites': The Art of the Meal," Sunday Book Review, *New York Times*, December 12, 2004, www.nytimes.com/2004/12/12/books/review/poet-of-the-appetites-the-art-of-the-meal.html?_r=0.

[40] Jan Morris in Fisher, *Long Ago in France*, ix–x.

[41] Elizabeth Moulton, "M. F. K. Fisher 1908–1992," *Sewanee Review* 108.3 (2000): 433.

[42] M. F. K. Fisher, *The Art of Eating*, 50th anniversary ed. (New Jersey: Wiley, 2004), 379.

[43] Ibid., 381.

singularity … A singularity, also insularity, is a decisive point and a place where perception is felt in movement.[44]

This description suits MFK to a tee. Her writing embraces the flow of words and things, places and tastes, people and loves. In the essay where she discovers that "oh anything" will never do, she describes herself as a "suddenly, big, moody [girl] full of undirected energies of a thousand kinds."[45] She has finished school and her parents want to keep her close to them at a university in Los Angeles. Aged nineteen, she rebels: "I fought against it instinctively as a person on the operating table fights against ether."[46] She gets her way, and her parents put her on a train to spend a semester in Illinois. She is accompanied by her uncle, the man who would not tolerate her "*gaucherie*" when she utters the dreaded "anything." On the train she learns to expand herself – she learns "that a menu is not something to be looked at with hasty and often completely phony nonchalance."[47] Her description of her uncle slides along well-oiled lateral lines: he used to love beer and good whiskey, and sometimes he sang or he wept when he had too much. During Prohibition he stopped drinking: "he was a teacher of law, and too honest to preach what he did not practice." MFK comments:

> Personally I regret his honesty, because I think he would have been a fine man to drink with, and by the time I knew how to, and the country could, it was too late. He had been killed by a drunken driver.[48]

In this movement, the later MFK comments on her younger self, and what she would have desired, in a train hurtling through the countryside – a Foucauldean heterotopia par excellence.[49] And then she comes to a full stop. "He had been killed by a drunken driver." *Point finale*. But not quite. She resumes her seat in the dining car, which was "an unusually good one rather the way the Broadway Limited was to be later, with an agreeable smooth dash to it." As the older MFK looks over the shoulder of her nineteen-year-old self, the uncle asks why she would want to order lamb chops. "'But you know what lamb chops taste like,' my uncle would say casually. 'Why not have something exciting? Why not order … uh … how

---

[44] Conley, "Singularity."
[45] Fisher, *Art of Eating*, 379.
[46] Ibid.
[47] Ibid., 380.
[48] Ibid.
[49] Foucault argues: "The heterotopia is capable of juxtaposing in a single real place several spaces, several sites that are in themselves incompatible." Michel Foucault, "Of Other Spaces," translated by Jay Miskowiec, *Diacritics* 16 (1986), 25. This, I would argue, is also a good summation of Fisher's writing, which brings together elements considered incompatible.

about Eastern scallops? Yes,' he would go on before I could do no more than gulp awkwardly, 'we will have scallops tonight, Captain, and I think an avocado cocktail with plenty of fresh lime juice …' and so forth."[50]

While MFK appreciates her uncle's choices, she doesn't yet get the import of his lesson. When they arrive in Chicago, the uncle's son meets them and they go for dinner at the station restaurant, which like the dining cars on trains in the 1920s would have been luxurious – featuring Lobster Newberg and other rather incredible American dishes.[51] Faced with overwhelming concoctions of lobster with cream, butter, cognac, sherry, eggs, and cayenne, MFK goes back to her old ways and "mumbled stiffly, 'Oh anything … anything, thank you.' "[52] To which the uncle responds "with a cold speculative somewhat disgusted look in his brown eyes."[53] This shakes her to the core. "I looked at my menu, really looked with all my brain, for the first time."[54] An eon passes but she finally says to her uncle, "without batting an eye, 'I'd like iced consommé, please, and then sweetbreads *sous cloche* and a watercress salad.' "[55]

This is momentous; not perhaps the act of ordering but the way in which Fisher's control of ordering is mirrored in her writing. The blur of movements, temporalities, and flows, of trains, and escaping, of family and growing up and away, are abruptly halted with the singular composition of a meal. This becomes a tactic Fisher uses often. She writes of how she would compose menus to deliberately and violently upset the quotidian:

> I spent hours in my kitchen cooking for people, trying to blast their safe, tidy little lives with a tureen of hot borscht and some garlic-toast and salad, instead of the fruit cocktail, fish, meat, vegetable, salad, dessert and coffee they tuck daintily away seven times a week.[56]

MFK Eats an Oyster[57]

Oysters are at the heart of two of Fisher's most lateral, most athwart texts, which is not surprising given how athwart a creature the oyster is. *Consider*

---

[50] Fisher, *Art of Eating*, 380.

[51] James D. Porterfield, *Dining by Rail: The History and Recipes of America's Golden Age of Railroad Cuisine* (New York: St. Martin's Press, 1993).

[52] Fisher, *Art of Eating*, 380.

[53] Ibid., 381.

[54] Ibid.

[55] Ibid.

[56] Ibid.

[57] For a much more developed argument about oysters, singularity, and taste in regards to Fisher's writing see Probyn, *Eating the Ocean*, Chapter 2; and Annemarie Mol's article "I Eat an Apple" from

the Oyster is a very queer little book, ranging over recipes, history, fiction passed off as real, and fact fictionalized.[58] The opening chapter, "Love and Death among the Molluscs" begins with the well-known lines: "An oyster leads a dreadful but exciting life."[59] She then describes how the oyster turns herself-himself-herself as easily as if she/he were a mobius strip.

> Almost any normal oyster never knows from one year to the next whether he is he or she, and may start at any moment, after the first year, to lay eggs where before he spent his sexual energies in being exceptionally masculine. If he is a she, her energies are equally feminine, so that in a single summer, if all goes well, and the temperature of the water is somewhere around or above seventy degrees, she may spawn several hundred million eggs, fifteen to one hundred million at a time, with commendable pride.[60]

Fisher writes almost guardedly about the oyster, aware of its fleeting life-span. But the essay also calls out to be read against the backdrop of its inscription: "For Dillwyn Parrish." Fisher wrote her text in the last year of Parrish's life, apparently to distract him from the pain that would lead to his suicide. Something of that milieu of writing seeps into her descriptions of the fate of the oyster at sea: "the starfish, which floats hungrily in all the Eastern tides and at last wraps arms around the oyster like a hideous lover and forces its shells apart steadily and then thrusts his stomach into and digests it." "The picture is ugly", she says.[61]

The other notable oyster text is "The first oyster," Fisher's tale of adolescent female sexuality and pashes in a Californian boarding school. As she builds her story wending around and around the figure of Mrs. Cheever, the cook, who produced unappreciated marvels of well-prepared food for the young ladies, it is above all a love story where a taste for oysters remarks on and then transcends class. Mary Francis tastes her first oyster: "Oysters, my delicate taste buds were telling me, oysters are *simply marvellous*! More! More!"[62] One can picture the scene. The girls in a bright room, seated at several long tables. There is of course a bad girl, there always is. In MFK's story, it is Inez, an upper-class girl slightly older than Mary Francis who has been making a play for the young MFK. The oyster still swelling in her, Mary Francis escapes her clutches and rushes into the kitchen. "The

---

which I take this subheading: Mol, "I Eat an Apple: On Theorising Subjectivities," *Subjectivity* 22.1 (2008): 28–37.
[58] M. F. K. Fisher, *Consider the Oyster* (New York: North Point Press, 1941/1954).
[59] Ibid., 3.
[60] Ibid.
[61] Ibid., 6.
[62] Fisher, *Art of Eating*, 375.

delightful taste of oyster in my mouth, my new-born gourmandize, sent me toward an unknown rather than a known sensuality."[63] There in the kitchen she stumbles upon a tableau of tenderness between the cook, Mrs. Cheever, and the unnamed nurse. The cook with tears "running bloodlessly down her soft ravaged cheeks" serves the nurse – her *amie* – a platter of oysters watching as "the old woman ate steadily, voluptuously, of the fat cold molluscs."[64] As I said, it is a tale of class order overturned by the taste for oysters. The teachers and students looked down on Mrs. Cheever – just a cook – and Mrs. Cheever affected disdain for the nurse, who was even lower on the pecking order. But through and with the oysters MFK affords a wrenching depiction of female care that grasps the two old women – perhaps lovers, perhaps long since just companions – in a kitchen, eating oysters. I see them as Fisher does, focused on their love of eating *oysters* – not the remains shunned by privileged young girls.

With this passage, Fishers performs a magnificent task of bringing together and then forcing apart taste, social distinction, old and young women's cares and love. And just as it might threaten to become saccharine, Fisher effects a stylistic equivalent of the starfish forcing apart the oyster's shell in order to digest it. No, food and eating is never just comfort.

Queering Food Writing

I've argued across this chapter that M. F. K Fisher is exemplary of a certain style. Her leaps, slides, stops, and changes of direction mean that the reader is forced off track. I characterize this as an athwart form of writing that forms rhizomatic connections. Whether or not she was queer, and whatever that would mean, her style, as I said at the outset, queers the genre *avant la lettre*, as she contributes to forging the genre. Her writing is caught up in and creates "continuing moment, movement, motive – recurrent, eddying, *troublant*," to quote Sedgwick again.[65] Her space of writing between memory and apprehension is temporally queer as she veers between the known and the unknown, memory and apprehension. Writing athwart means not knowing in advance the taste of things – meals, people, loves. And whether or not they will match up.

What can we take from Fisher's style in the overheated realm of food writing today? For all its omnipresence – on cable and free-to-air television, on social media, in traditional forms of print media, in millions of

[63] Ibid., 376.
[64] Ibid., 377.
[65] Sedgwick, *Tendencies*, 12.

cookbooks of all flavors, and of assorted nationalities (though dominated by Anglo-British productions) – there is a sameness to food writing. What may be lacking is Fisher's insistence on the forces of hunger and dread. Food writing is comfortable – it seeks to comfort us in an imagined realm where "home," "food," and "love" all meet in a heteronormative middle-class imaginary. Fisher's incisive, sometimes cruel, often full-of-herself writing punctures that imaginary. Or rather she fuels the hope that food and security and love – our basic needs – can be met, while she disappears behind the image she has produced. I hope here to have helped bring to the surface how Fisher makes us read athwart, and reading her begins to help us to eat athwart.

And of my tale with which I opened this chapter? Today as we prepare for what may be the penultimate move[66] until I get a shiny new kitchen, our bags are packed and my foodstuffs are reduced to a bottle of Sriracha, I give up the unequal task of cooking. Tonight we will join the Halloween crowds of zombies on the streets of the city. Surely there will be something to eat. Forced to be intimate with the skin of the Central Business District, as Australians call "downtown," I am on the look out for the unexpected. As MFK would say, I am sure it will be "queer and rude and exciting."[67]

BIBLIOGRAPHY

Alexander, Kelly. "The Daily Meal Hall of Fame: M. F. K. Fisher." *Daily Meal*, March 31, 2015. www.thedailymeal.com/eat/daily-meal-hall-fame-mfk-fisher.
Berlant, Lauren. *Cruel Optimism*. Durham, NC: Duke University Press, 2011.
Cantrell, Jaime. "Put a Taste of the South in Your Mouth: Carnal Appetites and Intersextionality." *Study the South*, September 10, 2015. southernstudies.olemiss.edu/study-the-south/put-a-taste-of-the-south-in-your-mouth.
Campbell, J. D. "M. F. K. Fisher and the Embodiment of Desire: A Study in Autobiography and Food as Metaphor." *Biography* 20.2 (1997): 181–202.
Conley, Tom. "Singularity." In *The Deleuze Dictionary*, edited by Adrian Parr. Edinburgh: Edinburgh University Press, 2010.
Deleuze, Gilles, and Félix Guattari. *A Thousand Plateaus*. Translated by Brian Massumi. London: Athlone Press, 1988.
Fisher, M. F. K. *The Art of Eating*. 50th anniversary edition. New Jersey: Wiley, 2004.
  Consider the Oyster. New York: North Point Press, 1941/1954.
  The Gastronomical Me. New York: North Point Press, 1934/1954.
  The Gastronomical Me. Reprinted in *The Art of Eating*. New York: Vintage, 1976.
  "Jumping from Bridges." *Paris Review*, May 26, 2016. www.theparisreview.org/blog/2016/05/26/jumping-from-bridges.

---

[66] It wasn't.
[67] Fisher, *Art of Eating*, 558.

Long Ago in France: The Years in Dijon. Englewood Cliffs, NJ: Prentice-Hall, 1991.

A Map of Another Town. 1964. Reprinted in *Two Towns in Provence.* New York: Vintage, 1983.

Foucault, Michel. "Of Other Spaces." Translated by Jay Miskowiec. *Diacritics* 16 (1986): 22–27.

Fussell, Betty. "She Spoke in Paragraphs." *Food Arts,* September 13 (2013). http://foodarts.com/news/views/28442/she-spoke-in-paragraphs.

Gilbert, Elizabeth. *Eat, Pray, Love: One Woman's Search for Everything Across Italy, India and Indonesia.* New York: Penguin, 2006.

Gilbert, Sandra M. "Feeding the Foodoir: Hunger Artistry." *Gastronomica: Journal of Food and Culture* 14.3 (2014): 74–82.

Helmreich, Stefan. *Alien Ocean: Anthropological Voyages in Microbial Seas.* Berkeley: University of California Press, 2009.

Kummer, Corby. " 'The Theoretical Foot' and 'The Arrangement.' " Sunday Book Review, *New York Times,* February 19, 2016. www.nytimes.com/2016/02/21/books/review/the-theoretical-foot-and-the-arrangement.html?_r=0.

McCrum, Robert. "The Best 100 Nonfiction Books," *Guardian,* October 10, 2016. www.theguardian.com/books/2016/oct/10/110-best-nonfiction-37-how-to-cook-a-wolf-mfk-fisher.

Mol, Annemarie. "I Eat an Apple: On Theorising Subjectivities." *Subjectivity* 22.1 (2008): 28–37.

Moulton, Elizabeth. "M. F. K. Fisher 1908–1992." *Sewanee Review* 108.3 (2000): 432–40.

Muhlke, C. "Kiss the Cook." *New York Times,* December 6, 1999.

Ozersky, Josh. "Consider the Food Writer." *Medium,* October 7, 2014. https://medium.com/@ozerskytv/m-f-k-fishers-invisible-empire-b7df8755e1a4#.j467f7cot.

Porterfield, James D. *Dining by Rail: The History and Recipes of America's Golden Age of Railroad Cuisine.* New York: St. Martin's Press, 1993.

Probyn, Elspeth. *Blush: Faces of Shame.* Minneapolis: University of Minnesota Press, 2005.

Carnal Appetites: FoodSexIdentity. London: Routledge, 2000.

Eating the Ocean. Durham, NC: Duke University Press, 2016.

Outside Belongings. London: Routledge, 1996.

Sexing the Self: Gendered Positions in Cultural Studies London: Routledge, 1993.

Reardon, J., and M. F. K. Fisher, "M. F. K. Fisher: A Celebration." In *The Art Of Eating* by M. F. K. Fisher. 50th anniversary ed. New Jersey: Wiley, 2004.

Sedgwick, Eve Kosofsky. *Tendencies.* Durham, NC: Duke University Press, 1993.

Shapiro, Laura. "'Poet of the Appetites': The Art of the Meal." Sunday Book Review, *New York Times,* December 12, 2004. www.nytimes.com/2004/12/12/books/review/poet-of-the-appetites-the-art-of-the-meal.html?_r=0.

Simmel, Georg. "The Sociology of the Meal." Translated by Michael Symons. *Food and Foodways* 5.4 (1994): 345–50.

Tamny, Elizabeth. "Secret Recipe." *Chicago Reader,* May 15, 2003. www.chicagoreader.com/chicago/secret-recipe/Content?oid=912078 15/5/2003.

Utilizing Food Studies with Children's Literature and Its Scholarship

Kara K. Keeling and Scott T. Pollard

Published in a variety of venues over the past four decades, children's literature scholarship that has focused on food demonstrates an uncanny likeness to the interdisciplinary growth of food studies scholarship. Such scholarship reflects the development of critical theory as an analytical tool over the latter half of the twentieth century and into the twenty-first, exploring with increasing sophistication food as a powerful and complex signifying force. Such scholarship illuminates food as a prime cultural mover that is acted upon (cooked, elaborated) but as a cultural force also acts. In 1980, Wendy Katz was the first to find culinary patterns among classic children's books in her article, "Some Uses of Food in Children's Literature." While not as theoretically sophisticated as later critical work, Katz nonetheless laid important groundwork in ascribing meaning to the presence of food in the lives of children, both characters and readers.

Subsequent scholars, pursuing the connections between the food in children's texts and the real world culture and history of food, have employed more contemporary and multidisciplinary theoretical strategies to articulate and develop those connections. In his 1990 article, "Maurice Sendak's Ritual Cooking of the Child in Three Tableaux: The Moon, Mother, and Music," Jean Perrot used Claude Lévi-Strauss' understanding of cooking as a civilizing trope to discuss a variety of Sendak's texts. Maria Nikolajeva devoted a chapter, "An Excursus on Significant Meals," in her 2000 book *From Mythic to Linear: Time in Children's Literature*, to applying the concepts from a variety of theorists from various disciplines (Claude Lévi-Strauss, Carl Jung, Vladimir Propp, and Algirdas Julien Greimas) to stories for children in order to explore the deep structures (mythic, archetypal) of children's literature through the consumption of food as significant, ritualized temporal markers that integrate the child into the community.

The next development in the scholarship of food in children's literature integrated sophisticated theoretical strategies with the work of food writers and scholars. Lynn Vallone's 2002 article, "'What Is the Meaning of All This Gluttony?': Edgeworth, the Victorians, C. S. Lewis and a Taste for Fantasy," began with Katz and Nikolajeva and then turned to Gian-Paolo Biasin (*The Flavors of Modernity: Food and the Novel*) and Margaret Visser (*The Rituals of Dinner*) to construct food as a metaphor for the integration of children into the adult world. In *Voracious Children: Who Eats Whom in Children's Literature* (2006), Carolyn Daniel pursued a feminist analysis and used theorists like Pierre Bourdieu, Julia Kristeva, Roland Barthes, Judith Butler, and Lévi-Strauss, along with food scholars like Mary Douglas, Norbert Elias, Peter Farb, and Sidney Mintz, to demonstrate how patriarchy constitutes food as a cultural signifier and indoctrinator. Susan Honeyman used a similar multidisciplinary mix of cultural theorists in *Consuming Agency in Fairy Tales, Childlore, and Folkliterature* (2010) to examine the material and imaginary cultures of food utopias as signifying regimes through which race, gender, and class structures position, pacify, and integrate children. Vallone, Daniel, and Honeyman represent not only the growing theoretical complexity of the field of children's literature food scholarship but the expanding reach of children's literature as a broad cultural lens. A recent collection – *Feast or Famine? Food and Children's Literature* (2014), edited by Bridget Carrington and Jennifer Harding – continues the arc of what is now this scholarly tradition.

As for our own work, as both writers and editors we have experienced a developmental arc that parallels the one delineated above. In our earliest article – "Power, Food, and Eating in Maurice Sendak and Henrik Drescher: *Where the Wild Things Are, In the Night Kitchen,* and *The Boy Who Ate Around*" (1999) – we made use of, what seemed at the time, a limited but intriguing set of food-oriented writers and scholars (M. F. K. Fisher, Mary Douglas, Julia Kristeva, Stephen Mennell) to understand food as a cultural signifier. In the second, "In Search of His Father's Garden" (2002), we added material culture – *Mrs. Beeton's Book of Household Management* (1861) – and Carolyn Korsmeyer's *Making Sense of Taste* (1999), which features an analysis of the food scenes in Herman Melville's *Moby Dick*. In the anthology we edited, *Critical Approaches to Food in Children's Literature* (2009), we were fortunate to bring together scholars who represented an array of approaches, which offered a significantly broadened theoretical palette (archival research, cultural studies, feminism and gender studies, material culture, metaphysics, popular culture, postcolonialism, post-structuralism, race, theology). In our more recent scholarship, "'The Key Is in the Mouth': Food and Orality in *Coraline*" (2012) and "Privilege and Exploitation: Food as Dual Signifier in Pamela Muñoz Ryan's *Esperanza*

Rising" (2016), we found the value of focusing on the histories of particular places, periods, and peoples. It is with this interpretive focus that we pursue here an analysis of Laura Ingalls Wilder's Little House books as a case study to demonstrate the possibilities of food studies scholarship in children's literature for those who may be unfamiliar with this particular field.

Introduction to Laura Ingalls Wilder and the Little House Books

Laura Ingalls Wilder's seven-book Little House series details a fictionalized account of the events of her childhood growing up on the American frontier of the 1870s and 1880s.[1] Published between 1932 and 1943, her books sold phenomenally well, received five Newbery honor awards, and became an integral part of the canon of American children's literature for reading audiences of the second half of the twentieth century. Any reader of *Little House in the Big Woods*, the first novel Wilder wrote, will notice Wilder's preoccupation with food: Pa hunts game and raises crops, while Ma tends a garden and preserves its bounty for the winter as well as fixing meals on a daily basis. Through all of the description of nineteenth-century American foodways runs the refrain, "Laura and Mary helped," suggesting the integral part that child labor played in frontier culture. As Wilder rehearses the processes of food production and preparation that the Ingalls adults taught her younger self, she simultaneously passes on to her readers an ideologically inflected set of food practices. These novels, produced for Depression-era audiences, reflect Wilder's anti-New Deal political stance – an ideological position not initially noticed by scholars who were themselves under the spell of historian Frederick Jackson Turner's dominant interpretation of the westward expansion of Anglo-American culture. Historians and cultural critics' later critiques of the underlying assumptions of Turner's vision of the west have also created scholarly reevaluation of Wilder's work. An examination of Wilder's portrait of food preparation and foodways within her books, in the context of these evolving critical ideas, reveals the interplay between the conventional nineteenth-century American foodways of the Ingalls family when Laura was a child and Wilder's politically

---

[1] We are including the seven novels about Laura's experiences growing up that were published in Wilder's lifetime: *Little House in the Big Woods, Little House on the Prairie, On the Banks of Plum Creek, By the Shores of Silver Lake, The Long Winter, Little Town on the Prairie,* and *These Happy Golden Years*. We are excluding *Farmer Boy*, the second book she wrote, which focuses on her husband Almanzo's experiences as a boy, and *The First Four Years*, based on an unedited draft found among Wilder's papers after her death.

conservative views as an author in the 1930s: a lifelong farmer's wife who believed in the self-sufficiency of the small family farm and who had no patience with what she viewed as government handouts.

Wilder's interest in food in the first book continues in the rest of the series: food always plays a large role in the Ingalls family's life. Writing in 1979, Barbara Walker observes in the introduction to *The Little House Cookbook: Frontier Food from Laura Ingalls Wilder's Classic Stories* that "Throughout this now classic series much of the action centers on food – hunting it, growing it, losing it to natural disasters, cooking it, preserving it, and eating it."[2] Walker makes this comment in the context of creating a rationale for her cookbook, but reexamination of the novels in the light of food studies scholarship suggests that grappling with the integral function of food in their lives and society yields a fuller understanding of Wilder's characters. Food within the series is not simply a plot element to be noted; rather, food and foodways are essential to Wilder's reproduction of historical context, the development of character and character relationships, as well as representing her conservative cultural politics.

Three interrelated patterns shape the function and signification of food's structuring power, both in the family life portrayed in Wilder's Little House books and in the form and trajectory of the series' narrative. First, food plays a central role in the series and in readers' reception of the books, which reflects the material culture of late nineteenth-century pioneer life and nostalgic modern recovery of historical foodways of the period. Second, within that larger frame the types and preparations of food manifest nineteenth-century Anglo-American cultural values, serving as an engine for the dissemination of "civilized" behavior into the wilderness. Third, paradoxically, despite Wilder's own political and gender conservatism, her books depict how food provided a significant means by which women created culture on the frontier – a contribution that historians and critics have consistently overlooked and devalued.

The Role of Food in the Little House Books

Although her analysis appears in the guise of a cookbook, Barbara Walker is really the first critic to look at food in the Little House books. In their survey of literary cookbooks for children, Jodie Slothower and Jan Susina evaluate "Walker's *The Little House Cookbook* … [as] perhaps the best

---

[2] Barbara M. Walker, *The Little House Cookbook: Frontier Food from Laura Ingalls Wilder's Classic Stories* (New York: Harper & Row, 1979), 3.

historical cookbook related to children's literature" because it successfully preserves and revives an aspect of material culture of pioneer life, stressing "the importance of the entire family's role in food preparation."[3] This observation is equally true of Wilder's original series: the Little House books are superb survival manuals because they offer exemplary and detailed instruction on how to manage life in the nineteenth-century American wilderness. Walker notes how "Laura Ingalls Wilder's way of describing her pioneer childhood seemed to compel [reader] participation."[4] The novels inspired Walker and her daughter Anna to try the food preparation shown within them, ultimately leading to the research required to recreate recipes and their historical contexts within the cookbook.

In *A History of Cooks and Cooking*, Michael Symons argues for cooks, cooking, and kitchens as the central disseminators of civilization. In one chapter of his book, he spends time on food's presence in literature, expressing a particular interest in nineteenth-century domestic adolescent literature: Susan Coolidge's *What Katy Did*, Wilder's *The Long Winter*, and L. M. Montgomery's *Anne of Green Gables*. Symons cites "the original meaning of *oikonomia* – from the Greek words *oikos* for 'house' and *nemo* for 'manage' – is 'household management.'"[5] In the nineteenth century, the meaning of economics expanded from its ancient household-centered definition and was applied metaphorically to describe a broad social science that eventually came to ignore and deprecate its domestic origins.[6] Symons' purpose is to restore that original understanding of economy by celebrating the detailed portrayal of the complex processes of food acquisition, preparation, and distribution within the novels he examines, including Wilder's novel about Laura's early adolescence. The omnipresence of food within *all* the Little House books suggests that Wilder chooses to entertain her readers by instructing them in these lost processes, fulfilling her own nostalgia for a lost way of life and creating it for readers; Walker comments on Wilder's success with her own daughter and other child readers.

The books provide abundant examples of such detail. One particularly elaborate example of instruction occurs in *Little House in the Big Woods*, in which Wilder spends eight pages describing making cheese. She goes from the milking to the acquisition of the required rennet from a relative,

---

[3] Jodie Slothower and Jan Susina, "Delicious Supplements: Literary Cookbooks as Additives to Children's Texts," in *Critical Approaches to Food in Children's Literature*, edited by Kara K. Keeling and Scott T. Pollard (New York: Routledge, 2009), 33–34.

[4] Walker, *Little House Cookbook*, xviii.

[5] Michael Symons, *A History of Cooks and Cooking* (Champaign: University of Illinois Press, 2004), 17.

[6] Ibid.

to the pressing of whey from the curd, to the curing and packaging of the ripened cheese. Though five-year-old Laura experiences some fear over the potential death of one of the family's calves to make rennet, that emotional crisis is resolved quickly and the scene moves on to the details of the cheese-making process. Wilder hooks the readers emotionally, sharing Laura's concern for the family calf, but she lets them off that hook by putting the death of the calf offstage: since both of the Ingalls family's calves are valuable heifers, Pa's brother agrees to kill his male calf to which Laura is not emotionally attached. The rennet derived from its stomach fulfills the needs of three related families. Cheese making is thus an event aided by social cooperation. Indeed, Wilder stresses the whole family's participation in the events: Ma labors daily to press and cure the cheeses with Laura and Mary "helping" (as always). Laura's dislike of her surreptitious taste of the whey turns into a family joke, prompting Pa to sing the folk song of Old Grimes and his wife who made skim-milk cheeses rather than cheese with some fat from cream content. He turns that example of poor cheese making into a compliment for his wife's good skill with more substantial cheese, perfect for a family doing hard manual labor in the wilderness and needing those extra calories to burn, which poor Old Grimes didn't get from his wife and thus he blew away. Ma in turn praises Pa's skill as a provider, rounding off the entire event.[7] The episode highlights the partnership between the spouses, Pa as the one who produces the raw materials of food and Ma as the one who processes them to make them edible, nutritious, and tasty.

Wilder's attention here to her family's cheese making in the 1870s resonates historically with the rise of dairy farming and cheese making as Wisconsin's primary products in the latter part of the nineteenth century. Through the confluence of immigrant streams from Germany, the Scandinavian countries, and New York state (where the Ingalls family hailed from), settlers' ancestral dairying and cheese-making skills became the engine that drove agricultural and economic development in the newly settled territory, resulting in the industrialization of cheese manufacturing as Wisconsin became the dominant cheese producer in the nation by the early twentieth century.[8] Although initially cheese was produced on family farms for personal use and sometimes for cash revenue, as demand rose

---

[7] Laura Ingalls Wilder, *Little House in the Big Woods* (1932; repr., New York: Harper Trophy, 1971), 186–93.
[8] Richard Nelson Current, *Wisconsin: A History* (Champaign-Urbana: University of Illinois Press, 2001), 73–78.

production centralized in factories to assure quality, because, as historian Richard Nelson Current notes, "cheese was difficult to make at home in good and uniform quality."[9] Current's assessment uncannily echoes Pa's story and compliment for Ma as someone who has mastered home cheese-making techniques. In this episode, Wilder portrays the beginnings of the larger food arc that Current discusses, plus she invokes nostalgia for the pre-industrial process of cheese making that has become uncommon by the time she composes her first book at the beginning of the 1930s, cele-brating the individual initiative and skilled ability of the frontier family farm.

Food as Disseminator of Anglo-American Values in Nineteenth-Century Westward Expansion

Wilder recognized her family story as embodying a particular and important American experience: "I realized that I had seen and lived it all – all the successive phases of the frontier, first the frontiersman, then the pioneer, then the farmers and the towns. Then I understood that in my own life I represented a whole period of American history."[10] In this comment and within the novels that she based on this epiphany, Wilder constructs the Ingalls family's movements westward in ways that correspond with the "frontier thesis" as formulated by Frederick Jackson Turner.[11] He argued that the development of the American frontier – and consequently of the American national character – depended on the movement and adaptation of European-derived cultures and peoples westward across the continent. Pioneers saw themselves as "winning a wilderness," in Turner's words, bringing civilization to transform the wild land.[12] Within the Little House books, the members of the Ingalls family use their labor to change woods and prairie to farm and household. Pa works both as hunter-gatherer fron-tiersman and as pioneering farmer; he enjoys the former role more but knows that it is a short-term method of feeding his family. As the land

---

[9] Ibid., 75.

[10] Janet Spaeth, *Laura Ingalls Wilder* (Boston: Twayne, 1987), 23.

[11] For lengthy discussions of the connection between Wilder and Turner, please see Elizabeth Jameson, "Unconscious Inheritance and Conscious Striving: Laura Ingalls Wilder and the Frontier Narrative," in *Laura Ingalls Wilder and the Frontier Narrative: Five Perspectives*, edited by Dwight M. Miller (Lanham, MD: University Press of America, 2002), 69–94; and the chapter "Laura Ingalls Wilder, Frederick Jackson Turner and the Enduring Myth of the Frontier," in John E. Miller, *Laura Ingalls Wilder and Rose Wilder Lane: Authorship, Place, Time and Culture* (Columbia: University of Missouri Press, 2008).

[12] Frederick Jackson Turner, *The Significance of the Frontier in American History* (New York: Martino Fine Books, 2014), 2.

settles and game grows scarce due to competition and ecological habitat change, his role shifts more and more to farmer. He inhabits both the wilderness and the settled lands with ease. Ma's role, by contrast, remains steady: she cooks and preserves whatever foodstuffs her husband brings home or raises, manages a garden when that is practical, keeps house, and trains her daughters to fulfill their domestic roles properly. As Holly Blackford notes, Ma "is a very steady machine of civilization ... [and] throughout the series Ma stands for the importation of Eastern standards of gentility" into the wilderness.[13]

Food, in its production, conservation, and preparation, is one of the primary engines by which the pioneers worked this historical transformation. Food studies scholarship offers a means of bridging Turner's conservative "manifest destiny" ideology with Blackford's feminist critique of Caroline Ingalls' means of disseminating and adapting "civilization" into life on the frontier, particularly through the set of axioms that food theorist Massimo Montanari offers in his book *Food Is Culture*. Using his principles helps explain why food has such cultural power in the Little House books. In his book's introduction, Montanari proposes that a set of actions humans perform with food – its production, preparation, and eating – creates a developmental arc leading to the enactment of cultural values and assumptions.

To begin, Montanari argues that "Food is culture *when it is produced*, even 'performed,' because man does not use only what is found in nature ... but seeks also to *create* his own food ... superimposing the action of production on that of predator or hunter."[14] Montanari creates a division here between food that is hunted or gathered and consumed in something close to its natural state and food that is deliberately produced through farming: hunting deer or bear or wild fowl versus the sowing and reaping of crops and garden produce, dairying, or raising and butchering livestock. Although Laura's Pa engages in hunting throughout the books, particularly when the family lives in locations remote from towns, as narrator Wilder spends little time after the first book dramatizing the effort he goes to in hunting game. Her choice is partly explained by the point of view: as a child and a girl Laura is not present when Pa is hunting. As Ann Romines notes in *Constructing the Little House*, the stories Wilder reproduces from her father, including the ones about his hunting, were the genesis of her novels: she initially wrote to preserve and share them "because they were

[13] Holly Blackford, "Civilization and Her Discontents: The Unsettling Nature of Ma in *The Little House in the Big Woods*," *Frontiers: Journal of Women Studies* 29.1 (2008): 152–53.
[14] Massimo Montanari, *Food Is Culture* (New York: Columbia University Press, 2006), vi.

too good to be altogether lost." Romines sees passing on these stories as the central purpose of the first novel, to which the impetus to tell "an autobio-graphical fiction written by a woman" played second fiddle.[15] The focus on Pa's stories as hunter-gatherer is attenuated in later novels, however, when Laura has taken center stage in this "autobiographical fiction." Thus later in the series Wilder generally confines herself to mentioning the results of his hunt with no discussion of his experiences while out hunting. The Ingalls family does enjoy the results of Pa's hunting: whether it is deer in Wisconsin, turkey for Christmas in Kansas, or ducks, geese, or jackrabbits in South Dakota, Ma skillfully cooks each offering from her husband.

But it is worth noting that Wilder in some ways also privileges food creation, as Montanari defines it, in her descriptions of food production throughout the series. While the dairying example discussed above is just one of many detailed accounts of such processes, perhaps more importantly Wilder always figures Pa as a raiser of crops, a creator, in the Montanarian sense, of foods not found in nature. Whether he is combatting "sprouts" that threaten to take over his fields in *Big Woods* or breaking prairie sod to sow wheat or corn in *Prairie*, *Plum Creek*, and *Little Town*, the amount of time and effort Pa puts into growing crops conforms to Montanari's axiom that humans "superimpose" agricultural production over hunting – at least in "civilized" society.

As much as Wilder focuses on the production of food, she spends far more time on the cooking of food. Her emphasis illustrates Montanari's second axiom on the intersections of human culture and food:

> Food becomes culture *when it is prepared* because, once the basic products of his diet have been acquired, man transforms them by means of fire and a carefully wrought technology that is expressed in the practices of the kitchen.[16]

This axiom applies to food in the series no matter what its source, whether it is carefully cultivated grains, vegetables, and meats, or foodstuffs hunted or gathered from the wild: most are carefully processed through cooking, drying, or other preservation techniques. Two outstanding examples of complex preparation and the effort involved occur in *Big Woods*: the smoking of the venison and the elaborate social production of maple sugar. Wilder spends nearly five pages describing Pa's creation of the smokehouse and Ma's work in smoking the meat over many days. While the meat is not

---

[15] Ann Romines, *Constructing the Little House: Gender, Culture, and Laura Ingalls Wilder* (Amherst: University of Massachusetts Press, 1997), 22–23.
[16] Montanari, *Food Is Culture*, vi.

"cooked," per se, and the process happens out of doors rather than in the domestic space of the house, the smoking process is an extension of the kitchen in its use of fire as the technological means by which to preserve the meat for later consumption. The roles Pa and Ma take on fit the gendered performances typical of their division of labor: Pa makes the smokehouse, gets it set up and ready to use (as he will build hearths in later little houses), then Ma takes over the labor of watching the fire, keeping it going but not too fast so that the meat smokes properly but does not burn.

Wilder begins the second example by having Pa describe to his daughters the details of Grandpa's harvesting the sap from the maple trees; Laura later observes for herself the long process of cooking down the sap into syrup.[17] Wilder spreads this equally detailed description over many pages, interspersed with all the social events happening simultaneously as the sap boils: supper, dressing up, and the dance. By intermixing the narrative of Grandma as prime cook of the syrup and the events occurring outside the kitchen, Wilder gives a realistic sense of how long the process takes: this is indeed "slow food." The story climaxes with the event of greatest interest to little Laura: creating maple sugar candy for the children, each of whom gets a "patty-pan" filled with the cooled syrup for herself. But the greatest drama that intermixes food production and social interaction comes when Grandma wins an impromptu dance competition with her son, George, and then she immediately afterwards saves the sugar syrup from burning, triumphing again and drawing everyone into the kitchen for the candy. Through the preparation of the maple candy, Grandma dominates the scenes with her cooking skills. Romines sees Wilder's representation of Grandma as "a tremendous danger to social order" because she deserts her kitchen to compete in a jigging contest with her son – and beats him; however, this scene can easily be read instead as the story of a capable and triumphant woman who can cook and dance simultaneously and succeed at both.[18] Romines interprets Grandma as a threat to the rule of patriarchal dominance of *Big Woods*, but, taking Montanari's second principle into account, the grandmother's story represents a powerful assertion of cultural dominance, because at this stage of maple syrup preparation Grandma controls the process that has brought everyone together for the social occasion. Her concurrent triumphs inside and outside the kitchen, as the

---

[17] The complex rendering of the maple syrup in the sugar snow episode contrasts with Pa's discovery of the honey bees. Although it takes ingenuity to harvest the honey for his own use (rather than let the competing bear and the bees themselves take it), once he successfully gathers the honey it needs no processing beyond storage in vessels "covered ... neatly with cloths." Wilder, *Big Woods*, 195.

[18] Romines, *Constructing the Little House*, 30.

center of everyone's attention, model an active path for female narratives rather than male, a perspective that Wilder makes the focal point in the subsequent novels. Although Romines' perspective is important to understand how patriarchy works within the novels, understanding how food functions as a cultural force demonstrates a female empowerment that Romines overlooks. Thus a complicated set of "performances" is inherent in the annual sugaring of the maples, which Pa immediately recognizes will begin when he sees the sugar snow and hurries off to help his father.

Cooking remains a central feature of food consumption even (or in Ma's view, especially) when the family lives geographically farthest from "civilization." Blackford sees Ma in *Little House on the Prairie* as "struggl[ing] to make order and meaning out of emptiness, which is for her the chaos of absence: of a female sphere, of housekeeping."[19] Despite the challenges of camping for weeks on end, even after they have reached their destination, Ma perseveres in using cooking techniques that speak to her of civilization. Though lacking the cookstove of Wisconsin, even on an open fire Ma has an iron bake-oven, in which she cooks cornmeal cakes over the coals, and a spider, a pan on legs in which she can fry the sliced fat salt pork they have brought with them.[20] The primacy of cooking technology as a cultural value is clear when Pa chooses to build the hearth for the cabin even before he digs the well that will provide fresh, clean water, moving cooking into the more conventionally domestic indoor space Ma prefers. Once Pa has built the fireplace and its mantle, Ma moves cooking operations inside immediately and "roast[s] a prairie hen for supper."[21] When the floor is also complete, Ma "spread[s] a red-checked tablecloth on the table" and remarks, "Now we're living like civilized folks again."[22] Ma's relief at being able to eat in a "civilized" fashion (in a house, with a wood floor rather than dirt, at a table) suggests how closely cultural values are tied to the means of consuming food. Manners are a particularly important sign of civilization to Ma, no matter where she is in the wilderness or what markers of civilization may be missing: "'You must mind your manners, even if we are a hundred miles from anywhere,'" she admonishes Laura, adding that "'it isn't good manners to sing at table. Or when you're eating,' … because there was no table."[23]

Ma's binary vision of the world, valuing "civilized" behavior, necessarily leaves out those who are not "civilized" in her view: the local Indian

---

[19] Blackford, "Civilization and Her Discontents," 179.
[20] Laura Ingalls Wilder, *Little House on the Prairie* (1935; repr., New York: Harper Trophy, 1971), 30.
[21] Ibid., 118.
[22] Ibid., 129.
[23] Ibid., 40.

population. Her exclusionary attitude reflects Montanari's point that "Food etiquette [becomes] a sign of social barriers and of the impossibility of breaking them down."[24] Three times Indians visit the house, and food provides the central point of contact: twice Ma fixes food for them, and once they take it, but each time the narrative describes how the Indians eat, crouching by the fire rather than sitting at the table, thus fulfilling Ma's expectations of them as "uncivilized." Her binary framework allows no possibility of seeing, much less of understanding, that the Osage come from a culture equally complex and full of manners that differ from her own. Pa can sit down to eat with one of them, crouching beside the fire, but ultimately he agrees with their neighbor Mrs. Scott that "the land belongs to folks that'll farm it," rather than the people whose hunter-gatherer culture uses the land for food production in a way that these Anglo-Americans will not recognize.[25] Pa fully expects the Osage to be moved off their reserve: Montanari's first axiom that "created" food has greater primacy than "hunted" food underpins his expectation.[26]

Not only are manners important for marking culinary events as meaningful and exclusive (and thus civilized), but the foods people choose to eat function similarly, demonstrating Montanari's third axiom:

> Food is culture *when it is eaten* because man, while able to eat anything, or precisely for this reason, does not in fact eat everything but rather *chooses* his own food, according to criteria linked either to the economic and nutritional dimensions of the gesture or to the symbolic values with which food itself is invested. Through such pathways food takes shape as a decisive element of human identity and as one of the most effective means of expressing and communicating that identity.[27]

What the Ingalls family chooses to eat – and even more to the point what they choose *not* to eat – is significant. Although grasshoppers are a source of protein, the idea of eating them never occurs to the Ingalls family, despite an overly plentiful supply on Plum Creek when the family experiences the great grasshopper plague of the 1870s. During the Hard Winter, the family chooses to make bread by grinding the wheat into flour by using the coffee grinder, despite the labor involved, rather than boiling the wheat as

[24] Montanari, *Food Is Culture*, 97.
[25] Wilder, *Little House on the Prairie*, 211.
[26] For further discussion of the problems with Wilder's depictions of the Osage, see Sharon Smulders, "'The Only Good Indian': History, Race, and Representation in Laura Ingalls Wilder's *Little House on the Prairie*," *Children's Literature Association Quarterly* 2.4 (Winter 2002): 199–202; Frances W. Kaye, "Little Squatter on the Osage Diminished Reserve: Reading Laura Ingalls Wilder's Kansas Indians," *Great Plains Quarterly* 20.2 (2000): 123–40.
[27] Montanari, *Food Is Culture*, vi–vii.

porridge or mush as Pa first thinks they might, because within their cultural tradition bread is the primary food. They unconsciously follow the pattern Montanari notes, that in famine situations people remain as close as possible to their traditional foodways through substitutions of foodstuff or technology, thus preserving their sense of cultural identity even when it is under threat.[28] Yet the Ingalls family is innovative as well: when blackbirds eat the corn and oat crops in *Little Town on the Prairie*, Ma turns into food the blackbirds Pa shoots as pests, first frying them, then substituting them for chickens in a delicious pie. The family finds that many birds on the wing are edible (except pelicans and swans!) but that grasshoppers on the wing are not.

The blackbird pie signifies our final point from Montanari: the confluence of tradition and innovation:

> What we call *culture* takes its place where tradition and innovation intersect. Tradition is made up of knowledge, techniques, values, which were handed down to us. Innovation exists insomuch as this knowledge, these techniques, these values modify the place of man in the environmental context, rendering him able to experience a new reality. *A very successful innovation*: that is how we define tradition.[29]

Pa brings in blackbirds from the field, saying he hasn't heard of people eating them, but "these must be good meat and they're fat as butter."[30] As a hunter, Pa has often brought home many birds to eat, of particular approved kinds (ducks, geese, turkeys, prairie chickens). At this moment, he sees a new link between "food" birds and "non-food" birds and thus suggests substituting the blackbirds into their meal. Though these birds fall outside her cooking traditions, Ma accepts the challenge and initially serves them fried, a conventional rendering of bird meat, and the family exclaims "that they were the tenderest, most delicious meat that had ever been on that table."[31] Ma's next foray into cooking blackbirds is more innovative: baking them in a meat pie, which Pa mistakes as chicken pie. Yet the family sings the nursery rhyme about blackbirds in a pie, as Ma serves hers up, so in fact they have a prior text that grants cultural permission for eating the birds and even supplies a kind of template recipe. Ma knows how to make a chicken pie; chicken pie is a staple when chickens are plentiful enough for killing and eating. Tradition thus also allows innovation. When new ingredients are available but conventional ones are

[28] Ibid., 106.
[29] Ibid., 7.
[30] Laura Ingalls Wilder, *Little Town on the Prairie* (1941; repr., New York: Harper Trophy, 1971), 102.
[31] Ibid.

not, Ma has the insight to make substitutions and surprise Pa with her inventiveness. As Ma says when trying to make a green pumpkin pie in *The Long Winter*, "we wouldn't do much if we didn't do things nobody ever heard of before."[32] Thus the Ingalls family can take advantage of a new reality – and eat it. They extend culture – though these two innovations do not seem to be so successful that they become permanent parts of their diet, at least not as written up in Wilder's books. The Ingalls family thus fits Montanari's final assertion: their blackbird and green pumpkin pies are a hit for a hungry family in lean times, but when food becomes more plentiful they shift back to traditional foods and preparation: the two pies are not such *successful innovations* that they become a permanent part of the family's foodways.

Food and Foodways: Women Create Culture on the Frontier

This paradigm of cultural innovation correlates with Frederick Jackson Turner's theory of westward expansion. At the end of the nineteenth century, he influentially argued that as European peoples (both US citizens and European immigrants) moved west, innovating to adapt to the frontier, these pioneers shaped the national character: "Little by little [the pioneer] transforms the wilderness, but the outcome is not the old Europe ... Moving westward, the frontier became more and more American."[33] Contemporary Wilder scholars have noted the close connection between Turner's ideology and Wilder's interpretation of the frontier in her stories. John E. Miller draws an explicit ideological connection between them: "She certainly was a Turnerian in the sense that she had imbibed many of his ideas from the culture around her and agreed with him on the central importance of the frontier in American life."[34] The Ingalls family embodies Turnerian values, particularly in their self-reliance. Blackford notes that in *Big Woods*, "The Ingalls family can make everything from bread to bullets, houses to music, clothing to sugar – and make it seem fun, too."[35] Elizabeth Jameson agrees, noting that Wilder's vision of the capable frontier family is based in "individualism, self-sufficiency and self-reliance," and she further aligns the Turnerian values with Wilder's

---

[32] Laura Ingalls Wilder, *The Long Winter* (1940; repr., New York: Harper Trophy, 1971), 32.
[33] Turner, *Significance of the Frontier*, 7.
[34] Miller, *Laura Ingalls Wilder and Rose Wilder Lane*, 95.
[35] Blackford, "Civilization and Her Discontents," 155.

anti-New Deal political stance in the 1930s, the decade during which Wilder composed most of the Little House books.[36]

Miller comes to a similar assessment, concurring that Wilder echoes Turner, but notes "a mystifying paradox" that suggests Wilder revises Turner's thesis along gender lines:

> she constructed a fictional frontier full of women's (as well as men's) activities and participation while Turner almost entirely excluded women from his analyses ... He [Turner] focuses upon male conquest, individualism, lawlessness, and the search for autonomy, while Wilder depicts a dual West, where men's actions are set off against women's interests in making gardens, building homes, and sustaining community, thereby providing an alternative vision of what the West was and could be.[37]

Thus, reflecting the new western historians' interrogation of Turner's white, male bias,[38] the Little House books suggest that despite her underlying agreement with the patriarchal, white, Turnerian vision of the west, simply by focusing her narrative on a young girl coming of age on the frontier, Wilder diversifies his mono-gendered view of western frontier experience. Many feminist critics of Wilder's work have missed this revision of the Turnerian thesis in their focus on how Wilder subordinates the importance of the roles the women play in the Ingalls family. For example, rather than seeing Wilder as privileging a women's arc to frontier history, Jameson makes the point that Wilder's focus on "family households – those 'primitive' social units – buried women in a history of the nation in which they were largely invisible."[39] Likewise, Blackford and Louise Mowder both rework Jameson's point as Wilder's strategy to "silence" her female characters, reducing their autonomy and agency to keep them subordinated to the patriarchal arc of pioneer history. In "Domestication of Desire: Gender, Language, and Landscape in the Little House Books," Mowder notes,

> Her novels relate the process of enculturation by which the voice of the female child is trained and restrained so that the child may become a proper lady. Woman here is characterized by her silence, even in the face

---

[36] Jameson, "Unconscious Inheritance," 76.
[37] Miller, *Laura Ingalls Wilder and Rose Wilder Lane*, 95–96.
[38] Both Miller and Jameson use new western historians. For an example of this work, please look to Patricia Nelson Limerick, *The Legacy of Conquest: The Unbroken Past of the American West* (New York: Norton, 1987).
[39] Jameson, "Unconscious Inheritance," 77.

of suffering, and her ability to perform her female duties regardless of that silence.[40]

Blackford agrees with Jameson and Romines that, in contrast to "Pa's avid storytelling of his childhood," Ma is comparatively silent: "Ma reveals little of her childhood, which, Jameson argues, is because we cannot really hear Ma." Blackford then goes on to nuance Jameson: "Ma's actions are legible, so legible they tend to take Laura's breath away and render her speechless."[41] The silencing of the protagonist starts young, according to these critics, and continues as Laura matures and internalizes Ma's regime of silence.

Jameson, Mowder, and Blackford produce insightful critiques of Wilder's attempts to rein in women's power: Wilder quiets that power in order to conform to her preference for a Turnerian, conservative patriarchal narrative of pioneer history and a boot-strapping strategy of taming the frontier that she believes has parallels for surviving a Depression-era economy. But a close examination of food within the series suggests that women have more power on the frontier than critics frequently give them credit for: their skills in the making, preparation, and creation of food give the women in the Little House books an expressive outlet which affords them power, legibility, and visibility, demonstrating their power and their position as a supplement to the traditional male narrative. Montanari's axioms reveal a fundamental creative cultural power that cannot be ideologically encased and suppressed.

This chapter has made three main interrelated points. First, food is a significant part of the Little House books, in part because it reflects historical reality. Wilder presents food production as the central form of work in daily frontier life, embedded in a complex familial and social structure for which food is a signifying network that makes that structure visible. The novels chronicle a long-term apprenticeship in food production for Laura, served under her knowledgeable and loving parents, who teach her all the techniques they know or invent, skills whose value she intends to pass on to her readers. Second, inherent in the techniques of cooking and proper consumption are the values of Anglo-American culture of the period. Third, ideologically, Wilder's aim fits with her anti-New Deal politics, but as Pamela Riney-Kehrberg's historical analysis in *Childhood on the Farm: Work, Play, and Coming of Age in the Midwest* makes clear, Wilder's experiences parallel those common for rural children of her time; working with her parents to produce and process food often led to close bonds

---

[40] Louise Mowder, "Domestication of Desire: Gender, Language, and Landscape in the Little House Books," *Children's Literature Association Quarterly* 17.1 (Spring 1992): 15.
[41] Blackford, "Civilization and Her Discontents," 148.

between parents and children, as it does with Laura and her parents.[42] This labor, required of all members of the family, made self-sufficiency possible in Wilder's nostalgic look backward. Walker notes that reading the novels makes clear for modern readers connections that Wilder knew intuitively:

> Connections among the food on the table, the grain in the field, and the cow in the pasture. Between the food on the table and the sweat of someone's brow. Between the winter and dried apple, the summer and tomatoes, the autumn and fresh sausage. Between the labors of the pioneers and the abundance we enjoy today. Between children and their elders. Between the preparation of a meal and the experience of love.[43]

Although Walker writes without the benefit of the new western historians' updated understanding of the multifarious agents that produced the history of westward expansion, she properly celebrates food – both recipes and preparation – as a powerful expressive force which impels community, change, and empowerment in spite of efforts to limit and reduce American identity to a core of white patriarchal privilege and dominance. Montanari argues that food is culture; Wilder demonstrates in spite of herself that food is power.

What we hope that we have demonstrated in this chapter is that an analysis of any children's text in which food plays a central role requires examination of food practices and their history, the representational uses of food (symbolism, ideology), and, finally, the evolving multidisciplinary practice of food studies as it intersects with literary and historical scholarship. Converging conventional literary scholarship on an author's work with food studies results in a synthesis that offers a richer, culturally based understanding of the work. Such an approach reveals, in this case, a more profound understanding of the complex (and at times even contradictory) social and historical contexts that underlie Wilder's story, in its setting, composition, and ideological underpinnings.

BIBLIOGRAPHY

Biasin, Gian-Paolo. *The Flavors of Modernity: Food and the Novel*. Princeton, NJ: Princeton University Press, 1993.
Blackford, Holly. "Civilization and Her Discontents: The Unsettling Nature of Ma in *The Little House in the Big Woods*." *Frontiers: Journal of Women Studies* 29.1 (2008): 147–87.

---

[42] Pamela Riney-Kehrberg, *Childhood on the Farm: Work, Play, and Coming of Age in the Midwest* (Lawrence: University Press of Kansas, 2005), 51–54.
[43] Walker, *Little House Cookbook*, xv.

Carrington, Bridget, and Jennifer Harding, eds. *Feast or Famine? Food and Children's Literature*. Newcastle upon Tyne: Cambridge Scholars, 2014.

Current, Richard Nelson. *Wisconsin: A History*. Champaign-Urbana: University of Illinois Press, 2001.

Daniel, Carolyn. *Voracious Children: Who Eats Whom in Children's Literature*. New York: Routledge, 2006.

Honeyman, Susan. *Consuming Agency in Fairy Tales, Childlore, and Folkliterature*. New York: Routledge, 2010.

Jameson, Elizabeth. "Unconscious Inheritance and Conscious Striving: Laura Ingalls Wilder and the Frontier Narrative." In *Laura Ingalls Wilder and the American Frontier: Five Perspectives,* edited by Dwight M. Miller, 69–94. Lanham, MD: University Press of America, 2002.

Kaye, Frances W. "Little Squatter on the Osage Diminished Reserve: Reading Laura Ingalls Wilder's Kansas Indians." *Great Plains Quarterly* 20.2 (2000): 123–40.

Katz, Wendy R. "Some Uses of Food in Children's Literature." *Children's Literature in Education* 11.4 (1980): 192–99.

Keeling, Kara K., and Scott T. Pollard. "Introduction: Food in Children's Literature." In *Critical Approaches to Food in Children's Literature*, edited by Kara K. Keeling and Scott T. Pollard, 3–18. New York: Routledge, 2009.

" 'The Key Is in the Mouth': Food and Orality in *Coraline*." *Children's Literature* 40 (2012): 1–27.

"Power, Food, and Eating in Maurice Sendak and Henrik Drescher: *Where the Wild Things Are, In the Night Kitchen,* and *The Boy Who Ate Around.*" *Children's Literature in Education* 30.2 (June 1999): 127–43.

"Privilege and Exploitation: Food as Dual Signifier in Pamela Muñoz Ryan's *Esperanza Rising.*" *The Lion and the Unicorn* 40.3 (September 2016): 280–99.

Korsmeyer, Carolyn. *Making Sense of Taste: Food and Philosophy*. Ithaca, NY: Cornell University Press, 1999.

Limerick, Patricia Nelson. *The Legacy of Conquest: The Unbroken Past of the American West*. New York: Norton, 1987.

Miller, John E. *Laura Ingalls Wilder and Rose Wilder Lane: Authorship, Place, Time, and Culture*. Columbia: University of Missouri Press, 2008.

Montanari, Massimo. *Food Is Culture*. New York: Columbia University Press, 2006.

Mowder, Louise. "Domestication of Desire: Gender, Language, and Landscape in the Little House Books." *Children's Literature Association Quarterly* 17.1 (Spring 1992): 15–19.

Nikolajeva, Maria. *From Mythic to Linear: Time in Children's Literature*. Lanham, MD: Children's Literature Association – Scarecrow Press, 2000.

Perrot, Jean. "Maurice Sendak's Ritual Cooking of the Child in Three Tableaux: The Moon, Mother, and Music." *Children's Literature* 18 (1990): 68–86.

Pollard, Scott, and Kara Keeling. "In Search of his Father's Garden." In *Beatrix Potter's Peter Rabbit: A Children's Classic at 100*, edited by Margaret Mackey, 117–30. Lanham, MD: Children's Literature Association – Scarecrow Press, 2002.

Riney-Kehrberg, Pamela. *Childhood on the Farm: Work, Play, and Coming of Age in the Midwest*. Lawrence: University Press of Kansas, 2005.

Romines, Ann. *Constructing the Little House: Gender, Culture, and Laura Ingalls Wilder*. Amherst: University of Massachusetts Press, 1997.

Slothower, Jodie, and Jan Susina. "Delicious Supplements: Literary Cookbooks as Additives to Children's Texts." In *Critical Approaches to Food in Children's Literature*, edited by Kara K. Keeling and Scott T. Pollard, 21–38. New York: Routledge, 2009.

Smulders, Sharon. "'The Only Good Indian': History, Race, and Representation in Laura Ingalls Wilder's Little House on the Prairie." *Children's Literature Association Quarterly* 27.4 (Winter 2002): 199–202.

Spaeth, Janet. *Laura Ingalls Wilder*. Boston: Twayne, 1987.

Symons, Michael. *A History of Cooks and Cooking*. Champaign: University of Illinois Press, 2004.

Turner, Frederick Jackson. *The Significance of the Frontier in American History*. New York: Martino Fine Books, 2014.

Vallone, Lynne. ""What Is the Meaning of All This Gluttony?": Edgeworth, the Victorians, C. S. Lewis and a Taste for Fantasy." *Papers: Explorations into Children's Literature* 12.1 (2002): 47–54.

Visser, Margaret. *The Rituals of Dinner: The Origins, Evolution, Eccentricities, and Meaning of Table Manners*. New York: Grove Press, 1991.

Walker, Barbara M. *The Little House Cookbook: Frontier Food from Laura Ingalls Wilder's Classic Stories*. New York: Harper & Row, 1979.

Wilder, Laura Ingalls. *By the Shores of Silver Lake*. 1939. Reprint, New York: Harper Trophy, 1971.

Little House in the Big Woods. 1932. Reprint, New York: Harper Trophy, 1971.

Little House on the Prairie. 1935. Reprint, New York: Harper Trophy, 1971.

Little Town on the Prairie. 1941. Reprint, New York: Harper Trophy, 1971.

The Long Winter. 1940. Reprint, New York: Harper Trophy, 1971.

On the Banks of Plum Creek. 1937. Reprint, New York: Harper Trophy, 1971.

CHAPTER 11

Avant-Garde Food Writing, Modernist Cuisine

Allison Carruth

Search online for the phrase "modernist cuisine" and over 390,000 unique results populate your browser.[1] Individual filter bubbles notwithstanding, you will likely encounter at the top the five-volume $625 tome *Modernist Cuisine: The Art and Science of Cooking* – followed by a bevy of stories, posts, social media feeds, and academic articles that tout the unorthodox experiments of the contemporary culinary phenomenon known as molecular gastronomy. In contrast, a search for "avant-garde food writing" yields a scant two unique results: a snippet from literary critic and food studies scholar Alice McLean's 2012 monograph *Aesthetic Pleasure in Twentieth-Century Women's Food Writing* and a series of posts from the *Average Food Blog*.[2] The point of departure for what follows is this asymmetry combined with skepticism about claims that the chefs and methods associated with molecular gastronomy represent the twenty-first-century successor to modernism writ large and to specific avant-garde movements, from absurdist theater to the Dada readymade.[3] In examining those claims, this chapter proposes that the culinary trend for which Catalan chef Ferran Adrià has been a leading figure should be reexamined in terms of its high-tech economics and also its particular investments in innovation, proto-typing, and data mining. Rather than modernist or avant-garde, *start-up cuisine* is an apt framework for apprehending the cultural origins and import of restaurant-incubators like Adrià's now shuttered elBulli.[4] My argument thus aims to distinguish the buzzword of modernist cuisine

---

[1] "Modernist cuisine," Google browser search, November 17, 2016.
[2] "Avant-garde food writing," Google browser search, November 17, 2016; Alice L. McLean, *Aesthetic Pleasure in Twentieth-Century Women's Food Writing: The Innovative Appetites of M. F. K. Fisher, Alice B. Toklas, and Elizabeth David*, Studies in Twentieth-Century Literature (New York: Routledge, 2012).
[3] Kevin Landis, "Culinary Pataphysics: Dining, Theatre, and the Avant-Garde," *Gastronomica: Journal of Critical Food Studies* 14.2 (2014): 50–53.
[4] I follow the spelling of elBulli that Adrià and the restaurant use; however, a number of journalists and critics spell it instead as El Bulli, and in citations I follow the convention of the source's author where it differs from Adrià's.

from the historical avant-garde, a project that invites cross-disciplinary approaches to the multiple forms and histories of modernism, on the one hand, and the social conditions of contemporary restaurants, on the other. It is in this sense that elBulli and its peers offer a rich area of inquiry for both modernist studies and critical food studies.

Food Politics of the Historical Avant-Garde

Culinary tropes and their political meanings preoccupy a range of canonical modernists from Henry James to Jean Toomer, Gertrude Stein to F. T. Marinetti – as Michelle Coghlan, Jennifer Fleissner, Catherine Keyser, and other scholars have shown.[5] As for modernist writers and artists whose work has been classed as avant-garde, food culture, when it arises as a central concern, often appears in a mutated form that operates to shake up capitalist structures of consumption, labor, and domesticity. A similarly critical alimentary strand also runs through histories and theories of the avant-garde. In the seminal *Theory of the Avant-Garde*, for example, Peter Bürger characterizes the Dada readymade as akin to the generic conventions and sociocultural function of recipes:

> It is no accident that both [Tristan] Tzara's instructions for the making of a Dadaist poem and [André] Breton's for the writing of automatic texts have the character of recipes. This represents not only a polemical attack on the individual creativity of the artist; the recipe is to be taken quite literally as suggesting a possible activity on the part of the recipient.[6]

Kenneth Goldsmith describes neo-Dada artists of the 1960s in kindred terms, noting that Sol LeWitt and others crafted a "recipe-based art" guided by the principle that anyone could adapt its creative procedures.[7] Finally, Sianne Ngai intimates that avant-garde aesthetics develop in part out of a relationship to consumerism that models what she describes as

---

[5] Michelle Coghlan, "Tasting Modernism: An Introduction," *Resilience: Journal of the Environmental Humanities* 2.1 (2015); Jennifer L. Fleissner, "Henry James's Art of Eating," *ELH* 75.1 (2008); Catherine Keyser, "Bottles, Bubbles, and Blood: Jean Toomer and the Limits of Racial Epidermalism," *Modernism/modernity* 22.2 (2015); Catherine Keyser, "An All-Too-Moveable Feast: Ernest Hemingway and the Stakes of Terroir," *Resilience: Journal of the Environmental Humanities* 2.1 (2014). See also Michel Delville, *Food, Poetry, and the Aesthetics of Consumption: Eating the Avant-Garde* (New York: Routledge, 2008); Cecilia Novero, *Antidiets of the Avant Garde: From Futurist Cooking to Eat Art* (Minneapolis: University of Minnesota Press, 2010).

[6] Peter Bürger, *Theory of the Avant-Garde*, translated by Michael Shaw, Theory and History of Literature (Minneapolis: University of Minnesota Press, 2002), 53.

[7] Kenneth Goldsmith, *Uncreative Writing* (New York: Columbia University Press, 2011), 128–29.

"gustatory" interventions in the all-too-palatable tastes of commodity culture.[8] Such interventions arguably tend to take an anti-humanist approach
to cuisine, conviviality, and taste, an approach that employs avant-garde
aesthetic practices to investigate biological processes of eating along with
the messy web of relations connecting human eaters to other bodies.

We see this disruptive food politics at work in an eclectic set of texts: the
catalogue of "drives and appetites" that Stein composes for the "FOOD"
section of *Tender Buttons* (1914), the weird meals and dishes that pervade
The Futurist Cookbook (1932), the satire of industrial agriculture found
in Lorine Niedecker's mid-century poems, the gastronomical parody
embedded within M. F. K. Fisher's World War II cookbooks, and the
compilation of surreal portraits of meals and actual recipes that comprises
Salvador Dalí's *Diners de Gala* (1973), to name a few.[9] An illustration of
Cecilia Novero's concept of the avant-garde's "anti-diets," Marinetti's *The
Futurist Cookbook* performs an especially provocative avant-garde rejoinder
to both cosmopolitan fine dining and regional foodways by collaging dis-
cordant images and ingredients that upend individual nostalgia and social
norms around food.[10] This zany work, in Ngai's sense,[11] lambasts Italian
culinary traditions and the centrality of pasta within those traditions,
which Marinetti and his collaborators decry in characteristically mascu-
linist terms for making Italian bodies "leaden" and "opaque."[12] In response
to this perceived national crisis, *The Futurist Cookbook* posits a prototype
for "a *new* way of thinking, which everyone considers *crazy*, but which
will henceforth establish the proper nourishment for a faster and even

---

[8] This idea informs Ngai's broader argument that part of what defines cultural production as avant-
garde is the particular, peculiar uses of "marginal"/"minor" aesthetic categories (specifically, the
categories of cuteness, zaniness, and the interesting) in order to resist the "ease with which market
society turns art into a culinary commodity." Sianne Ngai, "The Cuteness of the Avant-Garde,"
Critical Inquiry 31.4 (2005): 831, 834. See also Sianne Ngai, *Our Aesthetic Categories: Zany, Cute,
Interesting* (Cambridge, MA: Harvard University Press, 2015).

[9] Gertrude Stein, *Tender Buttons: The Corrected Centennial Edition*, edited by Seth Perlow (San
Francisco: City Lights, 2014); F. T. Marinetti, *The Futurist Cookbook*, translated by Suzanne Brill
(London: Trefoil, 1989); Lorine Niedecker, *New Goose*, edited by Jenny Penberthy (Berkeley,
CA: Rumor Books, 2002); M. F. K. Fisher, *Consider the Oyster* (1941; repr., New York: Farrar, Straus
and Giroux, 1988); M. F. K. Fisher, *How to Cook a Wolf* (1942; repr., New York: North Point Press,
1988); M. F. K. Fisher, *The Gastronomical Me* (1943; repr., New York: North Point Press, 1989);
Salvador Dalí, *Les Diners De Gala*, translated by Captain J. Peter Moore (1973; repr., Taschen, 2016).

[10] Novero, *Antidiets of the Avant Garde*.

[11] Beginning with an extended analysis of Lucille Ball's performance style, Ngai defines zaniness
capaciously as "a stressed out, even desperate" aesthetic category that, while it is "playful in all
its manifestations across genres, media, and cultural strata … is an aesthetic of action pushed to
strenuous and even precarious extreme." Ngai, *Our Aesthetic Categories*, 185.

[12] Marinetti, *Futurist Cookbook*, 36.

more airborne life."[13] More specifically, Marinetti lays out an agenda for refashioning Italian bodies to be like and also literally nourished by industrial materials.

To concretize this endeavor, the book concludes with a miscellany of variously artful, bizarre, and downright off-putting recipes that carry titles such as "Sculpted Meat," "Steel Chicken," "Network in the Sky," "Tyrrhenian Seaweed Foam [with coral garnish]," and "Atlantic Aerofood."[14] Collected in the section titled "futurist formulas for restaurants and quisibeve [sic],"[15] the recipes knit the revolutionary impulses of futurism to a pseudoscientific and "hygienic" vocabulary of cooking that maps eerily onto eugenic ideology, Enrico Cesaretti argues.[16] The recipes might remind some contemporary readers of the methods connected to molecular gastronomy, methods that adapt the chemistry equipment and synthetic goods of industrial food science (vacuum sealers and agar-agar, for instance) to the space of high-end restaurant kitchens. Foams, infusions, and reconstituted dishes are some of the mainstays featured on the menus of restaurants like elBulli. And like those menus, on the surface at least, Futurist "formulas" detail state changes that aim to disturb a diner's sensory associations of certain shapes, colors, and textures with specific edible ingredients and flavor profiles. A dish called "Italian Sea" thus calls for "geometric stripes of fresh tomato sauce and liquidized spinach" to be arranged on a "rectangular plate" with skyscraper-like "constructions" of boiled fish, banana, cherry, and dried fig,[17] while the recipe for "Tyrrhenian Seaweed Foam" transforms whole foods (such as "freshly-netted sea lettuce") into an airy liquid. The dish further messes with one's appetite for natural and seasonal foods by turning "clusters of piquant red peppers, slices of sea urchins caught at full moon, and a constellation of seeds from a ripe pomegranate" into an "architectural" structure meant to look like coral while smelling, feeling, and tasting nothing like that.[18]

---

[13] Ibid., 73 (emphasis in original).

[14] Ibid., 143, 51, 58, 61, 65.

[15] "Quisibeve" [or *qui si beve*] translates as "here one/you drink" and represents Marinetti's term for bars as a rejection of the use of French and other foreign terminology in Italian culture.

[16] Comparing *The Futurist Cookbook* to French utopian thinker Charles Fourier's writings (a comparison Marinetti would no doubt dislike for its transnational scope), Cesaretti contends that "the implied notion that the social body could be made healthier" in the cookbook shows "the intersections of [nineteenth-century Italian physiologist Paolo] Mantegazza's and, by extension, Marinetti's, hygienic utopia with the more extreme interpretations of the new science of eugenics ... which would constitute such a crucial subtext of the Nazi-fascist ideology in the first decades of the century." Enrico Cesaretti, "Recipes for the Future: Traces of Past Utopias in *The Futurist Cookbook*," *The European Legacy* 14.7 (2009): 851.

[17] Marinetti, *Futurist Cookbook*, 165.

[18] Ibid., 161.

However resonant with the techniques of molecular gastronomy, the farcical and deliberately inedible character of the Futurist recipes should give pause. In step with the 1909 Futurist manifesto published in *Le Figaro*, *The Futurist Cookbook*, Novero argues, "relentlessly advance[s] the call for progress and modernity" both through its formulas and through its performative descriptions of a series of Futurist "banquets" held at the Holy Palate Restaurant space in Turin.[19] Although Novero identifies an ironic register in the cookbook that "interferes with the self-importance of the fascist political agenda," she also acknowledges that the cookbook's culinary program imagines a form of "Futurist edible art that is nonorganic and avant-gardist but also chauvinistic."[20] Unlike the experimental cuisine of chefs who take cues from food scientists and product engineers, Futurist cuisine can be understood as a type of performative art that promotes simultaneously emerging technologies and regressive politics. Moreover, Marinetti's formulas connect cuisine to engineering in a manner that ultimately flouts the cultural history and meaningfulness of the recipe as a type of writing that is an implement of vernacular science and engineering. To cite Kyla Tompkins' elegant analysis, the recipe "morphs across time as foodways are handed down and changed," circulating among communities as a mode of person-to-person knowledge exchange.[21] Conversely, *The Futurist Cookbook* advocates for reengineering Italian cuisine around the fusion of edible and industrial materials in order to jettison both communal conviviality and cosmopolitan *gourmandise* in favor of what we might call steel-powered nationalism.[22]

Of course, avant-garde notions of and experiments with food are by no means uniform. Consider, as a counterpoint to *The Futurist Cookbook*, Niedecker's *New Goose* poems, which reject *gourmandise* and nationalism alike by crafting an edible assemblage that includes metaphors such as "the undigestible phrase" and fast-growing asparagus ("Capital's / miracles of profit") as well as material markers of malnutrition such as "quack-grass bread" and rotting apples.[23] This assemblage signifies, among other political matters, the exploitation of agricultural and domestic labor to power the economy and military as well as lived, rural experiences of famine and poverty.[24] One of the volume's organizing leitmotifs is a portrait of Midwestern US farmers going hungry during World War II while urban

[19] Novero, *Antidiets of the Avant Garde*, 9.
[20] Ibid., 43.
[21] Kyla Wazana Tompkins, "Consider the Recipe," *J19: Journal of Nineteenth-Century Americanists* 1.2 (2013): 440.
[22] Thanks to Routledge for granting permission to adapt this analysis of Marinetti and (below) Lorine Niedecker from Amy L. Tigner and Allison Carruth, *Literature and Food Studies*, Literature and Contemporary Thought Series (London and New York: Routledge, 2018), 157–159.
[23] Niedecker, *New Goose*, 13, 37, 75.
[24] Ibid., 13, 37, 75, 81.

elites dine on French food, as was in fact the case during the war, when hotel restaurants in New York and London functioned as bomb shelters and cultural oases for the affluent.[25] One lyric speaker in *New Goose* powerfully describes the "destitute" rural towns where everyday life during this period offers "Nothing nourishing."[26] Another poem repeats this figure of scarcity ("nothing") to characterize the shelves of a local grocery store, while yet another assails the "government men" charged with increasing agricultural yields on behalf of the Allied powers despite the ironic persistence of hunger in food-producing communities like Niedecker's own Fort Atkinson, Wisconsin.[27] Invoking the contradictory political discourses of food rationing and agricultural productivity, the volume questions the very premise of stockpiling commodities for "way off" battlefields – a project *New Goose* calls a "quack" idea that divides the rich from civilians who are "too hungry to flatter."[28]

This analysis highlights an alternative genealogy of avant-garde food politics to that of the Futurists, one that turns to agriculture and rural life rather than cooking and technological innovation and that employs modernist fragmentation and allusiveness to critique the relationships between capitalism, war, and consumerism. Divergent as they are in their political commitments, *The Futurist Cookbook* and *New Goose* also suggest commonalities in the ways that the historical avant-garde interfaces with food. Texts like these, penned during the era of international modernism and rapid modernization (not to mention during the rise of what the *Harvard Business Review* in 1956 termed "agribusiness"), make food politics a zone of disquieting embodiment and visceral satire – or what Novero terms "countergastronomy."[29]

The Celebrity of Modernist Cuisine

How, by comparison, might we apprehend the jubilant narrative of modernist cuisine? And as a corollary question, how might a critical food

---

[25] See John Burnett, *England Eats Out: A Social History of Eating Out in England from 1830 to the Present* (London: Pearson Longman, 2004); George Orwell, "The British Crisis: London Letter to *Partisan Review* [8 May 1942]," in *My Country Right or Left, 1940–1943*, edited by Sonia Orwell and Ian Angus (Boston: Nonpareil Books, 2000), 207–16.

[26] Niedecker, *New Goose*, 55.

[27] Ibid., 57, 75.

[28] Ibid., 118–19.

[29] Novero argues that central to the project of the historical avant-garde is "the translation of a visual aesthetic into countergastronomy," or what she also terms antidiets, that hinges on bodily provocation, discomfort, and disgust. Novero, *Antidiets of the Avant Garde*, xxiii.

studies approach help to contextualize and interpret the idea that a network of contemporary chefs have "ignited a culinary revolution" best understood as an extension of the most avant-garde strands of modernism?[30] To answer these questions requires taking stock of the terms on which modernist cuisine has been defined and celebrated. On the whole, the most prominent chefs and restaurants within this discourse are viewed as dispensing with the social norms and digestible products of traditional *haute cuisine* by making fine dining into a performance art that emotionally and sensorily consumes the diner. At the same time, what also makes these culinary trailblazers "modernist" is their use of expensive technologies and materials to disrupt received culinary genres: most notably, French bistro fare and Japanese *omakase*, the two traditions that defined the fusion aesthetic of *nouvelle cuisine* in the 1980s and 1990s. It is in this latter sense that modernist cuisine has become more or less synonymous with molecular gastronomy.

Writing for the journal *Gastronomica*, Kevin Landis draws parallels between the radical art practices of the early twentieth century and the contemporary restaurants aligned with modernist cuisine and molecular gastronomy: among them, Thomas Keller's Per Se (New York City), Heston Blumenthal's Fat Duck (Berkshire, England), Grant Achatz's Alinea (Chicago), and Adrià's elBulli (Costa Brava, Spain).[31] Landis compares these eateries, in particular, to absurdist writer Alfred Jarry's philosophy of pataphysics – which Jarry defined as "a complex science" (or artful pseudoscience more aptly) that pursues "imaginary solutions to imaginary problems."[32] Citing the 2006 "Statement on the 'New Cookery' " that Adria, Blumenthal, and Keller co-authored with science writer Harold McGee, Landis reasons that such chefs share creative DNA with avant-garde figures like Jarry.[33] In support of this argument, he cites several characteristics that the "new cookery" evinces: the production of outrage as an affective experience for the diner/audience, a strategy of embedding nonsensical (and in this case edible) objects squarely within a space of bourgeois consumerism, and an artistic commitment to "experiential and fleeting" forms.[34]

---

[30] Mitchell Davis, "A Time and a Place for a Peach," *The Senses and Society* 7.2 (2012): 147.

[31] Landis, "Culinary Pataphysics."

[32] Ibid., 46.

[33] Ferran Adrià et al., "Statement on the 'New Cookery,'" *Guardian UK*, December 10, 2006, www.theguardian.com/uk/2006/dec/10/foodanddrink.obsfoodmonthly. For a more recent such statement in the form of an entire cookbook, see J. Kenji López-Alt, *The Food Lab: Better Home Cooking Through Science* (New York: Norton, 2015).

[34] Landis, "Culinary Pataphysics," 47. Mitchell Davis makes a related comparison in connecting the same coterie of chefs and restaurants to midcentury performance art, building on 1950s American restaurateur Joe Baum's "maxim" that all restaurants produce theater. Davis, "Time and a Place."

However, this comparison of avant-garde movements such as Theater of the Absurd and a cuisine that costs upwards of $200 per person to partake of collapses what are in fact distinct categories of cultural experimentation: categories such as innovation, unconventionality, modernism, and the avant-garde itself.[35] Noting the broader tendency to apply the category of the avant-garde to this "food scene," Fabio Parasecoli unsettles laudatory accounts of executive chefs like those above as modernist, chefs who operate multimillion-dollar businesses that rely on low-wage and intern labor, cater to affluent patrons, and often attract venture capital investors.[36] Contradictions abound, in other words, when restaurant reviewers, cultural critics, and technology reporters variously hail such chefs at once as avant-garde artists who craft modernist cuisine and as savvy entrepreneurs who generate lucrative profits for silent partners. These contradictions come into focus in the conceptual fault lines running through the discourse of modernist cuisine in which keywords like modernist, avant-garde, and deconstructive intermix seamlessly with terms like innovation, prototyping, engineering, technology, and molecular gastronomy. Having coined the last of these terms in the 1980s to describe the empirical study of cooking techniques and dishes in lab settings, the French biochemist Hervé This has critiqued the use of molecular gastronomy as synonymous with modernist cuisine.[37] His critique underscores the tension between the artistic, scientific, and economic dimensions of the people and places identified with molecular gastronomy, who are arguably less concerned with reviving modernism in all its guises and more interested in adapting the business model of Silicon Valley to tackle the challenges of restaurant finances in high-rent, high-tech cities.

To this point, former Microsoft CTO Nathan Myhrvold has been among the most influential voices in popularizing "modernist cuisine" and linking it to molecular gastronomy – in part through his self-publication of

---

[35] As of the time of this chapter's composition, Alinea listed the prices of its three menus (the "intimate, immersive and cutting edge experience" of the Kitchen Table menu, the "multi-sensory 16-to-18 course" Gallery menu, and the "10–12 course" Salon menu) as, respectively, $385, $285 to $345, and $175 to $225 before service, tax, and wine; while Fat Duck's set menu was priced at approximately $320.

[36] Fabio Parasecoli, "The Chefs, the Entrepreneurs, and Their Patrons: The Avant-Garde Food Scene in New York City," in *Gastropolis: Food and New York City*, edited by Annie Hauck-Lawson and Jonathan Deutsch (New York: Columbia University Press, 2009), 116–31. See also Fabio Parasecoli, "Deconstructing Soup: Ferran Adrià's Culinary Challenges," *Gastronomica* 1.1 (2001): 60–73.

[37] See especially Hervé This, *Révélations Gastronomiques* (Paris: Belin, 1995); Hervé This, *Molecular Gastronomy: Exploring the Science of Flavor* (New York: Columbia University Press, 2008); Hervé This, *Building a Meal: From Molecular Gastronomy to Culinary Constructivism* (New York: Columbia University Press, 2009); Hervé This, *The Science of the Oven* (New York: Columbia University Press, 2012).

Modernist Cuisine. In "The Art in Gastronomy," Myhrvold contends that chefs who over the last two decades have melded engineering and food science with fine dining are "the true intellectual heir[s] to Modernism."[38] We should question the premise of this claim, which posits a monolithic understanding of modernism and also ignores what is a lively field of contemporary literature, art, and performance where we might also locate "intellectual heir[s]" to the past century's modernist movements. Furthermore, in classifying celebrity chefs as "true" modernists, Myhrvold glosses over the monetization of experimental restaurants on the model of tech start-ups and the attendant influx of venture capital into their operating budgets. It glosses over, that is, the influence of the industry in which Myhrvold earned the wealth that he has parlayed into patronizing molecular gastronomy restaurants and self-publishing a treatise on modernist cuisine. This is not to say that the chefs who penned the "Statement on the 'New Cookery'" and their compatriots are without artistry or intellectual roots. Rather, my point here is to highlight the financial realities that make experimental restaurants reliant on private equity and to acknowledge the social conditions that make cultural capital and celebrity most readily available to a select cadre of primarily white male restaurateurs.

This critique begs another question: how do celebratory accounts of modernist cuisine like Landis' and Myhrvold's compare to depictions of its evident antithesis of farm-to-table cooking? Anthropologist Amy Trubek offers a preliminary answer in suggesting that popular food discourse tends to correlate the "gustatory pleasure" that farm-to-table restaurants provide to a set of *a priori* commitments: commitments to local sourcing, fresh ingredients, urban agriculture, and simple culinary techniques that showcase the "taste of place."[39] In contrast, the established line of thought goes, modernist cuisine rejects traditional connections between *terroir* and technique and eschews conventional expectations about "gustatory pleasure" itself. In a compelling call for a new ethos within food studies and food activism that is open-minded to technological innovation, Rachel Laudan reinforces this binary of forward-looking modernist cuisine and rearguard farm-to-table and slow food proponents by identifying the latter with "culinary Luddism."[40] The problems with this binary portrait are

---

[38] Nathan Myhrvold, "The Art in Gastronomy: A Modernist Perspective," *Gastronomica: Journal of Food and Culture* 11.1 (2011): 20.

[39] Amy B. Trubek, *The Taste of Place: A Cultural Journey into Terroir*, California Studies in Food and Culture (Berkeley: University of California Press, 2009), 17.

[40] Rachel Laudan, "A Plea for Culinary Modernism: Why We Should Love New, Fast, Processed Food," *Gastronomica: Journal of Food and Culture* 1.1 (2001): 36.

several. First, the differences presumed in the political, operational, and gastronomical values of each term in the binary obscures what is a spectrum of culinary methods and values. Second, although I have elsewhere critiqued the literature around slow food for its own binary vision of environmentalist versus techno-utopian food, the blanket dismissal of farm-to-table cuisine neglects the cultural forces that celebrate self-consciously inventive chefs as creative geniuses while positioning environmentally minded chefs as participants within a collective social movement.[41] As evidence of this unevenness, the Wikipedia entry for "molecular gastronomy" features a growing list of individual chefs, while the "farm-to-table" page has no such section and mentions Chez Panisse's well-known executive chef Alice Waters only in the context of the slow food movement and the history of environmental activism in California. Charlotte Druckman has traced a similarly gendered pattern throughout the industries of professional cooking – from the institution of restaurant awards to the media of food television. However successful and innovative they may be, chefs who are not in the profession's longtime privileged group of European and Anglo-American men, Druckman argues, tend to "remain isolated and pigeonholed."[42]

The stratified distinctions maintained between "modernist" and "farm-to-table" cuisines are rhetorical and material, in other words. They are also reductive, I am suggesting, vis-à-vis both culinary modi operandi. Many chefs associated with molecular gastronomy source ingredients locally, while many farm-to-table proponents are innovative in combining familiar and rare ingredients and in mixing ethnic culinary traditions from the chef's local community and beyond. Put differently, the restaurants that "deconstruct" gastronomy often put as much stock in local procurement, regional culture, and edible biodiversity as farm-to-table restaurants put into aesthetic and technical experimentation. Indeed, a new generation of chefs hailed as this decade's culinary rabble-rousers are nothing short of zealous about hyper-local ingredients and ancient foraging and fermentation practices as these same chefs (René Redzepi, the Danish head chef of Noma, for one) intermingle those practices with the spheres, foams, and *sous vide* preparations that made others, like Adrià, famous. Moreover, it is this combination of painstakingly sourced ingredients and

[41] Allison Carruth, "Slow Food, Low Tech: Environmental Narratives of Agribusiness and Its Alternatives," in *The Routledge Companion to the Environmental Humanities*, edited by Ursula K. Heise, Jon Christensen, and Michelle Niemann (London: Routledge, 2017), 313–22.

[42] Charlotte Druckman, "Why Are There No Great Women Chefs?," *Gastronomica: Journal of Food and Culture* 10.1 (2010): 31.

novel methods that has distinguished "modernist cuisine" and in turn inspired a devoted following of patrons with the material means and the social network to secure reservations at restaurants like Noma and elBulli (which in its final season received over one million inquiries).[43] It is a privileged few who secure reservations so sought-after and who are eager to spend large sums for a meal that will alternately dazzle, satiate, frustrate, puzzle, and at points even outrage the diner.

Culinary Innovation and the Case of elBulli Lab

In an ethnographic study of molecular gastronomy research labs and allied restaurants, Sophia Roosth shows that the links between scientists like This (whose lab methodically tests "culinary dictums") and restaurants like elBulli have in part functioned to "bridge the socioeconomic distance between the food industry ... and the exorbitant menus of high-end restaurants."[44] More accurately, the result of this exchange has been to move the materials and methods of industrial agriculture, bioengineering, and flavor science into the professional kitchen – where chefs mix meticulously sourced and rare ingredients with what Roosth calls the "low cost" and "low prestige" foods of agribusiness (gelling agents, artificial colors, corn syrup, etc.). According to Roosth, the result is the marriage not of avant-garde and applied science but rather of "cultural discernment ... [and] scientific progressiveness."[45] We could refine this argument to observe that the cultural import of molecular gastronomy cuisine is not that it marries modernist art to applied science but rather that it interlaces a new mode of gastronomical connoisseurship with techie entrepreneurship.

The case in point is elBulli – the celebrated restaurant on Spain's Costa Brava that Catalan chef Adrià shuttered in 2011 to focus his energy on a Barcelona think tank by the same name. On July 30, 2011, elBulli served its final meal to fifty people who had traveled to Spain's Costa Brava to eat. Billed as "El Ùltimo Vals" ("The Last Waltz"), the forty-nine-course tasting menu was the product not only of the restaurant's usual huge staff but also visiting celebrity chefs such as Redzepi and Achatz. The meal began with a series of abstract, austere cocktails, such as the perversely titled "dry Martini" – perverse in that it comprised one essence-of-olive

---

[43] Ferran Adrià, *A Day at elBulli* (London: Phaidon, 2008).
[44] Sophia Roosth, "Of Foams and Formalisms: Scientific Expertise and Craft Practice in Molecular Gastronomy," *American Anthropologist* 115.1 (2013): 9.
[45] Ibid.

spherical globule placed on the diner's tongue and spritzed with gin and vermouth mists. At the meal's tail end was a decadent foil to this one-sip tidbit: the restaurant's signature "Box," an ironically banal name for what was an extravagant presentation of confections variously hand-crafted and technologically fabricated in the "Sweet World" of the elBulli kitchen.

The implausibility of ingesting so many sweets after nearly fifty courses helps to explain why Adrià has employed the terms "technique-concept" and "deconstructive" to describe elBulli's food (preferring them to molecular gastronomy).[46] The organizing rubric of a meal like "El Ùltimo Vals" is the theatrical display of countless technical expressions of often clashing conceptual takes on the stages of a meal (from aperitif to dessert), which together explode the expected parameters of fine dining. However, that analysis disturbs the notion that Adrià and fellow chefs are in fact leaders of a "culinary revolution" that is modernist, either in form or cultural impact.[47] For advocates like Myhrvold, these chefs topple the conventions of "fine dining" and, by extension, employ both artistic and technological tools to reject culinary traditions. But do such approaches make restaurants like elBulli modernist in the particular sense of avant-garde? Parasecoli has observed that a number of chefs have conveyed a distaste for both "molecular gastronomy" and "avant-garde" as labels for what they do.[48] And when we consider the historical avant-garde in its manifold attitudes toward and experiments with food (rather than employ the avant-garde as a catch phrase that is interchangeable with modernist, experimental, unconventional, innovative, etc.), we notice that many avant-garde works explore edible matter and acts of eating to produce the "image of something less easily consumable – a blistered, toothy, and staggering something that we would not want to put in our mouths at all," as Ngai writes about *Tender Buttons*.[49] By comparison, Adrià's technique-concept cuisine mixes kitchen science with architectural and theatrical food presentation to produce a consumable meal – however unusual or hyperbolic it may feel to the diner. Put differently, formal and cultural experimentation at elBulli and kindred eateries works in service of highly conspicuous consumption.

So if not as either modernist or avant-garde, how then might we interpret the innovations of a chef like Adrià and an institution like elBulli? Consider

---

[46] For an extended discussion of Adrià's "deconstructive cuisine" see Parasecoli, "Deconstructing Soup."

[47] Davis, "Time and a Place," 147.

[48] Parasecoli, "The Chefs," 125.

[49] Ngai, *Our Aesthetic Categories*, 91.

the media coverage of the restaurant's "last waltz." The evening made news around the world, as food critics who could barely contain their glee at having a seat recreated their experiences of the meal. However genuine their enthusiasm for elBulli's history and influence, these published accounts read together like a parody of gastronomical connoisseurship. "We'd been flown in from food capitals around the world by the Champagne company Dom Pérignon," wrote Adam Platt for *New York Magazine*, "the event's price tag, we giddily estimated, was at least $350,000."[50] As for the dishes themselves? They titillated the diners' "palates with gastronomical delights [that included] a 'golden egg' and 'icy quinoa of duck fois-gras,'" Anna Edwards observed in the *Daily Mail*.[51] These accounts add to an international archive of over 2,800 stories about the restaurant published since the late 1990s, when Adrià began to shift the restaurant from traditional Catalan fare to his methodology of technique-concept cuisine. Sifting through this archive reveals that "avant-garde" has been only one way that food critics and science and technology writers have hailed the inventiveness and unconventionality of elBulli's executive chef. That term circulates in a chorus of labels for Adrià, from "magician" to "engineer" – a plethora of identities that reflects longstanding ideas of male genius. At the same time, this media discourse reflects current relationships between creativity and celebrity, which Fred Turner and Cynthia Larson define, with a focus on the tech industry's self-fashioned pathbreakers, as "network celebrity."[52]

The archive of mostly admiring, sometimes skeptical journalism about elBulli reveals that Adrià gained celebrity not just by inventing new techniques and dishes but also by forging a novel business model for a

---

[50] Adam Platt, "Last Supper of the Food Hacks: A Chopper Ride to El Bulli for 'the Mother of All Boondoggles,'" *New York Magazine*, May 20, 2011, http://nymag.com/restaurants/features/el-bulli-2011-5.

[51] Anna Edwards, "Adios El Bulli! 'World's Best Restaurant' Serves up Extravagant 49-Course Last Supper as It Closes Its Doors Forever," *Daily Mail*, July 30, 2011, www.dailymail.co.uk/news/article-2020461/El-Bulli-closing-Restaurant-serves-49-course-supper-shuts-doors.html.

[52] Turner and Larson define network celebrity as follows: "Together, entrepreneurial research culture and digital technologies have dramatically amplified the power of social networking to produce both ideas and reputations. In [Norbert] Wiener, [Stewart] Brand, and [Tim] O'Reilly they have given rise to a newly influential kind of celebrity, the network intellectual. Unlike the mass media celebrities and public intellectuals with whom we're most familiar, network intellectuals build the social and intellectual communities that bring them fame. Within those communities, they help develop new social and institutional ties and, with them, new ideas and new turns of phrase. They then package this work in books and articles and speeches that promote the networks of people and ideas they've built and enhance their own standing, within and beyond them. For network intellectuals, celebrity is not so much a matter of spectacular." Fred Turner and Christine Larson, "Network Celebrity: Entrepreneurship and the New Public Intellectuals," *Public Culture* 27.1 (2015): 55.

destination restaurant and by building a global patronage network, a network in which he morphed from chef into public intellectual, entrepreneur, and visionary. Between 1987 and 2001, elBulli gradually scaled back its operations from ten to six months a year, as the 2010 documentary *Cooking in Progress* chronicles.[53] In the early 2000s, Adrià and his core leadership team took the further leap of narrowing the restaurant's offering from full lunch and dinner services to a single nightly seating. As a result, the restaurant evidently became a loss leader in that its gross revenues (approximately 2.4 million euros in 2009) did not cover its costs, while the celebrity elBulli generated for Adrià translated into six-figure speaking fees along with academic, foundation, and corporate funding.

The novel operational structure for the restaurant grew out of Adrià's drive to avoid copying others and repeating menus, informing a process of daily "creative sessions" and meticulous record-keeping (as the encyclopedic book *A Day at elBulli* documents).[54] To support these aims, the restaurant's full-time kitchen team also devoted the "winter closure" months to full-time recipe testing in Barcelona. These workshops, as they were termed, both built on and provided fodder for the creative sessions back in the elBulli kitchen. Through this two-part structure, Adrià worked out a theory of creativity rooted in a regimented approach to innovation. Central to that approach were scripted processes for testing new techniques, concepts, and dishes; routinized habits of cataloging, photographing, and rating all experiments and their results; and collaborative development of special projects, like the one shown in *Cooking in Progress* for which the Barcelona team charted the universe of possible ingredients, by month and category of dish, that were locally available to the restaurant during its open season. The protocols and procedures that came to define elBulli implicitly reject the open form of the recipe that Tompkins theorizes in favor of the structured approach to experimentation in STEM fields and the algorithmic logic of databases.[55] Put differently, Adrià linked culinary creativity to information technology as everything under the elBulli sun found its way into graphs, spreadsheets, flow charts, and diagrams.

The restaurant's closure in 2011 marked its reboot as the elBulli Foundation and Lab: a think tank for "deconstructing the entire process of creativity," in Adrià's words, that is funded by Madrid telecom giant

[53] *El Bulli: Cooking in Progress*, directed by Gereon Wetzel (Munich: if … Productions, 2010).
[54] Adrià, *A Day at elBulli*.
[55] Tompkins, "Consider the Recipe," 440.

Telefónica and a number of venture capital investors.[56] The think tank takes the data-centered, taxonomic practices of the elBulli restaurant and Barcelona workshops into a new transdisciplinary context. The current array of projects, for instance, includes the "elBulliPedia" (a public database for logging and classifying gastronomical lexicons, cuisines, dishes, and edible matter itself); a curated exhibition space for "revolutionary" and presumably tech-centered projects (edible and otherwise); and a museum planned for the restaurant's former location and called elBulli 1846 in honor of the exact number of different dishes served there under Adrià's tenure as executive chef. This evolution of elBulli suggests that modernism is an appealing but ultimately misleading framework for interpreting culinary innovation in the digital era, an era in which creativity and invention are domains that engineering and venture capital increasingly claim investment in and intellectual property over even as avant-garde food culture resurfaces at unexpected sites – from participatory art projects like those of the Center for Genomic Gastronomy's *Food Phreaking* zine and EcoArtTech's food fermentation workshops (projects that disrupt privatized food science and agribusiness) to art–science collaborations like the Washington State University Bread Lab (which brings together "open source" wheat breeding and experimental baking). By comparison with this *green avant-garde*,[57] the work of chefs like Adrià and restaurants like elBulli exemplify the rise of culinary labs and incubators – well-funded spaces located in the interstices of invention and documentation, gastronomy and engineering.

BIBLIOGRAPHY

Adrià, Ferran. *A Day at elBulli*. London: Phaidon, 2008.
Adrià, Ferran, et al. "Statement on the 'New Cookery.'" *Guardian UK*, December 10, 2006. www.theguardian.com/uk/2006/dec/10/foodanddrink. obsfoodmonthly.
Borden, Sam. "Ferran Adrià Feeds the Hungry Mind: The Former El Bulli Chef Is Now Serving Up Creative Inquiry." *New York Times*, January 2, 2015. www. nytimes.com/2015/01/04/business/ferran-adria-the-former-el-bulli-chef-is-now-serving-up-creative-inquiry.html?_r=0.

[56] Sam Borden, "Ferran Adrià Feeds the Hungry Mind: The Former El Bulli Chef Is Now Serving Up Creative Inquiry," *New York Times*, January 2, 2015, www.nytimes.com/2015/01/04/business/ferran-adria-the-former-el-bulli-chef-is-now-serving-up-creative-inquiry.html?_r=0.
[57] I have elsewhere elaborated on this concept of the green avant-garde and open source food culture: Allison Carruth, "The Green Avant-Garde: Food Hackers and Cyberagrarians," *Resilience: Journal of the Environmental Humanities* 2.1 (2014), www.jstor.org/stable/10.5250/resilience.2.1.005.

Bürger, Peter. *Theory of the Avant-Garde*. Translated by Michael Shaw. Theory and History of Literature. Minneapolis: University of Minnesota Press, 2002.

Burnett, John. *England Eats Out: A Social History of Eating Out in England from 1830 to the Present*. London: Pearson Longman, 2004.

Carruth, Allison. "The Green Avant-Garde: Food Hackers and Cyberagrarians." *Resilience: Journal of the Environmental Humanities* 2.1 (2014). www.jstor.org/stable/10.5250/resilience.2.1.005.

"Slow Food, Low Tech: Environmental Narratives of Agribusiness and Its Alternatives." In *The Routledge Companion to the Environmental Humanities*, edited by Ursula K. Heise, Jon Christensen, and Michelle Niemann, 313–22. London: Routledge, 2017.

Cesaretti, Enrico. "Recipes for the Future: Traces of Past Utopias in *The Futurist Cookbook*." *European Legacy* 14.7 (2009): 841–56.

Coghlan, Michelle. "Tasting Modernism: An Introduction." *Resilience: Journal of the Environmental Humanities* 2.1 (2015): 1–9.

Dalí, Salvador. *Les Diners De Gala*. Translated by Captain J. Peter Moore. 1973. Reprint, Cologne, Germany: Taschen, 2016.

Davis, Mitchell. "A Time and a Place for a Peach." *Senses and Society* 7.2 (2012): 135–52.

Delville, Michel. *Food, Poetry, and the Aesthetics of Consumption: Eating the Avant-Garde*. New York: Routledge, 2008.

Druckman, Charlotte. "Why Are There No Great Women Chefs?" *Gastronomica: The Journal of Food and Culture* 10.1 (2010): 24–31.

Edwards, Anna. "Adios El Bulli! 'World's Best Restaurant' Serves up Extravagant 49-Course Last Supper as It Closes Its Doors Forever." *Daily Mail*, July 30, 2011. www.dailymail.co.uk/news/article-2020461/El-Bulli-closing-Restaurant-serves-49-course-supper-shuts-doors.html.

El Bulli: Cooking in Progress. Directed by Gereon Wetzel. Munich: if . . . Productions, 2010.

Fisher, M. F. K. *Consider the Oyster*. 1941. Reprint, New York: Farrar, Straus and Giroux, 1988.

The Gastronomical Me. 1943. Reprint, New York: North Point Press, 1989.

How to Cook a Wolf. 1942. Reprint, New York: North Point Press, 1988.

Fleissner, Jennifer L. "Henry James's Art of Eating." *ELH* 75.1 (2008): 27–62.

Goldsmith, Kenneth. *Uncreative Writing*. New York: Columbia University Press, 2011.

Keyser, Catherine. "An All-Too-Moveable Feast: Ernest Hemingway and the Stakes of Terroir." *Resilience: Journal of the Environmental Humanities* 2.1 (2014): 10–23.

"Bottles, Bubbles, and Blood: Jean Toomer and the Limits of Racial Epidermalism." *Modernism/modernity* 22.2 (2015): 279–302.

Landis, Kevin. "Culinary Pataphysics: Dining, Theatre, and the Avant-Garde." *Gastronomica: Journal of Critical Food Studies* 14.2 (2014): 46–55.

Laudan, Rachel. "A Plea for Culinary Modernism: Why We Should Love New, Fast, Processed Food." *Gastronomica: Journal of Food and Culture*, 1.1 (2001): 36–44.

López-Alt, J. Kenji. *The Food Lab: Better Home Cooking Through Science*. New York: Norton, 2015.

Marinetti, F. T. *The Futurist Cookbook*. Edited by Lesley Chamberlain. Translated by Suzanne Brill. London: Trefoil, 1989.

McLean, Alice L. *Aesthetic Pleasure in Twentieth-Century Women's Food Writing: The Innovative Appetites of M. F. K. Fisher, Alice B. Toklas, and Elizabeth David*. Studies in Twentieth-Century Literature. New York: Routledge, 2012.

Myhrvold, Nathan. "The Art in Gastronomy: A Modernist Perspective." *Gastronomica: Journal of Food and Culture*, 11.1 (2011): 13–23.

Ngai, Sianne. "The Cuteness of the Avant-Garde." *Critical Inquiry*, 31.4 (2005): 811–47.

Our Aesthetic Categories: Zany, Cute, Interesting. Cambridge, MA: Harvard University Press, 2015.

Niedecker, Lorine. *New Goose*. Edited by Jenny Penberthy. Berkeley, CA: Rumor Books, 2002.

Novero, Cecilia. *Antidiets of the Avant Garde: From Futurist Cooking to Eat Art*. Minneapolis: University of Minnesota Press, 2010.

Orwell, George. "The British Crisis: London Letter to *Partisan Review* [8 May 1942]." In *My Country Right or Left, 1940–1943*, edited by Sonia Orwell and Ian Angus, 207–16. Boston: Nonpareil Books, 2000.

Parasecoli, Fabio. "The Chefs, the Entrepreneurs, and Their Patrons: The Avant-Garde Food Scene in New York City." In *Gastropolis: Food and New York City*, edited by Annie Hauck-Lawson and Jonathan Deutsch, 116–31. New York: Columbia University Press, 2009.

"Deconstructing Soup: Ferran Adrià's Culinary Challenges." *Gastronomica: The Journal of Food and Culture* 1.1 (2001): 60–73.

Platt, Adam. "Last Supper of the Food Hacks: A Chopper Ride to El Bulli for 'the Mother of All Boondoggles.'" *New York Magazine*, 2011. http://nymag.com/restaurants/features/el-bulli-2011-5.

Roosth, Sophia. "Of Foams and Formalisms: Scientific Expertise and Craft Practice in Molecular Gastronomy." *American Anthropologist* 115.1 (2013): 4–16.

Stein, Gertrude. *Tender Buttons: The Corrected Centennial Edition*. Edited by Seth Perlow. San Francisco: City Lights, 2014.

This, Hervé. *Building a Meal: From Molecular Gastronomy to Culinary Constructivism*. New York: Columbia University Press, 2009.

Molecular Gastronomy: Exploring the Science of Flavor. New York: Columbia University Press, 2008.

Révélations Gastronomiques. Paris: Belin, 1995.

The Science of the Oven. New York: Columbia University Press, 2012.

Tompkins, Kyla Wazana. "Consider the Recipe." *J19: Journal of Nineteenth-Century Americanists* 1.2 (2013): 439–45.

Trubek, Amy B. *The Taste of Place: A Cultural Journey into Terroir*. California Studies in Food and Culture. Berkeley: University of California Press, 2009.

Turner, Fred, and Christine Larson. "Network Celebrity: Entrepreneurship and the New Public Intellectuals." *Public Culture* 27.1 (2015): 53–84.

CHAPTER 12

Comic Books and the Culinary Logic of Late Capitalism[1]

Rohit Chopra

Food is violence. The act of uprooting from soil. The slash of the knife. The taking of life. The spilling of blood and guts. The consuming of one life to sustain another. Animals kill for food. People kill for food. In simplistic Darwinian understandings of social phenomena, the hunger for food, the most basic element required for survival, is often described as the force behind violence and crime. At the level of political economy, the vagaries of global food markets and the international economic order manifest themselves as structural violence. Farmers in Ghana, Ethiopia, or India might be encouraged to increase coffee production, only to find themselves dealing with a glut in the international markets a couple of years later, with their livelihood at stake as a consequence.

In the explosion of food culture in recent decades, which has been intertwined with an accompanying surge of media coverage in food, the violence of food has been simultaneously obscured and emphasized. The apparatus of industrialized food production, long under suspicion in the public eye for lack of transparency, the use of "food-like substances" in lieu of real food,[2] and unethical practices in the treatment of both animals and human employees, has sought to improve its public image by showing commitment to sustainability and cruelty-free harvesting and making clear every step of its supply chain in sourcing plant and animal materials. In contrast, the practice of hyper-local cooking, the return of traditional food sources and practices, and the emergence of new forms of culinary artistry have put the violence of cooking center stage. For instance, the art of butchering, hitherto a backstage activity in the preparation of beef, lamb, or pork products, has now become essential to the repertoire of the visible

---

[1] The reference to Frederic Jameson's *Postmodernism, or The Cultural Logic of Late Capitalism* (Durham, NC: Duke University Press, 1992) should be obvious.

[2] Tara Parker-Pope, "An Omnivore Defends Real Food," *New York Times*, January 17, 2008, https://well.blogs.nytimes.com/2008/01/17/an-omnivore-defends-real-food/comment-page-10.

skills that a chef must possess. This new form of expertise is symbolized in the figure of celebrity chefs like Fergus Henderson, author of the land-mark work *The Whole Beast*, the book that inaugurated the nose-to-tail eating movement.[3] While industrialized violence is sought to be hidden or made more palatable, the solitary chef who cooks with authentic, fresh ingredients, and stands as the antithesis of the system of industrialized food production, must be able to unflinchingly engage in acts of violence as part of his or her vocation. Paradoxically, the image of the celebrity chef, the person whose dedication to culinary art stands separate from and above materialistic concerns, is itself now a commodity, a product of a media-industrial complex that both reflects and feeds the globally resurgent interest in food culture. This highly mediated food culture takes the form of competitive shows on television like *Iron Chef*, *Top Chef*, *No Reservations*, and *Bizarre Foods*, a bounty of food blogs on the internet, and an increasingly widespread cultural practice of photographing food and posting it on social media platforms like Facebook, Instagram, and Twitter.

Capitalism, too, is violence, of course. As Marx saw it, the violence of capitalism, inevitable and cyclical, was powerful enough to need an equal or greater violence to counter it, the violence of revolution itself. Even if the prospect of proletarian revolution along the lines predicted by Marx appears dim, the fact that violence is essential to capitalism is generally recognized across ideological borders, whether it is valorized as "creative destruction" or criticized as producing massive social upheaval. Popular understandings of capitalist violence in the global public imagination typ-ically involve images of disenfranchised families, forlorn neighborhoods, and pioneering Starbucks cafés bravely venturing into these same desolate neighborhoods to which they seek to bring the benefits of gentrification.

These observations in broad brushstrokes already suggest a set of relationships between capitalism, food, and violence: while capital and food may each stake claim to its own, distinct form of violence, it is in the areas of the system of industrialized food production, the risks to the envir-onment, the commodification of taste, and the creation and marketing of celebrity chefs, typically through elaborately staged spectacles of intense competition, that the violence of the world of food merges with the violence of the domain of capital. It is this juncture as depicted in the form of the food comic, a subgenre of comics and the graphic novel, that I examine in this chapter. I look at the relationship between food, violence,

---

[3] Fergus Henderson, *The Whole Beast: Nose-to-Tail Eating* (New York: Ecco, 2004).

and capitalism in three comic book series on food, *Get Jiro!* and *Get Jiro! Blood and Sushi*, *Starve*, and *Chew*.[4]

Get Jiro!, co-authored by well-known chef and media personality Anthony Bourdain, was the first volume in the two-part series, with *Get Jiro!: Blood and Sushi* released later as a prequel, giving us the back story of Jiro, the sushi chef who is the protagonist of the tale. Jiro, born in a Yakuza family and heir to a mafia empire, is now in Los Angeles, serving and defending the honor and tradition of sushi. Each of the two volumes of *Starve* combine five issues respectively. Across the two volumes, they tell the complete arc of a story involving a celebrity chef, Gavin Cruikshank, fallen from grace in both his personal and professional life but seeking now to set things right after being forced to return to Manhattan to complete the remaining episodes of his hit television show named *Starve*. *Chew*, an award-winning, *New York Times*-bestselling, publication is a twelve-volume series, whose title is a pun on the name of the protagonist, Tony Chu, a police officer with the Philadelphia Police Department. Chu is the possessor of a rare gift; he is a cibopath, someone who can take a bite of any form of food (except beets) and instantly ascertain the entire history of that piece of food via powerful impressions. This talent, whose value for crime detection should be obvious, draws the attention of an undercover agent, Mason Savoy, who also happens to be a cibopath. Savoy enlists Chu in the service of the Food and Drug Administration of the US government where he works as well.

I argue that in these series, which share a number of important themes and representational tropes, food as the symbol of nature, unsullied human existence, and truth becomes a way to countenance the corrupting violence of capitalism. Food also serves as a symbol of an authentic human bond, one that is prior to and beyond capital. It stands as the basis of a critique of the violence of the contractual reason that is essential to capitalism. The protagonists, each of whom is necessarily an outsider figure, have a profoundly ambivalent relationship to food. Food has been a blessing and curse for them. It is a burden, yet also redeems them, just as each of them seeks to redeem food from the malevolent influence of capitalism. The

---

[4] Anthony Bourdain and Joel Rose, *Get Jiro!* (Burbank, CA: DC Comics, 2012); Anthony Bourdain and Joel Rose, *Get Jiro! Blood and Sushi* (Burbank, CA: DC Comics, 2015); Brian Wood, Danijel Zezelj, and Dave Stewart, *Starve*, Vol. 1 (Berkeley, CA: Image Comics, 2016); Brian Wood, Danijel Zezelj, and Dave Stewart, *Starve*, Vol. 2 (Berkeley, CA: Image Comics, 2017). Each volume of *Chew* combines several issues. In this chapter, I focus on the first volume, "Taster's Choice," which brings together the first five issues, each one designated as a chapter in the volume. See John Layman, *Chew*, Vol. 1: *Taster's Choice* (Berkeley, CA: Image Comics, 2017).

world of food in these works embodies the contradictory logic of late capitalism, in which food culture and the chefs are both hyper-commodified and hyper-mediated yet are the source of critique and opposition to the very culture that produces them.

Situating the Genre of the Food Comic

As a distinct form of literary and cultural expression, the food comic, as it may be termed, can be located within several traditions of representation. It is a relatively new subgenre within the broader genre of the comic book or graphic novel. Drawing on the work of Santiago Garcia, I use the terms interchangeably; the term "graphic novel," as popularized in the 1980s, was "an attempt to differentiate the product from what is evoked by the word 'comics': a cheap, disposable, and childish product."[5] The food subgenre of comic books also reflects the enormous surge of interest in food in global popular culture, taking shape in a range of textual and visual forms, including memoirs, recipe books, academic works, fictionalized accounts of important figures like Julia Child, coffee-table publications, film, television shows, magazines, and food websites. All of this reflects the fact that food culture has become a global culture industry of its own, meshing with the worlds of media, technology, art, cinema, and literature. Yet, it has perhaps not received the attention that it deserves in scholarship. As Fabio Parasecoli bemoans, while food "has become the object of a wide and ever-growing corpus of studies and analysis, from marketing to history, from nutrition to anthropology," many aspects of what food might mean "are left unexplored when it comes to phenomena that fall squarely under the heading of pop culture, especially the 'low brow' or even 'trash' kind."[6] Parasecoli's scholarly examination of the representation of food in popular culture is intended as a corrective to this lacuna. While his somewhat limited definition of pop culture as comprised of "any cultural phenomenon, material item, practice, social relation, and even idea that is conceived, produced, distributed, and consumed within a market-driven environment" can be replaced with a more expansive definition to incorporate independent or non-mainstream forms of popular culture such as underground comics, his general point about the academic devaluation of popular cultural forms is valid.[7]

[5] Santiago Garcia, *On the Graphic Novel*, translated by Bruce Campbell (Jackson: University Press of Mississippi, 2010), 21.
[6] Fabio Parasecoli, *Bite Me: Food in Popular Culture* (New York: Bloomsbury, 2012), 2.
[7] Ibid.

In contrast to the paucity of scholarly attention on the subject, there does appear to be a decent amount of journalistic and media attention paid to the relationship of food and popular (literary and visual) culture. In an article in the well-known food magazine *Lucky Peach*, globally renowned chef and media personality Mario Batali traces the origins of food *as* popular culture to a particular moment and place. Till the late seventies and early eighties, Batali notes, "Gastronomy was only important to, maybe, a small group of people, and even then, it was a frippery. No one cared about consuming the information as well as the food."[8] Batali locates the birth of food culture in the California cuisine revolution that occurred after the time of Julia Child but before the era of the Food Network channel. Today, however, as the result of the revolution inaugurated in California, people have a voracious appetite for both food and information about food.

Finally, the subgenre of the food comic can also be placed in a genealogy of the visual representation of food, from works of art, such as Goya's *Still Life: A Butcher's Counter*, which lay bare the violence involved in the preparation and consumption of food, to the kind of television show featured in *Starve*, which also features the same violence. All these features, reflecting the various traditions that the food comic draws on – combined with the fact that as a visual and textual form, the food comic engages at least two of our modalities of comprehension in its treatment of food – make the genre especially powerful and relevant for the examination of food culture.

Food as Ambivalent Substance and the Violence of Consumption

Consistent with a recognizable convention from the genre of the superhero and science fiction comic book, the volumes are set in a near future that is immediately recognizable as an amalgam of aspects of late twentieth- and early twenty-first century capitalist society, marred by urban sprawl, crumbling inner city neighborhoods, massive inequality, scarcity of natural resources monopolized by an elite, and populations that are the subject of various disciplinary mechanisms. All three series feature as protagonist a solitary figure, marginalized or alienated, who goes it alone in trying to redress the wrongs of a sordid world. This, too, of course, is a well-known trope of the superhero comic book genre. And all three series are drenched

---

[8] Mario Batali, "Food as Pop Culture," *Lucky Peach*, April, 17, 2016, http://luckypeach.com/how-food-became-pop-culture-mario-batali/?mc_cid=6c69ed73a0&mc_eid=c0f8c7df08.

in blood, from cover to cover. Against this dystopian, blood-spattered canvas that envelops the works collectively, each series offers a remarkable story that intertwines food, violence, and capitalism.

Get Jiro! introduces us to the mysterious Jiro, a sushi-chef who has just opened a nondescript sushi restaurant in a run-of-the-mill strip mall on the outskirts of Los Angeles. In the first course of the comic book, so to speak, Jiro has just decapitated a garden-variety Californian "bro," who has had the temerity to ask him for a California roll. Los Angeles is "ruled by two chef warlords … locked in battle with the other over culinary minutiae and arcane philosophical differences," which also translates into a competition over territory.[9] People wait years for a reservation at well-known restaurants. Eating at a prized restaurant or, even better, a secret one, is the ultimate currency, traversing class and occupation. Thugs and cops, as well as everyone in between, speak the language of global *haute* food culture, of secret invitations to secret and exclusive restaurants, of fashionably run-down holes in the wall that serve authentic food, of the importance of grating your own ingredients and sourcing fresh ingredients.

One of the two chefs, Bob, is part of a global food conglomerate, suggestive of a chef like Wolfgang Puck with his empire. His archenemy and antithesis, Rose, is a devout locavore, a sort of Alice Walters on steroids. A chef committed to the local, Rose gathers under her wing an ideologically flexible rag-tag bunch of vegans, hippies, organic farmers, and the like. Seeking to establish total dominance over the city, Rose and Bob also aim to monopolize scarce food resources, from tomatoes to tuna, between them, at any cost and by any means necessary. Rose, as one of her flunkies reminds her, has killed for the first tomatoes of the season.[10] In the bargain, as one of Jiro's friends, the chef Jean Claude, tells him, they "squeeze" the small independent chefs out of business.[11] Jiro, word of whose old-world sushi skills and dedication to his craft gets out, is sought out by both of the chef warlords. Their henchmen fight, they both threaten Jiro, seeking to enlist him on their side of the culinary war – initially, at least, till they can dispatch him. Jiro sets in motion a plan to play both off against each other and single-handedly exterminates numerous members of both organizations. The volume ends with Bob and Rose teaming up and Jiro back at his sushi restaurant, likely about to execute another ignorant innocent asking for a California roll.

---

[9] Bourdain and Rose, *Get Jiro!*, [19]. The comic book does not have page numbers. I have numbered pages assuming the text starts from [1].
[10] Ibid., [26].
[11] Ibid., [57].

In *Get Jiro! Blood and Sushi*, the prequel to *Get Jiro!* that features as much decapitation as the first volume, we learn more about where Jiro gets his cooking and fighting skills, as well as his honor and integrity, from. As one of the reluctant sons of a Yakuza boss, who is slotted to take over as chief instead of his wildly impetuous half-brother, he seeks refuge from the straitjacket of expectations by apprenticing secretly with a sushi chef, the vocation in which he finds self-fulfillment. Framed for the death of their father by his stepbrother and on the verge of being executed by him, Jiro is saved in the nick of time by his sushi teacher. He cuts his hair off and leaves for Los Angeles. Outed by his stepbrother for abandoning his duties to the family, and now in trouble because of his sushi skills, Jiro has been simultaneously doomed and saved by food.

All the self-indulgent excesses of contemporary foodie culture are clearly satirized in the works, especially the first volume. The volumes excoriate the pretentiousness of food culture, the affected performance of vocabularies and rituals of excitement and disappointment centered on food, and the irrational romanticization of the local, which in aiming to destroy the pathologies of commercialized *haute cuisine* has become indistinguishable from it. Indeed, Rose is as unethical as Bob. If the food that she wants is not local to Los Angeles, it is local somewhere, she surmises, and that is close enough for her. Yet this work is too enraptured with itself. Jiro uses violence effectively to combat what Bob and Rose represent, protecting the sanctity of food and speaking up for the small guy like Jean Claude, yet he cannot exist past violence. Given his Yakuza background, perhaps this is the albatross he must always carry around his neck. Whatever the reason, like Bob and Rose, he remains a type. Bob and Rose might, in fact, be seen as unethical and inconsistent versions of him. If his violence is in the cause of the purity of tradition and food, for them, at some point of time, power and violence have become ends in themselves not simply a means to serve food. This is summed up in a scene in which Bob insists on keeping a dish all white in contravention of tradition but valorizes it as a perverse tribute to that tradition. "You gotta know the classics … *Respect* the classics," he says, "Before you fuck with them."[12] Jiro, then, is but one trope in a clever set of volumes that get a number of tropes from noir, the tradition of the comic book, and present-day food culture into play with each other.

More self-aware of the seductions of violence and packing a more pungent critique is Brian Wood's grimly luminous set of volumes, *Starve*, about one-time rock star chef, Gavin Cruikshank, who is hiding out "somewhere"

[12] Ibid., [23].

in Southeast Asia, drinking Soju, eating Moo Ping, and watching fights.[13] Cruikshank, an erstwhile celebrity chef with his own successful television show, titled *Starve*, is hiding here, away from the world, after a global economic crisis shut the show down and left him stranded in Beijing with no access to money or credit. The crisis now having passed, Cruikshank is forced back by the network to Manhattan to finish up the eight episodes of the show that remain. He returns to a complicated personal situation as well; his long-estranged wife, Greer, has taken control of his assets after having him declared dead. Long the archetypal absent, drunk, and indifferent husband, late in their marriage Gavin has come out as gay. He has avoided a divorce for the sake of their daughter, Angie.

As he soon realizes, Gavin has returned to a world far more Darwinian in its capitalism than the one he left. Sheldon, the network executive who comes to fetch him back to the US, tells him that everything has been privatized in the wake of the crisis. Cruikshank's popular show, as conceptualized by him, was "a travelogue, a hip little show where [he] roamed the planet exploring local culture and technique."[14] Now the number one show on television, *Starve* is "a competition for the privileged elite," which with its obscene excess and challenges such as asking competitors to cook dog, mocks the 99 percent of the world who are separated from the 1 percent by a vast gulf.[15] To rub salt in his wounds, the show is now hosted by Cruikshank's one-time friend and now rival, Roman Algiers, with Cruikshank himself playing the part of contestant.

Cruikshank decides he will get all of it back, "my show, my money, my daughter," and then destroy the network.[16] And like Jiro, who seeks temporary refuge with chefs like Jean Claude who refuse to play the game, Cruikshank too has a friend, chef Dina Stern, who is the embodiment of the authentic chef, the counterpoint to celebrity television chefs. Dina helps him find ingredients that he needs to meet the challenges of the show. Assisted by his daughter, Angie, Cruikshank wins episode after episode, proceeding duly to the next stage. Yet, Cruikshank has also become prey. Greer plots to have him killed by Roman; when Roman is unable to do the deed, she stabs Cruikshank herself. He does not press charges and finally signs the divorce papers. Angie is offered a contract by the network, as the work boils toward its denouement.

---

[13] Wood, Zezelj, and Stewart, *Starve*, Vol. 1, 7.
[14] Ibid., 24.
[15] Ibid., 24.
[16] Ibid., 27, 28.

Personal violence, the violence of cooking, and the systemic violence of capitalism mingle in the texts of the two-part series like ingredients in a well-blended recipe. Cruikshank and his team, for instance, have to physically fight another chef's team for ingredients. In one episode, contestants have to butcher a pig live, in another, a dog's head, severed from its body, and its carcass stripped of its skin, greets us. Physical violence, however, is treated as a lesser evil than the violence of unethical consumption and the greed of the wealthy that engage in such acts of consumption. The work is unremitting in its critique of this invisible form of violence and of the marketing of food culture that both celebrates and enables it. Bluefin tuna, required for one of the show episodes, is "the perfect example of what *Starve* represents," in Cruikshank's view, that is, "*rich* people paying a premium to pretend the world's not broken."[17] The commodified world of food culture and media is seen as corrosive, infecting everyone who comes into contact with it, from Gavin Cruikshank to Roman Algiers and Sheldon. Dina implores Cruikshank not to debase himself on the show, to give up the "celebrity trash nonsense."[18] Cruikshank does ultimately walk away from it all, but not before setting things right with Greer and ensuring Angie doesn't fall prey to the same temptations as him. He also experiences a profound self-realization about his narcissism, even in his heroic project to teach the network a lesson. He is struck by the sudden knowledge that despite his intentions, he was "nearly seduced" by the rush of fame, attention, wealth and power the second time around as well. Food, which gives him his very identity, has saved him yet very nearly proven to be his downfall again.[19]

Like Jiro and Gavin Cruikshank, Tony Chu, the protagonist of *Chew*, is an outsider and reluctant hero, drawn into a mystery involving the US government. In the wake of a bird flu epidemic, chicken is contraband, replaced by an artificial substitute called Poultree. The official channels of demand and supply, however, are complemented by a black market for natural chicken. It is in the course of tracking down a dealer in illicit, natural, chicken meat that Chu is enlisted in the service of the Special Crimes division of the FDA, which happens to be the most powerful law enforcement agency in the world. While the critique of capitalism takes a different form here as compared to the depiction of extremes of affluence and deprivation

---

[17] Ibid., 41.
[18] Ibid., 42.
[19] Wood, Zezelj, and Stewart, *Starve*, Vol. 2, [112]. The second volume does not have page numbers. I have counted the page numbers, assuming [1] is the first page of the narrative, following front matter.

shown in the *Get Jiro!* volumes and *Starve* and from the direct moral commentary of the latter, it is nonetheless obliquely present in the scenes of abandoned, graffiti-strewn stores, and shabby fast food restaurants; these bring to mind the inner cities of the urban American landscape and the nondescript suburbs that operate as the hinterlands of capitalism.

Chu is burdened by food in his own particular manner as are Jiro and Cruikshank in theirs. Chu's ability to psychically intuit information from biting anything, including human flesh, is a terrible gift, especially when he is expected by his peers and superiors, and compelled by his own conscience, to chew unsavory objects, such as the face of a suspect.[20] Like the other series, *Chew* too is slathered in violence, from the routine violence encountered by Chu as a law enforcement officer to the memories of violent crimes that flood his consciousness when he takes a bite of any substance at the scene of a crime. By the end of Volume 1, Chu himself becomes a form of food subject to violence. When Chu figures out that the criminal who he has been tracking is none other than Mason Savoy, the fellow cibopath who recruited him into the FDA, he confronts the latter, only to have a part of his ear bitten off by his soon-to-be former colleague. Savoy does this so that he will always have a sense of Chu's location. The violence of his gift turns upon him, yet Chu persists in his job out of a sense of ethical obligation.

While all three series are concerned with the ethics of consumption, *Chew*, Volume 1 more so than the other works raises questions about the boundaries of what constitutes food and the notion of the edible. For Jiro, the limit of the edible is that which violates tradition, while for ideologues like Rose, a customer who demands caprese in January deserves punishment. For Chu, almost anything that can help him solve a case can be eaten. Food, then, in this sense, includes the plainly inedible, the unsavory, and the rotting. The volume perhaps deliberately brings us uncomfortably close to the Other of food, like rotting human flesh and body fluids, to force us to confront the question of whether artificial substances like Poultree can be considered food.

Food as Prepolitical Human Bond and Counter to Capitalist Contractuality

While each series, as described above, offers its own specific critique of the ambivalent power of food to damn and redeem, and its own take on

---

[20] Layman, *Chew*, Vol. 1, [19].

the violence of capitalism as manifested in the realm of food, there is one issue on which all three works appear unanimous. All of them offer an unflinching critique of a fundamental hypocrisy that is essential to the functioning of capitalism, that is, the idea that contemporary capitalist society is predicated on voluntary contractuality. Each work shows us that the voluntaristic nature of capitalism is a fiction and that voluntaristic contractuality can only exist when guaranteed and enforced by violence, legitimate or illegitimate.

In *Starve*, Gavin Cruikshank is dragged back from his self-imposed exile in Southeast Asia on the basis of his contract. When he violates his contract, however, he is initially subjected to the brute violence of thugs employed by the network. When he resorts to a similar measure, barging in to a board meeting with a baseball bat, charges are levied against him. Cruikshank's revenge, executed perfectly by his daughter Angie, is to refrain from playing the game at all. In the final episode of *Starve*, she refuses to compete, simply cracking an egg in lieu of undertaking the specified cooking task. Cruikshank, who still has not met the terms of his contract, goes to jail rather than reach a negotiation with the network or persuade his daughter to do a show.

In the *Jiro!* volumes too, we find the same argument. The violence of capitalism there is also seen as double-fold; it is systemic, leading to inequality and disempowerment, but also employs the mechanisms of the Yakuza. While the Yakuza are recognized as criminals, those who benefit from capitalism are not viewed as such. For Tony Chu, it is the contractuality of the system of law, meant to preserve society, that is similarly hypocritical. Whether it is his boss who considers him a freak and harasses him, or Mason Savoy, his new partner, who turns out to be a criminal, those on the side of enforcing contractuality turn out to be as unethical as those on the other side of the law.

In this regard, each of the three works also posits food, in its untarnished, natural state, as the counterpoint to the myth of voluntaristic capitalism. Food is the primordial bond of authentic collective life and society itself, food is the path to self-knowledge, and food is the path to truth about others. If food is politically overdetermined because of its relationship to power and violence, it is also paradoxically prepolitical at the same time, the basis of self and society that is prior to politics itself. Angie fulfills her contractual obligations by doing a documentary for the network and decides to devote her energies to her own restaurant. "The generation she represents," Cruikshank reflects, "is not going to participate in their old class warfare games."[21] Cruikshank himself starts a co-op restaurant in a decaying, blighted neighborhood and, reluctant to play the savior, steps away, letting it take root on its own. Food revives and nourishes a community here, with the potential of transforming a neighborhood outside the paradigm of profit and capital. Food is the basis of relationships that sustain Jiro, from the love he leaves behind in Tokyo to the sushi master who saves him in more ways than one. In Los Angeles, it is food that he aims to rescue from the clutches of commodification so that it can be the source of fulfillment and pleasure rather than a prop in a public theater of gratification. And for Chu, food is what leads to the truth, even if the cost it extracts from him is a heavy one. It is the source of facts, beneath the lies the government may or may not be telling about bird flu.

Conclusion

What then do we make of these series of food comics, violent, highly stylized, cleverly self-aware, drawing on and mixing idioms from other forms of popular culture, such as satire, noir, and social commentary? Certainly, these works do not exhaust the subgenre, for other well-known texts like *Seconds* do not conform to this model.[22] But the similarities between them in terms of tropes, idioms, and thematic concerns are strong enough to suggest that one of the key features of the subgenre is to critically comment on the self-indulgent excesses of what is sometimes called "foodie culture." The term refers to the late capitalist, postmodern celebration of food in which the rejection of mass consumption, the fetishization of the local, the public sharing of the intimate act of eating, and a whole series of routine activities from booking a table at a restaurant to reading a menu have been commodified or bureaucratized. The degree and nature of the critique varies across the series, of course. It covers the avowedly political polemics that cross Cruikshank's consciousness; the unequal, over-the-top world of Jiro about which we are left to draw our own conclusions; and the criticism quietly emanating from the pages of *Chew*, which seems designed to produce a sense of claustrophobia and discomfort among us.

As a popular culture form, then, the food comic book exceeds Parasecoli's definition of pop culture as something circumscribed by the logic of the market.[23] Rather, the subgenre is perhaps better understood as liminal to

---

[21] Wood, Zezelj, and Stewart, *Starve*, Vol. 2, 104.
[22] Bryan Lee O'Malley, *Seconds: A Graphic Novel* (New York: Ballantine Books, 2014).
[23] Parasecoli, *Bite Me*, 2.

market forces, seemingly marginal but autonomous – the self-awareness of popular food culture, if you will. Just as the chefs Jiro, Gavin Cruikshank, and the cibopath Tony Chew are outsiders, partly by choice and partly by circumstance, the genre seems to choose to stay at arm's length from the object of its depictions, eschewing the euphoria about the latest foodie fad and the uncritical adulation showered on television chefs and other food personalities in its stories. This may possibly have to do with the status of the comic as a countercultural form or with a deliberate desire to save food from the violence of capitalism, even if it is to celebrate the singular, distinct violence of food in its place.

BIBLIOGRAPHY

Batali, Mario. "Food as Pop Culture." *Lucky Peach*. April 17, 2016. http://luckypeach.com/how-food-became-pop-culture-mario-batali/?mc_cid=6c69ed73a0&mc_eid=c0f8c7dfo8.

Bourdain, Anthony, and Joel Rose. *Get Jiro! Blood and Sushi*. Burbank, CA: DC Comics, 2015.

   Get Jiro! Burbank, CA: DC Comics, 2012.

Garcia, Santiago. *On the Graphic Novel*. Translated by Bruce Campbell. Jackson: University Press of Mississippi, 2010.

Henderson, Fergus. *The Whole Beast: Nose-to-Tail Eating*. New York: Ecco, 2004.

Jameson, Frederic. *Postmodernism, or the Cultural Logic of Late Capitalism*. Durham, NC: Duke University Press, 1992.

Layman, John. *Chew*. Vol. 1, *Taster's Choice*. Berkeley, CA: Image Comics, 2017.

O'Malley, Bryan Lee. *Seconds: A Graphic Novel*. New York: Ballantine Books, 2014.

Parasecoli, Fabio. *Bite Me: Food in Popular Culture*. New York: Bloomsbury, 2012.

Parker-Pope, Tara. "An Omnivore Defends Real Food." *New York Times*, January 17, 2008. https://well.blogs.nytimes.com/2008/01/17/an-omnivore-defends-real-food/comment-page-10.

Wood, Brian, Danijel Zezelj, and Dave Stewart. *Starve*. Vols. 1–2. Berkeley, CA: Image Comics, 2016.

PART III

Applications

CHAPTER 13

Inebriation
The Poetics of Drink

Sandra M. Gilbert

The son of Semele,
Found out the grape's rich juice, and taught us mortals
That which beguiles the miserable of mankind
Of sorrow, when they quaff the vine's rich stream.
Sleep too, and drowsy oblivion of care
He gives, all-healing medicine of our woes.

Tiresias, in Euripides, The Bacchae

Civilization begins with distillation.

William Faulkner

Once drunk, a cup of wine can bring one hundred stanzas.[1]

Xiuxi Yin

I don't think anything worth reading was ever written by anyone who
was drunk when he wrote it.[2]

Eugene O'Neill

The poetics of drink is a poetics of conflict. On the one hand, there are
the bull-roarers of Bacchus, the orgiastic Maenads, the mystical priests
of the vine, the poets and prophets whose drinking songs or sacraments
celebrate the inspiring and perhaps entheogenic virtues of consciousness-
transforming intoxication. On the other hand, there are the Malvolios,
the hatchet-wielding Carrie Nations, the temperance workers, and – most
telling of all – the recovering alcoholics, who testify to the disease and disease of drunkenness. Where the acolytes of inebriation share the view of
Euripides' Tiresias that "the grape's rich juice" is an "all-healing medicine of
our woes,"[3] the members of AA hope that a "Power greater than ourselves

---

[1] Xiuxi Yin quoted in Blake Morrison, "Why Do Writers Drink?" *Guardian*, July 20, 2013,
www.theguardian.com/books/2013/jul/20/why-do-writers-drink-alcohol.
[2] Eugene O'Neill quoted in Robert M. Dowling, *Eugene O'Neill: A Life in Four Acts* (New
Haven: University of Yale Press, 2014), 264.
[3] Euripides, "The Bacchae," in *The Plays of Euripides*, vol. 2 (Maryland: Wildside Press, 2007), 8.

[can] restore us to sanity" – and sobriety.⁴ Summarizing these contradictions, Carl Jung argued that the "craving for alcohol [is] the equivalent, on a low level, of the spiritual thirst of our being for wholeness," explaining that "'alcohol' in Latin is *spiritus*, and one uses the same word for the highest religious experience as well as for the most depraving poison."⁵ By implication, then, in*spiration* equals in*toxication* and vice versa. Good cheer is of course also an issue for social drinkers who imbibe to keep their spirits up, as the saying goes. Drinking songs abound in almost every culture. "Come, thou monarch of the vine, / Plumpy Bacchus with pink eyne! / In thy vats our cares be drown'd": Shakespeare's lines from *Anthony and Cleopatra* summarize the gist of hundreds of lyrics, and Sir Toby Belch's taunt to Malvolio in *Twelfth Night* – "Dost think because thou art virtuous there shall be no more cakes and ale?" – dramatizes the dedicated drinker's defiance of what he considers puritanical sobriety.⁶

But spirits and inspiration? The confusion of spirit as alcohol with spirit as soul or breath helps explain why a poetics of drink seems to have shaped or shadowed the poetry – and fiction – of so many writers. For might the Romantic (and post-Romantic) poet's transformative possession by a muse or daimon parallel the hapless drinker's possession by the demon rum? The lists of alcoholic writers reiterated by commentators are long and varied, and among Americans they include a number of Nobel prize winners (Sinclair Lewis, Eugene O'Neill, Ernest Hemingway, William Faulkner). And beyond the Nobels, there are the usual suspects on both sides of the Atlantic: Hart Crane, F. Scott Fitzgerald, Louise Bogan, Dylan Thomas, Delmore Schwartz, Philip Larkin, Robert Lowell, John Berryman, Edna St. Vincent Millay, Raymond Carver, Elizabeth Bishop, John Cheever, Dorothy Parker – and on and on.

But these writers had nineteenth-century forebears, some who were addicted to opium or used laudanum (opium dissolved in alcohol) and others who merely meditated on the aesthetic visions induced by states of dream or trance. Coleridge, De Quincey, Elizabeth Barrett Browning, and Edgar Allan Poe all were users, or sometimes abusers, of consciousness-altering substances. Coleridge, most famous for his vexed relationship to opium, evidently also had a vexing relationship to drinking, even penning a poem titled "Drinking versus Thinking."⁷ The closing quatrain of "Kubla

---

⁴ Bill Wilson and Robert Holbrook Smith, *Alcoholics Anonymous* (New York: Penguin, 2014).
⁵ Carl Jung, "Letter to Bill Wilson," *AA Grapevine* (November 1974), 30–31.
⁶ William Shakespeare, *Anthony and Cleopatra*, in *The Norton Shakespeare*, edited by Stephen Greenblatt et al. (New York: Norton, 1997), 2.7.134–36.William Shakespeare, *Twelfth Night*, in ibid., 2.3.115.
⁷ Samuel Taylor Coleridge, *The Complete Poems of Samuel Taylor Coleridge* (New York: Penguin, 2004), 294.

Khan" – a poem notoriously written on drugs – celebrates the powers of one who "on honey dew hath fed / And drunk the milk of paradise."[8] What had this youth with flashing eyes and floating hair ingested? Opium *and* the "vine's rich stream"? To the extent that the poetics of Romanticism was a poetics of the imaginative metamorphoses induced by "wise passiveness" along with possession by an alien, visionary spirit, it was a shamanistic poetics of inebriation.

Keats, remember, yearned in his "Ode to a Nightingale" for a "beaker full of the warm South,"

> Full of the true, the blushful Hippocrene,
> With beaded bubbles winking at the brim,
> And purple-stained mouth;
> That I might drink, and leave the world unseen,
> And with thee fade away into the forest dim:[9]

Intoxicated by the bird's inhuman happiness, the speaker here longs to enter a realm of *difference*, where he can escape the "fever and the fret." Yet *nota bene*: he corrects his plan as his poem evolves, declaring that he will journey "*Not* charioted by Bacchus and his pards, / But on the viewless wings of Poesy," And yet, again: he reiterates his thirst for oblivion, imagining that it would be "rich to die" into the mystical anesthesia induced by real inebriation so that to the nightingale's "high requiem" he would "become a sod."

More comically, Byron confessed in *Don Juan* that he was writing one of his elegant ottava rima stanzas "reeling, / Having got drunk exceedingly today, / So that I seem to stand upon the ceiling."[10] Then after apologizing that "the future is a serious matter," he demanded "for God's sake – hock and soda water!"[11] Later in the century, in a similarly sardonic mode, A. E. Housman's well-known aesthetic manifesto – "Terence, this is stupid stuff" – elaborates on the relationship between alcohol and poetry, implying the superior beneficence of alcohol while accounting for its virtues in skillful verse.

> Why, if 'tis dancing you would be,
> There's brisker pipes than poetry.
> Say, for what were hop-yards meant,
> Or why was Burton built on Trent?

[8] Ibid., 250.
[9] John Keats, *Selected Poems* (New York: Penguin, 2007), 193.
[10] Lord George Gordon Byron, *Lord Byron: The Major Works* (Oxford: Oxford University Press, 2008), 478.
[11] Ibid., 478.

Oh many a peer of England brews
Livelier liquor than the Muse,
And malt does more than Milton can
To justify God's ways to man.
Ale, man, ale's the stuff to drink
For fellows whom it hurts to think:
Look into the pewter pot
To see the world as the world's not.
And faith, 'tis pleasant till 'tis past:
The mischief is that 'twill not last.[12]

Needless to say, some poets were even more extravagant in their praise of inebriation. Baudelaire advised readers to cultivate the intensity he associated with wine ("Be drunk!"), Rimbaud took intoxication as his theme ("The Drunken Boat"), Symonds investigated absinthe ("The Absinthe Drinker"), Apollinaire called poems "Alcools" (spirits? or as one translator suggests, "cocktails"). Perhaps the words of these writers helped shape the theories about alcohol intermittently espoused by the American philosopher William James, the French philosopher Gaston Bachelard, and even, at one point, Sigmund Freud. In *The Varieties of Religious Experience,* James rather ruefully conceded that drinking might actually inspire religious experiences, writing "Sobriety diminishes, discriminates, and says no; drunkenness expands, unites, and says yes. It is in fact the great exciter of the *yes* function in man. It brings its votary from the chill periphery of things to the radiant core. It makes him for the moment one with truth."[13] To be sure, he added that such bliss is available "only in the fleeting earlier phases of what in its totality is so degrading a poisoning."[14] Freud made a similar point in *Jokes and Their Relationship to the Unconscious,* where he observed that alcohol "makes accessible once again sources of pleasure which were under the weight of suppression."[15]

Elaborating on such themes in his phenomenological treatise *The Psychoanalysis of Fire,* Bachelard looked back nostalgically on his own childhood experiences with the making of a *brulôt* of burnt sugar and brandy during a winter festival as he began a discussion of "Alcohol: *The Water That Flames*" in the writings of E. T. A. Hoffmann, arguing that "the alcoholic unconscious is a profound reality."

[12] A. E. Housman, *The Collected Poems of A. E. Housman* (New York: Holt, 1971), 88.
[13] William James, *The Varieties of Religious Experience* (New York: Dover, 2013), 377.
[14] Ibid., 378.
[15] Sigmund Freud, *Jokes and Their Relationship to the Unconscious* (New York: Norton, 1960), 127.

One is mistaken if one imagines that alcohol simply stimulates our mental potentialities. In fact, it creates these potentialities. It incorporates itself, so to speak, with that which is striving to express itself. It appears evident that alcohol is a creator of language. It enriches the vocabulary and frees the syntax … Bacchus is a beneficent god; by causing our reason to wander he prevents the anchylosis of logic and prepares the way for rational inventiveness.[16]

The comments of James, Freud, and Bachelard may come as a shock to the recovering alcoholics of AA and the gurus of temperance who share the opinion, most notably propounded by Lewis Hyde in "Alcohol and Poetry," his censorious discussion of John Berryman's sad fate, that a "poet who has become wholly possessed by alcohol is no longer a poet," the victim of "a corporeal war between the powers of creation and the spirit of alcohol."[17] But all are articulating a view that has a long cultural history even while Bachelard in particular gradually expresses his awareness that, in Hyde's words, the addicted "drinker becomes alcohol in a human skin."[18] Historically, Bachelard notes, a number of scientists believed "the substantial concentration of alcohol in the flesh to be so strong that they … speak of a *spontaneous combustion,* so that the drunkard does not even need a match to set himself on fire."[19] Thus the inebriate – like the analyst of literary inebriation – must tread a fine line. For if the spirit of alcohol, judiciously imbibed, may enrich the vocabulary and free the syntax, it may also – injudiciously indulged – inflame the whole being of the drinker so that he self-destructs, literally or figuratively burning out. Fire water may set the soul alight but consume the flesh.

Far more than the foods of sobriety (bread, cheese, stews, grills, sweets), alcoholic beverages are themselves, like those who imbibe them, examples of striking metamorphoses. Certainly the fermentation that transforms grapes into wine, grains into beer, honey into mead, and potatoes into vodka is a primordial instance of thrilling, potentially perilous transmutation. Circe's special cocktail may have literally turned men into pigs, but most alcoholic drinks have the potential to bring out the beastly even before the combustible in those who overindulge. Simultaneously

[16] Gaston Bachelard, *The Psychoanalysis of Fire* (New York: Beacon Press, 1964), 87.
[17] Lewis Hyde, "Alcohol and Poetry: John Berryman and the Booze Talking," *American Poetry Review* (July/August 1975): 8.
[18] Ibid.
[19] Bachelard, *Psychoanalysis of Fire*, 95.

strengthening and even sacred as well as dangerously debilitating, wines and liquors are subject to quotidian abuse. If Christ's blood offers salvation in a wine chalice, Dionysus – the mysterious god of the vine and of drunkenness – brings both solace and frenzy, joy and rage, when he unleashes the power in the cup. For centuries alcoholic beverages were used as anesthetics and restoratives. Yet consider the fate of Pentheus, the righteous voyeur of Euripides' *Bacchae*: his own intoxicated mother tore him limb from limb when he spied on the ferocious celebrations of the Maenads. Consider, more generally, the madness represented by the Roman rites of the Bacchanalia and the Saturnalia. And consider, even to this day, the dangers of drink as outlined by protesters from the pious members of the Women's Christian Temperance Union to, more poignantly, the angry grievers of Mothers Against Drunk Driving.

D. H. Lawrence, a reasonably temperate man, had struggled with the spirit of alcohol since childhood, as he related in the various versions of *Sons and Lovers*, where young Paul Morel must cope with his coal-miner father's abusive drunkenness. Yet as a poet who identified deeply with the Romantic mystique propounded by a visionary company of nineteenth-century precursors, he continually sought for ways to commune with what Bachelard called "that which is striving to express itself" – the unconscious self just on the other side of some indefinable border.[20] A number of his strongest verses strive to cross that border, including "Medlars and Sorb Apples," and the late "Bavarian Gentians." But the most explicit one is "Grapes," which concludes almost as a manifesto against Prohibition:

> The grape is swart, the avenues dusky and tendrilled, subtly prehensile.
> But we, as we start awake, clutch at our vistas democratic, boulevards, tram-cars, policemen.
> Give us our own back
> Let us go to the soda-fountain, to get sober.
>
> Soberness, sobriety.
> It is like the agonised perverseness of a child heavy with sleep, yet fighting, fighting to keep awake;
> Soberness, sobriety, with heavy eyes propped open.
>
> Dusky are the avenues of wine,
> And we must cross the frontiers, though we will not,
> Of the lost, fern-scented world:
> Take the fern-seed on our lips,

Close the eyes, and go
Down the tendrilled avenues of wine and the otherworld.[21]

America, the place Lawrence once called "the evening land," is here the enemy of an "otherworld" as fertile as the Hades of "Bavarian Gentians," where Pluto and Persephone unite in a darker and darker blue not unlike the "swart" and "dusky" space of the grape. And sobriety, which was actually one of Lawrence's own characteristic states, seems here to be an American invention, like the soda-fountain and Whitman's democratic vistas. As in so many of his novels and poems, the writer of this work wants to go back to a primordial world that he imagines as transformative – although, to be sure, it is also a realm of unconsciousness, in which he too, like Keats, might "become a sod" to the high requiem of nature.

Of course, in his nasty allusion to "vistas democratic" Lawrence is pursuing his love–hate relationship with Walt Whitman, the author of *Democratic Vistas* and the American poet who most influenced his own versification. Among Whitman's earliest works was *Franklin Evans*, a temperance novel that he later dismissed as "rot" but about which Lawrence would most likely have known. At the same time, however, Lawrence is involved in a dialogue with Poe, whose drunkenness he deplored. As he wrote in *Studies in Classic American Literature,* Poe "tried alcohol, and any drug he could lay his hand on. He also tried any human being he could lay his hands on."[22] Whether or not this was the case, the statement locates Lawrence's own ambivalence toward both alcohol and America. Perhaps the "otherworld" to which the grape might transport the speaker of his poem is one that can be found nowhere but on the page? Certainly the writer himself tolerated drinking very badly. Memoirists and biographers repeatedly refer to a dramatic dinner at the Café Royal in 1923, when most of the guests, but especially Lawrence himself, got violently ill from too much wine: the author of "Grapes" vomited all over the table and had to be carried out of the restaurant by two close friends.

Unlike Lawrence, Bachelard, and Keats, most seriously addicted drinkers tend not to glamorize alcohol. To be sure, Hemingway and Fitzgerald portray hedonistic bacchanalias in *The Sun Also Rises* and *The Great Gatsby*, as if to illustrate Dorothy Parker's view that "Candy is dandy / But liquor is quicker." But *Tender Is the Night* is virtually Hogarthian in its delineation of Dick Diver's "progress" into dissolution and disintegration. And poets like Hart Crane, Delmore Schwartz, and John Berryman, themselves in

---

[21] D. H. Lawrence, *The Complete Poems of D. H. Lawrence* (New York: Viking, 1971), 286–87.
[22] D. H. Lawrence, *Studies in Classic American Literature* (Delhi: Atlantic, 1995), 77.

the grip of alcohol, wrote darkly and sardonically of their thirsts. Crane's phantasmagoric "The Wine-Menagerie" begins with the hope that wine "redeems the sight" and awakens a sleeping leopard in the speaker, but quickly declines into a blurry recognition that "Anguished [is] the wit that cries out of me."[23] Schwartz, when he first began seriously drinking, praised wine extravagantly. "Wine brings all things closer – vivider," he declared in 1942, noting that "Wine is my inspiration, exaltation, / Magic, Pegasus, and peerless peaks & heights," and adding that "With wine do I forgive my enemies."[24] As he was gradually overtaken by the manic depression and paranoia that ultimately (along with alcohol) consumed his literary career, his attitude grew more ironic. "Poor Schwartz! Poor Schwartz!," he exclaimed in a fragment titled "Doggerel beneath the Skin" (the title riffed on Auden and Isherwood's satiric play *The Dog Beneath the Skin* from the thirties).

> Love anyway to all of them!
> And may they leave to see the peace
> when no one has to drink to live
> And work without hysteria,
> Self-pity and insomnia,
> Poor Schwartz! Poor Schwartz!
> Self-doubt and sun deliria! ...
>   Poor Berryman! Poor Schwartz!
> All poet's wives have rotten lives,
> Their husbands look at them like knives[25]

The reference to Berryman here is especially telling, for the two had been close friends, literary companions-in-arms, and of course drinking partners. When Schwartz was found ignominiously dead outside an elevator in a Manhattan hotel, Berryman elegized him in ten poignant dream songs, "one solid block of agony." Obsessively brooding on "the scene of this same death," he produced one of his most desperately eloquent poems.

> There are all the problems to be sorted out,
> the fate of the soul, what it was all about
> during its being, and whether he was drunk
> at 4 a.m. on the wrong floor too

[23] Hart Crane, *The Complete Poems of Hart Crane* (New York: Liveright, 2000), 23.
[24] Quoted in James Atlas, *Delmore Schwartz: The Life of an American Poet* (New York: Farrar Straus Giroux, 1977), 199.
[25] Delmore Schwartz, *Once and For All: The Best of Delmore Schwartz* (New York: New Directions, 2016), 163.

fighting for air, tearing his sorry clothes
with his visions dying O and O I mourn
again this complex death
Almost my oldest friend should never have been born
to this terrible end, out of which what grows
but an unshaven, disheveled *corpse?*[26]

And though the piece concludes that "the young will read his young verse / for as long as such things go," he could not shake off the despair of his persona, "miserable Henry / who *knew* him all so long for better & worse / and nearly would follow him below."

Along with several other notable figures of their generation (Lowell, Bishop), Schwartz and Berryman were mid-century American *poètes maudit*. But of all this group, it was Berryman who wrote most frankly and most often about his fatal addiction to alcohol. *The Dream Songs,* with their hopped-up jazzy rhythms, acerbic minstrel-show dialogue between the sad-sack, cartoon-like Henry and his knowing foil Mr. Bones, function as both a definitive exploration of the modes and manners drink inflicts upon the poet and a surrealistic send-up of inebriation itself. Wise-cracking in the confessional, Berryman is neither a self-dramatizing Lowell nor a self-pitying Schwartz, although half the time his hand seems to be at his own throat and, like the Lowell of "Skunk Hour," he clearly believes his "mind's not right." That his pages are soaked in alcohol like a tipsy cake drenched in brandy is clear from the start. The fumes rise intermittently but strikingly; one can imagine Bachelard setting fire to them to create a *brulôt*. By the light of those flames, the poet sees himself clearly as the comic grotesque he claims he is.

Why drink so, two days running?
Two months, O seasons, years, two decades running?
I answer (smiles) my question on the cuff.
Man, I been thirsty.[27]

Or

Madness & booze, madness & booze,
Which'll can tell who preceded whose?[28]

Or

---

[26] "Song 157," in John Berryman, *The Dream Songs* (New York: Farrar Straus Giroux, 2014), 176.
[27] "Song 96," in ibid., 113.
[28] "Song 225," in ibid., 244.

> Books drugs razor whisky shirts
> Henry lies ready for his Eastern tour,
> swollen ankles, one hand,
> on reservations, friends at the end of hurts[29]

Or

> sad sights. A crumpled, empty cigarette pack.
> O empty bottle.[30]

Here, argues the critic and sometime temperance worker Lewis Hyde, we confront the debris of a life spent not just off but maybe even under the wagon. For though the Gaelic meaning of "usquebae" (whiskey) is supposedly "water of life," the fire water Berryman consumes has, in Hyde's opinion, burnt him out.

Or has it? Against Hyde's censorious view, Thomas Gilmore has argued eloquently, in his wide-ranging *Equivocal Spirits,* that Berryman "forged a distinctive poetic style and there is just as little doubt that his heavy drinking contributed to the development of this style – to its jazzy, jagged rhythms, its incoherences, its uninhibited (though of course calculated) use of colloquialisms and slang."[31] The price for this style, however, was high. In his introduction to Berryman's incomplete, posthumously published novel, *Recovery* – a barely fictionalized account of the poet's own experiences with AA groups – Saul Bellow brilliantly profiles the suicidal alcoholic in his last year of teaching at the University of Minnesota. Even when he was hospitalized for rehabilitation, Bellow explains, Berryman journeyed to campus to meet his Humanities class.

> He wore a huge Western sort of hat. Under the flare of the brim his pale face was long and thin. With tremulous composure, shoulders high, he stalked into the classroom … His first words were shaky, inaudible, but very soon other instructors had to shut their doors against his penetrating voice. He sweated heavily, his shaky fingers turned the numbered cards of his full and careful lecture outline … Then, peanut-faced, under the enormous hat and soaked in sweat, he entered the cab and was returned to [the hospital].[32]

By the time Berryman committed suicide by jumping off a bridge between St. Paul and Minneapolis, he had already annihilated his body with

---

[29] "Song 169," in ibid., 188.
[30] "Song 250," in ibid., 269.
[31] Thomas Gilmore, *Equivocal Spirits: Alcoholism and Drinking in Twentieth-Century Literature* (Chapel Hill: University of North Carolina Press, 1987), 171–72.
[32] Saul Bellow, "Foreword," in John Berryman, *Recovery* (Minneapolis: University of Minnesota Press, 2016), xiv.

whiskey, but he was not by any means what Hyde called "alcohol in a human skin" though he had – in Bellow's words – "the ruined drunken poet's God to whom he prayed over his shoulder."[33]

Poètes Maudit

From the texture of her work on the page and the tidy appearance she mostly presented, one would not be inclined to include Elizabeth Bishop in this category. Certainly Berryman himself appeared disinclined. In the dream song insouciantly beginning "Them lady poets must not marry, pal," he ranked Bishop with Dickinson, Sappho, Moore, and the Brontës:

> Miss Dickinson – fancy in Amherst bedding her,
> Fancy a lark with Sappho,
> a tumble in the bushes with Miss Moore,
> a spoon with Emily, while Charlotte glare.
> Miss Bishop's too noble O.[34]

Miss Dickinson, *Miss* Moore, *Miss* Bishop – three accomplished American poets are here represented as if they were prissy teachers in a girls' school. And yet, along with Sylvia Plath (who is described in the next stanza as now "not"), they constitute what Berryman calls "the lot" of "lady poets," implying some sort of minimal respect. And in her way Bishop herself returned that respect, reviewing *The Dream Songs* in 1969 with a "Thank-You Note" of four incisive lines in the *Harvard Advocate*.

> Mr. Berryman's songs and sonnets say:
> "Gather ye berries harsh and crude while yet ye may."
> Even if they pucker our mouths like choke-cherries
> Let us be grateful for these thick-bunched berries.[35]

Punning on Berryman's name while alluding to Herrick ("Gather ye rosebuds") and Milton ("berries harsh and crude"), Bishop seems to be tossing off a spirited, if ambiguous, tribute to the "thick-bunched" fruits of his imagination.

Spirited, though? Bishop was herself an alcoholic – a binge drinker, who struggled for most of her life with bouts of intoxication for which she often checked herself into hospitals like the rehab facility where Berryman went. But unlike Berryman, she almost never wrote about drinking; indeed unlike

[33] Ibid., xvi.
[34] "Song 187," in Berryman, *Dream Songs*, 206.
[35] Elizabeth Bishop, *The Complete Poems: 1927–1979* (New York: Farrar Straus Giroux, 1983), 207.

Berryman and Lowell, she was the opposite of a so-called confessional poet. "She was demure and reticent," in the words of a former student of hers at Harvard, dressed in "expensive Italian silk outfits and beautiful suits, and was immaculately put together" – as were her poems.[36] Yet in her carefully disciplined, highly polished work, Bishop did, as Brett Millier and others have noted, elliptically allude to her own drinking.[37] Most strikingly, in the sad and lonely revision of Defoe's *Robinson Crusoe* titled "Crusoe in England," arguably a sort of elegy for her lover Lota de Macedo Soares, she revived the imagery of her 1969 tribute to *Berry*man. Her Crusoe, recalling his years of isolation on a desert island featuring "fifty-two / miserable, small volcanoes" under "a sort of cloud-dump," discloses that he had comforted himself with "one kind of berry, a dark red."

> I tried it, one by one, and hours apart.
> Sub-acid, and not bad, no ill effects;
> and so I made home-brew. I'd drink
> the awful, fizzy, stinging stuff
> that went straight to my head
> and play my home-made flute …
> And, dizzy, whoop and dance among the goats.[38]

Dark red, sub-acid? The berries on this allegorical island eerily suggest the chokecherries of "Mr. Berryman's songs and sonnets," so astringent that they "pucker our mouths," though unlike Berryman's berries they are the source, not the consequence of alcoholic addiction.

Not only do chokecherries characteristically pucker the mouth, they can in fact be fermented to produce wine: according to one authority, they have "long been used for country wine-making because the fruits are plentiful and the wine-making easy."[39] In between playing on "his" (her?) "home-made flute" Bishop's Crusoe binges on the "awful, fizzy, stinging stuff" in bitter privacy, dizzily dancing among the mysterious goats who are the island's only other mammalian residents. And now, the speaker confesses, "I felt a deep affection for / the smallest of my island industries," then backtracks, "No, not exactly, since the smallest was / a miserable philosophy." In a kind of odd metonymy, the thick-clustered berries

[36] Peggy Ellsberg quoted in Gary Fountain and Peter Brazeau, eds., *Remembering Elizabeth Bishop: An Oral Biography* (Amherst: University of Massachusetts Press, 1994), 281.

[37] Brett Millier, *Flawed Light: American Women Poets and Alcohol* (Urbana-Champaign: University of Illinois Press, 2009).

[38] Bishop, *Complete Poems*, 164.

[39] G. K. Bayne, "How to Make Homemade Chokecherry Wine," Leaf Group, 2017, www.leaf.tv/articles/how-to-make-homemade-chokecherry-wine.

of Berryman's dream songs have mutated into Bishop's secret intoxicating "industry", inspiring her own spirited songs on a home-made flute.

Most commentators on Bishop's relatively small, painstakingly composed *oeuvre* have, of course, remarked that when this poet was seriously drinking she wasn't seriously writing. Like Hemingway, she herself might have confessed that she "drank to stop writing," unlike Berryman who perhaps drank to start writing. Yet her intermittent immersions in alcohol suggest a thirst that shapes her work from "A Man-Moth" to "At the Fish Houses." In a draft poem frankly titled "A Drunkard" she explains the etiology of this theme, recording a childhood memory of "the Salem fire" she witnessed at three, when she was "terribly thirsty but mama" – preoccupied with helping victims – "didn't hear me calling her."

> Since that night, that day …
> I have suffered from abnormal thirst –
> I swear it's true – and by the age
> of twenty or twenty-one I had begun
> to drink, & drink – I can't get enough
> and, as you must have noticed,
> I'm half drunk now … [sic]
>
> And all I'm telling you may be a lie … [sic][40]

Lying, drinking, dreaming, fantasizing, and – as Bishop wrote elsewhere – "poetry as an unnatural act," all are subtly linked here, as in "Crusoe in England." Art, Picasso once wrote, is a lie one tells in order to tell the truth. And the lie here may constitute just the truth that the demure and reticent "Miss Bishop" was "too noble O" to tell elsewhere.

Across the Atlantic, at a different, less prestigious university, the British writer Philip Larkin was rather more openly preoccupied with alcohol, although as the bespectacled, conservatively suited director of a library he too may have frequently appeared "demure and reticent." Describing himself in verse as "unchilded and unwifed," he lived mostly alone until nearly the end of his life, when he shared his house with Monica Jones, his heir and one of his three long-time mistresses.[41] Like him, Jones was an alcoholic, and Larkin's biographer, Andrew Motion, portrays the pair breakfasting on sherry or port at a point in those last years when the poet had virtually stopped writing. In any case, though he was renowned in England and always considered a candidate for the laureateship (which he

---

40 Elizabeth Bishop, *Edgar Allan Poe and the Juke-Box* (New York: Farrar Straus Giroux, 2007), 150.
41 "The View," in Philip Larkin, *Collected Poems* (New York: Farrar Straus Giroux, 1989), 195.

would have refused), Larkin's literary output was about as small as Bishop's, though considerably different in tone. As acerbic as Berryman, he loathed the "shallow violent eyes" of children, detested the thought of marrying (or partnering) anyone permanently, and in an ekphrastic verse titled "The Card-Players" that seems to have been inspired by a sixteenth-century Dutch genre painting, perhaps by Jan Lievens, celebrated the "secret, bestial peace" achieved by card playing drunks – comically named "Jan van Hogspeuw, Dirk Dogstoerd, and Old Prijk" – in their "lamplit cave."[42]

As his collected letters and various biographies have shown, in his own, secret, non-library life, Larkin was himself not just a drinker but a racist, a misogynist, and a collector of pornography. He was also, publicly, a Thatcherite and a jazz fan, who wrote eloquently on the subject. And both privately and publicly, he was obsessed with death, with "a black- / Sailed unfamiliar, towing at her back / A huge and birdless silence."[43] Perhaps, then, if Berryman drank not just to write but to dream of suicide, Larkin drank to quell the fears he so candidly dramatized in his poems. In his sardonic "A Study of Reading Habits," he punningly exaggerates his own peccadilloes ("with inch-thick specs, / Evil was just my *lark:* / Me and my cloak and fangs / Had ripping times in the dark"), then, perhaps not so comically, this nighttime version of the daytime librarian concludes "Get stewed: / Books are a load of crap."[44]

In Larkin's finest poems, his nighttime thoughts were far more serious. In "Sad Steps," a brilliant riff on Sir Philip Sidney's "With how sad steps, O moon, thou climbs't the skies," he wakens from the "secret, bestial peace" of drunkenness as "Groping back to bed after a piss," he parts "thick curtains" and is "startled" by the moon as it climbs the skies:

> One shivers slightly, looking up there.
> The hardness and the brightness and the plain
> Far-reaching singleness of that wide stare
>
> Is a reminder of the strength and pain
> Of being young; that it can't come again,
> But is for others undiminished somewhere.[45]

But where Sidney speaks of love ("O Moon, tell me … Do they above love to be loved … ?"), Larkin, in what seems to be a moment of luminous sobriety, broods on loss, implicitly comparing his own aging "singleness"

[42] "The Card-Players," in ibid., 177.
[43] "Next, Please," in ibid., 52.
[44] "A Study of Reading Habits," in ibid., 131 (emphasis mine).
[45] "Sad Steps," in ibid., 169.

to the Elizabethan sonneteer whose "Astrophil and Stella" is always and almost only about Petrarchan romance. His comment on the source poem is oblique and, for him, "confessional." The moon, he declares, is "High and *preposterous* and separate – / Lozenge of love! Medallion of art! / O wolves of memory! Immensements! No":[46] no, indeed. Sir Philip (his namesake) Sidney (his father's namesake) was an idealized courtier; in Yeats' words "Our Sidney and our perfect man."[47] Philip Larkin, in the dreary north-eastern town of Hull, is a thick-lensed librarian, groping "back to bed after a piss." "Aubade," the companion poem to "Sad Steps," may be one of the greatest hangover poems of all time and is certainly one of Larkin's most memorable works. Again, the title of the piece is allusively literary – and almost abusively anti-literary. An aubade is, of course, a dawn song meditating on the moment when lovers part. But here, as in "Sad Steps," the lover is Larkin and the beloved is Larkin's own life; there is no "significant other," no one to kiss and miss. Yet perhaps because of its isolation from love or even friendship, the work broods with greater clarity on the old medieval idea of *timor mortis* than almost any other contemporary poem. And it begins with inebriation, and an awakening from inebriation:

> I work all day, and get half-drunk at night.
> Waking at four to soundless dark, I stare.
> In time the curtain-edges will grow light.
> Till then I see what's really always there:
> Unresting death, a whole day nearer now,
> Making all thought impossible but how
> And where and when I shall myself die.
> Arid interrogation: yet the dread
> Of dying, and being dead,
> Flashes afresh to hold and horrify.[48]

Perhaps such candor can only be the consequence of unwilled sobriety, the dreadful recognition that comes to the drinker when inebriation has worn away and whatever might be real makes its claim in a dawn of sober consciousness. Any spirituality spirits have given to the alcoholic have here trickled away. The headache and existential Sartrean nausea of death impend. The elaborate confrontations of dawn cannot be avoided, including the "furnace-fear when we are caught without / People or drink" and "Courage is no good." In the end – the end of the poem, the end of the

---

[46] Ibid. (emphasis added).
[47] "In Memory of Major Robert Gregory," in W. B. Yeats, *The Wild Swans at Coole* (London: Macmillan, 1919), 4.
[48] "Aubade," in ibid., 208.

life, the dawn of truth – "Postmen like doctors go from house to house."
And there is sherry, or port, for breakfast.

Could Larkin – and his drinking contemporaries or forebears – have
confronted their fates and elaborated their fictions of selfhood without a
poetics of inebriation? That would be an unfair question, because hypo-
thetical: all were clearly shaped by the drinking they were driven to do. Yet
one could, after all, become what Emily Dickinson called an "inebriate of
air." Remember how she put it?

> I taste a liquor never brewed –
> From Tankards scooped in Pearl –
> Not all the Frankfort Berries
> Yield such an Alcohol!
>
> Inebriate of air – am I –
> And Debauchee of Dew –
> Reeling – thro' endless summer days –
> From inns of molten Blue –[49]

In western Massachusetts, a few decades after the English Romantics
drank the milk of paradise and other intoxicating substances, sobriety
itself could yield an alcohol of nature, not unlike the transcendence M. H.
Abrams has associated with natural supernaturalism. Dickinson says she
was drunk on the winds of her garden, drunk on the endless summer days
of her relatively short life. And yet – and yet – consider her (perhaps literally) fabulous recipe for "black cake," the kind baked "Only in Domingo."
It featured raisins, sugar, and at least a half pint of brandy ("not father's
best").

BIBLIOGRAPHY

Atlas, James. *Delmore Schwartz: The Life of an American Poet*. New York: Farrar
    Straus Giroux, 1977.
Bachelard, Gaston. *The Psychoanalysis of Fire*. New York: Beacon Press, 1964.
Bayne, G. K. "How to Make Homemade Chokecherries." Leaf Group, 2017.
    www.leaf.tv/articles/how-to-make-homemade-chokecherry-wine.
Bellow, Saul. "Foreword." In *Recovery* by John Berryman. Minneapolis: University
    of Minnesota Press, 2016.
Berryman, John. *The Dream Songs*. New York: Farrar Straus Giroux, 2014.
Bishop, Elizabeth. *The Complete Poems: 1927–1979*. New York: Farrar Straus
    Giroux, 1983.
    Edgar Allan Poe and the Juke-Box. New York: Farrar Straus Giroux, 2007.

---

[49] "214," in Emily Dickinson, *The Complete Poems of Emily Dickinson* (New York: Little, Brown,
1960), 98.

Byron, George Gordon, Lord. *Lord Byron: The Major Works*. Oxford: Oxford University Press, 2008.

Coleridge, Samuel Taylor. *The Complete Poems of Samuel Taylor Coleridge*. New York: Penguin, 2004.

Crane, Hart. *The Complete Poems of Hart Crane*. New York: Liveright, 2000.

Dickinson, Emily. *The Complete Poems of Emily Dickinson*. New York: Little, Brown, 1960.

Dowling, Robert M. *Eugene O'Neill: A Life in Four Acts*. New Haven: University of Yale Press, 2014.

Euripides. "The Bacchae." In *The Plays of Euripides*. Vol. 2. Maryland: Wildside Press, 2007.

Fountain, Gary, and Peter Brazeau, eds. *Remembering Elizabeth Bishop: An Oral Biography*. Amherst: University of Massachusetts Press, 1994.

Freud, Sigmund. *Jokes and Their Relationship to the Unconscious*. New York: Norton, 1960.

Gilmore, Thomas. *Equivocal Spirits: Alcoholism and Drinking in Twentieth-Century Literature*. Chapel Hill: University of North Carolina Press, 1987.

Housman, A. E. *The Collected Poems of A. E. Housman*. New York: Holt, 1971.

Hyde, Lewis. "Alcohol and Poetry: John Berryman and the Booze Talking." *American Poetry Review*, July/August 1975, 7–12.

James, William. *The Varieties of Religious Experience*. New York: Dover, 2013.

Jung, Carl. "Letter to Bill Wilson." *AA Grapevine*, November 1974, 30–31.

Keats, John. *Selected Poems*. New York: Penguin, 2007.

Larkin, Philip. *Collected Poems*. New York: Farrar Straus Giroux, 1989.

Lawrence, D. H. *The Complete Poems of D. H. Lawrence*. New York: Viking, 1971. *Studies in Classic American Literature*. Delhi: Atlantic, 1995.

Millier, Brett. *Flawed Light: American Women Poets and Alcohol*. Urbana-Champaign: University of Illinois Press, 2009.

Morrison, Blake. "Why Do Writers Drink?" *Guardian*, July 20, 2013. www.theguardian.com/books/2013/jul/20/why-do-writers-drink-alcohol.

Schwartz, Delmore. *Once and For All: The Best of Delmore Schwartz*. New York: New Directions, 2016.

Shakespeare, William. *Anthony and Cleopatra*. In *The Norton Shakespeare*, edited by Stephen Greenblatt, Walter Cohen, Jean E. Howard, and Katharine Eisaman Maus. New York: Norton, 1997.

    Twelfth Night. In *The Norton Shakespeare*, edited by Stephen Greenblatt, Walter Cohen, Jean E. Howard, and Katharine Eisaman Maus. New York: Norton, 1997.

Wilson, Bill, and Robert Holbrook Smith. *Alcoholics Anonymous*. New York: Penguin, 2014.

Yeats, W. B. *The Wild Swans at Coole*. London: Macmillan, 1919.

CHAPTER 14

Vampires, Alterity, and Strange Eating

Jennifer Park

Blood Drinking, Strange Eating

We might think of drinking blood as an act of strangeness. As a form of cannibalism, and a practice of eating typically condemned in the philosophy of the "civilized" West, vampiric feeding as blood ingestion pushes on the complications of what I call *strange eating* – to open up "taboo" eating to further dialogue.[1] Although the Victorianist vampire, exemplified in large part by Bram Stoker's *Dracula*, tends to serve as our reference point for vampiric feeding, this chapter attempts to provide another angle in our understanding of blood drinking in the context of food and literature. Specifically, I examine blood drinking as a form of strange eating, to argue that vampiric feeding, or the impulse to drink blood, manifests from the intersection of medicine, myth, and ideas of human difference to produce a diet that pushes on the boundaries of what constitutes humanity in the literary imagination. My intention here is to highlight the more obscure – and thus more urgent – alternative or marginalized histories and afterlives of vampiric feeding, before and beyond the Victorian vampire: blood lust as infant nourishment, medicinal ingestion, or eating disorder, with racial ramifications. These narratives span an historical range, from ancient epileptic blood drinking to early modern menstrual blood to the cross-pollination of blood drinking, disordered eating, and community building in the twenty-first century.

I begin by laying out the foundations for a proto-vampiric discourse about "flesh foods," to define vampiric feeding as a type of "strange eating."

---

[1] On the category of the "taboo" in eating, see Claude Lévi-Strauss, *The Raw and the Cooked* (Chicago: University of Chicago Press, 1983); Julia Kristeva, *Powers of Horror: An Essay on Abjection* (New York: Columbia University Press, 1982). On cannibalism, see Catalin Avramescu, *An Intellectual History of Cannibalism* (Princeton: Princeton University Press, 2009); Francis Barker, Peter Hulme, and Margaret Iversen, eds., *Cannibalism and the Colonial World* (Cambridge: Cambridge University Press, 1998).

By *strange eating*, I mean to evoke the various permutations of "strange" and "eating" placed side-by-side, permutations that include presumed aberrant or atypical eating habits – eating strange *things* and eating the strange or *strangers* – all of which serve to emphasize the function of diverging from the norm. Strange eating, in other words, is something foreign, whether the act of eating itself or that which is eaten. To this end, vampiric feeding is most easily categorized as a type of strange eating by virtue of the substance being consumed: human blood. As a human substance, the blood that constitutes the vampiric diet speaks to vampirism as thus a form, or subset, of cannibalism.

From my emphasis on marginalized narratives of vampiric feeding, what comes to light in the context of blood ingestion are the ways in which bodies of difference, "othered" bodies, figure as sources, cures, and antidotes to vampirism. This literalizes what scholars have identified as the metaphorics and theoretics of *eating the other*, in particular the black body as consumable.[2] It is through reading blood as food, and vampirism as eating, that the literal lust to consume blood is intimately concerned with sustenance, sexuality/reproduction, and the tensions of race and otherness in definitions of humanity. Tracing the histories of proto-vampiric feeding, I begin with ancient and early modern beliefs about blood drinking before moving to Zanche, the Ethiopian handmaiden in John Webster's *The White Devil* (1612), who offers up her drinkable blood as harnessing particular medicinal properties. These proto-vampiric narratives recast vampirism in light of premodern cannibalistic feeding and resonate in new ways with twenty-first century stories of racialized vampirism: through Ore, Helen Oyeyemi's queer, black narrator who becomes an example of blood lust to the white, xenophobic pica-vampirism that arises in her friend Miranda in *White Is for Witching*, and Shori, Octavia Butler's black vampire-human hybrid in *Fledgling*. I thus bring together two threads of food studies discourse in this study: the vampiric diet and the consumable black body.

Epileptic Vampires and Proto-Vampiric Feeding

According to the *Oxford English Dictionary*, the term "vampire" in the English language was not in use until close to the mid-eighteenth century, when it began to refer to "A preternatural being of a malignant nature (in

---

[2] See bell hooks, "Eating the Other: Desire and Resistance," in *Black Looks: Race and Representation* (Boston: South End Press, 1992), 21–39; Kyla Wazana Tompkins, *Racial Indigestion: Eating Bodies in the 19th Century* (New York: New York University Press, 2012).

the original and usual form of the belief, a reanimated corpse), supposed to *seek nourishment, or do harm,* by *sucking the blood* of sleeping persons," or, later, "a man or woman abnormally endowed with similar habits."[3] But the sucking of blood fits under Richard Sugg's "working definition of 'cannibalism'" as "consumption by mouth of those body parts or fluids which a donor cannot very easily do without."[4] While a case could be made that a donor could do without some amount of blood, it is useful to consider blood drinking as a form of cannibalism due to the taboos that surrounded it.[5] Thus, the ingestion of body parts and body fluids speaks to different forms of cannibalistic feeding, a phenomenon that extends well before the term "vampire" existed to describe one who indulges in a particular cannibalistic practice.

The history of what we might consider cannibalistic practices in the West, including the drinking of blood, includes what were widespread forms of "cannibalistic" feeding in premodern times – in accepted or common use, if also in contention. From the dietary theories of ancient Greece and Rome to early modern European physic, food and medicine were integrated, without the distinctions we form between the two today; ingested foodstuffs and ingredients all provided medicinal benefits in addition to nourishment. Thus, when we trace the history of blood drinking back into antiquity, we uncover the medicinal origins – indeed the medicinal benefits – of drinking blood.

Human blood was held to be a remedy for epilepsy. It was sometimes drunk "fresh and hot, seconds after a beheading; sometimes direct from a living donor's body."[6] In ancient Rome, after the death of a gladiator, one might find epileptic patients drinking blood "fresh from the wound" at the throat.[7] Epileptic patients, therefore, may have been the first vampiric feeders of the West. Not only were they early blood-drinkers, but additionally the etymological origins of the term epilepsy derived from the Greek verb, to be seized, connected to early belief in the "demonic origin of diseases."[8] Those with epilepsy were therefore thought to be

---

[3] "vampire, n." OED Online, September 2016, Oxford University Press, www.oed.com/view/Entry/221303 (emphasis mine). Fabio Parasecoli locates the term's beginnings in late seventeenth-century France; see Parasecoli, *Bite Me: Food in Popular Culture* (New York: Berg, 2008), 54.

[4] Richard Sugg, *Mummies, Cannibals and Vampires: The History of Corpse Medicine from the Renaissance to the Victorians,* 2nd ed. (London: Routledge, 2016), 11.

[5] Ibid., 11.

[6] Ibid., 6.

[7] Ibid., 15.

[8] Leo Kanner, "The Names of the Falling Sickness: An Introduction to the Study of the Folklore and Cultural History of Epilepsy," *Human Biology* 2.1 (1930): 111.

possessed by spirits, "suddenly overcome by a supernatural force," and the use of terms like "attack and seizure" still remain in medical descriptions.[9] As a "disease," epilepsy was thought in the Middle Ages to be contagious, to the point where in some areas "the saliva of epileptics is still considered poisonous."[10] If the epileptic patient provided an early paradigm for the proto-vampire, we find an early medicinal explanation for the phenomenon of blood drinking as a "potent remedy" for epilepsy – also called the falling sickness – a popular belief since the beginnings of "the history of therapeutics."[11] Ferdinand Moog and Axel Karenberg note the Roman "encyclopaedist" Aulus Cornelius Celsus as the first writer to describe blood drinking as an epileptic remedy; in his *De medicina* (40 AD), it is described that some epileptics have cured themselves "by drinking the hot blood from the cut throat of a gladiator."[12] This is echoed in Pliny the Elder's *Natural History*, in which he describes, with some judgment, the blood remedy for epileptics:

> The blood too of gladiators is drunk by epileptics as though it were a draught of life, though we shudder with horror when in the same arena we look at even the beasts doing the same thing. But – by Heaven! – the patients think it most effectual to suck from a man himself warm, living blood, and putting their lips to the wound to drain the very life, although it is not the custom of men to apply their mouths at all to the wounds even of living beasts.[13]

Indeed the Christian author Tertullian, writing in 197 AD, speaks to the same in his *Apologeticum*, writing of "those who, when a show is given in the arena, with greedy thirst have caught the fresh blood of the guilty slain, as it pours fresh from their throats, and carry it off as a cure for their epilepsy."[14] Once gladiatorial combat was prohibited, patients turned to other executed bodies for the same.

Medieval and early modern Europe continued to see the use of such corpse remedies, and the incorporation of body parts and body fluids into recipes. In a recipe for a "precious water" attributed to Albertus Magnus, an elixir is made by distilling the "blood of a healthful man," the virtues of which will heal "any disease of the body, if it be anointed therewith …

9 Ibid., 111.
10 Ibid., 118–19.
11 Ferdinand Peter Moog and Axel Karenberg, "Between Horror and Hope: Gladiator's Blood as a Cure for Epileptics in Ancient Medicine," *Journal of the History of the Neurosciences* 12.2 (2003): 138.
12 III 23, 7; quoted in ibid., 138.
13 Pliny, *Natural History*, vol. 8, translated by W. H. S. Jones (Cambridge, MA: Harvard University Press, 1963), book 28, 4–5.
14 Tertullian, *Apology*, IX.10, translated by T. R. Glover (Cambridge, MA: Harvard University Press, 1966), 50–51.

and all inward diseases by the drinking thereof," effectively treating the distilled human blood as a kind of panacea that "healeth all kinds of diseases."[15] Other recipes included preparing blood for various elixirs of life, speaking to the belief that the essence of life was contained in the blood, which could then be consumed. These beliefs corresponded to – and indeed merged – certain theories about the premodern diet, culminating in the early modern dietaries that promoted like-to-like thinking, a branch of Galenic dietetic thinking according to which foods most like the human body were more effectively assimilated into the body as well as the most beneficial for it. The Renaissance logic of this theory, taken to its extreme, would mean that human substances are most easily assimilated back into the human body making cannibalism the most ideal diet.[16]

While we might find this shocking to consider, this logic connects to early conception theories according to which our first food, effectively, would have been blood. These ancient theories, derived from Aristotle and Galen, were revitalized in early modern England, which promoted the idea that "[women] during the time [children] are in the Womb, feed and nourish the Child with the purest Fountain of Blood."[17] Essentially, the blood upon which the child feeds was believed to be the woman's menstrual blood which, in turn, was believed to transform into breastmilk upon the child's birth – what we more typically consider our first food. Women's milk was thus believed to be itself a form of blood, called white blood or "twice-concocted blood."[18] Since antiquity, human breast milk has been considered to be especially nutritive and more refined; thus, according to Marsilio Ficino's interpretation of the Galenic system, it was better to drink women's milk, "concocted from blood," than women's blood, a theory that spoke curiously to the possibility that both milk and blood were ingestible.[19] The power of breastmilk – and, in the womb, what was believed to be menstrual blood – for the nourishment of the child

[15] Quoted in Sugg, *Mummies, Cannibals and Vampires*, 17.
[16] See Ken Albala, *Eating Right in the Renaissance* (Berkeley: University of California Press, 2002), 68.
[17] *Aristoteles Master-Piece, Or, The Secrets of Generation displayed in all the parts thereof* (1684), 29.
[18] Ken Albala, "Milk: Nutritious and Dangerous," in *Milk: Beyond the Dairy*, Proceedings of the Oxford Symposium on Food and Cookery, 1999, edited by Harlan Walker (Devon: Prospect Books, 2000), 21.
[19] Valeria Finucci, "Introduction: Genealogical Pleasures, Genealogical Disruptions," in *Generation and Degeneration: Tropes of Reproduction in Literature and History from Antiquity through Early Modern Europe*, edited by Valeria Finucci and Kevin Brownlee (Durham, NC: Duke University Press, 2001), 2.

derives from an idea that blood contained a "force and vertue" needed for generation.[20]

This theory of vitalism in human blood held true for other variations of early modern European medicinal cannibalism.[21] If these various human substances were, according to dietary logic, the most easily assimilated into the human body, the "force and vertue" contained in these substances still offered another kind of threat: the threat of foreign contamination. In premodern and early modern dietetics, local foods were preferable to foreign foods because the domestic body was more accustomed to them; correspondingly, foreign foods were considered to be dangerous because the body was not accustomed to them, and ingestion thereof could cause indigestion or even poisoning. Furthermore, if the body did assimilate to "foreign" foods, the added danger was that these foods could change one's racial or ethnic identity altogether.[22] This idea of foreign pollution, or indeed transformation, was complicated by the system of human substances in premodern and early modern food and diet, precisely, it seems, because of the "force and vertue" of human-derived comestibles. In other words, human substances contained a kind of potency that, combined with their "easy" assimilation into the human body, had significant implications for the fear of the foreign. Breastmilk, for example, embodied a number of anxieties surrounding the use of wetnurses – women who might be of non-domestic origin, racially or ethnically, and who could easily transfer their racial qualities to the child that they fed through their breastmilk.[23] If foreign foods could alter one's bodily constitution, drinking *blood*, with its racially coded status and its "force and vertue," would seem to have significant power to transform the consumer.

Furthermore, the trade of foreign imports was deeply implicated in the phenomenon of medicinal cannibalism. Not only was medicinal cannibalism a form of strange eating, in that the act of ingesting human substances was distanced as taboo or "strange,"[24] but the bodies that

---

[20] *Aristoteles Master-Piece*, 33.

[21] For more on early modern medicinal cannibalism, see Louise Noble, *Medicinal Cannibalism in Early Modern English Literature and Culture* (New York: Palgrave Macmillan, 2012); Sugg, *Mummies, Cannibals and Vampires*.

[22] See Rebecca Earle, *The Body of the Conquistador: Food, Race and the Colonial Experience in Spanish America, 1492–1700* (Cambridge, UK: Cambridge University Press, 2012).

[23] See Rachel Trubowitz, "'But Blood Whitened': Nursing Mothers and Others in Early Modern Britain," in *Maternal Measures: Figure Caregiving in the Early Modern Period*, edited by Naomi J. Miller and Naomi Yavneh (Aldershot, UK: Ashgate, 2000), 84.

[24] Not to mention the "strangeness" of cannibalism ascribed to "savages" in the New World, a means of distancing cannibalism from its European practices. See Sugg, *Mummies, Cannibals and Vampires*; Catalin Avramescu, *Intellectual History of Cannibalism*.

constituted much of corpse medicine were, at least in theory, by and large foreign bodies. Mummy, or Egyptian mummy, for example, was at the time a substance sold at apothecary shops that was believed to derive from bodies anciently embalmed in Egypt, Syria, and other regions of the Middle East and Africa, brought to Venice, and "thence disperst over all Christendom."[25] These foreign bodies were believed to comprise what was called "true Mummie"[26] – in other words, the authenticity, and corresponding efficacy, of the corpse drug in early modern Europe depended on whether or not the bodies were of foreign origin. Thus the foreign origins of the bodies used in premodern and early modern European medicinal cannibalism begin to establish the connection that exists between vampiric (or cannibalistic) feeding and the consumable other. In early modern travel accounts, for example, one finds recipes for the preparation of corpse medicine using bodies from Ethiopia:

> take a captive Moor, of the best complexion; and after long dieting and medicining of him, cut off his head in his sleep, and gashing his body full of wounds, put therein all the best spices, and then wrap him up in hay, being before covered with a cerecloth; after which they bury him in a moist place, covering the body with earth. Five days being passed, they take him up again, and removing the cerecloth and hay, hang him up in the sun, whereby the body resolveth and droppeth a substance like pure balm, which liquor is of great price: the fragrant scent is such, while it hangeth in the sun, that it may be smelt.[27]

If the moor's body, here, constitutes the essential material needed to produce corpse medicine, the idea of the consumption of the other in the West has its roots in the very literal cannibalism of foreign bodies.

The foreign, consumable body and the history of blood drinking intersect significantly in John Webster's early modern macabre tragedy, *The White Devil*. We can use the history of these discourses, in proto-vampiric feeding and the consumption of othered bodies, to attend to the significances of a brief episode typically overlooked by literary scholars, when the Ethiopian handmaiden, Zanche, offers up her blood to be drunk for physic. Zanche, referred to in the play as "The Moor," recognizes the medicinal potential of her body in her blood at the same time that she acknowledges her body as a body of (racial) difference:

---

[25] Ambroise Paré, *The workes of that famous chirurgion Ambrose Parey translated out of Latine and compared with the French* (1634), 449.
[26] Ibid., 449.
[27] Samuel Purchas, *Purchas his pilgrimage* (1617), 849.

I have blood
As red as either of theirs: wilt drink some?
'Tis good for the falling-sickness. I am proud:
Death cannot alter my complexion,
For I shall ne'er look pale.[28]

What Zanche articulates here is her awareness of blood drinking as a remedy for epilepsy, also called "the falling-sickness." But furthermore, she gestures explicitly to her own blood as a source of medicinal remedy, a gesture further racialized by what precedes and follows that offer: her blood, she acknowledges, is "As red as either of theirs," referring to her white counterparts in the play; moreover, her body is racially marked by her "complexion," which cannot be altered, "For I shall ne'er look pale." Thus, Zanche here identifies her body of difference as consumable and as a particular source of remedy. To feed upon her vampirically, to drink her blood, will cure her presumably white or European consumer of epilepsy. Zanche's point here is worth considering: not only is the foreign body ingestible, but it appears in a form that reverses the standard narrative of the strange eating of cannibalism as itself something other, distanced from European eating habits. The moment of blood drinking here is intimately associated with Zanche as an "other," showing the implications of vampiric feeding in food studies to be directly correlated to ideas about foreign consumption.

What the vampire narrative contributes to food studies, then, is the conflation of the eater and the eaten in the human sphere as well as the gastronomic issue of the *pharmakon*. If the purpose of eating is for sustenance and nourishment, it is worth thinking about the strange eating of vampiric feeding as both troubling the idea of nourishment and extending beyond it to remedy. As I have attempted to point out, the early histories of blood drinking and medicinal cannibalism may have contributed to the idea of the cure-all. Blood drinking, after all, was seen as remedial – a form of physic. The power of medicinal cannibalism derived from the mysterious vital essences retained in human substances, believed to transfer to the consumer. The transference of healing potential to the consumer upon ingestion sees its more threatening counterpart in the form of infection or contagion. The threat of the latter, in the form of poisoning, and more dangerously transformation, is played out in the monstrous myth of the vampire and located in the bite, that foremost action of eating. The subsequent infection of vampirism manifests as a transference of the

[28] John Webster, *The White Devil*, edited by Christina Luckyj (London: Bloomsbury, 2008), 5.6.223–37.

vampire's strange eating habits upon the victim, who traditionally, in turn, then embodies vampiric eating habits.

Vampirism and Disordered Eating

In the figure of the Victorian vampire, and its exemplar in Bram Stoker's Dracula, the vampire is a paradigm of consumption, manifested in the monstrous appetite or the fear of foreign degeneracy that, as critics have examined, derives from a longer history of medicinal and cannibalistic feeding associated with the threat of the other. Psychoanalytical studies of Dracula and the Victorian vampire have focused, for example, on Freud's idea of the child's "blindly mechanical oral impulse" and the infant's "enjoyments of mouthing, ingesting, incorporating, and destroying."[29] According to critics, Dracula embodies this "desire to suck, eat, consume, consume utterly – even inappropriately" which manifests most extremely in "the appetite to eat (and destroy by eating) human flesh" which derives from the "infectious, communicable appetite" that humans attempt to repress.[30] The psychoanalyzed child's appetite finds grounding in early ideas of literal infant nourishment as the consumption of the mother's blood in its various pre- and postpartum forms. So, too, critics have argued that the vampirism of Stoker and his contemporaries is connected to ideas of degeneracy and degeneration that were circulating during the time of Dracula. These theories of degeneracy enabled critics to frame vampiric eating habits as symptomatic of other degenerate and "aberrant" gendered and sexualized behaviors. Examples include the "terrifying appetites" of women, their reputation as "sexually voracious,"[31] and what Renée Fox calls a generative queerness, specifically "a particularly female version of queer desire."[32] These threats of gendered and sexualized degeneracy manifest in the threat of infection or transference of presumed "aberrant," othered behaviors, categorized as strange, foreign, and dangerous. Indeed, Luise

---

[29] Dennis Foster, "'The little children can be bitten': A Hunger for Dracula," in Dracula: Complete, Authoritative Text with Biographical, Historical, and Cultural Contexts, Critical History, and Essays from Contemporary Critical Perspectives, edited by John Paul Requelme (Boston: Bedford/St. Martin's, 2016), 532.

[30] Requelme, Dracula, 517. See also the chapter "Of Breasts and Beasts: Vampires and Other Voracious Monsters," in Parasecoli, Bite Me.

[31] Riquelme, Dracula, 448; Parasecoli, Bite Me, 45.

[32] Renee Fox, "Building Castles in the Air: Female Intimacy and Generative Queerness in Dracula," in Riquelme, Dracula, 590–91. See also John Allen Stevenson, "A Vampire in the Mirror: The Sexuality of Dracula," PMLA 103.2 (1988): 139–49; Sos Eltis, "Corruption of the Blood and Degeneration of the Race: Dracula and Policing the Borders of Gender," in Riquelme, Dracula, 565–80.

White notes that "Vampire stories offer a better, clearer, more analytical picture of the colonial experience than other sources do," and that vampires, as "a separate race of bloodsucking creatures, living among humans on fluids that they extract from human bodies," thus "mark a way in which relations of race, of bodies, and of tools of extraction can be debated, theorized, and explained."[33] Here again, if vampirism is a mode of strange eating, whereby the dangers of transference take root, we can look to earlier contexts about the tensions of strange eating and the implicit and explicit threats of bodily harm or transformation that occur through the ingestion of the foreign. Thus, the longer cultural context of proto-vampiric feeding, informed by pre- and early modern historical phenomena, both resonates with and qualifies the work done on vampiric appetites and consumption in the Victorian era and beyond.

By starting with vampiric feeding as a paradigm for strange eating, with its roots in medicinal cannibalism and the consumption of the other, we can examine how vampirism figures in new experiments with ingestion. Oyeyemi's *White Is for Witching* (2009) and Butler's *Fledgling* (2005) both figure black, female, queer protagonists who are involved in vampiric feeding practices. Oyeyemi's Ore, a Nigerian transplant at Cambridge University, narrates her experience as friend and lover to the English Miranda, who inherits her eating disorder-turned-vampirism from generations of xenophobic nationalists in the maternal line of her family. Ore narrates, in other words, her experience as a black body that becomes the object of consumption. In contrast, Butler's Shori, a black vampire-human hybrid experiment and amnesiac victim of trauma, narrates her experiences of discovering who she is through her consumptive practices, as I will examine later.

In the opening prologue of *White Is for Witching*, we are told that "Miranda has a *condition* called pica she has eaten a great deal of chalk – she really can't help herself – she has been very ill – **Miranda has pica she can't come in** today, she is stretched out inside a wall she is feasting on plaster she has pica."[34] Oyeyemi begins with an eating disorder as the defining characteristic of her main protagonist. Miranda's "condition" is named three times, described as an illness, and defined by way of her acts of eating: "she has eaten a great deal of chalk ... she is feasting on plaster." Oyeyemi emphasizes the "condition" by providing a description

[33] Luise White, *Speaking with Vampires: Rumor and History in Colonial Africa* (Berkeley: University of California Press, 2000), 307.
[34] Helen Oyeyemi, *White Is for Witching* (New York: Riverhead Books, 2009), 3.

of Miranda's "disordered eating" as the opening of one of her first narrative sections:

PICA

is a medical term for a particular kind of disordered eating. It's an appetite for non-food items, things that don't nourish … I might remember Miri's special pastries as more elaborate than they really were, but Dad made some astonishing things for her. Flaky cones smothered in honey and coconut and chocolate and whatever else he could think of. He did a lot of soft foods, too, soups, and jellies with (eye) balls of peeled fruit staring out of them. What Miri did was, she crammed chalk into her mouth under her covers. She hid the packaging at the bottom of her bag and threw it away when we got to school. But then there'd be cramps that twisted her body, pushed her off her seat and lay her on the floor, helplessly pedalling her legs. Once, as if she knew that I was thinking of sampling her chalk to see what the big wow was, she smiled sweetly, sadly, patronisingly, and said to me, "Don't start, you'll get stuck."[35]

Oyeyemi both titles the section after "Pica" and uses the section to narrativize it. She moves from a strict definition of pica as "a medical term for a particular kind of disordered eating," specifically "an appetite for non-food items, things that don't nourish," to a description of the special foods Miranda, or "Miri," receives from her chef father who tries to feed her. The descriptions border on excess to depict the sensuous luxury of specialty pastries before moving, smoothly but suddenly, to foods that border on the cannibalistically sinister: from "Flaky cones smothered in honey and coconut and chocolate," to "jellies with (eye) balls of peeled fruit staring out of them." In other words, Oyeyemi moves from the gastronomically decadent to the unsettlingly human, gesturing to cannibalism by comparing jellies with fruit to eyeballs in similarly gelatinous or fleshly parts of bodies. The constitution of jellies from animal bones would not have been missed; jellies, or gelatin, have a long history extending to classical times, wherein "boil[ing] down animal parts (hooves, entire skeletons of poultry, or hides" was an explicit part of the process on the cook's part.[36] In other words, jellies housed the violent process of dissolving bodies into a strange but edible substance. Here, Oyeyemi plays upon jelly's correspondences with the body, reconstituting the jellies into metaphorized bodies that

---

[35] Ibid., 26.
[36] Wendy Wall, "Shakespearean Jell-O: Mortality and Malleability in the Kitchen," *Gastronomica: Journal of Food and Culture* 6.1 (2006), 41.

offer to Miranda another option to/from pica, setting the stage for the cannibalistic feeding to which Miranda will gravitate.

Miranda's pica, Oyeyemi notes, "runs in the family,"[37] and it is a generational inheritance rooted in the family's xenophobic ties to white British nationalism. Oyeyemi writes that Miranda's great-grandmother, Anna Good, "had it in 1938; a year before she became Anna Silver," and reveals an earlier iteration of the Silver women's pica as a kind of self-cannibalism and self-vampirism:

> there was another woman, long before you, but related. This woman was thought an animal. Her way was to slash at her flesh with the blind, frenzied concentration that a starved person might use to get at food that is buried. Her way was to drink off her blood, then bite and suck at the bobbled stubs of her meat. Her appetite was only for herself.[38]

Exemplifying a "related" eating disorder, this Silver ancestor hungered for herself with an obsessive addiction, "drink[ing] off her blood" and "bit[ing] and suck[ing] at the bobbled stubs of her meat," in a disordered appetite that "was only for herself." If pica evolved in the family line from a narcissistic vampirism, Oyeyemi shows that it was also self-destructive, in the way of a narcissistically xenophobic nationalism. Oyeyemi suggests here that vampirism and pica are related, integrally connected through the addiction to "non-food items, things that don't nourish." These vampiric tendencies trickle down through the generations. Miranda's mother, Lily, is mysteriously and violently killed when she visits Haiti, and her death is described in vampiric terms: "She dribbled blood, could not let it go, closed her eyes only for the length of time it took to drink it up again."[39] Lily's death connects her association with Haiti to vampiric feeding, an association that would play out in her daughter, Miranda, and her pica-turned-vampiric urges to consume Ore's black body.

Tellingly, Ore is flipping through critical essays of *Dracula* when she meets Miranda at Cambridge. As the two become involved, Oyeyemi suggests a kind of transference of Miranda's eating disorder, evident in changes in Ore's body which becomes malnourished despite her own efforts to eat. Ore, in other words, becomes a drained victim of vampiric feeding, at the same time that her eating becomes disordered as well: "I had never eaten so much," Ore observes, "I had never wanted to eat so much. But my clothes kept getting looser … first I would sleep alone,

---

[37] Oyeyemi, *White Is for Witching*, 26.
[38] Ibid., 26, 27–8.
[39] Ibid., 9.

later I would look for wounds."[40] Ore makes the connection to being a vampiric victim, drained by Miranda. Miranda's pica, in turn, evolves into vampirism by the thought of consuming Ore, and that transition, from pica to vampirism, speaks to Miranda's interpretation of Ore's black body as sexually and gastronomically consumable, manifesting in Ore as a kind of aphrodisiac. Miranda compares Ore's heart to an oyster, "living quietly in its serving-dish shell," an example both of a commonly regarded aphrodisiac and of a living creature ingested while still alive.[41]

The vampirism depicted in *White Is for Witching*, Aspasia Stephanou writes, "subverts the conventional and metaphorical associations of vampirism with the 'foreign' other."[42] Throughout the novel, Miranda's constant health problems derive from her disordered eating which, additionally, forms an addiction, a monstrous appetite that controls her more than she controls it. When waiting to be taken home from Cambridge, due to her illness, Miranda writes to herself, in her ancestor Anna's hand-writing, "*Manage your consumption*," and in other notes she tells herself "*I am lucky, Behave yourself,* and *Eat.*"[43] Afterwards, in "her own handwriting," she writes to remind herself that "*Ore is not food. I think I am a monster.*"[44] Miranda checks her disordered impulse to consume Ore. Miranda's vampiric appetite for Ore would seem to manifest as a permutation of her disordered eating rather than a solution to it. At the same time, however, her vampiric impulse runs counter to the xenophobia that defines the pica of the Silver women. As Miranda both befriends and becomes intimate with Ore, Miranda's ancestors react in shock and disgust, noting "The squashed nose, the pillow lips, fist-sized breasts, the reek of fluids from the seam between her legs. The skin. The skin."[45] Juxtaposed against Miranda's acceptance, and even invitation, of Ore – her parenthetical about "how much I like this / the way our skin looks together" – Anna and Jennifer (Miranda's grandmother) manifest their communal shock: "Disgusting. These are the things that happen while you're not looking, when you're not keeping careful watch. When clear water moves unseen a taint creeps into it – moss, or algae, salt, even. It becomes foul, undrinkable."[46] Miranda's vampirism, and her desire to consume Ore's black body, undoes the

---

[40] Ibid., 214.
[41] Ibid., 220.
[42] Aspasia Stephanou, "Helen Oyeyemi's *White Is for Witching* and the Discourse of Consumption," *Callaloo* 37.5 (2014), 1245.
[43] Oyeyemi, *White Is for Witching*, 221.
[44] Ibid., 221.
[45] Ibid., 223.
[46] Ibid., 223.

xenophobic tradition of the Silver family line, while still being disordered. To undo the disordered appetite to consume the black body, which is still a diversion from England's xenophobic impulses rather than a solution, Oyeyemi gestures to Miranda's sacrifice of herself to the vampiric house that puppeteers the Silver women, effectively saving Ore from Miranda's vampiric feeding while putting an end to the line of Silver women engaged in disordered eating.

Toward Symbiosis: Vampiric Feeding and the Productive Black Body

Whereas Oyeyemi's vision of vampiric feeding as disordered is reactive, attending to the problematics of casting the consumption of the other as an antidote to xenophobic tendencies, Butler presents a proactive vision of vampiric feeding, racialized through Shori and providing a means through which to build a new community. I end by turning to Butler's *Fledgling* to gesture to the possibilities that open up for reading vampiric feeding in light of the history of nourishment and the racialized consumption of othered bodies. *Fledgling* depicts, in Elizabeth Lundberg's words, "relationships that nourish and sustain themselves through the physical exchange of bodily fluids."[47] Lundberg argues that Octavia Butler's novel "biologiz[es] the social, recasting relational belonging as symbiosis or physical addiction";[48] here I would argue that vampiric feeding provides a productive way of reading consumptive symbiosis and addiction, merging sustenance and sexuality.

Butler begins with hunger. In the second line of the novel, Shori, the protagonist and narrator, announces, "I was hungry – starving!"[49] Like Oyeyemi, with Miranda Butler establishes Shori's hunger as her first and defining characteristic. But while Miranda's strange eating is immediately defined as disordered eating, Shori's strange eating is not initially marked as strange, but curious. As an amnesiac vampire-human hybrid, although she does not yet know this, Shori observes in her moments of feeding that the emphasis is not only on consumption, but on the formation of some form of pleasure and connection: "I stared down at the bleeding marks I'd made on his hand ... I ducked my head and licked away the blood, licked the

---

[47] Elizabeth Lundberg, "'Let Me Bite You Again': Vampiric Agency in Octavia Butler's *Fledgling*," *GLQ: Journal of Lesbian and Gay Studies* 21.4 (2015), 564.

[48] Ibid., 564.

[49] Octavia Butler, *Fledgling* (New York: Grand Central, 2005), 1.

wound I had made. He tensed, almost pulling away. Then he stopped, seemed to relax."[50] This will construct Shori's understanding of her feeding as a formation of ties that bind, paving the way for the process of mating; Ina mating ties – Ina is the name for the vampiric race in Butler's novel – begin when "an Ina female binds herself to a male Ina by biting him," transferring her venom, located in her saliva, which makes the Ina male "crav[e] his mate" only, gastronomically and sexually, making him "infertile with other female Ina."[51] Shori's black body is the result of experimenting among her maternal Ina family, and her evidence for being the first successful vampire-human hybrid is her black skin, which enables her to withstand sunlight during the day. The hope for Shori, and for the Ina race, lies in her ability to reproduce, to mate and create her own family and community which, in the context of Ina tradition, is accomplished through the act of vampiric feeding.

I began with an alternative history of alternative eating; the new methodologies I proposed, by way of proto-vampiric feeding, aim to construct a framework for reading later experiments with vampirism in alternative afterlives of the trope. If attending to lesser known histories of European blood drinking and medicinal cannibalism allows us to reposition vampirism in discourses about alterity and consumption, I conclude that examining early theories about blood as nourishment help us understand the possibilities Butler opens up in rewriting vampirism as a mode of *production* as much as consumption, reversing the trope of the consumable other to emphasize instead productive bodies of difference. I end, thus, with a gesture to an alternative future of alternative production, where the possibilities afforded by "vampiric" feeding, and strange eating, extend beyond the consumption of otherness, enabling instead the sustenance and growth of alterity.

BIBLIOGRAPHY

Albala, Ken. *Eating Right in the Renaissance*. Berkeley: University of California Press, 2002.
  "Milk: Nutritious and Dangerous." In *Milk: Beyond the Dairy*, Proceedings of the Oxford Symposium on Food and Cookery, 1999, edited by Harlan Walker, 19–30. Devon: Prospect Books, 2000.

[50] Ibid., 11.
[51] Therí Pickens, "'You're Supposed to Be a Tall, Handsome, Fully Grown White Man': Theorizing Race, Gender, and Disability in Octavia Butler's *Fledgling*," *Journal of Literary and Cultural Disability Studies* 8.1 (2014), 39.

Aristoteles Master-Piece, Or, The Secrets of Generation displayed in all the parts thereof. 1684.

Avramescu, Catalin. *An Intellectual History of Cannibalism.* Princeton: Princeton University Press, 2009.

Barker, Francis, Peter Hulme, and Margaret Iversen. *Cannibalism and the Colonial World.* Cambridge: Cambridge University Press, 1998.

Butler, Octavia. *Fledgling.* New York: Grand Central, 2005.

Earle, Rebecca. *The Body of the Conquistador: Food, Race and the Colonial Experience in Spanish America, 1492–1700.* Cambridge: Cambridge University Press, 2012.

Eltis, Sos. "Corruption of the Blood and Degeneration of the Race: *Dracula* and Policing the Borders of Gender." In *Dracula: Complete, Authoritative Text with Biographical, Historical, and Cultural Contexts, Critical History, and Essays from Contemporary Critical Perspectives*, edited by John Paul Riquelme, 565–80. Boston: Bedford/St. Martin's, 2016.

Finucci, Valeria. "Introduction: Genealogical Pleasures, Genealogical Disruptions." In *Generation and Degeneration: Tropes of Reproduction in Literature and History from Antiquity through Early Modern Europe*, edited by Valeria Finucci and Kevin Brownlee, 1–14. Durham, NC: Duke University Press, 2001.

Foster, Dennis. " 'The little children can be bitten': A Hunger for Dracula." In *Dracula: Complete, Authoritative Text with Biographical, Historical, and Cultural Contexts, Critical History, and Essays from Contemporary Critical Perspectives*, edited by John Paul Requelme, 531–48. Boston: Bedford/St. Martin's, 2016.

Fox, Renee. "Building Castles in the Air: Female Intimacy and Generative Queerness in *Dracula.*" In *Dracula: Complete, Authoritative Text with Biographical, Historical, and Cultural Contexts, Critical History, and Essays from Contemporary Critical Perspectives*, edited by John Paul Riquelme, 590–607. Boston: Bedford/St. Martin's, 2016.

hooks, bell. "Eating the Other: Desire and Resistance." In *Black Looks: Race and Representation*, 21–39. Boston: South End Press, 1992.

Kanner, Leo. "The Names of the Falling Sickness: An Introduction to the Study of the Folklore and Cultural History of Epilepsy." *Human Biology* 2.1 (1930): 109–27.

Kristeva, Julia. *Powers of Horror: An Essay on Abjection.* New York: Columbia University Press, 1982.

Lévi-Strauss, Claude. *The Raw and the Cooked.* Chicago: University of Chicago Press, 1983.

Lundberg, Elizabeth. " 'Let Me Bite You Again': Vampiric Agency in Octavia Butler's *Fledgling.*" *GLQ: Journal of Lesbian and Gay Studies* 21.4 (2015): 561–81.

Moog, Ferdinand Peter, and Axel Karenberg. "Between Horror and Hope: Gladiator's Blood as a Cure for Epileptics in Ancient Medicine." *Journal of the History of the Neurosciences* 12.2 (2003): 137–43.

Noble, Louise. *Medicinal Cannibalism in Early Modern English Literature and Culture.* New York: Palgrave Macmillan, 2012.

Oyeyemi, Helen. *White Is for Witching*. New York: Riverhead Books, 2009.

Parasecoli, Fabio. *Bite Me: Food in Popular Culture*. New York: Berg, 2008.

Paré, Ambroise. *The workes of that famous chirurgion Ambrose Parey translated out of Latine and compared with the French*. 1634.

Pickens, Therí. "'You're Supposed to Be a Tall, Handsome, Fully Grown White Man': Theorizing Race, Gender, and Disability in Octavia Butler's *Fledgling*." *Journal of Literary and Cultural Disability Studies* 8.1 (2014): 33–48.

Pliny. *Natural History*. Vol. 8. Translated by W. H. S. Jones. Loeb Classical Library. Cambridge, MA: Harvard University Press, 1963.

Purchas, Samuel. *Purchas his pilgrimage*. 1617.

Requelme, John Paul, ed. *Dracula: Complete, Authoritative Text with Biographical, Historical, and Cultural Contexts, Critical History, and Essays from Contemporary Critical Perspectives*. Boston: Bedford/St. Martin's, 2016.

Stephanou, Aspasia. "Helen Oyeyemi's *White Is for Witching* and the Discourse of Consumption." *Callaloo* 37.5 (2014): 1245–59.

Stevenson, John Allen. "A Vampire in the Mirror: The Sexuality of Dracula." *PMLA* 103.2 (1988): 139–49.

Sugg, Richard. *Mummies, Cannibals and Vampires: The History of Corpse Medicine from the Renaissance to the Victorians*. 2nd ed. London: Routledge, 2016.

Tertullian. *Apology*. Translated by T. R. Glover. Loeb Classical Library. Cambridge, MA: Harvard University Press, 1966.

Tompkins, Kyla Wazana. *Racial Indigestion: Eating Bodies in the 19th Century*. New York: New York University Press, 2012.

Trubowitz, Rachel. "'But Blood Whitened': Nursing Mothers and Others in Early Modern Britain." In *Maternal Measures: Figure Caregiving in the Early Modern Period*, edited by Naomi J. Miller and Naomi Yavneh, 82–101. Aldershot, UK: Ashgate, 2000.

Wall, Wendy. "Shakespearean Jell-O: Mortality and Malleability in the Kitchen." *Gastronomica: Journal of Food and Culture* 6.1 (2006): 41–50.

Webster, John. *The White Devil*. Edited by Christina Luckyj. London: Bloomsbury, 2008.

White, Luise. *Speaking with Vampires: Rumor and History in Colonial Africa*. Berkeley: University of California Press, 2000.

CHAPTER 15

Toast and the Familiar in Children's Literature

Frances E. Dolan

When Lewis Carroll's Alice ventures to taste the little bottle labeled "drink me," she finds that "(it had, in fact, a sort of mixed flavour of cherry-tart, custard, pine-apple, roast turkey, toffy, and hot buttered toast)," and, as a consequence, "she very soon finished it off."[1] Robert Hemmings, drawing attention to the "taste of nostalgia" in so-called golden age children's literature, points to the highly specific tastes and smells in this passage, which "are rich with associations of a privileged middle-class Victorian childhood, both Alice Liddell's and Charles Dodgson's: exotic fruit, desserts, a roast dripping with holiday associations, comforting toast, candy, nary a vegetable to wrinkle a child's nose."[2] The hot buttered toast Alice mentions, and Hemmings emphasizes as "comforting," would seem to be a prime example of nostalgia-invoking, non-vegetable, unobjectionable food. While it is "rich with associations of a privileged middle-class Victorian childhood," it also seems more accessible to a broader range of readers than, say, cherry tart or custard. It is less costly than any of the other foods Alice mentions. Barely needing to be cooked, it doesn't seem to require money, skill, time, or expertise. Surely almost anyone would have access to toast. It also promises to be a better time traveler than the other foods. Toast seems a food that readers now will recognize (as they do not, for example, the pickled limes in *Little Women*). Is it necessary, for instance, for an edition to provide a note for toast, to describe or define it? In its very familiarity, buttered toast might seem to be the perfect comestible to sum up the golden age of children's literature: it calls to mind the Victorian nursery, or at least a vision of that nursery that has been created precisely through

---

[1] Lewis Carroll, *Alice's Adventures in Wonderland* (New York: Penguin/Signet, 2012), 14. I am grateful to Elizabeth Crachiolo for her help researching this chapter.

[2] Robert Hemmings, "A Taste of Nostalgia: Children's Books from the Golden Age – Carroll, Grahame, and Milne," *Children's Literature* 35 (2007): 54–79, esp. 62. On food and nostalgia in children's literature, see also Perry Nodelman and Mavis Reimer, *The Pleasures of Children's Literature*, 3rd ed. (Toronto: Allen and Bacon, 2003).

such representations, yet it is recognizable to many a young reader today, creating another filament of connection between reader and characters and drawing the reader into the imagined world. In this chapter, I will make the familiarity of toast a question rather than an assumption, focusing on toast in *The Wind in the Willows* (1908), *Mary Poppins* (1934), the Harry Potter series (1997–2007), and *A Series of Unfortunate Events* (1999–2006). To what extent does toast connect readers across time and place and to what extent is it becoming an exotic comestible?

In another memorable moment from golden age children's literature in which food and nostalgia intertwine, the gaoler's daughter in Kenneth Grahame's *The Wind in the Willows* brings buttered toast to Toad when he is imprisoned. She proposes to tame Toad so that he will be a less sulky prisoner and even, perhaps, one more likely to purchase the "comforts, and indeed luxuries" her father hopes to sell the affluent Toad. "You let me have the managing of him," she tells her father. "You know how fond of animals I am. I'll make him eat from my hand, and sit up, and do all sorts of things." Ultimately, her attempt to domesticate the wild toad leads her to help him escape. But it begins with food. First, she offers to share her food with him, bringing in some of her own dinner, "hot from the oven."[3] It is bubble and squeak, a dish of cooked cabbage usually mixed with mashed potatoes, fried in a pan to form a crust. In the hot pan, the fat in which the patty browns bubbles and squeaks, giving the dish its name. It is one of those dishes that transforms leftovers into something transcendent. I find it comforting; Toad does not. While the dish's name emphasizes its sound, the narrator of *The Wind in the Willows* emphasizes its smell. There is no description of what bubble and squeak is or looks like. But, we learn, "its fragrance filled the narrow cell. The penetrating smell of cabbage reached the nose of Toad as he lay prostrate in his misery on the floor, and gave him the idea for a moment that perhaps life was not such a blank and desperate thing as he had imagined." Although Toad is perked up by the encouraging smell, he finally "refused to be comforted" and spurns this plebeian dish.[4] The narrator's reference to the smell of the cabbage, which lingers even after the dish has left Toad's cell, calls up the persistent associations of smelly cabbage with the poor and immigrant people who eat it.[5]

---

[3] Kenneth Grahame, *The Wind in the Willows* (New York: Aladdin/Simon and Schuster, 1989), 147.

[4] Ibid., 149.

[5] For the long history of these associations around cabbage, see Malcolm Thick, "Root Crops and the Feeding of London's Poor," in *English Rural Society*, edited by John Chartres and David Hey (Cambridge: Cambridge University Press, 1990): 279–96, esp. 288; Margaret Pelling, *The Common Lot: Sickness, Medical Occupations and the Urban Poor in Early Modern England* (London: Longman,

When the gaoler's daughter returns several hours later, she brings a meal that neither the narrator nor Toad can resist: a cup of "fragrant" tea and "a plate piled up with very hot buttered toast, cut thick, very brown on both sides, with the butter running through the holes in it in great golden drops, like honey from the honeycomb."[6] The reader can immediately imagine this toast. Fragrance is again paramount, as it is throughout this book because, as the narrator says in an earlier chapter, the word "smell" is inadequate to describe "an animal's intercommunications with his surroundings," the ways that he feels the olfactory with his whole body.[7] Just as the name "bubble and squeak" assigns a kind of voice to that dish, so the narrator grants the toast's smell a synesthetic ability to communicate: "the smell of that buttered toast simply spoke to Toad, and with no uncertain voice." The narrator then proceeds to elaborate on what that very particular toast said to Toad: it "talked of warm kitchens, of breakfasts on bright frosty mornings, of cozy parlour firesides on winter evenings, when one's ramble was over and slippered feet were propped on the fender; of the purring of contented cats, and the twitter of sleepy canaries."[8] As C. W. Sullivan has pointed out, the gaoler's daughter "provokes nostalgia from Toad for his home, for the first time, by bringing him the toast."[9] The toast, then, achieves something Toad's friends have failed to do. *The Wind in the Willows* is filled with picnics, impromptu suppers, hearty breakfasts, and banquets. Our protagonists and those they encounter tend to provision resourcefully and to eat everything set before them with relish. But it is the buttered toast, served to the despondent Toad in jail, that has the greatest impact.

This passage assumes that an expressive smell will speak to the reader as powerfully as it does to Toad, readily evoking cozy domesticity. For many readers, it still does. Many would need a gloss for bubble and squeak, although *The Annotated Wind in the Willows* glosses cabbage here but not bubble and squeak.[10] Even those who know the dish know it is unglossable,

---

1998), 38–62; Emma Cockayne, *Hubbub: Filth, Noise and Stench in England 1600–1770* (New Haven: Yale University Press, 2007), 84 and passim.

[6] Grahame, *Wind in the Willows*, 145–46.

[7] Ibid., 85–86.

[8] Ibid., 146.

[9] C. W. Sullivan, "'Chops ... Cheese, New Bread, Great Swills of Beer': Food and Home in Kenneth Grahame's *The Wind in the Willows*," *Journal of the Fantastic in the Arts* 15.2 (Spring 2005): 144–52, esp. 149. On food in *Wind in the Willows*, see also Humphrey Carpenter, *Secret Gardens: The Golden Age of Children's Literature* (Boston: Houghton Mifflin, 1985); Peter Hunt, *The Wind in the Willows: A Fragmented Arcadia* (New York: Twayne, 1994), who twice refers to hot buttered toast as a "nursery delight" (38, 87).

[10] *The Annotated Wind in the Willows* offers this gloss: "*Cabbage*. Compared to buttered toast and all the other food feasted upon at Toad Hall, cabbage would reek. It was also known to be the fare of

in a way, in that each bubble and squeak is a little different. If cold tongue, which appears several times in the novel, is the food that might not necessarily whet modern readers' appetites, "fantastic" rather than familiar food, toast would seem to be the foodstuff that is not in need of explanation or definition.[11] Toast is toast. And yet, as that vivid, even rapturous, description also makes clear, all toast is NOT toast. There are thinly sliced, under and over browned, inadequately buttered toasts. There is cold toast. At the end of the novel, when Toad and his friends have reclaimed Toad Hall, Toad "came down to breakfast disgracefully late" to find only the sad remnants of a breakfast, including "some fragments of cold and leathery toast."[12] Such toast would not jog Toad's memory or burnish his attachment to life. Frances Hodgson Burnett is reported to have said that "It is not enough to mention" that your characters have tea; "you must specify the muffins."[13] You must also specify whether the muffins are toasted and how well they are buttered, as Grahame's description of the toast that reattaches Toad to his life suggests.

While Toad's fortunes go up and down, he never makes his own toast. The toast Alice remembers was probably brought to her on a tray as well. This suggests both the freedom from labor and the dependency of those who do not make their own toast and must rely on the tender mercies of other toasters and risk the perils of toast not to their own specifications. In Mrs. Beeton's *Book of Household Management* (1861), she offers instructions first on how "To Make Dry Toast." To make it properly, she explains, "a great deal of attention is required; much more, indeed, than people generally suppose."[14] One must not use fresh bread, because it "eats heavy, and, besides, is very extravagant." Instead, "a loaf of household bread about two days old" is perfect. It should be "not quite ¼ inch in thickness," with crusts trimmed. The toast-maker must then

> put the bread on a toasting-fork, and hold it before a very clear fire. Move
> it backwards and forwards until the bread is nicely coloured; then turn it

a commoner." *The Annotated Wind in the Willows*, edited by Annie Gauger (New York: Norton, 2009), 188, n. 10.

[11] Peter Hunt, "Coldtonguecoldhamcoldbeefpickledgherkinsaladfrenchrollscresssandwidespotted-meatgingerbeerlemonadesodawater …: Fantastic Foods in the Books of Kenneth Grahame, Jerome K. Jerome, H. E. Bates and Other Bakers of the Fantasy England," *Journal of the Fantastic in the Arts* 7.1 (1996): 5–22.

[12] Grahame, *Wind in the Willows*, 248.

[13] Ann Thwaite, *Waiting for the Party: The Life of Frances Hodgson Burnett* (Boston: David R. Godine, 1991), 222.

[14] Isabella Beeton, *The Book of Household Management* (London: S. O. Beeton, 1861), 843. Searchable versions of this text are widely available and the recipes for toast are listed as entries 1725 and 1726.

and toast the other side, and do not place it so near the fire that it blackens. Dry toast should be more gradually made than buttered toast, as its great beauty consists in its crispness, and this cannot be attained unless the process is slow and the bread is allowed gradually to colour. It should never be made long before it is wanted, as it soon becomes tough, unless placed on the fender in front of the fire. As soon as each piece is ready, it should be put into a rack, or stood upon its edges, and sent quickly to table.[15]

The emphasis here on speed reminds us that these are instructions for making toast for other people and getting it to them in prime condition. The following recipe, for how "To make hot buttered toast" explains that one needs "nice even slices … rather more than ¼ inch in thickness."

Toast them before a very bright fire, without allowing the bread to blacken, which spoils the appearance and flavor of all toast. When of a nice colour on both sides, put it on a hot plate; divide some good butter into small pieces, place them on the toast, set this before the fire, and when the butter is just beginning to melt, spread it lightly over the toast. Trim off the crust and ragged edges, divide each round into 4 pieces, and send the toast quickly to table … It is highly essential to use good butter for making this dish.[16]

Toast is, then, a dish, and one that requires "household bread," "good butter," "a great deal of attention," a bright fire, and careful timing.

Has the invention of the toaster created a world in which even Toad might make his own toast? Dinah Bucholz's *The Unofficial Harry Potter Cookbook* explains that she "does not include a recipe for toast, although Victorian cookbooks [such as Mrs. Beeton] devoted chapters to the art of making toast properly. Today, with toasters and toaster ovens, it's pretty simple if you just pay attention."[17] By this account, toast is both easier to achieve and more familiar for us than it was for the Victorians. Toast is often taken as the gauge of basic culinary literacy and self-reliance. Novice cooks claim that all they can make is toast; the pithy description of someone who absolutely cannot cook is that he or she "can't even make toast." Toast is, then, beginner cooking. Parenting sites advise that "Toast is a great way to help children start 'cooking' on their own."[18] In Lemony

---

[15] Ibid.
[16] Ibid., 844.
[17] Dinah Bucholz, *The Unofficial Harry Potter Cookbook: From Cauldron Cakes to Knickerbocker Glory – More Than 150 Magical Recipes for Wizards and Non-Wizards Alike* (Avon, MA: Adams Media, 2010), 106.
[18] www.cozi.com/blog/10-snacks-kids-can-make-themselves. See also http://eats.coolmompicks.com/ 2016/08/13/easy-breakfast-recipes-kids-can-cook. A cookbook for children, Carol Odell and Anna Pignataro's *Once Upon a Time in the Kitchen: Recipes and Tales from Classic Children's Stories* (Ann Arbor: Sleeping Bear Press, 2010), assumes that its readers know how to make toast although it does advise that, should the reader wish to make toast as Doctor Doolittle did, by holding the bread on a

Snicket's *The Bad Beginning*, when the villainous Count Olaf challenges the Baudelaire orphans to make dinner for his friends, even the intrepid Violet feels at first that she might not be up to the challenge. "I don't know how to make anything except toast." As her brother Klaus reminds her, she doesn't even know how to do that. "Sometimes you burn the toast," he reminds her.

> They were both remembering a time when the two of them got up early to make a special breakfast for their parents. Violet had burned the toast, and their parents, smelling smoke, had run downstairs to see what the matter was. When they saw Violet and Klaus, looking forlornly at pieces of pitch-black toast, they laughed and laughed, and then made pancakes for the whole family.[19]

Here it is the memory of "pitch-black toast," and of the luxury of not having to eat it, that provokes nostalgia for the lost family and home, losses that, in the world of *A Series of Unfortunate Events*, cannot be recuperated. (With pantry staples and a cookbook from Judge Strauss, the Baudelaires do, however, pull off Pasta Puttanesca.) *A Series of Unfortunate Events* gestures back to the Victorian houses, to the orphans and villains, of golden age children's literature in lots of ways. In Klaus and Violet's memory here, we are informed that children do not generally cook for their parents, except on special occasions, and that the Baudelaire orphans, before finding themselves Count Olaf's drudges, were as privileged as Alice or Toad. They would not have made their own toast. The memory of the burnt toast is a memory of not needing to be competent, of trying to be the caretaker, failing, and not having it matter. The toast also stands for the "charred rubble" of the "enormous home they had loved," the house and parents destroyed by fire.[20] One might almost imagine Lemony Snicket interrupting to explain what the word toast here means.

If *A Series of Unfortunate Events* takes place in a hard-to-specify time and place, with cars and surveillance cameras but few other reminders of the modern day, the Harry Potter series takes place in an alternative reality that does not include the internet, cell phones, or iPads. Rowling's inventiveness in creating a fully realized world apart from our own extends to butter

---

fork in front of a fire, you must "be very careful not to toast yourself" (7). Lyn Stallworth provides a recipe for "Toad's Buttered Toast" in her cookbook *Wond'rous Fare* (Chicago: Calico, 1988), but it is actually a recipe for French Toast, as if buttered toast is a little too simple to require a recipe or constitute the "wond'rous."

[19] Lemony Snicket, *Series of Unfortunate Events #1: The Bad Beginning* (New York: HarperCollins, 1999), 28.

[20] Ibid., 12.

beer and the remarkable sweets at Honeyduke's. The food at Hogwarts is both fantastic and familiar. It is overwhelmingly abundant and appears and disappears magically – although it depends on the hidden labors of house elves.[21] It is also distinctly British, which would make it familiar to some readers but not to others. On his first night at Hogwarts, "Harry had never seen so many things he liked to eat on one table." What he likes, it appears, is meat and potatoes in varied forms, with the distinctly British addition of "Yorkshire pudding, peas, carrots, gravy, ketchup." For the first time, he is "allowed to eat as much as he liked."[22] If this is special occasion dining at Hogwarts, toast is daily fare. In *Chamber of Secrets*, for example, we learn that the breakfast tables in the Great Hall were "laden with tureens of porridge, plates of kippers, mountains of toast, and dishes of eggs and bacon."[23]

Given the international audience for the series, those mountains of toast may require some explanation, if not a recipe. The Harry Potter Wiki feels the need to define toast in its own entry: "Toast is bread that has been toasted. Toast is also a known flavour of Bertie Bott's Every Flavour Beans, and was served at breakfast time at Hogwarts."[24] The entry is accompanied by a picture of toast in a toast rack and the explanation that the house elves and probably Molly Weasley "manufacture" it. With its usual attention to detail, the Wiki also glosses bread and toaster, "a Muggle device used to toast Bread" owned by the Dursley family. In the global marketplace for the new golden age of children's literature, even toast, even bread, cannot go without explanation. But the Wiki also claims that, at Hogwarts, toast is "floating around between the tables" in the Great Hall so that students can just reach out and grab a slice. This is an appealing notion. Suspended in air, toast would seem magically unlimited (and, one hopes, perpetually hot), rising above the stodginess that threatens to weigh comfort foods (and their eaters) down. By floating, the familiar becomes just fantastic enough. Yet this claim seems to be invented or misremembered. In the books, we are never told that toast floats nor does it appear to float in the

---

[21] Jacqueline Corinth, "Food Symbolism in Three Children's Literature Texts: Grahame's *The Wind in the Willows*, Dahl's *Charlie and the Chocolate Factory* and Rowling's Harry Potter Novels," in *You Are What You Eat: Literary Probes into the Palate*, edited by Annette M. Magid (Newcastle upon Tyne: Cambridge Scholars, 2008), 260–83, esp. 272–73.

[22] J. K. Rowling, *Harry Potter and the Sorcerer's Stone* (New York: Scholastic, 1997), 123.

[23] J. K. Rowling, *Harry Potter and the Chamber of Secrets* (New York: Scholastic, 1998), 86. We are told that toast is part of Harry's breakfast at various other points, including *Sorcerer's Stone*, chapters 8 and 11, and *Prisoner of Azkaban*, chapter 9.

[24] http://harrypotter.wikia.com/wiki/Toast (accessed April 3, 2018). We learn about the flavor of beans in *Sorcerer's Stone*, page 104.

movies. In a fan-community obsessed with accuracy, this fantasy about a familiar food suggests, again, how toast is both familiar and fantastic, a given and in need of a gloss, a staple and an occasion for flights of fancy.

In its association with white foods and white people, with tea and the golden age of nursery repasts, toast sometimes stands as the food from which the increasingly ethnically diverse protagonists of children's literature depart. Pamela Munoz Ryan's *Esperanza Rising*, which in many ways rewrites earlier (toast-filled) precedents such as *A Little Princess*, never mentions toast. The book is organized around produce (which does not include wheat) and the characters make and eat tortillas but never toast. Critic Lan Dong emphasizes the "difference" of the protagonist in Jade Snow Wong's *Fifth Chinese Daughter* (1950) by describing what she doesn't eat: her "usual school-day breakfast is not cereal, milk, orange juice, toast, pancake, or omelet." Instead, she eats rice, soup, savory and spicy foods.[25] For many readers and protagonists, toast is not necessarily familiar.

Bread has a well-browned reputation as the staff of life, as a basic, unobjectionable, and irreplaceable food.[26] For example, writing in the seventeenth century, Thomas Moffett assumes "the dignity and necessity of Bread" and insists that it is one food everyone likes: "Bread is a food so necessary to the life of man, that whereas many meats be loathed naturally, of some persons, yet we never saw, read, nor heard of any man that naturally hated bread."[27] This is no longer true, since gluten-free and grain-free diets are in vogue, and bread has suddenly become a vilified foodstuff. Perhaps predictably it has simultaneously achieved a cachet that long eluded it. Artisanal loaves glow on the covers of food magazines, which promise that you can achieve such results at home. The current fashion for toast suggests how the mundane can become the fashionable and how prohibition prompts desire. Various bakeries offer what is called "artisanal toast." By one account, for example, "'Artisanal' toast is made from inch-thick, snow-white or grainy slices, lathered in butter and cinnamon or peanut butter and honey, then wrapped individually in wax paper."[28] This

---

[25] Lan Dong, "Eating Different, Looking Different: Food in Asian American Childhood," in *Critical Approaches to Food in Children's Literature*, edited by Kara K. Keeling and Scott T. Pollard (London: Routledge, 2009), 137–48, esp. 144.

[26] Scott Shershow, *Bread* (London: Bloomsbury, 2016).

[27] Thomas Moffett, *Healths Improvement: Or, Rules Comprizing and Discovering the Nature, Method, and Manner of Preparing All Sorts of Food Used in This Nation*, corrected and enlarged by Christopher Bennet (London, 1655), 265.

[28] Eliza Barclay, "We Didn't Believe in 'Artisanal' Toast until We Made Our Own," *The Salt*, *NPR*, April 22, 2014, www.npr.org/sections/thesalt/2014/04/22/305653252/we-didnt-believe-in-artisanal-toast-until-we-made-our-own.

description belies the freighted choices of bread and topping, choices that can paralyze. But while these vary, "artisanal toast" is distinguished by its thickness and its cost, infamously $4 a slice (and destined to rise) at Trouble in Oakland, California, one of the places credited with and blamed for this trend. As my niece and co-eater pointed out as we conducted research on this toast, "the topping goes all the way to the edge." No slapdash buttering and missed edges here. We watched four people carefully divide one piece of peanut butter toast, treating each quarter as a precious indulgence; but we also saw quite a few customers sheepishly approach the counter for a second round of pricey toast. The food of last resort has become a destination treat. The food you are supposed to be able to make for yourself is once again outsourced to experts. They serve us but we also have to count on them to get it right.

Once my mother, a legendary baker, asked her own mother, also a great baker, what treat she would most like for an upcoming holiday. My grandmother was, at that time, living in a nursing home (where she occasionally oversaw the baking of apple pies for the nuns, to great acclaim). Without hesitation, she announced that what she wanted, above all, was toast. Her request was a detailed denunciation of what was passing for toast at Villa St. Cyril and an unintentional homage to Mrs. Beeton. She wanted good bread (homemade, of course), well-toasted, lavishly buttered, and served HOT. So the centerpiece of that holiday meal was toast on demand. We would run the hot toast directly from the toaster to Gramma. She ate an unconscionable amount and damned the consequences. My point here is that just as toast can speak of comfort and contentment, it can also disappoint and dispirit. People have very strong opinions about toast.

A quick look at the etymology of toast suggests that it has always been lathered with associations and that it has steadily accrued meanings over time. The *Oxford English Dictionary* describes it as meaning, originally, "A piece of bread browned before the fire, often put in wine or ale." Because of that status as something to float in a beverage, toast evolved to mean "one to whom toasts are drunk" as in being "the toast of the town." This is, according to the *OED*, a figurative application of the noun toast, in that the name of the person being honored is "supposed to flavour a bumper like a spiced toast in the drink." There may also be a slide here from what floats in the cup to the person to whom the cup is lifted. As a verb, "to toast" is the act of browning and crisping the bread but also, by extension, the act of warming one's feet, or melting cheese, or of lifting a glass. The noun form has a long history of usage to describe physical comfort as in "to be warm (and dry) as toast." "Hot as toast" can mean eager or keen as well as cozy. The colloquial uses of toast suggest that it has a dark side. To be "had on toast" might mean to have been swindled; to have someone on toast is to have them at one's mercy. In specifically US slang, toast can refer to a "person or thing that is defunct, dead, finished, in serious trouble," apparently following from Bill Murray's ad lib in the 1983 film *Ghostbusters*, in which the script's "I'm gonna turn this guy into toast" became "This chick is toast."[29] Like "baked," "toasted" can mean intoxicated. This rich constellation of meanings provides further evidence that toast's status as "comfort food" is more complicated than it might at first appear. Is toast toast as in consigned to the past? Over? The vogue for artisanal toast suggests not. But toast makes its claims on our appetites and wallets for the same reason it works as a provocation in children's literature – because it seems to hearken back to lost consolations but also, like so much in children's literature, because it contains some uncertainty. The celebration of hot buttered toast warns that toast can be cold or burned; the delicious arrival of the gaoler's daughter relies on the awareness that she might not always turn up – with a generous portion of perfect toast.

In children's literature, toast takes its place on a table that is laden with fantastical sweets and body parts, feasts and famine.[30] While food is sometimes associated with comfort and nurture more broadly, it is often scarce or poisonous. Fairy tales famously rely on starvation, cannibalism, and hunger. They turn on mysterious and uncurbable cravings ("Rapunzel"), poisoned gifts of food ("Snow White"), and an astonishing amount of cannibalism ("Snow White," "The Juniper Tree," and "Sun, Moon, and Talia"). Growing out of this tradition, in Maurice Sendak's classic *Where the Wild Things Are* eating is both an expression of aggression, when Max threatens his mother that "I'll eat you," and of love, when the wild things beg him not to leave them: "We'll eat you up we love you so."

Considering toast in the context of other foods in children's literature, it's easier to see that since food is never simply comforting, toast might be more complicated as well. I want to conclude by considering the small detail that Mary Poppins is said to smell like toast. The first reference to this appears quite late in the first book, in the Bad Tuesday chapter. Michael

---

[29] William Safire, "History Is Toast," *New York Times Magazine*, April 20, 1997, www.nytimes.com/1997/04/20/magazine/history-is-toast.html.

[30] On food in children's literature, see also Bridget Carrington and Jennifer Harding, *Feast or Famine?: Food and Children's Literature* (Newcastle upon Tyne: Cambridge Scholars, 2014); Carolyn Daniel, *Voracious Children: Who Eats Whom in Children's Literature* (New York: Routledge, 2006). Note that food is not one of the headings in Philip Nel and Lissa Paul, eds., *Keywords for Children's Literature* (New York: New York University Press, 2011).

wakes up in a foul mood and is naughty all day until Mary rescues him from the menacing specters of creatures they have visited that day. This is the one chapter of the book that was revised. Modern editions specify that this chapter is the "revised version." For decades after its publication in 1934, critics objected to the racial stereotypes in this chapter, in which Mary uses a magical compass to take the children around the world to visit Eskimo, Chinese, African, and Native American families. P. L. Travers finally revised the chapter, turning humans into animals; the illustrator Mary Shepard revised the illustration of the compass as well. But the revision is haunted by the racist content it has tried to banish or ameliorate. This is the climactic moment in the original version:

> A noise behind the chair startled him and he turned round guiltily, expecting to see Mary Poppins. But instead there were four gigantic figures bearing down towards him – the Eskimo with a spear, the Negro Lady with her husband's huge club, the Mandarin with a great curved sword, and the Red Indian with a tomahawk. They were rushing upon him from all four quarters of the room with their weapons raised above their heads, and, instead of looking kind and friendly as they had done that afternoon, they now seemed threatening and full of revenge. They were almost on top of him, their huge, terrible, angry faces looming nearer and nearer. He felt their hot breath on his face and saw their weapons tremble in their hands.[31]

The revised version says that: "there were four gigantic figures bearing down upon him – the bear with his fangs showing, the Macaw fiercely flapping his wings, the Panda with his fur on end, the Dolphin thrusting out her snout. From all quarters of the room they were rushing upon him, their shadows huge on the ceiling. No longer kind and friendly, they were now full of revenge."[32] In both versions, Michael's fear leads him to call out for Mary Poppins – "Mary Poppins, help me!" – and his request for her help breaks the spell, banishing his assailants and his fears about what they might be "planning to do to him." This rescue enables him to make his peace with his dependence on Mary Poppins. "And, oh, the burning thing that had been inside him all day had melted and disappeared."[33] It is at this point in both the original version and the revised one that we learn for the first time in the series how Mary Poppins smells: "He could smell her crackling white apron and the faint flavor of toast that always hung about her so deliciously."[34] The burning thing that is his own resistance to

[31] P. L. Travers, *Mary Poppins* (Orlando: Harcourt/Odyssey, 1934), 65.
[32] P. L. Travers, *Mary Poppins*, revised ed. (Orlando: Harcourt/Odyssey, 1981), 100.
[33] Ibid., 102.
[34] Ibid.

her authority melts into the savor of toast that attaches to her, browned but not burned. The possibility that Michael could eat Mary Poppins replaces his fear that he will be killed or even eaten by the terrifying creatures and accompanies his relief at her rescue. This savor of toast – simultaneously a smell and a "flavor" – then becomes a feature of descriptions of Mary throughout the series, always touched on in passing.[35]

The association of Mary with toast would seem to reinforce her status as a source of comfort. But Mary is never simply that. When she first arrives, Michael asks "you'll never leave us, will you?"[36] Mary responds by looking "very fierce" and warning "One more word from that direction … and I'll call the Policeman." She promises only that "I'll stay till the wind changes" and that's what she does. Caitlin Flanagan argues that Michael's question is "the great question of childhood, the question upon which all the Mary Poppins books turn: is the person on whom a child relies for the foundation of his existence – food and warmth and love at its most elemental – about to disappear?"[37] What makes the series so fascinating is that the answer is yes. She will leave. But then again, she will also come back. Mary's appeal to the children is not that she is safe but that she is remarkable. "Michael suddenly discovered that you could not look at Mary Poppins and disobey her. There was something strange and extraordinary about her – something that was frightening and at the same time most exciting." "She's different. She's the Great Exception," the Starling confirms.[38]

Food is one of the ways that Mary marks herself and her associates as extraordinary and unsettling. When she first meets the Banks children, she doses them with a cordial that adapts to suit each consumer, ignoring Jane's worry that the infant twins, John and Barbara, are too young and serving it to them as well. In the second chapter of the novel, Mary has a day out, reminding readers that she has a life separate from the children, who appear only in the chapter's frame, and that she particularly likes raspberry-jam cakes. When she takes Jane and Michael to have tea with her uncle, Mr. Wigg, they all float up and enjoy their tea in the air. What's more, Mr. Wigg announces that, rather than beginning with the

---

[35] In the next book in the series, *Mary Poppins Comes Back*, we learn that "she smelt deliciously of newly made toast." P. L. Travers, *Mary Poppins Comes Back* (1935; reprint, Boston: Houghton Mifflin Harcourt, 1997), 23. See also P. L. Travers, *Mary Poppins Opens the Door* (New York: Harcourt, Brace and Co., 1943), 23; P. L. Travers, *Mary Poppins in the Park* (New York: Harcourt, Brace and Co., 1952), 105–6.

[36] Travers, *Mary Poppins*, revised edition, 14.

[37] Caitlin Flanagan, "Becoming Mary Poppins: P. L. Travers, Walt Disney, and the Making of a Myth," *New Yorker*, December 19, 2005, www.newyorker.com/magazine/2005/12/19/becoming-mary-poppins.

[38] Travers, *Mary Poppins*, revised edition, 12, 142.

bread-and-butter, "we will begin the wrong way – which I always think is the *right* way – with the Cake!"[39] On a visit to Mrs. Corry's shop, Mrs. Corry does not feed the twins from the glass cases of gingerbread. Instead, "She broke off two of her fingers and gave one each to John and Barbara. And the oddest part of it was that in the space left by the broken-off fingers two new ones grew at once."[40] Food is everywhere in this first book in the Mary Poppins series. But it often serves to emphasize the inversion of expectations rather than simply comfort or nurture.

This is most clear in the chapter in which Mary Poppins takes the children on a night visit to the zoo when her birthday falls on a full moon. There they find a world turned upside down, with human beings in the cages and talking animals on the prowl. The Hamadryad, who turns out to be related to Mary Poppins, reflects on the relationship between eating and being eaten.

> "Tonight the small are free from the great and the great protect the small. Even I – ," he paused and seemed to be thinking deeply, "even *I* can meet a Barnacle Goose without any thought of dinner – on this occasion. And after all," he went on, flicking his terrible little forked tongue in and out as he spoke, "it may be that to eat and be eaten are the same thing in the end. My wisdom tells me that this is probably so. We are all made of the same stuff, remember, we of the Jungle, you of the City. The same substance composes us – the tree overhead, the stone beneath us, the bird, the beast, the star – we are all one, all moving to the same end. Remember that when you no longer remember me, my child."[41]

The Hamadryad is Mary Poppins' "first cousin once removed – on the mother's side."[42] He sends her, for her birthday, one of his own cast skins, to wear as a belt. At the end of the chapter, Mary is wearing this belt as she makes toast at the fire – the only cooking she does. Just as, in *Alice's Adventures*, the pigeon fears that the long-necked Alice is a serpent who will eat her eggs – "You're a serpent; and there's no use denying it. I suppose you'll be telling me next that you never tasted an egg!" – here we are reminded that Mary both smells good enough to eat and is related to predators.[43] She is a feeder, an eater, and a comestible. Considered in the context of the novel as a whole, the claim that Mary Poppins smells like

[39] Ibid., 41.
[40] Ibid., 118.
[41] Ibid., 170.
[42] Ibid., 169.
[43] Carroll, *Alice's Adventures in Wonderland*, 44.

toast contributes to the characterization of her as magnetic, drawing the children to her, but also unpredictable.

Making toast in her snakeskin belt, she sums up the complex associations of toast with comfort and despair, sensuality and dependency, female nurture and authority, domesticity and the occult. Mary Poppins is a kind of witch, able to fly, to communicate with animals, and to defy the rules that govern other people's possibilities. As a servant who promptly takes charge, her paradoxical status resembles that of many accused witches, who were both socially subordinated and assigned enormous power. Mary Poppins also resembles the familiar, the small animal who acts as a witch's agent. Keith Thomas has called the familiar a "peculiarly English" feature of witchlore.[44] These small animals – weasels, mice, toads, and cats, among others – might seem unthreatening and unimportant. But precisely for that reason they could easily insinuate themselves into domestic spaces. What made these creatures familiar is precisely what made them dangerous: they were intimate with the witch, acting as extensions of her agency; they might not provoke suspicion because of their tiny size and resemblance to domesticated animals or vermin, familiar occupants of human spaces, and so could go anywhere. The familiar is the creature who belongs but remains strange, the creature we recognize but cannot really know or trust. Toast in children's literature, I have been arguing, is familiar in this sense. It is a known quantity. It is nugatory. But it can also be strange, alienating, inspiring – even powerful. It is both daily fare and an exotic dish that requires a recipe, a special occasion, a trip, and $4. While the smell of buttered toast still speaks to many readers, what it has to say is not necessarily simple, predictable, or intelligible.

BIBLIOGRAPHY

Barclay, Eliza. "We Didn't Believe in 'Artisanal' Toast until We Made Our Own." The Salt. *NPR*, April 22, 2014. www.npr.org/sections/thesalt/2014/04/22/305653252/we-didnt-believe-in-artisanal-toast-until-we-made-our-own.

Beeton, Isabella. *The Book of Household Management*. London: S. O. Beeton, 1861.

---

[44] Keith Thomas, *Religion and the Decline of Magic: Studies in Popular Beliefs in Sixteenth and Seventeenth-Century England* (New York: Scribner's, 1971), 445–46. See also Frances E. Dolan, *Dangerous Familiars: Representations of Domestic Crime in England, 1550–1700* (Ithaca, NY: Cornell University Press, 1994); James Sharpe, "The Witch's Familiar in Elizabethan England," in *Authority and Consent in Tudor England: Essays Presented to C. S. L. Davies*, edited by G. W. Bernard and S. J. Gunn (Aldershot, UK: Ashgate, 2002), 219–32, esp. 226.

Bucholz, Dinah. *The Unofficial Harry Potter Cookbook: From Cauldron Cakes to Knickerbocker Glory – More Than 150 Magical Recipes for Wizards and Non-Wizards Alike*. Avon, MA: Adams Media, 2010.

Carpenter, Humphrey. *Secret Gardens: The Golden Age of Children's Literature*. Boston: Houghton Mifflin, 1985.

Carrington, Bridget, and Jennifer Harding. *Feast or Famine?: Food and Children's Literature*. Newcastle upon Tyne: Cambridge Scholars, 2014.

Carroll, Lewis. *Alice's Adventures in Wonderland*. New York: Penguin/Signet, 2012.

Cockayne, Emma. *Hubbub: Filth, Noise and Stench in England 1600–1770*. New Haven: Yale University Press, 2007.

Corinth, Jacqueline. "Food Symbolism in Three Children's Literature Texts: Grahame's *The Wind in the Willows*, Dahl's *Charlie and the Chocolate Factory* and Rowling's Harry Potter Novels." In *You Are What You Eat: Literary Probes into the Palate*, edited by Annette M. Magid, 260–83. Newcastle upon Tyne: Cambridge Scholars, 2008.

Daniel, Carolyn. *Voracious Children: Who Eats Whom in Children's Literature*. New York: Routledge, 2006.

Dolan, Frances E. *Dangerous Familiars: Representations of Domestic Crime in England, 1550–1700*. Ithaca, NY: Cornell University Press, 1994.

Dong, Lan. "Eating Different, Looking Different: Food in Asian American Childhood." In *Critical Approaches to Food in Children's Literature*, edited by Kara K. Keeling and Scott T. Pollard, 137–48. London: Routledge, 2009.

Flanagan, Caitlin. "Becoming Mary Poppins: P. L. Travers, Walt Disney, and the Making of a Myth." *New Yorker*, December 19, 2005. www.newyorker.com/magazine/2005/12/19/becoming-mary-poppins.

Grahame, Kenneth. *The Annotated Wind in the Willows*. Edited by Annie Gauger. New York: Norton, 2009.

The Wind in the Willows. New York: Aladdin/Simon and Schuster, 1989.

Hemmings, Robert. "A Taste of Nostalgia: Children's Books from the Golden Age – Carroll, Grahame, and Milne." *Children's Literature* 35 (2007): 54–79.

Hunt, Peter. "Coldtonguecoldhamcoldbeefpickled-gherkinsaladfrenchrollscresss andwidespottedmeatgingerbeerlemonadesodawater …: Fantastic Foods in the Books of Kenneth Grahame, Jerome K. Jerome, H. E. Bates and Other Bakers of the Fantasy England." *Journal of the Fantastic in the Arts* 7.1 (1996): 5–22.

The Wind in the Willows: A Fragmented Arcadia. New York: Twayne, 1994.

Moffett, Thomas. *Healths Improvement: Or, Rules Comprizing and Discovering the Nature, Method, and Manner of Preparing all Sorts of Food Used in this Nation*. Corrected and enlarged by Christopher Bennet. London, 1655.

Nel, Philip, and Lissa Paul, eds. *Keywords for Children's Literature*. New York: New York University Press, 2011.

Nodelman, Perry, and Mavis Reimer. *The Pleasures of Children's Literature*. 3rd ed. Toronto: Allen and Bacon, 2003.

Odell, Carol, and Anna Pignataro. *Once Upon a Time in the Kitchen: Recipes and Tales from Classic Children's Stories*. Ann Arbor: Sleeping Bear Press, 2010.

Pelling, Margaret. *The Common Lot: Sickness, Medical Occupations and the Urban Poor in Early Modern England*. London: Longman, 1998.

Rowling, J. K. *Harry Potter and the Chamber of Secrets*. New York: Scholastic, 1998.
Harry Potter and the Sorcerer's Stone. New York: Scholastic, 1997.

Safire, William. "History Is Toast." *New York Times Magazine*, April 20, 1997. www.nytimes.com/1997/04/20/magazine/history-is-toast.html.

Sendak, Maurice. *Where the Wild Things Are*. New York: HarperCollins, 1984.

Sharpe, James. "The Witch's Familiar in Elizabethan England." In *Authority and Consent in Tudor England: Essays Presented to C. S. L. Davies*, edited by G. W. Bernard and S. J. Gunn, 219–32. Aldershot, UK: Ashgate, 2002.

Shershow, Scott. *Bread*. London: Bloomsbury, 2016.

Snicket, Lemony. *Series of Unfortunate Events #1: The Bad Beginning*. New York: HarperCollins, 1999.

Stallworth, Lyn. *Wond'rous Fare*. Chicago: Calico, 1988.

Sullivan, C. W. "'Chops … Cheese, New Bread, Great Swills of Beer': Food and Home in Kenneth Grahame's *The Wind in the Willows*." *Journal of the Fantastic in the Arts* 15.2 (Spring 2005): 144–52.

Thick, Malcolm. "Root Crops and the Feeding of London's Poor." In *English Rural Society*, edited by John Chartres and David Hey, 279–96. Cambridge: Cambridge University Press, 1990.

Thomas, Keith. *Religion and the Decline of Magic: Studies in Popular Beliefs in Sixteenth- and Seventeenth-Century England*. New York: Scribner's, 1971.

Thwaite, Ann. *Waiting for the Party: The Life of Frances Hodgson Burnett*. Boston: David R. Godine, 1991.

Travers, P. L. *Mary Poppins*. Orlando: Harcourt/Odyssey, 1934.
Mary Poppins. Revised ed. Orlando: Harcourt/Odyssey, 1981.
Mary Poppins Comes Back. 1935. Reprint, Boston: Houghton Mifflin Harcourt, 1997.
Mary Poppins in the Park. New York: Harcourt, Brace, and Co., 1952.
Mary Poppins Opens the Door. New York: Harcourt, Brace, and Co., 1943.

CHAPTER 16

Food, Humor, and Gender in Ishigaki Rin's Poetry

Tomoko Aoyama

When I wipe my mouth
Scattered about the kitchen
Carrot tails
Chicken bones
My father's guts

Ishigaki Rin, "Living"

Food and literature are, as Terry Eagleton pointed out, "endlessly inter-pretable," and each "looks like an object but is actually a relationship."[1] To understand this endlessly interpretable food in endlessly interpretable literature, then, it is essential to consider various types of relationships, including socio-political, cultural, (inter)textual, gender, and familial. When the food and literature belong to, or involve, another culture and language, it further complicates the discussion. Added to each kind of "rela-tionship" are issues of translatability, cultural hegemony and assumptions, shifts in norms, and so on. All this affects the understanding of humor: what is funny in one culture or to a certain group of people or at a certain point in time may not necessarily be regarded as funny in another context. This chapter attempts to clarify some of the relationships that comprise and construct food, gender, and humor in the works of the Japanese poet Ishigaki Rin (1920–2004).[2] Rather than applying Western theories – such

---

[1] Terry Eagleton, "Edible Écriture," in *Consuming Passions: Food in the Age of Anxiety*, edited by Sian Griffiths and Jennifer Wallace (Manchester: Mandolin, 1998), 204–5.

[2] In this chapter I cite Japanese names in Japanese order, with the surname (e.g. Ishigaki) first, followed by personal name (Rin) in the body of the text. When citing a Japanese name as the author of a publication originally written in English and published in the anglicized order (e.g. Hiroaki Sato), however, I use that order. In footnotes, anglicized name order is used for all items to comply with the designated reference style and avoid confusion. Some of Ishigaki's works have been translated into English: Leith Morton, *Poems of Masayo Koike, Shuntarō Tanikawa, Rin Ishigaki* (Sydney: Vagabond Press, 2013), 85–111; Rin Ishigaki, "The pan, the pot, the fire I have before me," translated by Hiroaki Sato, *Chicago Review*, 25.2 (1973): 108–9; Rin Ishigaki and Hiroaki Sato, "Ishigaki Rin," *Poetry Kanto*, 22 (2006), http://poetrykanto.com/issues/2006-issue/ishigaki-rin-2; Rin Ishigaki, "Five poems," translated by Yukie Ohta and Rie Takagi, *positions* 3.3 (1995): 723–27; Janine Beichman, "Poem Provides Advice about Identity: A Translator Explains What a Poem

as those of Hélène Cixous and Julia Kristeva – of food, gender, and humor in literature to Ishigaki's case, or comparing her to writers who are more widely known outside Japan, I will concentrate on clarifying the relevant relationships mostly within specific Japanese contexts. Food-related motifs infuse Ishigaki's poetry from her very first collection, *Watashi no mae ni aru nabe to okama to moeru hi to* (In front of me the pot and ricepot and burning flames, 1959). Humor is another prominent feature of her poetry. Both food and humor are overtly and covertly connected to gender issues, which, in turn, are linked to other sociocultural and political issues, historical events, and her personal situation.

Ishigaki belongs to the generation of Japanese who experienced prewar, wartime, and postwar hardships. Unusually for a poet, especially for a woman poet, she worked full-time in a major bank in Tokyo, the Industrial Bank of Japan, which played an important role in the Japanese economy throughout the twentieth century. In 1934, aged only fourteen, Ishigaki started as an apprentice clerk, and she continued to work at the bank until she reached the mandatory retirement age of fifty-five in 1975. Her working life spanned Japan's military aggression, defeat, the Allied Occupation, and the postwar democratization, economic recovery, and expansionism, all of which was deeply connected to the question of food production and consumption.

Complex family issues also greatly affected Ishigaki's life and work. She was born in Akasaka, central Tokyo, as the eldest daughter of Hitoshi and Sumi. When the devastating earthquake hit Tokyo in September 1923, Sumi was seriously injured; she died the following March, after giving birth to another child in January. Rin's father married Sumi's younger sister in 1927 but she, too, died in 1929. He married again in 1931 and had three children with this third wife before they divorced in 1937. His fourth marriage lasted from 1938 until his death in 1957. Thus, by the age of eighteen Rin had four mothers and several siblings, two of whom also died young.

Means to Her," *Trends in Japan*, March 20, 2002, http://web-japan.org/trends01/article/020320fea_r.html; Janine Beichman, "Ishigaki Rin, the Venus of Tokyo," in *Across Time and Genre: Reading and Writing Women's Texts*, edited by Janice Brown, Brad Ambury, and Sonja Arntzen, Conference Proceedings (Edmonton: University of Alberta, 2002), 301–4; Janine Beichman's translations included in J. Thomas Rimer and Van C. Gessel, eds., *The Columbia Anthology of Modern Japanese Literature*, vol. 2 (New York: Columbia University Press, 2007), 415–17; Lee Friederich, "Through Beastly Tears: Devouring the Dead in the Poetry of Ishigaki Rin," *Japanese Language and Literature* 43.1 (2009): 27–54; Makoto Ōoka, compiler, Paul McCarthy, trans., and Janine Beichman, ed., *101 Modern Japanese Poems* (London: Thames River Press, 2012): 25–27; Hajime Kijima, *The Poetry of Postwar Japan* (Iowa: University of Iowa Press, 1975), 56–59; James Kirkup, *Modern Japanese Poetry* (St. Lucia: University of Queensland Press, 1978), 166–70; and Rin Ishigaki and John Solt, "Life," *Mānoa: Pacific Journal of International Writing* 3.2 (1991): 32.

The family house was burnt down in the air raid of May 1945. Ishigaki remained single, and supported her aging parents and younger siblings. She lived with her family until 1970, when she moved to an apartment.

Although not very prolific by Japanese standards, with only four original collections of poetry, she was, as Leith Morton writes, "the first postwar woman poet generally acknowledged by readers and critics alike as making a powerful impact on the Japanese consciousness as a distinctly feminist writer."[3] Ishigaki's second collection of poetry, *Hyōsatsu nado* (Nameplates etc., 1968) received the prestigious Mr. H. award for emerging poets. The major poetry journal, *Gendaishi techō* (Contemporary Poetry Notebook), published a special obituary volume to Ishigaki in 2005. The book included tributes by a number of leading contemporary poets. Ibaragi Noriko (1926–2006), who was often compared and contrasted to Ishigaki, affectionately acknowledged their thirty-year friendship as well as their heated discussions. Shinkawa Kazue (b. 1929) adopted the title of Ishigaki's obituary for another poet-artist, Tsuji Makoto (1913–1975): "Mako-chan ga shinda hi / watashi wa gohan tabeta" (On the day Mako died / I had my meal). On the morning after Ishigaki's death, Shinkawa "chewed the lines along with breakfast: 'On the day Rin died, I had my meal.' "[4] She finds strong cathartic power in Ishigaki's poetry:

> Even when a close friend or a dear family member has died, one gets hungry and eats. Ishigaki expressed this sense of the pathetic and unbearable sadness of human beings as living creatures superbly in a few laconic, unembellished words.[5]

Food in Ishigaki's texts is linked to the gender issues faced by women and girls in diverse roles and situations – as survivors of the war, as waged and domestic workers, as (step)daughters and (step)mothers, as single women, and as young, middle-aged, and elderly women. This is widely recognized in Japan. Equally well known is the importance of humor in her life and work. On the front and back covers of the *Gendaishi techō* volume are photographs of Ishigaki's round, smiling face, one mature and the other young. The book comes with a CD that contains an hour-long recording of a poetry reading and talk she recorded live in March 1999. Sprinkled throughout this performance are her soft, cheerful, and almost

[3] Leith Morton, "Feminist Strategies in Contemporary Japanese Women's Poetry," *Journal of the Association of Teachers of Japanese* 31.2 (1997): 79; Leith Morton, *Modernism in Practice: An Introduction to Postwar Japanese Poetry* (Honolulu: University of Hawaii Press, 2004), 89.
[4] Gendaishi techō, ed. *Ishigaki Rin* (Tokyo: Shichōsha, 2005), 16.
[5] Ibid., 16–17.

girlish giggles, which somehow still seem to fit the mature, sensible, and thoughtful voice of the seventy-nine-year-old poet. There is nothing outrageous or showy in her voice, appearance, or personality. This modest, gentle humor can be found in her poetry and essays, too, but more prominent in her work is a different kind of humor – black, brutal, confrontational, and abject – as we will see in detail below. Although Ishigaki is usually regarded as a poet who represents the post-World War II era, there are important links to earlier twentieth-century literary modes and ideas. At the same time, her work maintains and has even increased its relevance in contemporary society. This chapter identifies the links between Ishigaki's "written food" and other prominent examples of food in modern and contemporary Japanese literature and culture, and highlights her originality, with a particular focus on her humor. The bilingual, cross-cultural, and cross-generational approach not only connects Japanese-language scholarship in Ishigaki studies with translation and reception studies but also clarifies the diversity and the workings of humor in Ishigaki's poetic food.

Poems to Eat à la Ishigaki Rin

As already mentioned, Ishigaki started work at the bank when she was fourteen. She was twenty-five at the end of the war. As her friend Ibaragi Noriko wrote in one of her most well-known poems, "When I was at my prettiest / My country lost the war."[6] In the postwar period Ishigaki was involved in the bank workers' union movement. Unlike in the prewar and wartime eras, labor unions were not only legalized but actually promoted by the Allied GHQ as part of the democratization of Japan. Ishigaki published a number of overtly socially engaged poems in union publications on topics ranging from war, pollution, and poverty to industrial accidents. The poem "Genshi dōwa" (An atomic fairy tale), written in September 1949, for example, depicts a post-apocalyptic world in which the only survivors are the crews of the two airplanes that dropped atomic bombs simultaneously on each other's country.[7] "How sadly / and affectionately they lived together – / / Perhaps this may / become a new myth."[8]

---

[6] Ōoka, McCarthy, and Beichman, *101 Modern Japanese Poems*, 54.
[7] Friederich discusses this and another poem on the atomic bomb in Hiroshima. Friederich, "Through Beastly Tears," 32–36. Although she has translated *dōwa* as "lullaby," I prefer to use the literal translation of the word, "fairy tale." Ishii's original texts quoted in this chapter are mostly from the 2015 collection of her poetry edited by Itō Hiromi. Unless otherwise noted, the translations are mine.
[8] Hiromi Itō, ed., *Ishigaki Rin shishū* (Tokyo: Iwanami Shoten, 2015), 10–11.

As Morton identified, irony is a key strategy Ishigaki uses in her poetry.[9] In the 1999 live recording, her clear, gentle voice further enhances the ironic effect of the fairy tale form. After reading this poem on the recording, she notes the significance of the date attached to the poem in a humorous way, by quoting a critic's comment, which had been published "only recently":

> "On September 25, 1949, the media reported the Soviet Union's success in testing an atomic bomb. It can be surmised that upon hearing this report, the poet felt a sense of crisis, a different kind of crisis from the time when the US was the only nation that possessed nuclear weapons, and wrote this poem." And the poet herself feels that it *"can be surmised"* like that.[10]

The last brief remark is met by laughter from Ishigaki and her audience. This is one form of Ishigaki's humor: while expressing her thoughts and social conscience in clear and accessible language, using fairy tale narrative techniques in the poem, she foregrounds and teases the slightly pompous "can be surmised" (*de arō ka*) of the well-meaning critic, who is unnamed here but we are tempted to think "can be surmised" to be a male critic. The joke does not come through as effectively in translation, partly because of the syntactic difference between English and Japanese. In the Japanese version the phrase *de arō ka* comes at the very end of the quotation and hence just before Ishigaki's repetition of it in her personal aside. Italics are the best option I could find to suggest the subtle emphasis in her voice when repeating the phrase. This is a reminder of the limitation of translations and written texts, which, combined with cultural and historical differences, makes it difficult to discuss humor in another language.

Ishigaki wrote a poem titled "Mayu" (Cocoon) in July 1954, shortly after the construction of the world's first nuclear power plant in Obninsk, USSR. In the poem, the world is "devoured by an unknown power," like mulberry leaves eaten by a silkworm.[11] In another poem, "Nikki yori" (From a diary), Ishigaki refers to the news that the Japanese government has decided to allow toxic "yellowed rice" to be mixed with the rice to be distributed for general consumption. "The plan to distribute 56,956 tons / 4.8 billion yen worth of toxic rice / has passed with no problem in one country's politics."[12] The news is juxtaposed in the poem with the nuclear testing at Bikini Atoll as well as the death of one of the tubercular patients who participated

---

[9] Morton, "Feminist Strategies," 81; Morton, *Modernism in Practice*, 91.

[10] Rin Ishigaki, *Ishigaki Rin sakuhin rōdoku CD*, appended to Gendaishi techō, ed. *Ishigaki Rin* (Tokyo: Shinchōsha, 2005), track 2, 1:00–1:20.

[11] Itō, *Ishigaki Rin shishū*, 26–27. English translation in Ishigaki, "Five poems," 723–24.

[12] Itō, *Ishigaki Rin shishū*, 46.

in a sit-in protest outside the Tokyo Metropolitan Government Office. Another poem from this period depicts the death of "yet another" construction worker: "He climbed high to a dangerous place / not because he wanted to build a high rise / but to eat / or to let his family eat."[13]

Food and eating in these poems can be regarded as what the poet-critic Ishikawa Takuboku advocated in 1909 when he coined the phrase "poems to eat" – that is, "poetry written with both feet firmly planted on the ground, poetry written with feelings that are inseparable from real life," and "necessities" for everyone rather than delicacies or a feast for the privileged. This is not simply a revolt against the conventional poetic style, diction, and subjects but an advocacy for relevance to contemporary life and for everyday vernacular and accessible language.[14] In postwar Japan many women have led the way in producing socially engaged literature in various genres. Ishigaki's atomic bomb "fairy tale" may not be as widely known as the works of novelist Hayashi Kyōko (b. 1930); nor do her poems on pollution have as great an impact as the sustained work of poet/novelist Ishimure Michiko (b. 1927) on Minamata disease (severe mercury poisoning) or the major non-fiction work, *Fukugō osen* (Compound Pollution, 1975) of novelist/dramatist Ariyoshi Sawako (1931–84). Nevertheless, it is clear that Ishigaki's "poems to eat" are connected to, and open to, the wider world and the issues confronting it, which in itself poses a challenge to the myth that circulated until relatively recently among misogynistic and homosocial literary critics and journalists that women's literature is narrow, inward-looking, emotional, and so on.[15]

Devoured Workers and the "Shit-Pot"

Ishigaki's poetic "food" also shares some motifs and characteristics with the proletarian literature of the 1920s and 1930s, which often used the metaphor of cannibalism to depict the exploitation and inhumane conditions of factory workers. In Sata Ineko's (1904–98) 1928 short story "Kyarameru kōjō kara" (From the caramel factory), for example, a twelve-year-old girl factory worker is exploited both at work and at home. The girl in the

---

[13] Ibid., 40.
[14] See Tomoko Aoyama, *Reading Food in Modern Japanese Literature* (Honolulu: University of Hawaii Press, 2008), 46–47, for a more detailed discussion of Takuboku's notion of "poems to eat." Ishikawa is the poet's surname, but he is usually referred to by his pen name (*gagō*, i.e. elegant sobriquet), Takuboku.
[15] See Rebecca L. Copeland, ed., *Woman Critiqued: Translated Essays on Japanese Women's Writing* (Honolulu: University of Hawai'i Press, 2006) for ample examples of misogynistic essentialist comments.

story, Hiroko, is forced to leave primary school to work in a factory to support her family. The factory produces caramel, which was regarded at the time as a modern, Western-style consumer food targeted at the children of the growing middle class. Hiroko and her fellow child workers are excluded from this consumption, except for the broken fragments of caramel that they are allowed to eat occasionally. The factory is so far from home that commuting there on a tram packed with adult workers is hard and exhausting. "Hiroko squeezed herself in between adult legs. She, too, was a worker – a fragile, little worker, like grass eaten by a horse."[16] At the end of the narrative, the father finds Hiroko another job as a live-in waitress at a small Chinese noodle shop. When Hiroko receives a letter from her former teacher, she takes it to the shop's toilet so that she can have some privacy. The teacher urges her to complete her elementary school education. Although sympathetic, the teacher has no idea of Hiroko's situation. Hiroko weeps in the dark toilet.[17]

In another canonical proletarian text, *Kani kōsen* (The crab cannery ship, 1929) by Kobayashi Takiji (1903–33), the workers on a factory boat off Kamchatka are brutally treated by the company and live in inhumane conditions. Their living quarters below decks are called the "shit-hole" as they are airless and unsanitary. "Barely alive human beings shivered with cold as though they'd been mistaken for salmon and trout and thrown into a refrigerator."[18] Many of the people in this "shit-hole" have experienced and witnessed abusive treatment in other industries.

> Each railroad tie in Hokkaido was nothing but the bluish corpse of a worker. Posts driven into the soil during harbor reclamations were laborers sick with beriberi buried alive like the ancient "human pillars." The name for workers in Hokkaido was "octopus." In order to stay alive, an octopus will even devour its own limbs. It was just like that![19]

Horrendous violence and torture await those workers who attempt to escape. The novel depicts groups of workers rather than individuals. The author, Kobayashi, selected the crab cannery factory as it was "a type of exploitation typical of colonies and undeveloped areas," and it suited his purpose of clarifying not only "the conditions of Japanese workers" but also the "international, military, and economic relations" that gave rise to

---

[16] Quoted and translated in Aoyama, *Reading Food*, 66.
[17] See note 62 in ibid., 225.
[18] Takiji Kobayashi and Zeljko Cipris, *The Crab Cannery Ship and Other Novels of Struggle* (Honolulu: University of Hawai'i Press, 2013), 31.
[19] Ibid., 54.

those conditions.[20] Kobayashi himself, coincidentally, worked in a bank, the Otaru branch of the Hokkaido Colonial Bank, from 1924 until his dismissal in 1929 because of the publication of this novel and his involvement in strikes and other political activities. Just a few years after he wrote this novella, Kobayashi was tortured and killed by the Special Higher Police.

Ishigaki's poetry does not contain this kind of violence. The working conditions in the postwar metropolitan bank and other offices were far from those of the cannery workers in the Sea of Okhotsk or the caramel factory of the mid-1910s. Nevertheless, the metaphor of workers being eaten appears frequently in her poems. In the 1956 poem "Kakedasu" (Start running), for example, the noise of people running to get to work on time makes the poet think: "Who is about to devour me? / My roasted heart / Roasted till obsequious, tiny, and dry / This serious / fainthearted / timid worker / Who is going to eat bunches of us up?"[21] In Kobayashi's work, capitalism, the military, and the emperor system are identified as the interconnected sources and framework of exploitation and discrimination. Ishigaki, too, presents this in a less brutal manner. In the title poem of the third collection, "Ryakureki" (CV), she describes her life precisely with these three elements: "born in a regiment town," "worked in a place with a cashbox," and "grew older in the town of the Imperial Palace."[22]

As we have glimpsed, in *The Crab Cannery Ship*, abject imagery in connection to the food production industry abounds. Even in the much less horrible working conditions of "From the caramel factory," the final scene shows that the only private space in the noodle shop is the toilet. The juxtaposition of food and excrement is a recurrent motif in postwar literature as well, especially in literature that depicts the brutal milieu of the military and the marginalization of certain groups of people.[23] Somewhat surprisingly, the toilet is an important topos in Ishigaki's poetry. A lighthearted example is titled "Gehinna shi" (A vulgar poem), which was first published in the August 15, 1955 issue of a workers' union magazine. It depicts an incident that occurred about ten years earlier. The narrator-persona was on a train, which was, typically of the time, incredibly crowded – so crowded that people were standing on the seats. One day, however, she was "lucky" enough to stand in a toilet cubicle with three other passengers. An old Japanese-style toilet in a public space would,

[20] Ibid., 7 (Kobayashi's letter to his friend and comrade, Kurahara Korehito cited by Komori Yōichi in his "Introduction" to *The Crab Cannery Ship*).
[21] Itō, *Ishigaki Rin shishū*, 224–25.
[22] Ibid., 148–49.
[23] Aoyama, *Reading Food*, 80–88.

under normal circumstances, be regarded as one of the least desirable places. It would be a "vulgar" topic, too. The concluding lines declare: "I'm completely shameless / though ten years have passed."[24] There is no shame about the "vulgarity" or about having enjoyed this "privilege." Thus the poem subverts "vulgarity," "shame," and "luxury." In a later poem titled "Public" that is included in the 1968 collection, a "relatively clean" public toilet in a new station building is an "oasis" between work and home that "after working for thirty years / I have found."[25] The "public" is the only "private" space – reminding us of the young working girl of half a century before in Sata's story. The most well-known, and the most powerful, toilet poem by Ishigaki is a ten-line poem with the shocking title "Kinkakushi," which is the common, though now almost obsolete, word for the porcelain squat toilet.[26] This is attached to the longer poem "Ie" (Family). The cesspool below the *kinkakushi* stinks of "intimacy between my father and my stepmother / which makes me want to pinch my nose / the filth sinks into my body."[27] To understand the power of this poem it is necessary to discuss the significance of family, gender, and sexuality in Ishigaki's poetry.

The Devoured Woman, the Devouring Woman

Food and family in Ishigaki's works are often confrontational rather than comforting, and associated with exhaustion, solitude, death, and the abject. Black humor and cutting satire are everywhere. Being devoured by the family is a familiar theme in Ishigaki's poetry. In "Haete kuru," translated by Friederich as "Ready to sprout," the narrator likens herself to an octopus whose tentacles keep sprouting even after her "loving" family eats one after the other.[28] As in many other poems, the narrator needs to assume the unbearable burden of providing the family's living, but her two legs can no longer support the slipping roof. She is forced to pluck out and let go of "things like hopes, ideals, and happiness" that constitute her essential bone structure. Since even her "backbone" has been removed, she has become limp like an octopus. This octopus daughter cannot communicate with her "human" family members. The level of destitution here

---

[24] Itō, *Ishigaki Rin shishū*, 213.

[25] Ibid., 135.

[26] The word has a comic and vulgar ring to it as the "kin" is from *kintama*, the golden ball/s, the slang word for testicles, and "kakushi" is the noun form of the verb to hide.

[27] Itō, *Ishigaki Rin shishū*, 72.

[28] Ibid., 140–43; Friederich, "Through Beastly Tears," 42–43. The following summary and translations of some phrases are mine and differ from Friederich's.

is not as extreme as that in *The Crab Cannery Ship*, in which exploited workers are compared to self-munching octopuses. Ishigaki's focus is on the burden of the dependent family and the sacrifice and isolation of the daughter. Although depressing and disturbing, the poem has a Kafkaesque kind of humor in its description of the octopus daughter despairing of communicating with her human (yet inhumane) family.

The octopus poem is included in Ishigaki's second collection, *Nameplates etc.*, which was published when she was forty-eight. Many other poems in this volume have anthropophagic motifs. The poem entitled "Living" starts with the line "I can't survive without eating."[29] Listed as the essential foods for survival are rice, vegetables, meat, and so on, as well as parents, brothers and sisters, and teachers. The eater/food relationship is reversed here. At the same time, as Morton points out, this is "an ironic cannibalism where the narrator/persona as dependent ... devours those she is dependent upon."[30] The poem concludes: "My fortieth sunset / For the first time the tears of a wild beast filled my eyes."[31] In the recorded reading Ishigaki makes an interesting comment. Pointing out that the list of foods does not include friends, she cites a comment her friend made about the last line "What do you mean, '*fortieth* sunset,' Rin!?" Ishigaki was closer to fifty than forty at the time. "Japanese language is ambiguous, and poetry is even more ambiguous," says the poet, suggesting that "40 no higure" (the fortieth twilight) could also mean the twilight of the forties. She then makes a more serious point about the final line and her "intention" in writing this poem. I quote these words not because I believe in the "intention" of the poet but because the poetry reading as performance adds another interesting layer to our reading of the poem.

> I was born and brought up as a human being, and educated as a human being. So I thought the tears I shed were human tears. But in the twilight of my forties, I appreciated for the first time the sorrow of the beast that "can't survive without eating."[32]

Cannibalism motifs and related imagery are not uncommon in modern Japanese literature, including pre-war and postwar women's writing.[33] In Ishigaki's poetry, metaphor or imagery around eating human beings is

[29] Morton, *Poems of Masayo Koike, Shuntarō Tanikawa, Rin Ishigaki*, 95. This is one of the most frequently translated Ishigaki poems: Beichman and Solt have translated it as "Life," whereas Morton's and Friederich's translations are titled "Living," and Kirkup's "To Live."
[30] Morton, "Feminist Strategies," 84.
[31] Morton, *Poems of Masayo Koike, Shuntarō Tanikawa, Rin Ishigaki*, 95.
[32] Ishigaki, *Ishigaki Rin sakuhin rōdoku CD*, track 3, 2:40–3:00.
[33] See Aoyama, *Reading Food*, 94–130.

usually associated with work and family rather than sexuality. In "Dōyō" (A nursery rhyme, translated as "A child's song" by Friederich), the narrator/ persona is a boy, who "realized that Dad didn't taste so good at all, / bad to the point of choking us with tears." Like a nursery rhyme, this "song" contains repetitions. After the father's will come the mother's, and then the boy's own death: "I will die more beautifully, / like those high-class meals / under a white cloth." The final lines of the poem are: "Fish poultry beasts / all dying their very tasteful, tasteful deaths."[34] While the beasts echo the last line of "Living," the choice of the boy persona makes us wonder about the irony of these "tasteful deaths."

"Oni no shokuji" (Feast of the Ogres) captures a black comic moment in the ritual of a Japanese funeral. With the words "Sorry to have kept you waiting," the freshly cremated ashes are laid out in front of the mourners. As is the custom, "the mourners picked up their chopsticks," to place some bones into the urn, but the poem reminds us that the gesture is "as if to eat," and concludes: "Without the formal attire / it would not have been a seemly act."[35] Here, the solemn but common ceremony is defamiliarized and transformed into a horrible yet comic "ogres' feast." The cremator's words sound like those of a waiter, and are faintly reminiscent of the wildcat waiters in Miyazawa Kenji's classic children's story, "Chūmon no ōi ryōriten" (The restaurant of many orders, 1924). As poet Yamamoto Tarō suggested, the words of apology could also be interpreted as coming from the cremated person.[36] The reader may also think of Itami Jūzō's film, *Osōshiki* (The funeral, 1984), which is an elaborate comic study of the incongruity of funeral conventions that Ishigaki captured in this poem.

One of the most powerful poems to contain a devouring woman's image is found in "Shijimi" (Clams). The first of its three short stanzas describes clams (not *hamaguri* clams but the smaller and cheaper *shijimi*) in the kitchen corner at midnight, "alive / with their mouths open."[37] The second stanza is a brief quotation: " 'When morning comes / *I'll eat you up / each and every one.*' "[38] The horror reaches its climax in the third stanza: "I laughed – / a witch's laugh," and then suddenly comes to an anticlimactic

---

34 Friedrich, "Through Beastly Tears," 48.
35 Ishigaki, "Five Poems," 727.
36 In Ishigaki, *Ishigaki Rin*, 155.
37 Ishigaki, "Five Poems," 725. For the Japanese text, see Itō, *Ishigaki Rin shishū*, 97–98.
38 Ishigaki, "Five Poems," 725. There are at least five different translations of this poem: by Beichman, Morton, Ohta and Takagi, McCarthy, and Sato. Morton uses "them" instead of "you" in the middle line of the second stanza, whereas all of the other translators use "you." Italics are added to the quoted text to indicate that these lines are shown in the original Japanese text in katakana script, which is normally used for loan words, onomatopoeia, and emphasis.

and yet in a sense even scarier conclusion: "After that / mouth faintly open / I had nothing to do with my night but sleep."[39] The uncanny witch-like woman grinning and declaring she will devour the poor clams looks exactly like her victims. The witch's laughter strongly reminds us of the devouring women in Japanese myths and folktales, in particular, the *yama-uba* (mountain witch) and variations such as "The Woman Who Eats Nothing."[40] These horrifying, devouring women also have demure, nurturing, and productive aspects and are associated with motherhood. Although reference to motherhood is absent from "Clams," the ambivalence of the devouring woman is a key feature not only of this poem but of much of Ishigaki's poetry.

While the search for liberation from family appears frequently in Ishigaki's work, we also find poems that celebrate women's work and solidarity. One of her most well-known poems and the title poem of her first collection, "In front of me the pot and ricepot and burning flames," recognizes the significance and value of the cooking done by "our mothers and grandmothers and their mothers also" and makes reference to their techniques and utensils as well as the "love and faithfulness" they poured into their pots and pans. However, this is certainly not a poem of nostalgic yearning for grandma's cooking: the poem proposes that women study "politics and economics and literature" in front of the beloved pots and pans, and pour just as much love into these pursuits, not for self-promotion or pride, or just for their families, but for "all humanity."[41]

Ishigaki explains the background to this poem in her essay and her recording.[42] With the postwar advocacy for women's liberation and gender equality, some women rejected tasks conventionally assigned to women such as making the tea for their work colleagues and cooking for the family. Ishigaki says she felt like saying to her friends "Wait a minute, everyone. Is the kind of work women have been doing really so worthless?" The poem, published in the union newsletter, was welcomed more enthusiastically by men than by women.[43] Yet, she insists, she wanted to send a message to women rather than to men:

---

[39] Ishigaki, "Five Poems," 725–26.

[40] Hayao Kawai, *The Japanese Psyche: Major Motifs in the Fairy Tales of Japan* (Dallas: Spring, 1988), 27–45.

[41] Morton, *Poems of Masayo Koike, Shuntarō Tanikawa, Rin Ishigaki*, 88–89. Japanese text in Itō, *Ishigaki Rin*, 40–43.

[42] Rin Ishigaki, *Yūmoa no sakoku* (Tokyo: Chikuma Shobō, 1987), 165; Ishigaki, *Ishigaki Rin sakuhin rōdoku CD*, track 2, 4:25–5:03.

[43] See Morton, "Feminist Strategies," 83 for a sample of comments by male critics such as Suzuki Shiroyasu, Miki Taku, and Tamura Keiji.

By the time I wrote this, I had worked [in the bank] for about ten years, observing men's world, and appreciated the difficulties they had to face and the great trouble they had to go through to obtain power and promotion. [in a lower, slightly mischievous voice] I never wished to become a man ... I really wanted to say to women, why can't we combine the old and the new, the best things from each to build a new world.[44]

Combining the best things from the old and the new to build a new world and literature is exactly what Ishigaki achieved with her poetry, which has continued to appeal to generations of women and men. With its easy diction and gentle giggles peppered with irony and cutting criticism, the poetic food she offers is accessible, nutritional, and appealing.

Bilingual Feminists Eating Ishigaki's Poetic Dishes

In this final section, I will discuss how bilingual, bicultural feminist poets, scholars, and critics have responded to Ishigaki's poetry in more recent years. Norma Field, whose scholarship spans *The Tale of Genji* to proletarian literature, finds "horror" in Ishigaki's works, especially the leftover tempura in her poem "Mazushii machi" (The poor part of town, in the 1968 collection). The poem depicts an evening scene when the narrator-persona comes home after a day's work. In a shop selling cheap cooked food there is some tempura that hasn't been sold. "I have on hand / a little bit of time / left to me. / Tired, cheerless time, / time that is like tempura that has gone cold." Just as the family that runs the shop will eat its leftover food for their supper, "I will eat my tired time." In the final stanza "I" wonders about those who bought the best part of her day.[45] As Field suggests, Ishigaki's poetry, which is written in easy, everyday language, has the power to make one shudder as it captures the mechanism of capitalism that forces the buying and selling of time – which is life – and at the same time tries to distract us from this fact. In contemporary society this "horror" is still very relevant. Other kinds of "horror" that Ishigaki depicted – atomic war, pollution, industrial accidents, and so on – are also still very real.

Feminist scholar, Mizuta Noriko, who spent decades in the USA from the early 1960s before returning to Japan in 1985, describes Ishigaki as a "diaspora" trying to survive by fleeing from sexuality and family.[46] As Itō Hiromi comments in the anthology she edited, Ishigaki did attempt to

---

[44] Gendaishi techō, *Ishigaki Rin*, CD track 2, 7:20–8:03.
[45] Norma Field, "Iki no ii jikan: Ishigaki Rin 'Mazushii machi' ni yosete," *Quarterly Zen'ya* 4 (Summer 2005): 6–11. For the poem in question, see Itō, *Ishigaki Rin*, 116–18.
[46] Gendaishi techō, ed., *Ishigaki Rin*, 111–12.

deal with women's sexuality in some poems.[47] Unsurprisingly for a poet who pursues a radical and innovative treatment of themes such as women's corporeality, sexuality, and motherhood, Itō finds Ishigaki's attempts lukewarm. In her view, Ishigaki is unwilling to reveal herself and hence her poems tend to be "too verbose with too many metaphors and common onomatopoeia … she can write about her parents' sex but she doesn't want to write about her own sex." Even so, Itō admits: "these, too, represent women's being. They, too, represent honest and vivid ways of living as a woman."[48] In contrast, what Itō really admires is the "devastating reality" that abounds in many of Ishigaki's other poems, such as "Kinkakushi." "Simple, laconic, subversive, and honest. What other goal is there for those of us who have chosen to write modern poetry?"[49]

Just as Field finds profound meaning in the leftover tempura, Itō pays attention to a particular food that appears in "In front of me the pot and ricepot and burning flames": "crushed fish."[50] Puzzled by the word "crushed," Itō asked her older poet friend, Ishimure Michiko, whose Minamata-disease poetry was mentioned above, about it. Ishimure thought it might be a reference to the coarse chopping and crushing of small fish with bones such as sardines before putting them into a mortar to grind them and make fish balls for soup and frying. Itō apparently found this explanation so convincing that she could almost picture women crushing fish in a dimly lit kitchen.[51] This pursuit of "crushed fish" illustrates generations of women poets who have poured their love and passion into cooking as well as writing, "not for the sake of pride or worldly fame but / in order for these things to be offered to all humanity."[52] The act of "crushing" requires the appropriate tool, power, and technique. Citing the great charms of this poem – that is, "women's intelligence, sorrow, and determination … and even toughness, their wild animal-like nature, vitality … all these good things about women" – which would be greatly appreciated by men, Itō suspects that Ishigaki wanted to make men feel relaxed and unguarded so that she could take them down with a bang.[53] This theory that Ishigaki strategically ambushed her male readers is amusing and convincing. Itō cites the toilet poem, "Kinkakushi," as one example of such a bang. After an acute analysis of the rhythm, sounds, and freedom of the poem, Itō points out

---

[47] Itō, *Ishigaki Rin*, 301–2.
[48] Ibid., 303.
[49] Ibid., 307.
[50] Morton translates this as "diced fish" but "tataki tsubusareta" is, as Hiroaki Sato has translated it, "crushed fish."
[51] Itō, *Ishigaki Rin*, 295–97.
[52] Morton, *Poems of Masayo Koike, Shuntarō Tanikawa, Rin Ishigaki*, 89.
[53] Itō, *Ishigaki Rin*, 298.

in her frank, comic, subversive style that "Some women have no children, some no sex, some no job, and some don't cook; but there's no woman who doesn't go to the toilet. There's no woman who isn't a daughter, either."[54] She relates the seemingly personal story of Ishigaki's narrator-persona to "other women, to 'us.'"[55] This is yet another example of Ishigaki's poetic legacy taking on new life through other women's reading and writing.

We have seen some examples here of cultural issues in translation, especially of humor and food in poetry. Are Ishigaki's poems only accessible, in the end, to those who read Japanese? In response, I quote Janine Beichman's comment about her experience translating "Nameplates":

> But like all the best poetry, her poem works in more than its original context. One of the satisfactions of translation is transplanting a poem into a new context and then seeing it flower there. In this case, the poem flowered in a rather unusual way for me.[56]

This reminds us of Walter Benjamin's notion of the "afterlife" of a literary text through translation.[57] There is no single and finite "original" text that reigns over translation; rather, the text transforms and finds new life in different languages and contexts. And this applies not only to translation but to reading and rewriting. Thus the endlessly interpretable text and food in it continue to multiply and explore new relationships. Ishigaki's poetry attracts and demands our attention to specific linguistic, socio-historical, and political issues. The charm and power of her "crushed fish" dish, however, invites each reader and cook to reinvent the dish with the available ingredients across generations and geo-cultural boundaries.

BIBLIOGRAPHY

Aoyama, Tomoko. *Reading Food in Modern Japanese Literature*. Honolulu: University of Hawai'i Press, 2008.
Beichman, Janine. "Ishigaki Rin, the Venus of Tokyo." In *Across Time and Genre: Reading and Writing Women's Texts*, edited by Janice Brown, Brad Ambury, and Sonja Arntzen, 301–4. Conference Proceedings. Edmonton: University of Alberta, 2002.
"Poem Provides Advice about Identity: A Translator Explains What a Poem Means to Her." *Trends in Japan*, March 20, 2002. http://web-japan.org/trends01/article/020320fea_r.html.

---

[54] Ibid., 299–300.
[55] Ibid., 300.
[56] Beichman, "Poem Provides Advice," *Trends in Japan*, March 20, 2002, http://web-japan.org/trends01/article/020320fea_r.html.
[57] "The task of the translator" [first printed as introduction to a Baudelaire translation, 1923], in Walter Benjamin, *Illuminations*, translated by Harry Zohn; edited and introduced by Hannah Arendt (New York: Harcourt Brace Jovanovich, 1968), 69–82.

Benjamin, Walter. *Illuminations*. Translated by Harry Zohn. Edited and introduced by Hannah Arendt. New York: Harcourt Brace Jovanovich, 1968.

Copeland, Rebecca L., ed. *Woman Critiqued: Translated Essays on Japanese Women's Writing*. Honolulu: University of Hawai'i Press, 2006.

Eagleton, Terry. "Edible Écriture." In *Consuming Passions: Food in the Age of Anxiety*, edited by Sian Griffiths and Jennifer Wallace, 203–8. Manchester: Mandolin, 1998.

Field, Norma. "Iki no ii jikan: Ishigaki Rin 'Mazushii machi' ni yosete." *Quarterly Zen'ya* 4 (Summer 2005): 6–11.

Friederich, Lee. "Through Beastly Tears: Devouring the Dead in the Poetry of Ishigaki Rin." *Japanese Language and Literature* 43.1 (2009): 27–54.

Gendaishi techō, ed. *Ishigaki Rin*. Tokyo: Shichōsha, 2005.

Ishigaki, Rin. "Five Poems." Translated by Yukie Ohta and Rie Takagi. *positions* 3.3 (1995): 723–27.

Ishigaki Rin. Gendaishi bunko, 46. Tokyo: Shichōsha, 1971.

Ishigaki Rin sakuhin rōdoku CD. Appended to Gendaishi techō, ed. *Ishigaki Rin*. Tokyo: Shinchōsha, 2005.

"The pan, the pot, the fire I have before me." Translated by Hiroaki Sato. *Chicago Review* 25.2 (1973): 108–9.

Yūmoa no sakoku. Tokyo: Chikuma Shobō, 1987.

Ishigaki, Rin, and Hiroaki Sato. "Ishigaki Rin." *Poetry Kanto* 22 (2006): n.p. http://poetrykanto.com/issues/2006-issue/ishigaki-rin-2.

Ishigaki, Rin, and John Solt. "Life." *Mānoa: Pacific Journal of International Writing* 3.2 (1991): 32.

Itō, Hiromi, ed. *Ishigaki Rin shishū*. Tokyo: Iwanami Shoten, 2015.

Kawai, Hayao. *The Japanese Psyche: Major Motifs in the Fairy Tales of Japan*, Dallas: Spring, 1988.

Kijima, Hajime. *The Poetry of Postwar Japan*, Iowa: University of Iowa Press, 1975.

Kirkup, James. *Modern Japanese Poetry*, St. Lucia: University of Queensland Press, 1978.

Kobayashi, Takiji, and Zeljko Cipris. *The Crab Cannery Ship and Other Novels of Struggle*. Honolulu: University of Hawai'i Press, 2013.

Mizuta, Noriko. *Nijusseiki no josei hyōgen* [Women's self-expression in the twentieth century]. Tokyo: Gakugei Shorin, 2003.

Morton, Leith. "Feminist Strategies in Contemporary Japanese Women's Poetry." *Journal of the Association of Teachers of Japanese* 31.2 (1997): 73–108.

Modernism in Practice: An Introduction to Postwar Japanese Poetry, Honolulu: University of Hawai'i Press, 2004.

Poems of Masayo Koike, Shuntarō Tanikawa, Rin Ishigaki, Sydney: Vagabond Press, 2013.

Ōoka, Makoto, compiler, Paul McCarthy, trans., and Janine Beichman, ed. *101 Modern Japanese Poems*. London: Thames River Press, 2012.

Rimer, J. Thomas, and Van C. Gessel, eds. *The Columbia Anthology of Modern Japanese Literature*. Vol. 2. New York: Columbia University Press, 2007.

CHAPTER 17

Food, Hunger, and Irish Identity
Self-Starvation in Colum McCann's "Hunger Strike"
Miriam O'Kane Mara

Twentieth-century self-starvation episodes in Ireland point to the recurrence of hunger in Irish history and culture. For example, medieval *troscud* – fasting to protest an injury – has a history in Ireland long before the 1980s IRA hunger strikes. After the Great Famine, the use of starvation to proclaim complaint gains resonance, because so many Irish people starved against their will. Hunger strikes provide a way for political prisoners to declare grievances against the colonial power and thus gain access to Irish identity. In Colum McCann's novella "Hunger Strike," self-starvation appears to provide this connection to Irish identity.[1] McCann's representation of self-starvation in "Hunger Strike" expands representations of anorexia, emphasizing the political nature of all self-starvation.

McCann's novella proceeds from the historical reality of hunger strikes in the prisons of Northern Ireland during the 1980s, when Margaret Thatcher's policy of criminalizing sectarian political violence infuriated nationalist populations in Northern Ireland. Bobby Sands and nine others died in Her Majesty's Maze or Long Kesh prison carrying out the hunger strikes.[2] In "Hunger Strike" McCann uses a boy and his hero-worship of an uncle in prison to crystallize significance in their behavior, and their denial of food is vested with heroism. Yet, McCann also suggests the futility of the hunger strike, comparing it to a game of chess. In the novella, the boy and his mother leave war-torn Derry for a "holiday" in Galway to escape the horrific situation of the uncle's impending hunger strike. The narrative revolves around the boy, who is too young to fully understand the politics and the tactics of adults. He wishes to understand his uncle's

---

[1] I have argued elsewhere that Irish women who starve themselves seek (and are denied) political meaning as a path to Irish identity. Rather they are ignored or overly pathologized. See Miriam O'Kane Mara, "The Geography of Body: Borders in Edna O'Brien's *Down by the River* and Colum McCann's 'Sisters,'" in *The Current Debate about the Irish Literary Canon: Essays Reassessing "The Field Day Anthology of Irish Writing,"* edited by Helen Thompson (Lewiston: Edwin Mellen Press, 2006).

[2] Bobby Sands ran for Parliament while in prison, and died on hunger strike as an MP.

decision and attempts to replicate his physical sensations by not eating. The young protagonist seems to work in the direction of maturity with his behaviors, and many scenes in the novella describe strained mealtimes as a struggle between the boy and his mother. The boy's attempts to gain nationalist identity coincide with his efforts to distance himself from his mother, who wants to offer her son a nonviolent identity detached from sectarianism. Alternately, his uncle represents Irish nationalism and efforts of the colonized Ulster men to gain masculinity (and Irishness) through armed struggle. The boy stands between these opposing poles and tries to form a subjectivity of his own. His halting movement toward maturity becomes a frustrated coming of age story.

In a text addressing identity, the narrator also withholds the boy's name. Using dialogue to convey character, his mother on occasion identifies him as Kevin. The boy is not wholly nameless in the text, but he is unnamed by himself or the "all-knowing" narrator who tells us everything else. The boy's attempt to find an identity for himself seems linked to his own refusal – as well as the narrator's – to accept his given name. The boy in the novella needs to establish identity partially by creating boundaries around his body. The war, his immaturity, and his position in between two countries all create fear of invasion. The colonizer remains in Northern Ireland, and, especially during the troubles of the 1970s and 1980s, conducts its business on the bodies of Irish people through combat, crossing their body boundaries while artificially bolstering the created boundary between North and South. In *Formations of Violence* Allen Feldman suggests that the political prisoners exemplify the larger colonial imprisonment, arguing that the prisons "encapsulated a wider colonial power which has imprinted discourses of domination upon their bodies. There was a semantic and historical equivalence between the colonization of Ireland and the colonization of the Blanketmen's bodies."[3] The young boy in "Hunger Strike" struggles against both geographic and corporeal boundaries in an attempt to understand how foreign others can be in control of the border lines in his own homeland. His confusion and questioning respond to Ireland's historical inability to decide their own borderlines and markers.

His situation underlines how identity is contingent on consumption of language, food, and the language of food. The boy's political identity is troubling in the Republic and Northern Ireland. He agonizes over his inability to fit into the new environment of Galway, knowing that he did

---

[3] Allen Feldman, *Formations of Violence: The Narrative of the Body and Political Terror in Northern Ireland* (Chicago: University of Chicago Press, 1991), 227.

not fit well in Derry either. In his musing, "He thought to himself that he was a boy of two countries with his hands in the dark of two empty pockets."[4] By repeating "two" McCann connects the sets of countries and pockets; he indicates that both countries *contain* an emptiness. Young Kevin, with a hand in either pocket and a foot in each country, walks in a void; neither place gives him appropriate answers, or provides him an easy identity. McCann indicates Kevin's lack of opportunity for development of subjectivity in either space.

These two spaces differ in language as well. Early in the narrative the boy notices the differences between the North, where use of Irish could be dangerous, and the Republic where Irish appears on almost all road signs and government documents. Seemingly for the first time, he is faced with the (Irish) language that might have been his own: "He stopped and looked at the sign that gave the name of the town in two languages – he could not make the connection between them, the English being one word, the Irish being two. He tried to juggle the words into each other but they would not fit."[5] Confronting the question of identity through language, McCann's protagonist grapples with the same tundish as Stephen Dedalus.[6] The sign evokes more than difference in both a splitting and rehybridization of identity. It attempts to acknowledge the reality of the English language in Ireland and the importance of (re)integrating Irish. The young protagonist makes sense of earlier suppression of the Irish language in Ireland and the subsequent appropriation of English, as well as attempts to recover Irish there. The words do not fit and yet they exist together on the sign, just as they do in the postcolonial Republic.

Non-verbal communication, and the language of food and eating become important symbols of political identity. When the boy reminisces about his mother playing the guitar and singing in the pub back home, he contrasts his previous experience with the Galway pub where she sings now. Looking back at the pub in the North, the closed nature of the place surprises him: "They [pub-goers] were conspiratorial. They didn't talk loud or address each other by the clue of their first names. They hunched over their plates. It seemed to the boy that even the food was under siege."[7] For practical reasons of shielding their identities (names, and accents,

---

[4] Colum McCann, "Hunger Strike," in *Everything in this Country Must* (New York: Picador, 2000), 49.
[5] Ibid., 47.
[6] See James Joyce's *A Portrait of the Artist as a Young Man*, edited by Richard Ellmann (New York: Viking Press, 1964). The protagonist, Stephen Dedalus, encounters similar language questions when an English priest asks him whether the word tundish, meaning funnel, is Irish. The term is English.
[7] McCann, "Hunger Strike," 70.

can identify a person's religion and much else in Northern Ireland), the customers avoid names and keep voices down. Yet the food, too, becomes consequential to meaning in eating, and in fasting. Indeed food (like language and place) becomes so important in this text that it is *under siege*. Every scene containing foodstuffs becomes a battleground for Kevin, a space of tension where he uses food for communication. In these moments the text reveals the necessity of food, sustenance, as well as spiritual food, in the transmission of meaning or identity.

Within the family especially, behaviors at mealtime can be important modes of communication. Donnalee Frega explains: "As a language, food-related behavior is multifaceted, uniting both biological desire for food and the more complicated longing for less tangible 'foods' that humans crave: acceptance, respect, love, support, security, self-determination."[8] In "Hunger Strike," the boy makes the communicative function of food more obvious, turning his food into a makeshift alphabet. Rather than eating his bread, he sculpts it into a chess piece, the knight. In the midst of avoiding ingestion, "The boy began to mold the bread quickly. He moved it around the plate with the knife and it soaked up more sauce, took on a definite form. He thought of his uncle in prison: a single cell, the darkness outside, the sound of boots along a metal catwalk, the carving of days into a wall."[9] In the boy's mind food immediately reminds him of his uncle. When his mother "told him the knight [chess piece] looked delicious," he replies "It's not for eating, Mammy."[10] Not for eating but for communication and diversion, the chess piece instead becomes a marker in the boy's multi-modal silent conversation, including his refusal to eat. In this scene Kevin creates a material sign and makes manifest the language of food and starvation, creating a physical signifier for a symbolic act. In this moment, the rejection of food takes on a tangible shape, and the boy tries to reach his mother, who had wanted to play chess. In addition to his denial of food, now there is another reminder in the doughy chess piece.

McCann's text here suggests the importance of play in the language. The transformation from non-verbal communication to material marker hints at a Derridean fluidity of signifiers.[11] At the same time, the boy's choice of markers implies that the politics in Northern Ireland have been reduced to

[8] Donnalee Frega, *Speaking in Hunger: Gender, Discourse, and Consumption in Clarissa* (Columbia: University of South Carolina Press, 1998), 1.
[9] McCann, "Hunger Strike," 54.
[10] Ibid.
[11] Jacques Derrida explains play in Derrida, "Différance," in *Margins of Philosophy*, translated by A. Bass (Chicago: University of Chicago Press, 1982).

a sort of game. The boy wants to play with the meaning of food. For him, language has partially broken down and he must find an alternative, a better way to convey meaning. First, he uses his own body and his rejection of food to make meaning, and then the body of the knight, a replica of other bodies who have died in European wars. Using a game of strategy and a metaphor for war with chess, the boy shows his understanding of starvation both as a tactical move and as a sign of war or weapons. He refuses to connect the signifying chess piece to one specific meaning and explain himself, forcing both his mother and the reader to provide explanation.

Like the boy's early encounters with language, his uncle in prison, too, finds words linked to his identity. If food and eating (or not eating) seem linked to spoken language and the ability to communicate with words, McCann also creates a link to literacy and literature. After the uncle goes on hunger strike, language and books become a form of solace as: "he was reading books for the first time in years, poetry and a play by W. B. Yeats."[12] This uncle, on hunger strike, finds access to Irish culture and literature as a result of his starvation. Clearly, the absence of attention to bodily worries like caloric intake and maintaining appropriate body weight make way for more mental and spiritual pursuits like reading. This Jansenist response in the uncle reveals the continued belief in the separation, and perhaps opposition, of body and spirit in Irish culture. Yet it also reflects subtle conjunction between communication through language and the politics of food and eating.

Although Kevin cannot yet find himself through language or landscape, the text offers him another avenue toward growth. In the first scene of the narrative, the boy looks out of the window to view an older couple launching a kayak: "The kayak glided out … a bright yellow speck on the gray cloth of the sea."[13] It fascinates him, and his growth during the narrative connects to the kayak, as it provides access to the borderland ocean boundary of Ireland. The terrors and potentials of language reappear, when the boy finally speaks to the Lithuanian kayak owners. He again realizes the association between food and the manners and mores of mealtimes. He first wonders if their accent might be English, but rejects that theory, thinking that "English people … delivered their words on silver tongs. They spoke as if each word were being served with scones and china cups."[14] Language creates identity, just as food and mealtime

---

[12] McCann, "Hunger Strike," 96.
[13] Ibid., 45.
[14] Ibid., 105.

rituals establish cultural identity. The older couple with their difficult accents represent other, but not a dangerous other to Kevin. Of course, his thoughts link language with typical English fare like tea and scones.

Despite his interest in the kayak and his new surroundings, the base reality of food and mealtimes quickly intrude into the young boy's inner musings. The young protagonist problematizes food long before he mimics his uncle's hunger strike:

> The boy pushed his penknife into his plate and it slid among the beans and he thought it looked like an absurd kayak in a sea of red. He lifted it up and licked the handle and began spearing individual beans. They broke at the weight of this knife until he learned to pierce them lightly, and he held them in the air, on the tip of his knife, staring at them. He didn't eat at all.[15]

Even before Kevin decides to imitate his uncle, he feels annoyed at the necessity of nourishing his body. Instead of eating, the boy plays with his food, rendering it disgusting and unappetizing. Like language and space, food also becomes a possible (failed) venue for determining identity. The scene represents traditionally English beans as ugly or absurd, as if McCann's entire text has become anorexic. The boy views the knife like a kayak, referring to his new-found interest, but not even the boat metaphor can bring him freedom to eat. At the same time, the knife imagery establishes Kevin's new preference for masculine-coded items, potentially used for violence, over food.

His mother regards and notes the refusal to eat, but she has no appropriate response. Instead she carries on: "She poured two mugs of tea from the pot and began eating her own meal, feigning indifference."[16] Although the text suggests the mother can understand this non-verbal cue, she responds to it with the maternal urge to feed. She observes, "you haven't eaten all day. I bet you could eat that whole thing in, oh, two minutes flat."[17] As mother, she is expected to provide sustenance for her child, and his refusal to eat encroaches on her role as mother/feeder. The battle over Kevin's developing identity begins at the table. The boy both communicates and frustrates communication with his mother as part of his growth.

This movement toward a more adult identity becomes confused by the political conflict, which the characters cannot ignore. Soon after Kevin's creation of bread chessmen, the boy and his mother receive the news. The uncle takes the place of another prisoner, as Kevin's mother conveys: "He's

---

[15] Ibid., 50–51.
[16] Ibid., 51.
[17] Ibid.

on [hunger strike]."[18] The youngster tries to comprehend the choice his uncle has made, as he muses: "He was one of four prisoners on the strike – already, for each man dead another had replaced him and the boy found it strange that the living were stepping into the bodies of the gone."[19] In Kevin's view, the bodies of the men on hunger strike fuse into one body, as they allow the boundaries of their bodies to overrun those of the already dead revolutionaries. However, they disallow such fluidity of body borders, when the oppressors try to invade them with food. They shut out the prison food from their bodies in the same way they try to shut out the British governance of Northern Ireland. Those shifts in body borders and identity provide a complicated model for Kevin, who wants to shape his own identity using his body through their examples.

Their ongoing dissent complicates Irish identity, while working to build it. The boy knows that before the prisoners resorted to hunger, they engaged in another form of protest to the same end – to gain the status of political prisoner. Kevin reflects, "The men had their cells sprayed down by prison guards once a week and sometimes their bedding was so soaked they got pneumonia. When the protest failed they cleaned their cells and opted for hunger instead."[20] This "Dirty Protest" involves all of the unpleasant, foul emanations of the corporeal body. The guards confined them to the small space of the cell, with no freedom, no power, and no recourse. They realize that the body can itself be a weapon of communication and revert to abjection when all other avenues are gone.[21] Feldman describes the tactics of the prisoners: "The Blanketmen viewed the 1981 Hunger Strike as a military campaign and organized as such. For them, it was a modality of insurrectionary violence in which they deployed their bodies as weapons."[22] The boundaries of their homeland and now the boundaries of their identity are consistently broken, and they begin to use body boundaries to protest. First, they attempt to utilize the border where body becomes waste. Sweat and urine and feces break out of the body, naturally crossing the body boundaries, to become something else. As the abject they are ideal tools. Next, the prisoners turn to another border, the mouth, where food enters and becomes human, accepted into the body and transformed into cells

---

[18] Ibid., 55.
[19] Ibid., 57.
[20] Ibid., 58.
[21] Julia Kristeva conceptualizes abjection in Kristeva, *Powers of Horror: An Essay on Abjection* (New York: Columbia University Press, 1982).
[22] Feldman, *Formations of Violence* (Chicago: University of Chicago Press, 1991), 220.

of the body. The body with all of its inherent abjection becomes the focus and the weapon.

In his imaginings of starving bodies, the boy turns to visualizing his uncle's prison cell. In these attempts to take part in that assertion of identity, Kevin creates a jail for himself with artificial borders, "stak[ing] out a cell in the caravan, one window, one bed, a jug of water, a florescent light, a chair, a galvanized bucket for a chamber pot. He stayed in the space, not breaking its borders, hungry for three hours."[23] In recreating the space of the prison cell, the boy creates artificial borders, mirroring those of the prison. Somehow he understands the boundaries in the prison as a recreation of partition and its boundaries. The colonizers and jailers, like the architects of Partition, create a space where Irish Catholics are a powerless minority, and they contain the people they oversee.

When the boy's mother returns from her new job singing, the tension between hunger and plenty reemerges. He has been sitting in the cell of his own making feeling the pangs of hunger, and she comes in "carting groceries: sausages, eggs, cheese, black pudding, three fresh loaves of bread."[24] His mother wants to feed him, threatening the boy's uneasy relationship with food. The pressures of war, internment, and hunger strike have not diminished her role as provider and comforter; she still wants care for her family, but the boy's ability to accept her offerings grows more problematic. The hunger strike makes Kevin unwilling to pretend that food and mealtimes are normal. He wants his mother to understand that part of his identity is linked to the struggle in the North, while she wants to keep him separate from it.

Despite his mother's attempts to keep the boy safe and untouched by the troubles, she relates news of her brother-in-law's battle against hunger. She also describes the jailer's tactic of placing "food in his cell … I heard it's better food than they ever gave him before. And they count every last chip and pea."[25] British guards reverse English actions during the famine, when they removed available food from a starving island. Now, prison guards provide appetizing food for the strikers. The boy recognizes this perverse situation and feels the unfairness of tempting prisoners, calling the guards "'Pigs."[26] The boy's troubled relationship with food reflects the tensions of political hunger strike, and even his choice of epithets for the guard

---

[23] McCann, "Hunger Strike," 71.
[24] Ibid.
[25] Ibid., 72–73.
[26] Ibid., 73.

implies gluttonous animals. Similarly, the information deepens his existing aversion to food; knowing how others are tortured merely by the presence of food in their vicinity strengthens a growing revulsion about eating.

As a way of connecting, the youth imagines himself in his uncle's position. He creates detailed images of the prison in his mind by again moving into his own prison space at the back of the caravan. He visualizes the torturous presentation of delicacies that entice the hunger strikers and imagines "his stomach beginning the first of its small and poignant rumblings. A plate of cod appeared on the table beside him, with a slice of lemon and a big heaping of chips. An apple tart with ice cream. Packets of sugar for the tea. Milk in tiny little cartons."[27] The mental images of appetizing food displayed in the hunger strikers' cells serves to confuse and anger Kevin. He envisions the details of the meal and the surroundings to empathize with his uncle, but it does not provide any solace. Of course, prison guards provide the food not for nourishment, but for pain. Their supposed care for their captives represents a trap to interrupt the political aims of the Northern Irish prisoners.

Kevin, too, sees the food his mother provides as a trap; it forces him to examine the meanings of bodies and food and his ability to maintain a controlled relationship with food. Instead of appreciating the love and care that went into the meal's preparation, he resents the notion that they should enjoy food, when others are choosing to starve. He does not refuse the food yet, but he struggles with the idea of consumption. Kevin notes the traditional Northern Irish meal, observing that "she had prepared a full fry, which he pushed away at first but then he speared the sausages and broke the skin of the eggs and dunked the fresh bread and ate with an anger that gave him a stomachache."[28] The meal she prepares, often called an Ulster fry, complicates his eating even more with its connection to place and culture. Due to his uncle's suffering, food and eating are loaded with meaning and tensions that create impossible choices. For the young boy, enjoying food seems shameful in the context of a willfully starving man, "When he looked at his empty plate he imagined it full and then he threw his prison blanket across it and groaned and tried to stop the hunger pains and all the quiet necessary shiverings."[29] The boy again imagines that he has not eaten, that he does not enjoy the feast placed temptingly before him. The uncle's hunger strike places a burden of mindfulness about food

---

[27] Ibid., 74–75.
[28] Ibid., 76.
[29] Ibid.

that recreates the pain of the famine at the same time. He feels guilt and anger for eating, because it seems right to deny his body the food that others are strong enough to refuse. The hunger strikes also subtly reinforce messages about the weakness of flesh taught by Catholics. In the context of mortifying the flesh by denial and suppression of bodily appetites, restricting food intake seems a logical choice.

The tensions of mealtime seem to build together with the political tension. The boy cannot separate the hunger strike from his daily understanding of the world and from his own meals. He listens to the news while avoiding his dinner: "At the table he looked at his meals, pushed the food around on his plate. Every day there was news of an impending reconciliation, but always the talks broke down and even the radio announcers sounded tired."[30] For Kevin politics and food have been linked, and he cannot effectively disconnect them. The move from disinterested follower of the news to bodily participant in the struggle begins. Although he has no way of affecting the political situation, Kevin "decided he would not take food. When his mother wasn't watching, he swept the chicken and rice off his plate and he stuck only to water."[31] By mimicking his uncle's hunger strike, the young boy feels involved. Rebecca Graff-McRae agrees that "Kevin literally incorporates and embodies the strike, he also seeks ways to act out (as performance and as misbehavior) his experience of personal and political turmoil."[32] In what seems a simple act of mimicry, this youngster taps into the anorectic's need for control. Frega explains: "It is essential that such struggles for autonomy [refusals to eat] be understood as a means both of self-expression and of communication."[33] Anorectics cite the desire to maintain discipline over some aspect of their world as a prime motivator in the decision to avoid or limit food.[34] For Kevin, limiting food becomes one small mode of response to a world that seems mostly outside of his influence.

Like anorectics and unlike prison protestors, Kevin maintains his behavior in secret. He hides his wasted food and his hunger from his mother, when "At breakfast he took his cornflakes outside and dumped them in the long grass."[35] While the young boy may feel like his struggle against

---

[30] Ibid.
[31] Ibid., 77.
[32] Rebecca Graff-McRae, "Fiction, Encryption, and Contradiction: Remediation and Remembrance of the 1981 Hunger Strikes," *Nordic Irish Studies* 13.1 (2014): 27.
[33] Frega, *Speaking in Hunger*, 3.
[34] See Susan Bordo, *Unbearable Weight* (Berkeley: University of California Press, 1993).
[35] McCann, "Hunger Strike," 77.

food and his body's appetite works in conjunction with his uncle's battle, he does not publicly starve himself for ostensibly political ends. Instead he makes no demands, and he gives no objective, other than solidarity with his uncle. Neither the boy nor the reader knows exactly what might cause him to end his forced starvation. As Graff-McRae notes, "even as it [Kevin's protest] upholds the dominant narrative of communal identification and political unity, this vicarious memory permits individual agency, difference, and division."[36] As the boy continues to avoid food, he looks for evidence of community meaning in his efforts, even as he differentiates from his mother through starvation. While he eschews eating, he obsesses about the physical changes caused by starvation as "he stretched out his torso and thought about how flat his belly was becoming. The boy looked for clues to his uncle's body in his own: the chest concave, the ribs taut, the arms bare and rippled. His mother caught him staring in the mirror but she said nothing."[37] His body in some way becomes a marker for the sense of place and belonging that has eluded his similar search through language. It symbolizes more than his identity; it merges with an Irish fellowship of starvation and sacrifice with the IRA prisoners, the hunger strikers, and even the victims of the famine. The normal changes of adolescence become augmented by the alterations resulting from his fasting. By watching his body grow thin as a result of restricting calories the boy begins to understand the power of the body in staking individuality within identification.

Part of the new identity that the boy creates is the façade of control. His ability to deny his body's cravings connects with a new-found willingness to evade or mislead his mother:

> At dinnertime he asked if he could eat outside on his own, and when his mother agreed he walked out, feeling lightheaded, with a dull throb in his stomach now.
> He threw the plateful in the grass beside the morning's cornflakes, most of which had already been picked over by seagulls.[38]

After fasting for over a day, Kevin experiences the power of autonomous decisions about his corporeality. He continues to avoid calories in secret rather than making his aims known or even understanding those aims. He not only controls the body he has been forced to accept, he evades the authority and watchful eye of his mother. Thus, the autonomy of growing up and separating from parental control becomes perversely connected

[36] Graff-McRae, "Fiction, Encryption, and Contradiction," 31.
[37] McCann, "Hunger Strike," 77.
[38] Ibid., 78.

to his decision to avoid food. For many anorexia patients, refusing food responds to desire for control, and Kevin's rejection conforms to this trigger. Yet he considers his decision not to eat as a hunger strike, similar to the prisoners. As the "church bells struck eleven chimes," he muses that "He had been on hunger strike for thirty-four hours now."[39] In naming his fight to starve his body of nutrients "hunger strike," the youth maintains his relevance to his uncle's cause. Using food behavior, he can participate in that limited Irish identity without getting arrested.

Kevin's *decision* to break the hunger strike or fast is made in secret, just as the avoidance of calories had been secret. The young boy sneaks to the chip shop rather than eating in front of his mother. The young woman minding the shop comments that Kevin is "the first customer of the morning,"[40] remarking on his unusual, early-morning binge. He responds by "nod[ing] and look[ing] at his reflection in the stainless steel frontispiece of the counter. It made his face alternately fat and thin."[41] Even as he decides to break his fast, the boy notices his body as something separate from his mind, a thing to be observed, illustrating the Cartesian split. His musings also "reflect" the conflict in him, whether to give in to hunger and eat or to go on starving. His face in the counter shows "fat" and contented, alternating with "thin" and peaked, strained with the denial of basic human needs. The struggle of mind and body reflects in the countertop.

Kevin rejects food *at home*, but he cannot find strength to abstain completely. He breaks down and eats, full of regret. The narrator observes, "When he finally came out of the chip shop he was weeping, the vinegar so pungent that afterward he could smell it on his hands for days."[42] In his inability to remain on hunger strike in solidarity with his uncle, Kevin weeps at his betrayal, and at the fragility of human will. The food has nourished his body and his guilt, but it also removes one access to Irish identity through hunger strike. The boy has failed at his attempt to martyr himself to match his Christ-like uncle. Now the symbol of his failure reminds us of the vinegar offered to Christ when he was thirsty on the cross.

Even though he grudgingly eats, the boy continues to maintain secrecy as a tactic to retain his supposed autonomy over food from his mother. He still hides his anorexic attitudes; despite being "badly constipated after

---

39 Ibid.
40 Ibid.
41 Ibid.
42 Ibid., 79.

his hunger strike[,] he had not told her the reason why."[43] The boy subtly knows that his struggle with hunger is taboo, both because food is readily available – making him wasteful – and because he cannot define his self-starvation. While he slyly allows his mother to see and know some of his distress, he does not explain it or give her any reassurance. Such manipulative behavior reflects the youngster's conflicting feelings about autonomy and support, about strength and weakness. He uses his control over eating habits to substitute for true autonomy and maturity.

The old couple with the kayak feed the boy, sharing their traditional foods to create community and bridge the gap between them. For them eating is a non-threatening part of the day-to-day routine, but Kevin reflects that: "it was the worst soup the boy had ever tasted in his life, yet still he told her it was lovely."[44] In the insignificance of their rituals, the boy pretends that eating is normal. He still understands the need to equivocate and attempt to appreciate the food. And yet mealtimes make him uncomfortable, as a "feeling of emptiness hit his stomach and he put his teacup down on the table and asked to be excused."[45] The boy cannot accept the normalcy of sharing a meal with this couple. To him it seems unnatural to feel comfortable eating, to enjoy both food and company without examining their meaning.

The continuing conflict between normal behavior and the tensions of sectarian issues resurfaces at mass on Sunday. The social importance of shared meals grows to include confusion about the Last Supper and its reenactment during the Eucharist. During the consecration for communion, the boy cannot forget about his uncle's struggle: "For the first time he properly heard the words: This is the body of Christ. He wondered if the hunger strikers who had already died had taken the last rites and, if they had, did they receive bread before they died?"[46] In the conundrum of communion as sustenance, the boy stumbles upon another vital question of identity. He wonders if hunger strikers remain Catholic when they do not participate in the sacrament of communion and whether their slow suicide is a sin.[47] As he struggles with identities, he questions the connections between Irishness and Catholicism, between revolutionary and church supporter. As Kevin begins to understand, attempting to preserve an Irish Catholic identity may, in fact, diminish the prisoners' religious affinity.

[43] Ibid., 80.
[44] Ibid., 137.
[45] Ibid.
[46] Ibid., 117.
[47] The Catholic church concluded that the hunger strikes were not suicide.

The boy continues to wonder about the intricacies of taking last rites (communion) while on hunger strike. He becomes fascinated with the interconnection between physical and spiritual in the sacrament: "He found himself tortured by the question and he had visions of emaciated men walking around the prison hospital with single patches of white on their tongues wondering whether they should swallow or not."[48] Astutely noting that the very basis of Catholicism reflects consumption of both physical and spiritual food in the Eucharist, McCann's text hints at another core of nutritive tensions in Ireland. The tradition of the Last Supper remains central to Catholicism. By offering his body and blood as spiritual food for his followers, Jesus combined the sacred with the base. The ritual of the mass replicates his realization that sharing food with loved ones is a significant aspect of humanness. Although Catholicism in its Jansenist form demands a denial of bodily appetites, and imposes separation between physical and spiritual, the tradition of the Last Supper in the sacrament of communion contradicts this split. The church insists on the actual physicality of God's body through transubstantiation, reflecting the importance of the corporeal aspect of the sacrament and the very tangible meal that Christ and his apostles shared.

Beyond communion, all food remains difficult for Kevin, as his uncle grows weaker and begins losing his sight. When his mother prepares pancakes, both Kevin and his mother respond to the food oddly: "They sat at the table, both of them cutting up the pancakes into smaller and smaller pieces," attempting to make palatable portions of the pancakes, trying to assimilate the food and their life situations, neither of which will go down easily.[49] Attempting to break through his anorexic reaction, the boy tries to eat: "To make her happy he poured some syrup on the pancakes and ate them with as much relish as he possibly could. The syrup tasted exceedingly sweet and he washed it down with quick mouthfuls of tea. For a moment he felt he might vomit."[50] The pleasant feelings often related to food and eating have been replaced with a fear and loathing of both the food and the act of eating. This youngster experiences almost physical illness with the feel and taste of pancakes in his mouth, but he also feels compelled to placate the mother/feeder who communicates love with food.

In the final scene of the novella, Kevin's uncle has died, and he feels an inability to form an appropriate response. Instead he lashes out in anger at

[48] McCann, "Hunger Strike," 117–18.
[49] Ibid., 141.
[50] Ibid.

the people and the hobby, which have given him solace, a solace for which he feels guilty:

> He picked up a larger rock and flung it, and again it just bounced away from the kayak and he cursed the boat's resilience … His whole body was trembling now. He was on a street. He was at a funeral. He had a bottle of fire in his hands. He was in a prison cell. He pushed a plate away from his bedside.[51]

Even in these moments of complete abandon to his hostility, the refusal of food creeps into his thoughts. The last sentence seems an odd place to end his musings, except that food and its rejection becomes the focal point of this work, echoing the starvation of the Great Famine in both the hunger strikers in prison, refusing food for political reasons, and in the young boy's budding anorexia, refusing food because it cannot be trusted in an Ireland with such a history.

In "Hunger Strike" the representation of deliberate starvation becomes the focal point. McCann's novella represents a frustrated bildungsroman where the child does not quite develop into an adult and gain a place in society, just as Northern Ireland remains the stepchild of partition between Ireland and England. By describing a young boy's attempts to understand and create an identity, both by starvation and other more traditional methods, McCann addresses complex political issues surrounding food in Ireland. The boy's movement toward Irish identity emphasizes the double-edged use of self-starvation as a means to political action.

BIBLIOGRAPHY

Bordo, Susan. *Unbearable Weight*. Berkeley: University of California Press, 1993.

Derrida, Jacques. "Différance." In *Margins of Philosophy*, translated by A. Bass. Chicago: University of Chicago Press, 1982.

Feldman, Allen. *Formations of Violence: The Narrative of the Body and Political Terror in Northern Ireland*. Chicago: University of Chicago Press, 1991.

Frega, Donnalee. *Speaking in Hunger: Gender, Discourse, and Consumption in Clarissa*. Columbia: University of South Carolina Press, 1998.

Graff-McRae, Rebecca. "Fiction, Encryption, and Contradiction: Remediation and Remembrance of the 1981 Hunger Strikes." *Nordic Irish Studies* 13.1 (2014): 19–39.

Joyce, James. *A Portrait of the Artist as a Young Man*. Edited by Richard Ellmann. New York: Viking Press, 1964.

---

[51] Ibid., 150.

Kristeva, Julia. *Powers of Horror: An Essay on Abjection.* New York: Columbia University Press, 1982.

Mara, Miriam O'Kane. "The Geography of Body: Borders in Edna O'Brien's *Down by the River* and Colum McCann's 'Sisters.'" In *The Current Debate about the Irish Literary Canon: Essays Reassessing The Field Day Anthology of Irish Writing,* edited by Helen Thompson. Lewiston: Edwin Mellen Press, 2006.

McCann, Colum. "Hunger Strike." In *Everything in this Country Must.* New York: Picador, 2000.

CHAPTER 18

Postcolonial Hungers

Deepika Bahri

Zimbabwean writer Tsitsi Dangarembga's 1988 novel *Nervous Conditions* introduced the world of letters to a formidable array of women characters struggling under the yoke of colonial and patriarchal domination in pre-independence Rhodesia. The novel memorably features Nyasha, the anorexic daughter of England-educated patriarch Babamukuru, and her country cousin Tambu, the narrator who believes that education will deliver her from the privations of the rural homestead.[1] Hunger and alimentary scarcity emerge as the engine powering Tambu's escape from the homestead, while Nyasha's emaciated frame betrays sociogenic symptoms of a disturbed order in which the imbricated discourses of food, hunger, and power enact their drama on living bodies. Having promised a story about "my escape and Lucia's … my mother's and Maiguru's entrapment; and … Nyasha's rebellion … [which] may not in the end have been successful," the novel nonetheless ends inconclusively as Tambu, the narrator, ruminates on "being young then," and promising a sequel in the suggestive phrase, "seeds do grow."[2] That sequel materialized in the far more pessimistic *The Book of Not* (2006) with a calmer, medicated Nyasha, and Tambu as a scholarship student anxious about full access to the foods and other facilities allowed her as "a biologically blasphemous person" at the majority white Sacred Heart Convent during Zimbabwe's struggle for independence.[3] This chapter of Tambu's student life is followed by a disillusioning stint at an advertising firm in the newly independent Zimbabwe where her award-winning copy for the hair product "Afro-Shine" is stolen by her white boss, much as her brother Nhamo had stolen the maize she was growing to pay for her school fees in *Nervous Conditions*. The novel ends with the escapee at a loss, wondering "what future there was for me, a new Zimbabwean."[4]

---

[1] Tsitsi Dangarembga, *Nervous Conditions* (London: Women's Press, 1988), 179.
[2] Ibid., 1, 203.
[3] Tsitsi Dangarembga, *The Book of Not* (Banbury, UK: Ayebia, 2006), 64.
[4] Ibid., 246.

The seeds of Dangarembga's debut novel, growing into the bitter harvest of independence manqué in *The Book of Not*, bear strange fruit years later in an unexpected surrogate sequel. Published more than a quarter century after *Nervous Conditions*, NoViolet Bulawayo's *We Need New Names* (2013) introduces us to Darling, one more escape artist, driven by hunger from twenty-first century postcolonial Zimbabwe to her diet- and exercise-obsessed Aunt Fostalina's home in "America," a country that has converted "the stroll into exercise and food into calories."[5] At the start of Bulawayo's novel, we learn that hungry children have been stealing guavas from the trees in an area called Budapest, where the rich live, in a stratified town in Zimbabwe. In graphic, scatological passages, Bulawayo describes the experience of painful excretion resulting from the chewing of guava seeds as akin to "trying to give birth to a country."[6] These are some of the seeds making their way through the alimentary tracts of hungry children in an oblique reminder of Tambu's much more hopeful promise, "seeds do grow," near the conclusion of *Nervous Conditions*. In Bulawayo's novel, years after she leaves her home in Zimbabwe and finds herself in Michigan, Darling will welcome the receipt of a package of guavas – her constipating madeleine from a hungry childhood. Each bite unleashes her involuntary memory, as she finds herself "back in my Paradise, my Budapest" where the great hunger continues unabated.[7] More and more "children of the land" are leaving home with "hunger in their stomach and grief in their footsteps" so "their hunger may be pacified in foreign lands." In "America," the immigrants eat "like wolves, like dignitaries … like kings," past the point of hunger, eating for those "still back there." But in Darling's neighborhood in America, gunshots ring out, a neighbor drowns her children in a bathtub, and there are poor people "who lived on the streets, holding up signs to beg for money."[8] Bulawayo's long scream of a novel turns its fury upon colonial *and* indigenous tyrants, who are ranged in a global lineup of forces responsible not only for postcolonial hungers in the "kaka places" of the world, but the concomitant production of "Destroyedmichygen" (Detroit, Michigan in a cunning use of kenning) in real, developed "country-countries" plagued by the same corrupt neoliberal order, and its implication in global wars and poverty.

[5] NoViolet Bulawayo, *We Need New Names* (New York: Back Bay Books, 2013); Max Horkheimer and Theodor W. Adorno, *Dialectic of Enlightenment: Philosophical Fragments,* translated by Edmund Jephcott (Stanford: Stanford University Press, 2002), 196.
[6] Bulawayo, *We Need New Names*, 18.
[7] Ibid., 188.
[8] Ibid., 148, 241, 190.

This chapter explores the hunger narrative as a species of *postcolonial literary and political enjambment,* an intertextual phenomenon typified by two different writers taking up a temporally discontinuous but thematically connected screed on postcolonial hungers, food, and power. The inaugural gesture of the postcolonial hunger narrative arraigns history for its failure to meet humanity's most fundamental need, what Theodor Adorno describes as "the coarsest demand: that no one shall go hungry anymore."[9] The "engines of a great hunger," in the words of Dambudzo Marechera in his 1978 collection of stories, *The House of Hunger,* nonetheless grind on in many parts of the world, and leave us with Doris Lessing's overwhelming question in her last novel: "What will our descendants blame us for as we now blame the slave traders? Surely that is easy enough. They will say that one half of the world stuffed itself with food while the other half was hungry."[10] In expanding Darling's narrative into "America," Bulawayo indicts the collective betrayal of colonialism, native elites after independence, *and* the global regime of neoliberal capitalism which continues to divide the world into the hungry and the well-fed. Moreover, in the perverse logic of simultaneously economic and cultural globalization, famine and scarcity coexist with the global meme of ascetic thinness as an aesthetic ideal for women, promoting voluntary starvation despite plenty. The escape artists of Dangarembga's and Bulawayo's novels and their anorexic female hunger artists ask for a reckoning with the politics of food, food distribution, and women's voluntary self-denial as signs of "the malign order ... of a disturbed universe."[11] As I argue, the postcolonial hunger narrative ultimately showcases the alignment of power and foodways by asking us to consider not only who eats, how much, and in what order, but also whether the pleasures of food and eating are distributed equally, especially for women, immigrants, and other alimentary sub-citizens in the gastropolitical order.

Although this chapter examines postcolonial hungers through a focus on Zimbabwean literature, the ethical questions raised by these texts are relevant to a broader consideration of alimentary subalternity. The

---

[9] Theodor Adorno, *Minima Moralia,* translated by Edmund Jephcott (London: Verso, 2005), 156.

[10] Dambudzo Marechera, *The House of Hunger* (Oxford: Heinemann, 1978), 140; Doris Lessing, *Alfred and Emily* (New York: HarperCollins, 2008), 238.

[11] Marechera, *House of Hunger,* 18. See also Thanassis Cambanis on the "bread politics" underlying recent events such as the Arab Spring in Egypt, which he describes a "revolution of the hungry." Cambanis observes that "the ruler who controls the main staples of life – bread and fuel – often controls everything else, too." Cambanis, "The Arab Spring Was a Revolution of the Hungry," *Boston Globe,* August 23, 2015, www.bostonglobe.com/ideas/2015/08/22/the-arab-spring-was-revolution-hungry/K15S1kGeO5Y6gsJwAYHejI/story.html.

stereotypical association of hunger and famine with Africa and South Asia (and once with the Soviet Union, China, and Ireland) obscures the extent to which food insecurity is experienced more pervasively. The scandalous reappearance of hunger in independent twenty-first century Zimbabwe might seem at first to fit all too snugly within a predictable narrative of the unsuitability of the colonized for self-rule,[12] or of the phenomenon of "the mourning after" decolonization described by Neil Lazarus, and predicted by Frantz Fanon who understood that "natives, like the erstwhile colonizers, do not lose sight of the main chance."[13] Dangarembga's *Nervous Conditions*, *The Book of Not*, and Bulawayo's *We Need New Names* illuminate the itinerary of hunger in Rhodesia/Zimbabwe as a product of colonial *and* native corruption, now working in tandem with global arrangements of capital. The postcolonial hunger narrative thus challenges a lazy understanding of the postcolony as uniquely incompetent and corrupt, while also unexpectedly exposing divides within the first world. In the shared penumbra of global capitalism, Aijaz Ahmad's words ring ever truer today:

> we live not in three worlds but in one [China, Russia included] ... this world includes the experience of colonialism and imperialism on both sides of [Frederic] Jameson's global divide ... the different parts of the capitalist system are to be known not in terms of a binary opposition but as a contradictory unity – with differences, yes, but also with profound overlaps.[14]

Postcolonial hungers, then, far from substantiating tired clichés of third world scarcity and ineptitude, should be understood within a corrupt system of appropriation and various forms of theft in a globe girdled by capital and corporation in the phase following imperialism as a special stage of capitalism.

   Both Dangarembga and Bulawayo detail explicit scenes of stealing in their novels – unpunished and unprosecuted crimes that are tolerated, even routine. The trope of theft, and justifications for it, deployed and detailed variously in the novels, provides a structural matrix for examining the problem of hunger on the one hand, and rampant robbery of the right to food, rightful portions, the pleasures of eating, as well as the right to the fruits – literal and figurative – of one's own labor on the other. Foucauldian

[12] See Dipesh Chakrabarty's discussion of the politics of historicism to validate colonial decisions to deny self-rule to the colonized in Chakrabarty, *Provincializing Europe: Postcolonial Thought and Historical Difference* (Princeton: Princeton University Press, 2000).

[13] Neil Lazarus, *Resistance in Postcolonial African Fiction* (New Haven: Yale University Press, 1990), 211; Frantz Fanon, *The Wretched of the Earth*, translated by Constance Farrington (New York: Grove Weidenfeld, 1991), 144.

[14] Aijaz Ahmad, "Jameson's Rhetoric of Otherness and the 'National Allegory,'" *Social Text* 17 (Autumn 1987), 9.

notions of "a margin of tolerated illegality [illegalism]" offer a seemingly relevant theoretical model for this exploration.[15] In recent years, the concept of illegalisms has been explored with regard to money-laundering, corporate crime, and a range of economic and financial illegalisms, with a turn away from Foucault's focus on the law and toward the unprosecuted and rampant misappropriation of resources by plutocrats today. The idea of tolerated illegalisms is valuable for a postcolonial inquiry, not only in the relevant arena of the law and corporate and financial infractions, but I argue, in the hitherto unexplored arena of the domestic sphere in which it is *custom* that makes the law. Aristotle's propositions about the embeddedness of the *oikos*, the household, within the *polis*, the city-state, connect these realms. In the polis and the home, order implies a pecking order. What is tolerated, even *required*, in a system in which scarce resources are necessarily distributed unevenly, is the theft of someone else's right.

Dangarembga's detailing of the politics of the *oikos* – expanding from the homestead, Tambu's uncle's mission, and the Sacred Heart Covent to Tambu's hostel and her advertising firm – amplifies the gendered, colonial dimensions of these forms of robbery. *Nervous Conditions* begins by invoking a moral universe in which guilt and responsibility are simultaneously assumed but disavowed in the thirteen-year-old narrator Tambu's admission that she "was not sorry when [her] ... brother [Nhamo] died."[16] Nhamo dies of an illness while studying at their prosperous, England-educated Uncle Babamukuru's mission in Umtali. He has gone there in a bid to "distinguish himself academically" and allegedly to eventually lift Tambu's father Jermiah's branch of the family "out of the squalor in which ... [they] are living" on their rural homestead. Nhamo, however, soon begins to behave as if the homestead "no longer had any claim on him," refusing to help with chores and lording it over his younger sisters.[17] The novel's inception, in an admission that should but does not prompt apology or guilt in the narrator, leads to a narrative in which we come to learn why Tambu, far from regretting Nhamo's death, finds that it removes one of many impediments to her own advancement, since she is now next in line of succession for further education. In a morally disturbed universe, Nhamo's ill-treatment of his sisters is answered by Tambu's concomitant consideration and rejection of the expected regret that should attend his untimely death. Learning that her brother and father are to be provided

[15] Michel Foucault, *Discipline and Punish: The Birth of the Prison*, translated by Alan Sheridan (New York: Random, 1977), 82.
[16] Dangarembga, *Nervous Conditions*, 1.
[17] Ibid., 4, 7.

with sumptuous provisions as they prepare to go and receive Babamukuru and his family on their return home from England, Tambu expresses her desire to be part of this welcome party in terms of full alimentary citizenship: "I wanted to eat fresh cornbread, ashy roast peanuts and salty boiled chicken on the train at midnight too"; but she is told to curb her "unnatural inclinations."[18] Nhamo's gender-based birthright to the hope of a better future and a bigger portion, then, is founded in a system that robs Tambu of her share, even of the right to desire it, because it cannot be accommodated within the "natural" order.

The perennial hunger and malnutrition at the homestead, its deplorable, feces-splattered latrine, the constant labor of cultivating and harvesting an unyielding stony patch of land by hand, the preparation and serving of the choicest portions of food to the patriarchy, and the hasty consumption of remains by the women are some of the many burdens borne by women. Along with the privations of the homestead, the women endure routine appropriation of their labor in the service of men. Nhamo's sisters, Netsai and Tambu, must labor at the homestead and help their mother so their brother can attend school. On his occasional visits home, Nhamo makes his little sister carry his bags in a literal lightening of his own burden by unloading it on Netsai's young shoulders. Female labor is not withheld for fear of punishment; Netsai's solitary refusal to carry her empty-handed brother's bags at Tambu's suggestion, for instance, results in a sound thrashing and her conclusion that she should have just done it "in the first place."[19] Robbed of the power of refusal for fear of corporeal punishment, Netsai, needless to say, never refuses to carry his bags again. Even Tambu, who appears to demonstrate a keen sense of outrage at the injustice of a patriarchal order which simultaneously exploits and devalues her labor, participates in all the labor-intensive tasks on the homestead while the men await service. When Nhamo comes home, it is the sisters who must trap, kill, pluck, and prepare the chicken reserved for his return. Tambu "naively" entertains the thought that "the next time he wants to eat the chicken, Nhamo will catch it himself ... and kill it. I will pluck it and cook it. This seemed a fair division of labor." Tambu quickly admits to her naivety as she recalls that "Netsai's beating because of the luggage should have made it clear to me that Nhamo was not interested in being fair. Maybe to other people, but certainly not to his sisters, his younger sisters for that matter."[20] Moreover, on some of his

[18] Ibid., 33.
[19] Ibid., 10.
[20] Ibid., 12.

visits home, their brother returns with tea and sugar, "more often than not a gift from my aunt to my mother," but these too "Nhamo kept ... for himself."[21] Tambu nonetheless absolves Nhamo of any special brand of obnoxious behavior, explaining that he was "doing no more than behave, perhaps extremely, in the expected manner." Because of the division of labor at home, Tambu is "in Standard Three in the year that Nhamo died, instead of in Standard Five" as she "should have been by that age."[22] Compounding the injustice, Tambu's brother and father both rob her of the opportunity for advancing her education. Nhamo brazenly steals Tambu's maize, which she has been growing in her scant spare time to buy an education, and squanders it in gifts to friends, while her father steals the money Babamukuru has sent him for Tambu's fees. Later he attempts to steal the money donated to Tambu by a white couple for her education. In the face of this routine theft and her mother's acquiescence, albeit with "lips pressed tight," Tambu's affective detachment from her brother's death and her dislike of "everybody" represents her rejection of a patriarchal order in which alimentary subalternity is one sign among many of her subordination.[23] In a novel structured as a bildungsroman, however, it is the most potent sign of a disturbed order in which Tambu's growth and formation, physically and otherwise, are threatened by a chronic state of malnourishment.

The accident of Nhamo's illness and death allows Tambu to advance to the head of the line, out of order as it were, to step into Babamukuru's car, the vehicle of her eventual transport to "a better everything."[24] On their way to the mission, Tambu catalogs her "tight, faded frock," her calloused feet, the "scales on ... [her] skin ... due to lack of oil" and "short, dull tufts of malnourished hair," markings of her labor and her alimentary subalternity written on a body and person she hopes to leave behind. Beyond "mere sustenance of the body," a hitherto unavailable luxury, Tambu hopes to have the leisure and resources to nourish her spirit and consciousness.[25] Exulting at the prospect of a future self that is well fed, healthy, and groomed, Tambu comes upon the dining-room "with its large, oval table spacious enough to seat eight." Tambu reads in its "shape and size" an elaborate scripting of "the amount, the calorie content, the complement of vitamins and minerals, the relative proportions of fat, carbohydrate and protein of the food that would

[21] Ibid., 9.
[22] Ibid., 12.
[23] Ibid., 7, 12.
[24] Ibid., 179.
[25] Ibid., 58–59.

be consumed at it." "No one who ate from such a table could fail to grow fat and healthy," she muses, unaware that it is this very table, and its appropriation as a sign of Babamukuru's authority and control over his wife and daughter, that her sensitive cousin Nyasha will reject, responding to this control with anorexic and bulimic behaviors that imperil her very being in the alternative bildungsroman on offer in the novel.[26]

Along with conventional education at the mission, there are other lessons in store for Tambu, who quickly learns of the elaborate rituals at mealtimes under her Uncle Babamukuru's gastropolitical regime. Naomi Wolf writes that "food is the primal symbol of social worth ... publicly apportioning food is about determining power relations." "Crossculturally," Wolf concludes, "men receive hot meals, more protein, and the first helpings of a dish, while women eat the cooling leftovers."[27] This pattern is made amply clear at the Christmas reunion at the homestead where Babamukuru and his wife Maiguru provide the victuals. Maiguru jealously guards the meat, insisting that the patriarchy eat the meat stored in the small refrigerator while the remaining rotting meat is cooked and served to the women. The women cook and serve the dwindling food, eating last and little, without complaint. In Babamukuru's household, women may eat well but must wait till he is served. At the table, Aunt Maiguru replicates some of the practices of the homestead, fawning over her husband and eating his leftovers. Babamukuru puts out a token protest at her servility, following it up with a rebuke to Nyasha for helping herself to the rice before he has been served. Indeed, it is at the table that Tambu first witnesses Nyasha's confrontations with her father's authority. Later, Tambu learns that Maiguru is just as educated as Babamukuru, and that her wages are just as instrumental in helping to maintain the mission lifestyle and ample table that bedazzles Tambu, but her unacknowledged education and labor have been annexed to serve a societal order which awards their fruits and associated prestige to Babamukuru, lending him authority over the entire extended family. Babamukuru, in effect, has stolen her labor to enhance his position. We can assume from Maiguru's trajectory and Tambu's pursuit of further education along the same lines that she will continue to be schooled in the ways of a societal economy that will use her labor to support and enable the colonial and patriarchal order which will deny her, as it has Maiguru,

---

[26] Ibid., 69.
[27] Naomi Wolf, *The Beauty Myth: How Images of Beauty Are Used against Women* (New York: Anchor-Doubleday, 1991), 189–91.

the fruits of that labor. In the absence of inspiring female role models who can show her how to protest these indignities, Nyasha, unable to challenge Babamukuru's unfair governance of the microphysics of her behavior through control over her reading material, clothing, and social activities, chooses to launch an attack on her own body by denying it the food necessary to its survival by way of protest.[28] Psychosocial and cultural factors thus impede access to the pleasures of eating for alimentary subalterns even when food is plentiful. At the Sacred Heart Convent school where Tambu expects to find "better equipment, better teachers, better furniture, better food, better everything" in the closing pages of *Nervous Conditions*, there are even more sobering lessons in store about the politics of food.[29] A perverse sense of racial inferiority has so penetrated the sensibility of the black "nannies," or meal-servers, at Sacred Heart that "when they set a jug or plate before Ntombi or me" – the black children at a majority white school – they "smack it down with a jut of the chin and spills, as though slapping a hard, crushing thing down on obnoxious crawling objects."[30] In newly independent Zimbabwe, where her white landlady cannot tell the black residents in her hostel apart, even the black "tea boy" at the advertising agency that employs her "snarl[s]" at Tambu in Shona, putting her in her place by declaring: " 'I'm not your boy, I'm not your servant, he!' "[31]

So far, so patriarchal. So African, so postcolonial. As Chimamanda Adichie observes, however, "start the story with the arrows of the Native Americans, and not with the arrival of the British, and you have an entirely different story. Start the story with the failure of the African state, and not with the colonial creation of the African state, and you have an entirely different story."[32] If the patriarchal sociocultural complex comes in for sustained criticism in *Nervous Conditions*, Dangarembga nonetheless also targets the colonial order, detailing how it suffuses the mission, manifesting in its furniture, living arrangements, the table Tambu had found so impressive – complete with its many dishes and foods covered with "thick, white, tasteless gravy" and utensils the child finds a barrier to

---

[28] Unable to influence her decisions through argument, Tambu's mother also abjures food to protest her departure for the mission at first, and then Sacred Heart, because she thinks education and Englishness will kill Tambu as it has Nhamo. Dangarembga, *Nervous Conditions*, 184. In Bulawayo's novel, it is Uncle Kojo who abjures food when his son is sent to fight for the US in Afghanistan.

[29] Dangarembga, *Nervous Conditions*, 179.

[30] Dangarembga, *Book of Not*, 46.

[31] Ibid., 219.

[32] Chimamanda Ngozi Adichie, "The Danger of a Single Story," www.ted.com/talks/chimamanda_adichie_the_danger_of_a_single_story?language=en.

its actual consumption.[33] The *collusion* of patriarchal and colonial systems, moreover, is duly noted, particularly in Nyasha's revolt against colonial education, even as she is simultaneously battling her father's authority by refusing the provisions of "his" table. Finally, Dangarembga also makes the reader privy to a beginning prior to the novel's inaugural in 1968. Long *before* the conflicts at the table, *before* Babamukuru has access to a dining table and the amenities of the mission, *before* he leaves for England with his wife, *before* he is born, there is a prior history and a totally "different story" to be told, available in the brief accounts given by Tambu's grandmother who divulges what "could not be found in the textbooks." It transpires that the family was once wealthy "in the currency of those days." Her great-grandfather had

> cattle and land, goods to trade, and provided well for his many strong chil-
> dren until wizards well versed in treachery and black magic came from the
> south and forced the people from the land. On donkey, on foot, on horse,
> on oxcart, the people looked for a place to live. But the wizards were avar-
> icious and grasping; there was less and less land for the people. At last the
> people came upon the grey, sandy soil of the homestead, so stony and barren
> that the wizards would not use it. There they built a home.[34]

This abject story in the novel has a verifiable historical analogue. In 1888, Cecil John Rhodes' emissaries Charles Rudd, James Rochfort Maguire, and Francis Thompson, some of the aforementioned "wizards," persuaded King Lobengula of the Matabeleland kingdom to sign the Rudd Concession, granting exclusive mining rights throughout the country. This initial annexation was the foundation for the royal charter granted by the United Kingdom to Rhodes' British South Africa Company in October 1889, and thereafter for the Pioneer Column's occupation of Mashonaland in 1890, which marked the beginning of white settlement, administration, and development in the country that eventually became Rhodesia, named after Rhodes, in 1895. Under the settler colonial regime, land was divided such that forty-five million acres went to African people and forty-five million to Europeans.[35] Thirty-nine of the forty-five acres allotted to Africans were defined as Tribal Trust Lands, and comprised the least arable land in the country, the "stony and barren" patches referred to by Tambu's grandmother.

---

[33] Dangarembga, *Nervous Conditions*, 82.
[34] Ibid., 17–18.
[35] Sylvia Hill, "Facing Social Reconstruction in Zimbabwe," *The Black Scholar* 11.5 (1980): 40.

Until the dawn of independence, the *Christian Science Monitor* reported in 1980, "the country's mineral and agricultural riches had primarily bene-fited its 230,000 whites," and "the management of the country has been almost exclusively white."[36] While Tambu is groomed as a "woman with a future" at the Sacred Heart Convent – a promise that seems to be belied by the conclusion of the novel, her sister Netsai and others have been fighting for freedom and a more just distribution of resources.[37] On her visits home in *The Book of Not*, Tambu sees insurgents with "malnourished arms where the body had eaten its own meat in order to survive," and children with "cheekbones jutting like precipices."[38] These are the bodies built by empire, and its regime of depriving the moiety of its native subjects. After its hard-won independence, Zimbabwe had been promised that Britain would fund land reforms to redress old historical wrongs, but Britain reneged repeatedly, using various excuses. In the wake of Britain's vacillations, Mugabe's chaotic seizure of white farms, use of "land reform … as a tool of political patronage,"[39] redistribution of land to party cronies without the requisite farming experience or smaller African farmers without the capital to pay for fertilizer and equipment, the reluctance of foreign banks to extend necessary capital, and devastating drought followed by torrential rains, large numbers of Zimbabweans are facing chronic deprivation. A Bloomberg News report in early 2017 indicated that "some 4 million Zimbabweans, about a quarter of the population, need food aid, according to the government."[40] Zimbabwe has come to exemplify Fanon's dismal image of the postcolony, a place where "the people struggle against the same poverty, flounder about making the same gestures and with their shrunken bellies outline what has been called the geography of hunger."[41]

In opening the novel *We Need New Names* with a chapter entitled, "Hitting Budapest," Bulawayo does not begin her exploration of the geography of hunger at the impoverished site of a fictional Zimbabwean shantytown, "Paradise," where the poor live precariously. Instead, Darling, the narrator, begins with a tale of underage marauders on a mission: "There

[36] Robert Rotberg, "And Now – to Share Zimbabwe's Bounty." *Christian Science Monitor* April 17, 1980, www.csmonitor.com/1980/0417/041742.html.

[37] Dangarembga, *Book of Not*, 11.

[38] Ibid., 12, 19.

[39] Kevin Sieff, "Zimbabwean Farmers." *Guardian*, September 25, 2015. www.theguardian.com/world/2015/sep/25/zimbabwe-land-reforms-mugabe-white-farmers.

[40] "Rural Zimbabwe Empties as Mugabe Land Reform Policy Unravels." *Bloomberg News*, February 28, 2017, www.bloomberg.com/politics/articles/2017-02-28/rural-zimbabwe-empties-as-mugabe-s-land-reform-policy-unravels.

[41] Fanon, *Wretched of the Earth*, 97.

are guavas to steal in Budapest," a neighborhood with "big, big houses with satellite dishes on the roofs ... and the big trees heavy with fruit that's waiting for us."[42] Bulawayo redraws the Zimbabwean geography of hunger through the split portrait of Budapest/Paradise. Ten years old at the start of the story, Darling points the reader first to a place of spectacular wealth that may as well be a foreign country. Borrowing her nickname for this prosperous neighborhood from the name of a European capital, Bulawayo's choice employs a suggestive parapraxis in the slide between hungry and Hungary. The stolen vowel in the ellipsis points the reader to a young rabble *in extremis*, a condition that implicitly justifies a mission devoted to theft. The center, the source, and the recourse of the condition of hung[a]ry children is the capital, rich part of town. Here, in homes where rich whites and Africans live, are fridges full of "bread, bananas, yogurt, drinks, chicken, mangoes, rice, apples, carrots, milk ... things whose names [the children] don't even know," and people who brag about being on "the Jesus diet" and throw food away, criminally unaware that the desperately hungry children would have gladly eaten the leftovers.[43] The Manichean dichotomy of colonial urban planning is reproduced in the postcolony where native elites replicate an uneven economic order.[44] Fanon accurately divined the native's desire to take the settler's place, one secured by theft and exploitation disguised as industry and entrepreneurial acumen. Because "the iniquitous fact of exploitation can wear a black face," Fanon predicted, "the question which is looming on the horizon, is the need for a redistribution of wealth. Humanity must reply to this question, or be shaken to pieces by it."[45]

Bulawayo locates the children's petty larceny within a corrupt post-colonial regime emergent from the epic larceny involved in colonialism. Darling compares the children's theft with the grand theft of colonialism when recalling the death of her grandfather killed by white people "during the war for feeding and hiding the terrorists who were trying to get [her] country back because the white people had stolen it." If you must steal, she muses, it is better to steal something "small and hideable ... like guavas. That way, people can't see you with the thing to be reminded that you are a shameless thief and that you stole it from them." Marveling at the

---

[42] Bulawayo, *We Need New Names*, 6.
[43] Ibid., 131, 10, 12.
[44] Fanon writes that "The settlers' town is a strongly built town, all made of stone and steel. It is a brightly lit town" while "The native town is a hungry town, starved of bread, of meat, of shoes, of coal, of light." Fanon, *Wretched of the Earth*, 39.
[45] Ibid., 145, 98.

effrontery, she says, "I don't know what the white people were trying to do in the first place, stealing not just a tiny piece but a whole country. Who can ever forget you stole something like that?"[46] The point, of course, is that this criminal past is routinely forgotten, and compensation for victims rarely follows. Darling invokes the moral economy of shame and shamelessness, ostensibly to justify the children's decision to steal guavas without regret, much like Tambu who fails to be sorry in the wake of the death of her petty tyrant of a brother, Nhamo. Toggling between the *oikos* and the larger economic order, Darling positions the children's petty crimes within the theft of a whole country, its resources, its way of life, and of food from the bellies of a generation of colonized people forced to eke a living out of stony ground.

Although Bulawayo does not let us forget colonial theft, her ire is directed no less at native leaders who quell protests brutally, steal elections, terrorize their own subjects, and collude with emergent regimes of neoliberal capitalism. Darling recalls two distinct phases of postcolonial Zimbabwe ("home before [the ironically misnamed] Paradise, and home in Paradise, home one and home two") in her young life, one with "plenty of food to eat. Clothes to wear," a time of prosperity, jobs, dancing, parties, and happiness.[47] The new phase of hunger and turmoil well *after* independence, resulting in part from lack of capital and in part from Mugabe's chaotic and corrupt land reforms, indicts its "home grown" character as well as contemporary arrangements of capital.[48] Fanon predicts the withdrawal of capital which has been part of the production of Zimbabwe's geography of hunger. Fanon explains, "the newly independent people ... may see colonialism withdrawing its capital ... the colonial power says: 'Since you want independence, take it and starve' ... The spectacular flight of capital is one of the most constant phenomena of decolonization."[49] Farms held by natives in Zimbabwe have languished for lack for investment and capital, while the *return* of capital in the neoliberal order promises no respite. Coming from China, "a red devil looking for people to eat so it can grow fat and strong," investment is now directed not toward building "a school ... Flats ... [or] a clinic," but a "big, big mall" with "Gucci, Louis Vuitton, Versace."[50] The redirection of capital from land development,

[46] Bulawayo, *We Need New Names*, 22.
[47] Ibid., 193.
[48] David Smith, "NoViolet Bulawayo Tells of Heartbreak of Homecoming in Mugabe's Zimbabwe," *Guardian*, September 4, 2013, www.theguardian.com/world/2013/sep/04/noviolet-bulawayo-homecoming-mugabe-zimbabwe.
[49] Fanon, *Wretched of the Earth*, 103.
[50] Bulowayo, *We Need New Names*, 49.

education, housing, and health care toward consumption mahals for the rich works in cahoots with the interests of the native elite. In sum, it takes a world of corruption to starve Darling and her friends who were to have been the promise of the future of Zimbabwe after independence.

Although the withdrawal of the state from investment in services for the poor is not confined to former colonies, third world hunger and abjection nonetheless reconfirm stereotypes about the fabled lands of famine and corruption while obscuring domestic problems in the "real" places of the world such as America or their role in the production of the geography of hunger. Before Bulawayo sends Darling to America, with its own conflicted politics of food and power, she presents us with the spectacle of hunger in Zimbabwe as part of the geography of what Nigerian writer Teju Cole describes as "The White Savior Industrial Complex." Cole summarizes NGO and Western aid ventures in a crisp tweet: "The White Savior Industrial Complex is not about justice. It is about having a big emotional experience that validates privilege."[51] Bulawayo presents the reverse gaze of children upon their alleged benefactors in a searing description of the voyeuristic benevolence of the "NGO people" who "like taking pictures" when they arrive with their lorry full of goodies. The children "prefer they didn't do it" because they are "embarrassed by" their "dirt and torn clothing," but they don't complain because "after the picture-taking comes the giving of gifts."[52] In exchange for modeling the plight of the postcolony in a version of poverty porn that robs the children of any semblance of dignity, Darling is rewarded with "a toy gun, some sweets, and ... a T-shirt with the word *Google*."[53] Although it also carries "small" packets of food for adults, the NGO lorry transports goods with a problematic history: toy guns emblematic of the American military industrial complex; candy that points to the sugar industry with forgotten roots in the history of slavery; and a T-shirt sporting the telltale sign of the global reach of American power in the logo of a search engine that mediates much of our knowledge of the world today. A search for famine on Google, for instance, will readily yield images of a predictable geography of hunger in Africa and other places populated by the wretched

---

[51] Teju Cole, "The White-Savior Industrial Complex," *Atlantic*, March 21, 2012, www.theatlantic.com/international/archive/2012/03/the-white-savior-industrial-complex/254843. Later in the novel, Darling attributes her employer Eliot's enhanced benevolence toward her to the same video that provoked Cole's twitter response: "ever since the Kony video came out, he's been nice to me like I'm from Uganda." Bulawayo, *We Need New Names*, 271.

[52] Ibid., 54.

[53] Ibid., 57.

of the earth without any of the historical and neocolonial coordinates Bulawayo exposes.[54]

To escape this geography, Darling is sent to America where she will eat "real food," "all types and types of food," "all that food," but where eating disorders nonetheless prevail, where immigrants must eat their strange foods in secret, and where, moreover, "sometimes was the bang-bang-bang of gunshots in the neighborhood" and the homeless "holding up signs to beg for money."[55] Darling's journey also brings her into contact with immigrants fleeing not only from that part of Africa "where vultures wait for famished children to die," but also other "place[s] of hunger and things falling apart," with their colonial and neocolonial histories mined under.[56] Including references to Chinua Achebe's chronicle of the arrival of colonization, Vasco da Gama's discovery of India, US adventures in Iraq and Afghanistan, Bulawayo remaps the cartographic imaginary of the first and third worlds. The routes of contemporary migration are thus reconnected not only with the history of postcolonial corruption but also with the pernicious history of colonialism, and its neoliberal incarnations in a world torn apart by unbridled capitalism and the war complex. The deficient, ego-driven ministrations of the white-savior industrial complex unwittingly gesture at these imbrications while refusing to acknowledge them openly.

The refugee flees, moreover, to a place where refuge may be precarious, belying the promise held in popular imagination. In America, "they," who leave with "hunger in their stomachs" for the land of plenty, may eat "like kings," but will live in fear of detection if illegal, working at dangerous, ill paid jobs, and leave their traditions behind for the privilege of doing so.[57] Moreover, the immigrant escape artists will rediscover new hungers, no matter how much they eat, for a lost home and their own foods. Or they will walk away unsated from plentiful tables because the unfamiliar utensils are cumbersome, as Darling does at a wedding, exposing the table as a paradoxical source of hunger, or reduce themselves to bones voluntarily to approximate the increasingly powerful global ideal of feminine beauty, like her aunt, Fostalina. For every exemplar of "American fatness," like Dumi's bride at the wedding, or her cousin TK who "eats in one day"

---

[54] Cole co-implicates the aid industry with neo-imperial policies: "the white savior supports brutal policies in the morning, founds charities in the afternoon, and receives awards in the evening." Cole, "White-Savior Industrial Complex."

[55] Bulawayo, *We Need New Names*, 12, 155, 240, 190.

[56] Ibid., 239, 245, 51.

[57] Ibid., 148, 241.

what Darling and her grandma would in three, there is a "Miss I Want to Be Sexy" Kate, her employer Eliot's daughter, who has "a fridge bloated with food" – like the wealthy in Budapest – but restricts herself to "five raisins, one little round thing, and a glass of water" for breakfast, robbing herself of necessary nutrition, like Dangarembga's anorexic Nyasha, and the thirty-three year-old visitor to Budapest from London who looks "only fifteen, like a child" to Darling and her friends, because she has been on "the Jesus diet."[58]

The imbricated narratives of food and power acquire a broad gloss in Bulawayo's novel, positioning the scandal of twenty-first century hunger within the tradition of anti-colonial writing as well as a more complex geopolitical scape of the hunger narrative. Darling is "embarrassed" by the homeless and hungry in Destroyedmichygen, because "they made America not feel like My America, the one I had always dreamed of back in Paradise."[59] Darling reintroduces the moral horizon of shame in her encounter with American hunger and poverty, an emotion invoked earlier with regard to the theft of guavas and the colonial appropriation of Zimbabwe, knitting them together. Reading *Nervous Conditions*, *The Book of Not*, and *We Need New Names* as a thematically connected screed on postcolonial hungers, food, and power challenges the usual boundaries of the geography of hunger by disclosing overlaps between real and "kaka" (aka "third world") places, as well as between the domestic and public spheres. These novels ask for an accounting of the politics of inclusion and exclusion that attends the availability, distribution, and consumption of food as well as the psychosocial dimensions of eating disorders. When Ariel complains that it's "evil to play with [Alonso, Gonzalo, and Sebastin's] hunger" as well as "their anxieties and their hopes" in *A Tempest*, Aimé Césaire's postcolonial rewriting of the Shakespearean play, Prospero explains, "That is how power is measured. I am Power."[60] The stories of Nyasha, Fostalina, Kate, the woman on the "Jesus Diet," and Darling's hunger in Paradise/Budapest are specific to their circumstances, but their diverse hungers, and those of the nameless beggars in Darling's America, bear witness to a gastropolitical order in which individual bodies are but a measure of power, whether of patriarchal systems, the state, or the pitiless forces of contemporary capitalism.

---

[58] Ibid., 173, 156, 270, 10.

[59] Ibid., 190. The National Public Radio series on "Hunger in America," and novels such as T. C. Boyle's *The Tortilla Curtain* furnish images of a hungry America which Darling unveils briefly in her comment.

[60] Aimé Césaire, *A Tempest*, translated by Richard Miller (New York: TCG Translations, 2002), 32.

BIBLIOGRAPHY

Adorno, Theodor. *Minima Moralia: Reflections on a Damaged Life.* Translated by Edmund Jephcott. London: Verso, 2005.

Ahmad, Aijaz. "Jameson's Rhetoric of Otherness and the 'National Allegory.'" *Social Text* 17 (Autumn 1987): 3–25.

Bulawayo, NoViolet. *We Need New Names.* New York: Back Bay Books, 2013.

Cambanis, Thanassis. "The Arab Spring Was a Revolution of the Hungry." *Boston Globe,* August 23, 2015. www.bostonglobe.com/ideas/2015/08/22/the-arab-spring-was-revolution-hungry/K15S1kGeO5Y6gsJwAYHejI/story.html.

Césaire, Aimé. *A Tempest.* Translated by Richard Miller. New York: TCG Translations, 2002.

Chakrabarty, Dipesh. *Provincializing Europe: Postcolonial Thought and Historical Difference.* Princeton: Princeton University Press, 2000.

Cole, Teju. "The White-Savior Industrial Complex." *Atlantic,* March 21, 2012. www.theatlantic.com/international/archive/2012/03/the-white-savior-industrial-complex/254843.

Dangarembga, Tsitsi. *The Book of Not.* Banbury, UK: Ayebia, 2006.

Nervous Conditions. London: Women's Press, 1988.

Fanon, Frantz. *The Wretched of the Earth.* Translated by Constance Farrington. New York: Grove Weidenfeld, 1991.

Foucault, Michel. *Discipline and Punish: The Birth of the Prison.* Translated by Alan Sheridan. New York: Random, 1977.

Hill, Sylvia. "Facing Social Reconstruction in Zimbabwe." *The Black Scholar* 11.5 (1980): 37–47.

Horkheimer, Max, and Theodor W. Adorno. *Dialectic of Enlightenment: Philosophical Fragments.* Translated by Edmund Jephcott. Stanford: Stanford University Press, 2002.

Lazarus, Neil. "Great Expectations and the Mourning After." In *Resistance in Postcolonial African Fiction,* 211–24. New Haven: Yale University Press, 1990.

Lessing, Doris. *Alfred and Emily.* New York: HarperCollins, 2008.

Marechera, Dambudzo. *The House of Hunger.* Oxford: Heinemann, 1978.

Rotberg, Robert. "And Now – to Share Zimbabwe's Bounty." *Christian Science Monitor,* April 17, 1980. www.csmonitor.com/1980/0417/041742.html.

"Rural Zimbabwe Empties as Mugabe Land Reform Policy Unravels." *Bloomberg News,* February 28, 2017. www.bloomberg.com/politics/articles/2017-02-28/rural-zimbabwe-empties-as-mugabe-s-land-reform-policy-unravels.

Sieff, Kevin. "Zimbabwean Farmers." *Guardian,* September 25, 2015. www.theguardian.com/world/2015/sep/25/zimbabwe-land-reforms-mugabe-white-farmers.

Smith, David. "NoViolet Bulawayo Tells of Heartbreak of Homecoming in Mugabe's Zimbabwe." *Guardian,* September 4, 2013. www.theguardian.com/world/2013/sep/04/noviolet-bulawayo-homecoming-mugabe-zimbabwe.

Wolf, Naomi. *The Beauty Myth: How Images of Beauty Are Used against Women.* New York: Anchor-Doubleday, 1991.

Afterword

Darra Goldstein

When I entered graduate school in the mid-1970s, I planned to write my dissertation on food in Russian literature. The books I had read revealed a profoundly different way of apprehending the world, of appreciating it. I aspired to use food as a means of getting at an essential Russianness, what in those days we still rather naively called "the Russian soul." Even my first, most tentative, analyses of the Russian classics revealed that when food is used as a narrative element, it often doubles as shorthand for larger characterizations, whether of individuals or of society at large. I was struck by seemingly offhand remarks such as those uttered by the character Shabelsky in Chekhov's play *Ivanov*: "Since the world began scholars have thought and thought but still haven't come up with anything better than a pickle to accompany vodka."[1] Though these words sound like banter, they in fact disclose an entire history of the Russians' dueling tendencies toward hope and despair: the resolve to preserve against hardship; the urge to seek escape and oblivion from it. When I revealed my plans to my professors, they were aghast: How could I even consider writing on anything as trivial as food? How could I ever expect to be taken seriously, to get an academic job? They were unwilling to support work on such a topic and intimated that in proposing this topic, I myself was unserious. But what did "unserious" actually mean: light, slight, female, domestic, possibly divergent, possibly unworthy of a Stanford PhD?

Today, a dissertation exploring the uses of food in literature hardly seems groundbreaking, let alone academically revolutionary; and by that marker alone, we are in a better place, one that is enhanced by the appearance of this volume, which solidly establishes literary food studies as an acceptable mode of intellectual inquiry. As Gitanjali Shahani states in her introduction, the significance of food is a given, and we no longer have to be

---

[1] Spoken by the character Shabel'skii in Anton Chekhov, *Ivanov*, Act 3, Scene 1, www.ilibrary.ru/text/964/p.3/index.html. My translation.

defensive or apologetic about taking it as our subject. It is tempting to give a feminist reading to this evolution in thinking. In France, once the great male critics of the Annales School turned to daily life and its meanings, the study of food acquired gravitas; and when Claude Lévi-Strauss and Roland Barthes began theorizing food, it gained even more weight, so to speak. But attributing the development of the field merely to male hegemony is too pat. In a passage from *Blockade Diary*, her semi-fictional account of the nearly 900 days of siege Leningrad endured during World War II, the brilliant literary critic Lidiya Ginzburg put her finger on deeper reasons for the ultimate acceptance of food among the intelligentsia. The Blockade precipitated a rapid leveling of society: each person standing in line for rations was equal, no matter their upbringing or level of education. Although commensality had disappeared along with the food, people still shared as they stood in line awaiting their meager 125 grams of bread; except that now knowledge and experience were what they communicated, stories and instructions that could materialize only back in the kitchen. They learned how to boil old gopher-fur coats to yield broth with some small degree of nourishment, and to make aspic from joiner's glue. The "soul" of these queues lay in the conversations people had:

> This conversation [about eating], which had previously drawn down the scorn of men and businesswomen (especially young ones) and which she [the housewife] had been forbidden to inflict upon the thinking man – this conversation had triumphed. It had taken on a universal meaning and importance, paid for by the terrible experience of the winter. A conversation on how it's better not to salt millet when boiling, because then it gets to be just right, had become a conversation about life and death (the millet expands, you see). Reduced in range (siege cuisine), the conversation became enriched with tales of life's ups and downs, difficulties overcome and problems resolved. And as the basic element of the given life situation, it subsumed every possible interest and passion.[2]

"The basic element of the given life situation." These are words worth rereading. In Robert Appelbaum's formulation in Chapter 6, food serves as an "index of being." Like the conversations about siege cuisine, the chapters in *Food and Literature* speak to our profound interests and passions, to the very stuff of life. They explore the meanings of commensality; the phenomena of taste and disgust; the artistry of food writing; patterns of consumption, both economic and somatic; issues of ethics and race; political ideologies; technology and modernism in the culinary and literary

---

[2] Lidiya Ginzburg, *Blockade Diary* (London: Harvill Press, 1995), 43.

realms; the uses of food as a comic device and as a measure of cruelty in literary investigations of hunger, famine, colonialism, racism, and cannibalism. Food marks meanings and identities that shift across centuries, cultures, styles, and genres. It is, as Maud Ellmann states in *The Hunger Artists*, "the epitome of all creative and destructive labour."[3] This volume demonstrates the power of literature to express the creative and destructive power of food.

As I celebrate this publication, I recall how in the mid-1990s several of us in the nascent (though not yet named) field of food studies – including Krishnendu Ray, Ken Albala, Warren Belasco, and Fabio Parasecoli – discussed how to make the study of food acceptable within academia. Perhaps because we came from vastly different fields (literature, sociology, history, and politics), we agreed that we needed to formulate a common methodology. But the more we spoke, the more we realized that the excitement and promise of the field lay precisely in its multidisciplinary nature – that the study of food transcended traditional (read: entrenched) disciplinary bounds. We also worked hard to come up with a name for what we were doing, one that would encompass the various fields we were drawing on. The existing term "culinary history" seemed limited to domestic and cultural outlooks rather than able to embrace the societal and political issues we also wanted to explore. So early on we discarded the word "culinary" as too fettered, both etymologically and actually, to the kitchen, to cuisine. We then considered "gastronomy." In many ways, this word is ideal, arising as it does from the Greek roots for "knowing eater," as Denise Gigante notes in Chapter 4. Furthermore, gastronomy encompasses not only the idea of knowledge but those of connoisseurship and practice. But we ultimately concluded that the word sounded too elite, suggesting French gastronomers such as Brillat-Savarin and Grimod de la Reynière who spent more time philosophizing than considering real-life issues. And so, with some reluctance, we opted for the down-to-earth Anglo-Saxon word "food," fodder, so to speak, for the studies attached to it, and general enough to embrace anything we might want to include in this new field of research.

The term stuck. In 1999 the *Chronicle of Higher Education* observed that "Food studies has puttered along the margins of anthropology and folklore for more than a decade. Now it is gaining momentum among sociologists and scholars in the humanities."[4] That statement was encouraging,

[3] Quoted in Terry Eagleton, "Edible Ecriture," *Times Higher Education*, October 24, 1997, www.timeshighereducation.com/features/edible-ecriture/104281.article.
[4] Jennifer K. Ruark, "A Place at the Table," *Chronicle of Higher Education*, July 9, 1999, A17.

balanced, and apt. But today, nearly two decades later, the balance has tilted, with food studies largely commandeered by the social sciences. This development has partly to do with broader trends in education that privilege the STEM disciplines. Social sciences come next in the hierarchy (the designation as a type of "science" certainly helps), while the humanities languish where no Table of Literary Elements is likely to save us from being considered only marginally relevant to the practical concerns of contemporary American society (like getting a job). In applauding the rise of food-related courses in academia, a 2015 post on the blog *Civil Eats* reveals the consequences: "As the food movement grows, the demand for college and university classes focusing on food systems is exploding."[5] Most of these courses deal with food justice, policy, nutrition, and "sustainability" and have little or nothing to do with the humanities. That issues surrounding food are increasingly salient and politicized is important for the health of our country and of the world, and the disclosure of unethical and unhealthy practices in food production, distribution, and consumption has contributed to the betterment of people's lives, as well as to the respectability of scholarly studies of food. But in the process the study of food, once criticized as being too feminine, too domestic in its underpinnings, has been (safely) masculinized. Food studies is now about systems rather than people, while the starting point for all studies of food – the crucible that is the hearth – is overlooked in favor of data and statistics. And yet, as scholars like Richard Wrangham have argued, it is the mastery of cooking that makes us human.[6]

I have been fretting about this trend for some time. In a 2010 editorial on the state of food studies for the journal *Food, Culture and Society*, I noted how far our field had come but rued the loss of something essential: "Food carries enormous intellectual weight, but it is, essentially, visceral. If the study of food becomes too academic, its most vital characteristics could very well evaporate. Only the blend of the sensual with the cerebral, the tangible with the abstract, can make the study of food truly exciting and rich."[7] Simply put, what's missing in food studies is the sensory and now, I would add, the literary, which is closely linked. With the appearance of this important volume, I want to take the opportunity to plea for putting more literature back into food studies.

---

[5] "Majoring in Food: Colleges Offering More Courses, Degrees," Civil Eats, civileats.com/2015/09/22/majoring-in-food-colleges-offering-more-courses-degrees.
[6] Richard Wrangham, *Catching Fire: How Cooking Made Us Human* (New York: Basic Books, 2009).
[7] Darra Goldstein, "Food Scholarship and Food Writing," *Food, Culture and Society* 13.3 (2010): 319–29.

Nothing else comes as close to offering models for "being" as literature does in its reflections on what makes us human. In representing our collective experience, literature seeks less to analyze the world than to provide us with a means of understanding it. Stories are one of the most potent, participatory ways in which we express ourselves, and food has always been a natural part of that storytelling. Literature brings us back from impersonal systems to characters, to individual expression. The role of the literary food scholar is to offer up an imaginative perspective – not exactly as a corrective to the current work in food studies, but as another, equally important frame of reference. As Sarah Churchwell has cogently stated, "The humanities are where we locate our own lives, our own meanings; they embrace thinking, curiosity, creation, psychology, emotion. The humanities teach us not only what art is for, but what life might be for, what this strange existence might mean."[8]

The chapters in this broadly conceived volume make the case for the importance of literature as a guide for living – not merely a reflection of cultural and societal ideals but also a means of shaping them. Kara K. Keeling and Scott T. Pollard demonstrate that Laura Ingalls Wilder's *Little House on the Prairie* reads not simply as a charming pioneer tale for children but as an ideological anti-New Deal tract that promotes conservative values, while Valérie Loichot elaborates on the uses of food in French postcolonial literature: "When the political hurts, the customary resists. The stronghold of customary resistance is culinary expression. The privileged site of ethical resistance is the scene of eating together." The volume's close readings of literary texts and explorations of larger ideas about narrative invite readers to consider not only how to write about food in literature, but what the possibilities are for thinking about food through the literary imagination, through the speculations and leaps of fancy that are considered anathema in fields insisting on precise, often quantifiable, documentation.

The spinning of tales – an act of fabrication – may be "consciously representing the false as true," as Kant writes of metaphorical speech. But as Denise Gigante notes in Chapter 4, we should also recall that Dante refers to the poet as a *fabbro*, a maker or inventor. In the kitchen, "fabrication" refers to the breaking down of a carcass into primal cuts, from which recipes, and dishes, are eventually conjured. Literary language encourages fabrications, from metaphors to double entendres to neologisms. Literature

---

[8] Sarah Churchwell, "Why the Humanities Matter," *Times Higher Education*, November 13, 2014, timeshighereducation.com/comment/opinion/sarah-churchwell-why-the-humanities-matter/2016909.article.

further offers something unavailable to most other fields within food studies: a sensorial, and often sensual, experience of the world. Both language and food offer immediate entry into the sensorium, involving as they do the tongue, the organ of production for language as well as the receptor for food. Words and foods engage our senses of sight, hearing, smell, taste, and touch, mediating our encounters with the material world and allowing us to experience not only the present but to travel via memory or fantasy through space and time. Both are, in their analogous ways, primal.

Take, for example, Harry Mathews' brilliant story-cum-recipe, "Country Cooking from Central France: Roast Boned Rolled Stuffed Shoulder of Lamb (*Farce Double*)."[9] Imitating the methods of ethnography and anthropology, and toying with the promise of "authenticity," the narrator playfully, painstakingly, enumerates the minutest details of how to prepare lamb according to an arcane French tradition.

> If the traditional ways of enveloping the quenelles are arduous, they are in no way gratuitous. On them depends an essential component of *farce double*, namely the subtle interaction of lamb and fish. While the quenelles (and the poaching liquid that bathes them) must be largely insulated from the encompassing meat, they should not be wholly so. The quenelles must not be drenched in roasting juice or the lamb in fishy broth, but an exchange should occur, definite no matter how mild. Do not *under any circumstance* use a baggie or Saran Wrap to enfold the quenelles. Of course it's easier. So are TV dinners. For once, demand the utmost of yourself: the satisfaction will astound you, and *there is no other way*.

As readers we are caught up in the wonder of the recipe, the frisson of entering so deeply into the intimate secrets of another culture. It is only when the descriptions veer into the comic and the extreme that we realize the author is offering up less a recipe than a double farce, in the form of the Auvergnat *farce double*, a roast with two stuffings:

> I mentioned this misuse of plastic to a native of La Tour Lambert. My interlocutor, as if appealing for divine aid, leaned back, lifted up his eyes, and stretched forth his arms. He was standing at the edge of a marinating trough; its edges were slick with marinade. One foot shot forward, he teetered for one moment on the brink, and then down he went. Dripping oil, encrusted with fragrant herbs, he emerged briskly and burst into tears.

Mathews presents us with an exaggerated, parodic technique for making quenelles, creating a context that links the practice to ancient times:

---

[9] Originally written in 1977. Reprinted in Daniel Halpern, *Not for Bread Alone: Writers on Food, Wine, and the Art of Eating* (New York: Ecco Press, 1993), 144–45.

There are two methods. I shall describe the first one briefly: it is the one used by official cooks for public banquets. Cawl (tripe skin) is scraped free of fat and rubbed with pumice stone to a thinness approaching nonexistence. This gossamer is sewn into an open pouch, which is filled with the quenelles and broth before being sewn shut. The sealing of the pouch is preposterously difficult. I have tried it six times; each time, ineluctable burstage has ensued. Even the nimble-fingered, thimble-thumbed seamstresses of La Tour Lambert find it hard. In their floodlit corner of the festal cave, they are surrounded by a sizable choir of wailing boys whose task is to aggravate their intention to a pitch of absolute, sustained concentration. If the miracle always occurs, it is never less than miraculous.

Even if Mathews is teasing us, how palpable his description is! We taste the roasted lamb jus and the fish broth, and imagine the saltiness of the interlocutor's tears. We feel the slipperiness of the marinating trough and unctuous fat as well as the graininess of the pumice stone. We smell the fragrance of the herbs; adjust our eyes from the dark to the floodlit corner of the cave; and hear the wailing of the boys. All of our senses are engaged: taste, touch, smell, sight, and sound come together through language in a miraculous way that will yield a miraculous dish. The intensely real comingles with the overtly artificial.

The exaggeration inherent in farce aligns it with satire, even if irony is rarely present. So it's worth lingering on the idea of "visceral satire" that Allison Carruth explores in Chapter 11, on the historical avant-garde and contemporary cuisine. Having attended all too many temples of high gastronomy, I fully agree that "food politics [has become] a zone of disquieting embodiment and visceral satire," and that "formal and cultural experimentation at elBulli and kindred eateries works in service of highly conspicuous consumption." But let's also consider one of the reasons these over-the-top culinary performances have prevailed, which is not just diners' aspirations but also their delight. One trait that outré literary and culinary performances share is an impulse toward excessive display and posturing. When this kind of pretentiousness masquerades as art, it invites disdain. Today's staged meals are only the most recent iteration of conspicuous displays that have characterized elite dining for centuries; until the fashion for naturalism took over in early seventeenth-century France, artifice was arguably the most highly prized principle of culinary aesthetics.[10] The ability to skin and roast, then reconstruct, a peacock by replacing its feathers, creating an armature for its neck, and covering its

---

[10] Jennifer Davis, "Masters of Disguise: French Cooks between Art and Nature, 1651–1793," *Gastronomica: Journal of Food and Culture* 9.1 (Winter 2009), 36.

beak with gold leaf led to extraordinary feasts for the eye (if not for the palate).[11] And any cook who could create edible trompe l'oeil fantasies, or work sugar into spectacular *trionfi* and *pièces montées*, was greatly esteemed.

Thus, without ignoring underlying ethical and political motivations, it is also useful to talk about aesthetic ones, which in their own way are revelatory of culture. We can apply this approach to discussions of food in literature. In academic food studies, the current tendency to favor the issue-driven and ideological at the expense of the sensory, especially the gustatory, means that we risk limiting what literary food studies might yet achieve. J. Michelle Coghlan takes up this idea in her chapter on Elizabeth Pennell when she writes of "the modern disavowal of gustatory matters by those who seem most invested in reading them." Rather than privileging the theoretical, perhaps we as literary scholars could pay more attention to our organoleptic responses and revel in the very texture of writing, the sounds of words, the communication of taste through verbal agility. Unlike other fields of food studies, literature can claim language as a key element in conveying sensory perceptions. In his preface to Brillat-Savarin's *The Physiology of Taste*, Roland Barthes asserts that

> B.-S. is certainly linked to language – as he was to food – by an amorous relation: he desires words, in their very materiality. He comes up with an astonishing classification of the tongue's movements as it participates in manducation: there are, among other oddly learned words, *spication* (when the tongue takes the shape of a stalk of wheat) and *verrition* (when it sweeps) ... Neologisms (or very rare words) abound in B.-S.: he employs them without restraint, and each of these unexpected words (*irrorator, garrulity, esculent, gulturation, comessation*, etc.) is the trace of a profound pleasure which refers to the tongue's desire: B.-S. desires the word as he desires truffles, a tuna omelette, a fish stew ... we can say that B.-S.'s language is literally *gourmand*: greedy for the words it wields and for the dishes to which it refers.[12]

I'm not suggesting that we resort to using obscure words à la Brillat-Savarin to make the case for writing about food – that would only distance our readers rather than bring them into the fold. I ask instead for a renewed focus on creative fabrication, on the making of literature, and the impact that craft has on the reader. The interaction between reader and writer occurs in the gap between our seeing actual stars in the sky and reading someone else's imaginary experience of them. Through language, lyricism,

---

[11] See Barbara Wheaton, "How to Cook a Peacock," *Harvard Magazine* 82 (1979), 63–66.
[12] Roland Barthes, "Reading Brillat-Savarin," in *The Rustle of Language*, translated by Richard Howard (New York: Hill and Wang, 1984), 258–59.

and participation one mind can meet another. As Adam Gopnik has noted in relation to food writing: "The space between imaginary food in books and real food is the space where reading happens."[13] I would argue that this space also offers the greatest opportunity for sensory engagement. The sensuality of language and our participation in it as readers can lead to "a profound pleasure" that manages to solve the basic problem of literature, that we are one degree removed from the making of the work.

Here's an example. In Seamus Heaney's poem "Oysters" the briny tang of the bivalves links the palatable and the palatal, uniting us with language, with earth and with sky:

> Our shells clacked on the plates.
> My tongue was a filling estuary,
> My palate hung with starlight:
> As I tasted the salty Pleiades
> Orion dipped his foot into the water ...
>
> ... I ate the day
> Deliberately, that its tang
> Might quicken me all into verb, pure verb.

How much closer to eating an oyster can we get without actually slurping one ourselves? Here taste merges with language, becoming energy, not solely as a metaphor, but as a physical reaction. This union makes sense: like food, language is both material and symbolic. Yet in our eagerness to understand the symbolic, we too often overlook the primary material, the oyster, the taste. Terry Eagleton, in his oft-cited essay "Edible Ecriture," states: "Food looks like an object but is actually a relationship, and the same is true of literary works."[14] And of course he is right: We must continue to discover the relationships, the ideas beyond the object. But we also need to ground these ideas in the essential, in the stuff itself. We need to think about the food and its intrinsic properties, the cooking methods that can transform it, the equipment used to prepare and serve it. We need to train ourselves not just in narrative strategies but also in culinary methodologies, to understand the mechanisms not just of language but of the materials it describes.

The past decade has seen a proliferation of studies on individual foodstuffs,[15] which usefully demonstrate the multivalent lenses through

---

[13] Adam Gopnik, "Cooked Books," *New Yorker*, April 9, 2007, newyorker.com/magazine/2007/04/09/cooked-books.

[14] Eagleton, "Edible Ecriture."

[15] Most notable is the "Edible" series from Reaktion Books. The first title, *Pancake: A Global History*, appeared in 2008. Volume 68, *Honey: A Global History*, came out in May 2017, with more titles to

which we can look at food, among them race, gender, ecology, economics, biology, and chemistry. What I'm suggesting here is that the anxiety of disciplinary mandates, once crucial to the development of literary food studies, now risks fettering it if the text serves only as handmaiden to "larger" ideas. To reclaim our field we need to make use of the gift we have been given as literary scholars: the text itself, as it stimulates our organ of language and taste. Now that literary food studies has achieved respectability, we can feel secure enough to revel in the essence of our subject, and not only use it as a means to a more purposeful end. This is not to say that we should abandon the kind of important multidisciplinary analyses that are evident in this book. But we might also linger on the words themselves, to celebrate language, the essence – the distillate, if you will – of writing. As Mark Strand puts it:

> Ink runs from the corners of my mouth.
> There is no happiness like mine.
> I have been eating poetry.[16]

BIBLIOGRAPHY

Barthes, Roland. "Reading Brillat-Savarin." In *The Rustle of Language*, translated by Richard Howard, 258–59. New York: Hill and Wang, 1984.

Chekhov, Anton. *Ivanov*. www.ilibrary.ru/text/964/p.3/index.html.

Churchwell, Sarah. "Why the Humanities Matter." *Times Higher Education*, November 13, 2014. timeshighereducation.com/comment/opinion/sarah-churchwell-why-the-humanities-matter/2016909.article.

Davis, Jennifer. "Masters of Disguise: French Cooks between Art and Nature, 1651–1793." *Gastronomica: Journal of Food and Culture* 9.1 (Winter 2009): 36–49.

Eagleton, Terry. "Edible Ecriture." *Times Higher Education*, October 24, 1997. www.timeshighereducation.com/features/edible-ecriture/104281.article.

Ginzburg, Lidiya. *Blockade Diary*. London: Harvill Press, 1995.

Goldstein, Darra. "Food Scholarship and Food Writing." *Food, Culture and Society* 13.3 (2010): 319–29.

Gopnik, Adam. "Cooked Books." *New Yorker*, April 9, 2007. newyorker.com/magazine/2007/04/09/cooked-books.

Mathews, Harry. "Country Cooking from Central France: Roast Boned Rolled Stuffed Shoulder of Lamb *(Farce Double)*." In *Not for Bread Alone: Writers on Food, Wine, and the Art of Eating*, edited by Daniel Halpern. New York: Ecco Press, 1993.

---

follow. See reaktionbooks.co.uk/results.asp?SF1=series_exact&ST1=EDIBLE&DS=Edible&SORT =sort_title.

[16] Mark Strand, "Eating Poetry" (1968), in *Selected Poems* (New York: Alfred A. Knopf, 1991), poetryfoundation.org/poems-and-poets/poems/detail/52959.

Ruark, Jennifer K. "A Place at the Table." *Chronicle of Higher Education*, July 9, 1999.

Strand, Mark. "Eating Poetry." In *Selected Poems*. New York: Alfred A. Knopf, 1991.

Wheaton, Barbara. "How to Cook a Peacock." *Harvard Magazine* 82 (1979).

Wrangham, Richard W. *Catching Fire: How Cooking Made Us Human*. New York: Basic Books, 2009.

Index